THE ECONOMICS OF THE EURO-MARKET

The Economics of the Euro-Market

History, Theory and Policy

R. B. Johnston

St. Martin's Press   New York

All rights reserved. For information, write:
St. Martin's Press, Inc., 175 Fifth Avenue, New York, NY 10010
Printed in Hong Kong
First published in the United States of America in 1982

ISBN 0–312–23295–0

Library of Congress Cataloging in Publication Data

Johnston, R. B.
   The economics of the Euro-market.

   1. Euro-dollar market.   I. Title.
HG3897.J63   1982   332.4′5   82–10300
ISBN 0–312–23295–0

Contents

Preface

This book is intended as a systematic treatment of the economics of the Euro-market. Its aim is to get to grips with the theory of this market and the policy implications. Several themes are developed: the evolutionary nature of the Euro-currency system, the integrated and competing relationship between Euro- and domestic money markets, and the need to look at the market in a segmented fashion to understand its overall significance. The reasons for Euro-market growth, the determination of Euro-currency interest rates and lending spreads and the market's macroeconomic implications are subjects examined in detail. The Euro-market is emphasised because of its role as a centre of international banking flows and because, in recent years, it has been the subject of international policy discussions. The importance of other international banking flows and their relationships with the Euro-market are also investigated.

As well as examining the theory, an attempt has been made to seek out evidence to test and illustrate the workings of the Euro-market. Emphasis is laid on practical aspects of the market's development and on an examination of relevant statistics. An amount of new research is included and econometric results are sometimes called upon when they help elucidate the discussion. There are, however, data problems, so that these results can only be indicative of the processes involved.

The examination of the Euro-market involves aspects of several branches of economics, and some knowledge of money and banking theory and international economics, though not essential, will be helpful. The main readership of this book will probably be advanced undergraduate or graduate students of international finance who wish to have a more detailed treatment of the economics of the Euro-market than is generally available in other texts. However, it is hoped that the book will also appeal to bankers and other practitioners in the Euro-market and that my fellow researchers and central bankers will find it of interest.

The book evolved from four years I spent working on international financial market questions with the Bank of England, and it was written while I was on secondment to the Bank for International Settlements in Basle. I am very grateful to the Bank of England for allowing me to write it and to the Bank for International Settlements for accommodating me for a period of over one year while I worked on the drafts and for providing valuable technical assistance. I am especially indebted to D. G. Holland, Professor A. Lamfalussy, and C. W. McMahon for their support and for arranging that this could be possible.

I have learnt a great deal during my years with the Bank of England and this book has benefited greatly from my discussions with, and the work of, my colleagues and friends. Helmut Mayer provided a most stimulating input while I was at the Bank for International Settlements. Many of my colleagues also gave generously of their time and provided much-needed comments on earlier drafts. Clive Briault, John Ellis, Susan Howson and Jackie Whitley looked through several of the drafts and their comments helped me shape my thinking and stopped me going too far astray. David Holland made penetrating comments on a number of chapters, Charles Freeland kept me from making even more errors in Chapter 11, and John Bispham kindly read some of my more final versions. While I am very grateful to all these people and to all others who gave assistance, I have not always accepted their points of view and I am solely responsible for the final version. In particular, nothing that I have written should be taken to reflect the views of either the Bank of England or the Bank for International Settlements.

The job of typing the many drafts was undertaken by Rosie Munday and Julie Sowerbutts and supervised by Mlle. Conrad. They carried out what must have seemed an endless task with great speed, efficiency and cheerfulness and produced an excellent typescript. Frl. Capaul was responsible for much of the art work and Steve Arthur helped me look out data. I am grateful to all of them and to everyone else who made my stay in Basle such a valuable one.

Finally I would like thank Pat, my wife, for her encouragement and support towards the completion of this book.

May 1982   R. B. JOHNSTON

1 Introduction

Since its emergence some twenty years ago the Euro-currency (or simply the Euro-) market has grown to play an increasingly important role in international monetary relations and to be a source of some concern to various national authorities. This text examines the economics of the system and its policy implications. The emphasis of the book is on the Euro-currency money market, that is, an international market for non-bank and interbank deposits and short- and medium-term bank credits. In this market all major currencies are actively borrowed and lent. The US dollar is, however, overwhelmingly the most important − in the form of Euro-dollars. The activities of banks in this market are known as Euro-currency banking and are distinguished from other types of banking activities. This introductory chapter defines some of the characteristics of Euro-banking and outlines the text.

1.1   A CLASSIFICATION

It is possible to classify banking activities according to the currency composition of bank deposits and loans and the residency of borrowers and depositors. As we shall see below, the distinction between the functions of the different banking activities is not clear cut, but the schema of classification provides a useful formal starting-point. It is illustrated in Figure 1.1.

Domestic banking, while not easily defined, may be taken to refer to the activities of banks within the purely closed economy; within the schema of classification it is the taking of deposits and making of loans with *residents* of, and in the *domestic currency* of, the country in which the bank is located.

Traditional foreign banking (TFB) operations refer to bank activity with agents resident in other countries − *non-residents* − in the *domestic currency* of the country in which the bank is located. It is dubbed 'traditional' because of the long history of banks providing domestic currency facilities for foreigners for the finance of trade transactions.

Euro-currency banking activities are essentially those conducted

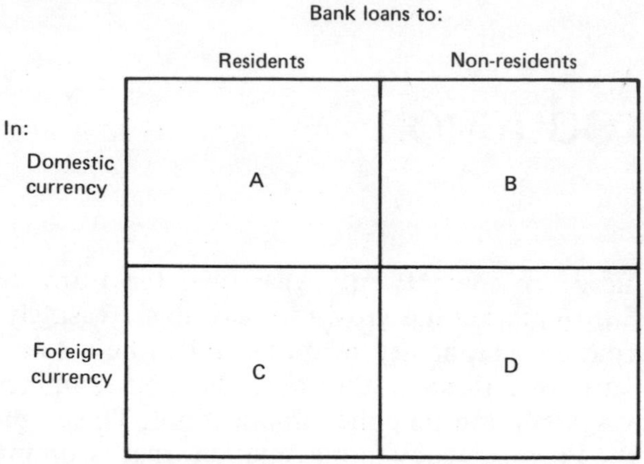

Bank loans to:

Residents   Non-residents

In:

Domestic
currency   A   B

Foreign
currency   C   D

A   'Domestic' lending
B   'Traditional foreign' lending
C + D   'Euro-currency' lending
B + D   'International' lending

(B + C + D is also sometimes known as 'International banking operations', and D
is known as 'entrepôt' business when loans are funded out of non-resident foreign
currency deposits.)

**Figure 1.1   Classification of bank lending by residence of borrower and currency
of loan**

by banks in *foreign currencies*, i.e. currencies other than those of the
country in which the bank is located. Transactions by banks in foreign
currencies with both residents and non-residents are included in the
classification.

The term 'Euro-currency' is itself rather misleading. It derives
from the original location of the Euro-currency market in the main
European financial centres, principally London. Today the market is
global in nature. Machlup (1972) has suggested the alternative name
'Xeno-currency' (from the Greek for foreign) and the term 'offshore'
is frequently used synonymously, though this has also a more specific
meaning. The name 'Euro-currency' is retained here as it is the most
familiar and because the largest volume of transactions continues to
be centred in Europe.

International bank lending describes banking activities with *non-
residents* in both domestic and foreign currency. It thus includes
banks' TFB activities but not all Euro-currency transactions. It is
thus both a broader and narrower concept than Euro-currency
banking. To confuse matters further, the composite of TFB and all
Euro-currency transactions, i.e. those with residents and non-residents,
is sometimes called 'international banking operations'. Presumably

this term is used because Euro-currency transactions with residents in foreign currencies have also an international dimension.

Finally, when banks take foreign currency deposits from non-residents and lend them back to other non-residents, the activity is sometimes known as *'entrepôt'* or 'turntable' business. It is distinguished because, unlike the other banking concepts, it has no specific domestic dimension, being conducted neither in domestic currencies nor with domestic residents.

1.2 SOME MARKET CHARACTERISTICS

First, the Euro-currency market should not be confused with the foreign exchange market. The distinction is that while banks buy and sell currencies in the foreign exchange market they borrow and lend currencies in the Euro-market — there are, however, some important links between the foreign exchange and Euro-currency markets. Indeed, it is the 'active' intermediation function of banks in foreign currencies between borrowers and lenders that is the primary characteristic of Euro-banking. Euro-markets are also predominantly 'wholesale' money markets in that only very large amounts are transacted, mostly not smaller than one million currency units. Small savers and borrowers are generally excluded from participating in the active Euro-market because of the size of transactions, and the main operators are commercial banks followed by central banks, industrial and commercial enterprises, institutional investors and some wealthy individuals. The majority of deposits are also fixed-term time deposits, though a market in negotiable time deposits has grown rapidly in recent years. The fixed-term nature of deposits means that Euro-currency balances are generally short- to medium-term investments rather than balances which are specifically held to meet current expenditures. Euro-currency deposits may nevertheless have a transactions role. The interest rates on deposits and loans are set in a highly aggressive free-market environment and frequently differ from those in national money markets: short-term Euro-currency interest rates are often somewhat higher than domestic currency interest rates because of the market's regulatory and institutional characteristics. The geographical location of borrowers and depositors in the Euro-market is diverse and the passing of funds from one foreign source to another — entrepôt banking — accounts for the largest share of business. The banking institutions which make the market are also drawn from many different countries.

A brief examination of some figures on the geographical uses (lending by banks in the Euro-market) and sources (deposits held with banks in the Euro-market) of Euro-currency deposits at European banks serves to illustrate the dimensions of the system. Of the total increase of about $400 billion in European banks' Euro-currency loans (uses) and deposits (sources) recorded during the years 1975–80, nearly three-quarters are accounted for by transactions with borrowers outside Europe (see Table 1.1). The figures in the table also show how the structure of flows has changed over time. Oil-exporting country placements in the market surged in 1976 and again in 1979 and after, while the borrowing of Euro-currencies by developing countries expanded rapidly in 1979 and 1980. In these respects the Euro-market is performing a *global* intermediation function between different economic and geographical groupings. On both the sources and uses side of the market the largest single group of transactors are, however, European non-banks. The Euro-market provides *regional* investment and borrowing facilities in foreign currencies for residents in its local area. When residents place and borrow their own domestic currency from banks in the Euro-market, the Euro-market also performs a *domestic* intermediation function. Resident transactions in their domestic currencies with banks in the Euro-market are a substitute for transactions with domestic banks. In this respect the sharp increase in the use of the Euro-currency market by US residents in 1979 was largely a substitute for transactions with US domestic banks. (We can make this statement since we know that the overwhelming volume of Euro-deposits takes the form of Euro-dollars and US residents' transactions in the Euro-market are therefore most likely to be conducted in their domestic currency.)

1.3   SIMILARITIES AND DIFFERENCES

Euro-currency banking overlaps with other banking activities in many ways. The currencies traded in the Euro-market are no different from those traditionally borrowed and lent by banks in domestic markets. The major differences are that the market is located outside the country of the currency concerned and deposits and loans are remunerated at different rates of interest to those in national money markets.

1.3.1   *TFB and Euro-banking*

It is particularly difficult to make an analytical or even statistical distinction between traditional foreign banking (TFB) and Euro-currency banking.

Table 1.1
Changes in estimated net sources and uses of Euro-currency funds ($ billion)

	Reporting European Area Banks	Non-banks	USA	Other developed countries*	Eastern Europe	Offshore banking countries	Oil-exporting countries	Developing countries	Total†
A USES									
1975	− 0.8	+ 2.3	− 1.7	+ 7.4	+ 5.8	+ 8.9	+ 1.8	+ 3.8	+ 28.0
1976	+ 4.2	+ 7.9	+ 1.7	+ 8.6	+ 4.9	+ 5.2	+ 4.3	+ 5.2	+ 42.0
1977	+ 5.7	+ 18.4	+ 2.8	+ 6.7	+ 3.0	+ 2.9	+ 6.0	+ 5.3	+ 53.0
1978	+ 11.9	+ 17.2	+ 3.3	+ 9.8	+ 5.7	+ 11.1	+ 8.6	+ 9.8	+ 77.0
1979	+ 15.0	+ 16.8	+ 12.1	+ 14.2	+ 4.6	+ 12.5	+ 6.1	+ 15.0	+ 98.0
1980	+ 12.7	+ 32.4	+ 5.0	+ 24.5	+ 2.9	+ 6.5	+ 3.4	+ 15.9	+ 100.0
Total 1975–80	+ 48.7	+ 95.0	+ 21.2	+ 71.2	+ 26.9	+ 47.1	+ 30.2	+ 55.0	+ 398.0
B SOURCES									
1975	+ 9.6	+ 2.1	+ 3.5	+ 1.4	+ 0.3	+ 4.0	+ 5.5	+ 0.7	+ 28.0
1976	+ 1.8	+ 6.3	+ 2.6	+ 1.4	+ 1.0	+ 8.3	+ 10.6	+ 5.1	+ 42.0
1977	+ 11.6	+ 9.4	+ 6.1	+ 5.3	—	+ 3.1	+ 8.8	+ 8.2	+ 53.0
1978	+ 13.1	+ 14.1	+ 11.6	+ 7.4	+ 1.8	+ 12.0	+ 0.2	+ 10.2	+ 77.0
1979	+ 6.6	+ 22.9	+ 13.5	+ 5.5	+ 4.2	+ 7.4	+ 26.3	+ 8.0	+ 98.0
1980	+ 5.7	+ 31.3	+ 9.2	+ 8.7	− 0.2	+ 15.2	+ 28.8	− 1.2	+ 100.0
Total 1975–80	+ 48.4	+ 86.1	+ 46.5	+ 36.2	+ 7.1	+ 50.0	+ 80.2	+ 31.0	+ 398.0

* Includes Canada and Japan.
† Includes an amount of unallocated funds.
Source: Bank for International Settlements quarterly press releases.

Banks have traditionally held working balances in foreign currencies and borrowed in foreign money markets, e.g. the US domestic market, for the purposes of financing their customers' foreign trade or other foreign exchange transactions. Although this business is conducted by the bank in foreign currencies, it is more correctly classified as traditional foreign banking rather than Euro-currency activities. The bank is mainly acting as an agent for its customer in the foreign exchange or money market and the deposits and borrowing are being remunerated at the interest rates set in the foreign money market. In the Euro-currency market, banks actively bid for foreign currency deposits and seek profitable outlets for foreign currency loans, and deposits and loans are remunerated at the interest rates set in the Euro-currency market.

Both Euro-currency and TFB activities involve geographically diverse borrowers and lenders of funds. They are competing – or, more precisely, complementary – segments of the international money market. For this reason international banking will often be the more appropriate variable for investigation rather than the narrower activities of banks in the Euro-currency market. The links between the segments of the international money market, the rates of interest and the reasons for transacting business in one market rather than another are themselves subjects of some interest and ones to be examined in detail.

1.3.2 *Institutions*

Institutionally, there are close links between Euro-market banks and domestic banks. The main operators in the Euro-market are the branches and subsidiaries of well-known commercial banks which may be located in a foreign country – Bank of America's branch in London or Paris – or in the same country as the parent bank – Lloyds Bank International (London) is a wholly owned subsidiary of the Lloyds UK Banking Group. Some banks may be established specifically to transact in Euro-currencies. Consortium banks may be set up by an international group of banks to pool together their individual resources; although each bank may be important in its own domestic markets, it may lack the size or expertise to operate on its own effectively in international markets. When banks arrange their international activities through foreign branches or even foreign subsidiaries in the Euro-market, the parent bank in the domestic market may well maintain close institutional links with its foreign affiliates which affect the affiliates' operational decisions. Unlike foreign branches, subsidiary and consortium banks have a legal identity distinct from their parent organisations but parental interest may well extend beyond that of simply shareholders in a company. The parent bank may accept 'moral' responsibility for its activities or channel funds to it at preferential interest rates. The 'Euro-bank' is more a conceptual than a real entity: it is that part of a bank's overall operations which concentrates on Euro-market activities and these activities may well be influenced to a greater or lesser extent by the operational decisions of parent banks. The analysis has therefore to examine the implications of these institutional relationships.

1.3.3 *Regulations*

One important difference between domestic and Euro-currency banking is the regulatory framework of banking activities. It is usually the case that banks' Euro-currency business — and most especially their entrepôt business — is less closely regulated for monetary control purposes than banks' domestic currency business. When banks conduct entrepôt business, funds are placed in the market from one foreign source and lent to another without 'touching' the domestic economy. The activity is neutral from the point of view of any direct impact on the balance of payments, the exchange rate and the liquidity in the country where the bank is located. This 'neutrality' means that authorities in Euro-currency centres have little need directly to control banks' Euro-currency activities and there are often regulatory asymmetries, of some degree, as regards banks' domestic and Euro-currency business. These asymmetries have led to concern about the macroeconomic effects of the Euro-market, as Euro-currency transactions may escape direct monetary regulation altogether, and to calls for direct monetary regulation of the Euro-market.

1.4   OUTLINE OF THE BOOK

The next two chapters provide the historical and statistical background to the analysis of the Euro-currency market; the following four examine some important theoretical questions, and the final four look at policy issues.

Chapter 2 reviews the post-war history of the Euro-market. The rapid expansion of Euro-currency banking owes much to historical circumstances, and a historical perspective is a useful one for introducing the main actors and terminology. There are many statistical measures of the Euro-currency market and international banking activity which are a source of considerable confusion.

Indeed, more confusion about the economic implications of the Euro-market has perhaps resulted from the incorrect interpretation of Euro-currency data than from any other source. Chapter 3 reviews two sets of statistical data and their economic implications.

The main theoretical analysis begins in Chapter 4 with an examination of some of the economic reasons for the existence of the Euro-currency markets. Since the Euro-currency system is a diverse one the analytical framework is rather untidy, and other important reasons for the market's existence are also examined in Chapter 6. This chapter is concerned with the relationship between global payments imbalances and financial intermediation. Chapters 5 and 7 deal with two specific questions: the determination of short-term Euro-currency interest rates (Chapter 5) and the determination of Euro-currency lending rates (Chapter 7).

An overview of the issues in the debate about the macroeconomic implications of the Euro-market is the subject of Chapter 8. This chapter also examines the impact of the market on exchange rates and the interdependence of national monetary policies. Chapter 9 looks at one of the most controversial questions: the ability of the Euro-market to expand the world money stock autonomously; and Chapter 10 surveys the implications of the market for national monetary policies and examines a proposal for direct control of the system. Chapter 11 discusses the question of international banking stability.

2 From Little Acorns...
(A Short Post-war History of International Banking)

2.1 THE EMERGENCE OF A EURO-DOLLAR MARKET

In the immediate post-war years the foreign currency business of banks consisted mainly of traditional services such as payments abroad and financing of national foreign trade. Sterling continued as an important, if not the predominant, vehicle for the invoicing of world trade flows,[1]* and London remained a centre of trade finance and for the discount and acceptance of trade bills. Because of restrictions on the convertibility of currencies, this activity was, however, largely confined to 'Sterling Area' countries. With the post-war reconstruction of Europe and large US balance-of-payments surpluses, there was a period of dollar shortage and several countries imposed controls on the import of goods as a means of conserving scarce dollar foreign exchange reserves.

Towards the end of the 1950s two important developments altered the organisation of international financial flows. Following a series of foreign exchange crises between 1955 and 1957, the British authorities in 1957 placed restrictions on the use of sterling in external transactions and in particular prohibited the sterling financing of non-UK trade and also limited the sterling refinancing of trade credits. By the late 1950s there had been a significant turnaround in the US balance of payments. The large foreign trade surplus gradually disappeared and this was compensated by increasing foreign holdings of dollars and capital inflows into the USA. The growing availability of the dollar in Europe and elsewhere greatly ehhanced its role as the predominant international reserve currency and its use as an international vehicle currency in the financing and invoicing of international transactions.

It was normal for banks in Europe when conducting their traditional trade financing and foreign exchange business with the USA

* For notes, see end of each chapter.

and dollar area countries to seek to provide dollar facilities for their customers. Such business was not in itself new. Initially, however, British banks, restricted in their external use of sterling, began more actively to seek dollar deposits for use in their external operations. When this met with a readily available supply from, among others, central banks in Europe, South-East Asia and oil-producing countries in the Near East, and even private corporations including foreign subsidiaries of US corporations, banks were more actively able to offer their customers and correspondent banks dollar facilities to take the place of the sterling credits. By mid-1958 a European market in dollar deposits and loans had become established. There are several reasons why investors might have preferred to hold their dollar balances in Europe rather than the USA (see Chapter 4). An often-quoted view traces the origin of a market for dollar deposits in Europe to the desire of several eastern European banks, fearful of having their dollar balances with US banks blocked during the political tensions of the cold war, and nervous of the strength of sterling, to hold their working balances in dollars with their correspondents in Paris and London. One of the earliest depositors of dollars appears to have been the Banque Commerciale de l'Europe du Nord, a Soviet-owned bank in Paris (cable address EUROBANK) together with its London sister unit Moscow Narodny Bank. However, by itself such a precautionary allocation of working balances would not have led to the growth of an active market in dollars, and subsequently other currencies, if it had not been for a number of favourable structural and economic factors.

In December 1958 Western Europe removed the remaining foreign exchange restrictions on the conversion by non-residents of current earnings in Western Europe currencies and returned to full convertibility of currencies. Prior to that time Western European banks had been granted considerable freedom to do business in foreign currencies and with the return to full convertibility more active and integrated foreign exchange markets emerged which provided links between the emerging market in dollar deposits, other foreign currency deposits and national money markets. These links enhanced the range of possibilities for the use of dollars for trading purposes and, as exchange controls on capital movements were relaxed, as a supplement to and outlet for liquidity in national money markets. Central banks in West Germany, Italy, Japan and Switzerland supplied dollars to their banks in the form of foreign currency swaps as a way of influencing domestic liquidity, and several countries encouraged dollar borrowing to supplement domestic credit and for the financing of trade. The scope of the external currency market began to broaden and deepen and by the early

1960s it had become known as the Euro-dollar, or more broadly the Euro-currency, market. Interest rates were regularly quoted for dollar deposits at a range of maturities. As the market widened, Italian, French, Canadian, West German, Japanese and British banks, as well as the branches of US banks abroad, became important participants, standing ready to accept deposits and provide credits in a number of foreign currencies – pounds sterling, Swiss francs, Deutsche Marks and Dutch guilders. The dollar, however, remained and remains overwhelmingly the most important.

2.2   EVOLUTION IN THE 1960s AND 1970s

Throughout the 1960s, and indeed the 1970s, the Euro-currency market grew at a remarkable pace. In September 1963 – the earliest date for which systematic data are available on the foreign currency activities of European banks[2] – the total short-term foreign currency assets of the commercial banks of nine countries[3] reporting to the Bank for International Settlements was $12.4 billion (of which $9.3 billion was in US dollars). By the end of the decade this aggregate had grown by over 500 per cent to $63.4 billion (of which $53 billion were US dollars), i.e. at an annual compounded rate of around 31 per cent per annum. The totals for the gross volume of foreign currency lending by European banks were, nevertheless, still small by comparison with national bank lending. In the USA, for example, the total assets of all commercial banks amounted to $527.6 billion at end-1969. But not only was the rate of growth of the Euro-curency market exceptional by the standards of national banking and credit aggregates – although when compared with the rate of expansion of world trade it was less remarkable – during the decade and in the early 1970s the world's banking system underwent a significant structural change. National banks began to set up networks of subsidiaries and branches abroad specifically to operate in foreign money and Euro-currency markets, and the scope of the Euro-currency market widened both geographically, to become a global market, and in the range of financial instruments and facilities provided. Several regulatory and economic factors, as well as the innovative nature of the banks themselves, contributed to this phenomenal evolution and internationalisation of the world's banking industry.

At the economic level world trade and income increased rapidly during the decade under the impetus of trade liberalisation, currency convertibility and technological advance. Economies became more closely interdependent and the capital needs of industry and the movement of long-term capital across national boundaries increased.

A feature of these developments was the growth of multi-national corporations and the increasing internationalisation of manufacturing industry. Banks saw advantages in setting up branches and subsidiaries abroad to serve the local financial needs of their corporate clients, such as foreign exchange and asset management services and as a local source of short- and longer-term finance.

An additional incentive for banks was to replace their networks of foreign correspondent banks. A correspondent bank, which is usually, but not always, a native to the foreign market, agrees to act as the agent for the bank in a foreign market on behalf of the bank or its customers. In this way a bank can take advantage of the local knowledge and expertise of the correspondent bank when carrying out its business in a foreign country. Generally these relationships continue to exist where the amount of business is small; however, where it is large it may pay the domestic bank to set up its own branch or subsidiary. Once abroad many of these banks become active participants as suppliers and takers of funds in the Euro-currency market both for use by their own clients and on behalf of their parent banks.

2.2.1   *The influence of national regulations*

Capital controls. This internationalisation of banking and the growth of the Euro-currency market was importantly stimulated by national controls and regulations introduced in the 1960s and early 1970s to restrict the international flow of short- and longer-term capital. These controls shifted locus of international transactions to the Euro-currency markets and away from national banking systems. In early 1965 the introduction of the Voluntary Foreign Credit Restraint Program (VFCR) in the USA severely limited the ability of US domestic banks to lend directly to foreigners. The VFCR, which was part of a larger programme, including the Interest Equalization Tax (IET), introduced in July 1963, and the Foreign Direct Investment regulations (FDI), aimed at improving the worsening US balance of payments by curbing capital outflows. Under the VFCR banks (and other non-bank financial intermediaries) in the USA were asked to keep their loans to foreigners and other foreign assets within a certain ceiling limitation, and during the period up to 1970 the foreign credits of US banks varied within a narrow range of $9.25 billion to $9.75 billion.[4] However, as the programme applied only to the operation of US-based banks and not their foreign branches, it had the effect of shifting the foreign operations of US banks to their foreign branches and the demand for international finance to overseas markets, particularly the Euro-currency market.

Brimmer and Dahl (1975) document the very rapid expansion of the foreign branches of US banks which accompanied these controls. As shown in Table 2.1, at end-1964 only 11 US banks had established branches abroad, operating 181 foreign branches; however, by end-1973, just before the controls were taken off, there were 125 banks with a total of 699 foreign branches, and the total assets of these branches had risen from $7 billion to $118 billion. There was also a sharp increase in the so-called 'Edge Act and Agreement' corporations, which are domestically organised subsidiaries that serve as a vehicle for foreign banking and investment. The number of these rose from 38 in 1964 to 104 in 1973 and their assets from $0.9 billion to $6.9 billion.

Table 2.1
International operations of US banks:
selected indicators, 1964–73

Category	1964	1970	1973
I. *US offices*			
Bank Credit to Foreigners ($ bn)	9.4	9.7	17.2
II. *Overseas branches of US banks*			
Number of banks with overseas branches	11	79	125
Number of overseas branches	181	536	699
Assets of overseas branches ($ bn)	6.9	52.6	118
III. *'Edge Act/and Agreement' Corporations*			
Number	38	77	104
Assets ($ bn)	0.9	4.6	6.9

Source: Brimmer and Dahl (1975).

Another effect of the restraint programme was the influence the Interest Equalization Tax (and FDI) had on the growth and development of an international or Euro-bond market and to a lesser extent on the growth of conventional foreign issues on a single European market. ('International' issues are typically underwritten by an international group of banks for placement on a number of different markets. 'Foreign' issues are loans designed for placement on a single national market and are normally denominated in the currency of the market of issue. Unlike international issues they are normally subject to the permission of the national authorities concerned.) Effectively, the IET made it unattractive for foreigners to issue bonds in the USA, while the Foreign Direct Investment regulations limited the amount of overseas direct investment by US firms unless this was financed by funds raised abroad. Both measures shifted the demand for longer-term finance away from New York to European capital markets and provided an incentive for the growth of a Euro-bond market.

Among other capital controls influencing the growth of the Euro-currency market were restrictions on the holding of deposits by non-residents in domestic currencies. In Switzerland and West Germany banks were at times prohibited from paying interest on non-resident deposits and they were required to hold larger cash reserve balances against foreign liabilities. These regulations, which were used during the 1960s and the early 1970s to reduce the upward appreciation of these countries' currencies by discouraging foreign inflows, encouraged non-residents to hold Deutsche Mark and Swiss franc deposits with banks in the Euro-currency market which were not subject to the regulations.

Monetary regulations. In the USA, under Regulation Q, ceilings were imposed on the level of interest rates banks were permitted to pay on deposits in the USA (but not their branches abroad). When credit was tight in the USA and market interest rates moved above the Regulation Q ceilings, banks in the Euro-currency market had an interest-rate advantage in attracting dollar deposits. The impact of these ceilings on the growth of the Euro-dollar market was particularly marked in 1968 and 1969 as interest rates rose during a period of credit restraint. At that time US banks, in seeking to offset large losses of time deposits, which in part had moved to banks in the Euro-dollar market who were paying higher dollar interest rates, turned themselves to the market and their branches abroad as a source of funds. Between end-1964 and end-1969 the Euro-currency claims of the European reporting banks on US residents, mainly banks, increased from $3 billion to $18 billion. The influence of Regulation Q ceilings is illustrated by Figure 2.1. This shows a close correlation between the impact of the ceilings on the relative competitiveness of US banks and Euro-banks in attracting dollar deposits (as measured by the difference between the six-month US domestic market rate and the Regulation Q ceiling), US bank borrowing from their foreign branches and the expansion of the Euro-dollar market.

By restricting the competitive ability of US domestic banks to attract new funds, the Regulation Q ceilings were used as a way of limiting the flow of bank finance to corporate borrowers during periods of credit restraint. The ceilings enhanced the constraining influence of high interest rates on economic activity. However, by turning to the Euro-dollar market as an alternative source of funds outside the interest rate ceilings, US banks were better able to finance

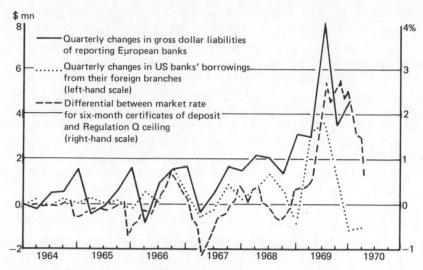

Source: Bank for International Settlements, *Fortieth Annual Report*, June 1970, p. 148.

Figure 2.1   Growth of the Euro-dollar market

the borrowing needs of domestic corporations. To control this Euro-dollar borrowing, the Federal Reserve Board introduced a 10 per cent reserve requirement in September 1969 on net increases in US bank borrowing from their foreign branches and on the increase of foreign branch loans to US residents. However, this occurred only after there had been a large inflow of funds to the US market. In Western Europe domestic corporations also used Euro-markets as a source of funds when the supply of domestic credit was restricted. Under tight monetary conditions West German enterprises were reported to have obtained about one-third of their total borrowing needs from abroad in 1970; and UK business firms borrowed heavily in the Euro-currency market during 1969–70 when there were quantitative limitations on the supply of domestic bank credit. In both countries controls on the import of capital had to be tightened to insulate the domestic market from external flows. On the other hand, the Italian authorities gave active encouragement to Euro-dollar borrowing by Italian corporations as a way of financing Italy's external payments deficit and as a supplement to domestic savings.

Other monetary regulations favoured the growth of the Euro-currency market. Unlike the situation in the US and West German domestic markets, Euro-banks were free from the requirement of holding non-interest-bearing reserve balances against deposits. These balances are held primarily for the purposes of domestic monetary control in these countries. The absence of these domestic regulations in the Euro-market enabled banks to offer higher deposit rates, and short-term Euro-dollar interest rates were usually some ½ per cent higher than in the US domestic market. Moreover, while it was illegal in the USA to pay interest on demand deposits and time deposits of less than thirty days, there were no such restrictions in the Euro-market. It was also reported that in making loans Euro-banks could operate on narrower lending margins, determined in a freely competitive market, than in national markets, where lending rates tended to be partly administered. This general freedom that the Euro-market enjoyed from regulatory constraints and the associated advantageous interest-rate terms it offered to both depositors and borrowers, the different constellation of geographical, sovereign and institutional risks in the Euro-market compared with national money markets, the relative freedom of capital movements and an emerging desire by wealth-holders to internationalise their investments, all added to the attractiveness of the Euro-currency markets to depositors and thus to the supply of foreign currency deposits to banks.

2.2.2 *Innovative banks in an efficient market*

The innovative nature of the banks themselves and the type of instruments they developed enhanced the market's attractiveness. A highly efficient market for deposits between banks – the interbank market – developed which ensured that deposits were allocated to wherever they could be most profitably employed. Typically, prime name banks would lend funds between themselves for margins as low as one-sixteenth (and sometimes one-thirty-second) of 1 per cent and in the interbank market interest rates were quoted on narrow 'bid' (the rate at which a bank is willing to pay for funds in the interbank market) and 'offer' (the rate at which a bank is willing to lend funds to other banks in the Euro-market) spreads. The London interbank offered rate (LIBOR) – an average of the rates at which several banks lend between themselves in the London Euro-currency market – developed into a particularly important reference rate for loans. A feature of this interbank dealing was the movement of large amounts of funds between markets and currencies in response to even small interest-rate differentials. Reflecting the close relationship between the Euro-currency market and the foreign exchange market and the absence of any restrictions on the movement of funds between currencies in the Euro-market, interest-rate arbitrage in the Euro-market ensured that Euro-currency interest rates rarely deviated from interest-rate parity conditions, unlike the usual situations between interest rates in different national money markets (see Chapter 5).

In 1966 the first negotiable Euro-dollar time deposits – a London Dollar Certificate of Deposit (CD) – was launched to fill the gap between the fixed-term time deposits offered by banks in the Euro-dollar market and longer-term instruments available in the Euro-dollar bond market. These negotiable instruments, which already existed in the US domestic market, became an integral part of the Euro-currency deposit market and an important cash management tool for corporations, institutions and banks.

In the capital markets, banks began to experiment with floating rate bonds or notes (FRNs). Unlike conventional fixed-rate bonds on which the interest rate (the coupon) is fixed for the life of the loan when the bond is issued, on FRNs the interest rate is allowed to vary with short-term market interest rates, being linked to a fixed margin usually over the six-month interbank lending rate in the Euro-currency market (six-month LIBOR). These bonds were used particularly by banks as a means of raising medium- to long-term funds and capital to support their growing international operations. In the bank credit markets, loans also developed on a floating rate or a 'roll-over' basis. On a 'roll-over' loan the price of the credit is altered every three, six or twelve months in line with ruling short-term interest rates in the interbank market. These credits have the advantage that they reduce the risk faced by longer-term borrowers and lenders that they will find themselves locked in to paying more or receiving less than current interest rates when market rates change. They are attractive to the banks as they pass on to the borrowers the interest-rate risks involved when funding medium-term loans with short-term deposits in what could be a volatile deposit market. To borrowers medium-term bank credits are generally a more flexible source of funds than bonds and are available for shorter periods. Bond issues are frequently used for long-term (capital) investment projects with the expected receipts coinciding with and being used to meet debt repayments. Bank credits are frequently not specifically related to any particular project. At times the bond markets can also suffer from periods of 'indigestion', because of the large volume of new issues, and completely 'dry up' when short-term interest rates rise, or during periods of currency unrest. At such times uncertainty about the future capital value of investments makes it unattractive for investors to buy fixed-interest bonds.

An important development in the early 1970s was the emergence of the technique of syndicating Euro-bank credits among an international group of banks. These loans are normally medium-term (i.e. three to ten years), though their maturity has lengthened during periods of easy credit conditions in the Euro-market, and are also priced on a 'roll-over' basis, having a fixed spread or margin – which

varies with, among other things, the creditworthiness of the borrower –
over a floating interest rate, usually tied to LIBOR. In addition to
the advantages the roll-over structure of the loans have in reducing
interest-rate risks, the technique of syndicating allows a greater
sharing of borrower risks between banks than non-syndicated credits
and increases the size of loans available to borrowers (without
necessarily increasing the risks to individual lenders). These instruments – syndicated medium-term Euro-credits – are attractive to
certain types of borrowers, particularly sovereign borrowers, who
wish to raise large loans in a single borrowing. 'Jumbo' loans, in
which between $1 billion and $3 billion is raised in a single loan, are
not unknown in the market. The United Kingdom, for example,
raised $2.5 billion in a single loan in 1974. This market became a
major factor in the markets' evolution in the 1970s. In the late
1970s the currency composition of Euro-currency bank deposits
and loans began to change. Banks began to experiment with multicurrency loan packages and to offer deposits in international units
of account, such as the International Monetary Fund's Special
Drawing Right (SDR) or the European Communities' European
Currency Unit (ECU) – which are baskets of different national
currencies. In June 1980 the first SDR Certificate of Deposit was
issued and in 1981 the first medium-term credit to include an option
to draw funds in SDRs was launched.

2.2.3   *Geographical widening through 'offshore' centres*

Towards the end of the 1960s and in the early 1970s the geographical
location of the market also began to change from being mainly
Western European to expand world-wide. Banks began setting up
'offshore' branches in a number of countries in the Caribbean Area,
Latin America, the Near East and South-East Asia. These countries
became known as 'offshore banking centres'.

An offshore banking centre may be defined as being typically a
small territory[5] in which the conduct of international banking
business is facilitated by favourable and/or flexibly administered tax,
exchange control and banking laws, and in which the volume of
banking business is totally unrelated to the size and needs of the
domestic market. Offshore banking activity is essentially entrepôt
business with foreign currency funds being deposited in a given
centre from one foreign source and then on-lent to another foreign
borrower. The overwhelming majority of the activity is wholesale
interbank business on both the deposit-taking and the lending sides.
Frequently much of it will be conducted either directly with or on

behalf of domestic parent banks or with branches in other Euro-currency centres. Loans, for example, may be arranged and funded at the domestic parent bank and then simply 'booked' through the offshore branch, because of tax or other regulatory advantages. However, some offshore activity is also likely to be the retail business of on-lending to final users in that part of the world where the centre is situated. A financial centre such as London exhibits some of the characteristics of an offshore centre, notably the large proportion of international business and the absence of direct monetary regulations on Euro-currency deposits (but not of favourable taxation). However, it can legitimately be distinguished from offshore centres proper on the grounds that it has evolved gradually as a principal international financial centre supported by the general business activities of a major trading and industrial nation. London certainly cannot be regarded as simply an entrepôt centre for the booking of loans.

In 1969 the Federal Reserve Board began to approve the creation of Nassau 'brass plate' offices, primarily with the objective of pro-viding smaller banks with a means of obtaining access to the Euro-dollar market to serve their foreign customers outside the restrictions of the VFCR guidelines. This was followed by the development of an offshore market in the Cayman Islands and in Singapore and Hong Kong, where an 'Asian'-dollar market developed. Brimmer and Dahl (1975) report that, by the end of 1973, US banks had 177 foreign branches in the Caribbean area, and 110 in Asia and the Pacific area, compared with 156 in Europe.

An 'Asian'-dollar is in principle the same as a Euro-dollar. The dis-tinction is based on the fact that these are US dollars held with banks in Asia (basically the Far East) and traded by market operators many of whom (e.g. certain Chinese-owned banks) would be less well known in the Euro-dollar market. Some market participants operate in both the Asian-dollar and Euro-dollar markets and arbitrage by these operators ensures that interest rates do not generally diverge widely between the two markets, though time differences mean that the functioning of the two markets hardly overlaps. The growth of offshore markets in different time zones means, that there is effec-tively twenty-four-hour trading in the main international currencies across the globe. About 90 per cent of deposits in the Asian-dollar market are in US dollars, though most freely convertible currencies are actively traded too.

These offshore banking centres benefited, as had the Euro-currency market, from the lack of restrictions on external banking activities. However, particular features, such as low or nil taxation, have given additional impetus to the growth of business in such centres and it has developed rapidly since 1970, even in comparison with the Euro-currency market. For example, the total liabilities of branches of US banks in the Bahamas and Cayman Islands grew from $4.8 billion in 1970 to $121.8 billion by end-1980, while during the same period the external foreign currency liabilities of European reporting countries rose from $79.3 billion to $800.5 billion.

A feature of this geographical widening of the market was the emergence of new funding techniques by banks as they moved towards the funding of their overall lending portfolios on a worldwide basis, taking funds wherever they were cheapest and on-lending them wherever the return was greatest. This feature of the operation of banks, which was an extension of interbank trading in a single market to interbank trading between markets, was to become increasingly important as regards the behaviour of large US banks with the removal of US capital controls in the 1970s. By the end of the 1960s the Euro-currency market was a well-developed international market for short-term funds denominated mainly in dollars, but also other major currencies, and longer-term finance through the operations of the Euro-bond markets, and the market for medium-term bank credit was rapidly emerging. The range of depositors, borrowers and operators in the market had widened significantly, and through its role in facilitating the movement of short-term funds the Euro-market had begun to play a role in the design and conduct of national monetary policy.

2.3   INTEGRATION AND MATURITY

The 1970s and early 1980s have seen a further major increase in the volume and scope of international banking. By end-1980 the overall gross volume of international banking flows exceeded $1,300 billion and the external foreign currency assets of banks in the European Euro-currency market exceeded $750 billion. During this period the operation of international banking evolved to a stage that can no longer be regarded as marginal when compared with national banking activity and to play an increasingly integrated role in the organisation of both national and international monetary relations. This move to what might be regarded as a degree of maturity in international banking activity — although a feature of the market was its continuing growth, flexibility and adaptibility — reflected a series of important new developments in the 1970s. Among these, two are perhaps most important: the removal of restrictions on capital movements in a number of countries; and the impact of oil price rises and the 're-cycling' burden this imposed on financial markets. Additionally, banking crises influenced developments and a fourth element —

less easy to assess, but nevertheless important – was the breakdown of the Bretton Woods system of fixed-exchange-rate parities and the evolution of the international monetary system to one of looser international arrangements.

2.3.1   *Capital controls and international bank lending*

In January 1974 the USA removed the series of capital controls it had imposed in the 1960s. Somewhat paradoxically, because of the influence these controls had in stimulating the Euro-currency market in the 1960s, their removal enhanced the standing and organisation of the Euro-market. By allowing US banks and wealth-holders freely to transfer funds to the Euro-currency market, the lifting of the controls significantly increased the interest-rate linkages between the US domestic and Euro-dollar markets and permitted these markets to become much more closely integrated than previously. Although Euro-dollar interest rates had been fairly closely correlated with *market* interest rates in the USA, such as rates on US Treasury bills, prior to the rescinding of US capital controls, they had tended to be somewhat more volatile, reflecting the smaller size and less well developed nature of the Euro-dollar deposit market. With the removal of restrictions on capital movements, however, US banks began to arbitrage between interest rates on domestic time deposits (especially large negotiable certificates of deposit – CDs) and Euro-dollar interest rates, and to move large amounts of funds between the markets whenever interest-rate differentials made this profitable. This arbitrage process (see Chapter 5) equalised the marginal effective cost of funds to banks in each market and ensured that even small changes in liquidity in one market were very rapidly transferred to the other. US banks became in effect residual suppliers to and takers of liquidity from the Euro-dollar interbank market. The removal of restrictions on capital flows into West Germany in 1974, and later exchange controls in the United Kingdom in October 1979, had similar influences as regards the integration of the Deutsche Mark and sterling segments of the Euro-market with their respective national money markets.[6] These linkages between the Euro-currency and national banking systems enhanced the standing and attractiveness of the Euro-markets to both depositors and borrowers, who began to regard the risks of doing business there to be little greater than in national banking systems.

The increasing integration of financial markets and the closer substitutability between domestic and offshore money markets raises, however, important questions for the conduct of national monetary policy. Domestic monetary regulations, such as reserve requirements on domestic bank deposits, which do not extend to Euro-currency deposits, have given varying interest-rate advantages to banks in the Euro-market in attracting deposit flows out of national banking systems. The closer integration of the markets has increased the potential for such flows, which have tended to complicate the implementation of domestic monetary policies (see Chapter 10).

The removal of US capital controls, and controls in other countries, also influenced the volume of international bank lending booked directly out of national markets in domestic currencies, and through 'shell' branches in offshore centres. The counterpart of the increasing integration of the Euro-currency market with national markets was a reduction of the Euro-market's role as the centre of international banking flows. At the time of the removal of US controls some commentators indeed believed that this would significantly reduce the importance of the Euro-currency markets, as the international business of banks would be attracted back 'on-shore'. While this did not generally happen, there was a very large surge in lending overseas in domestic currencies by banks in the USA and elsewhere; and by end-1980 lending abroad in domestic currencies and through offshore centres was nearly as large as external foreign currency lending by banks in the European Euro-currency market.

The construction and economic interpretation of international banking and Euro-currency statistics is relatively complex and detailed discussion of the data is thus delayed until the next chapter. The figures in Table 2.2 illustrate, however, the developments in international banking over the period 1974–80. Row (1) of the table shows the growth in gross foreign currency lending to non-residents by banks in the European Euro-currency market. Throughout the seven years this expanded by $550 billion or by nearly 300 per cent on the amount outstanding in 1973 to reach $750 billion by the end of 1980. Even more dramatic was the increase in international lending in domestic currencies by banks in the USA (row 4) and in other countries (row 5), and foreign currency lending by offshore branches of US banks (row 3), which largely acted as an alternative channel for international lending by US banks. These aggregates grew by between 500 per cent and 570 per cent in the six years, or by nearly twice the rate of expansion of lending to non-residents through the Euro-currency market. The table also provides estimates of the *net* volume of international bank lending (row 7). These estimates basically make adjustments to the total international banking flows for the double-counting of items due to the redepositing of funds between banks, to arrive at a figure for the volume of credit extended by the international banking system to final users (see Chapter 3 for a further explanation). During the 1970s the net international banking aggregate also showed a very rapid expansion.

In part, the rapid expansion in international bank lending, particularly as regards the operation of US banks in 1974, was a catching-up process following the removal of capital controls. However, the question of why overall international banking aggregates and the Euro-currency market have continued to expand is altogether more complex. It is the subject of many of the subsequent chapters. A sizeable proportion of international banking flows are short-term in nature and respond to factors such as national interest-rate differentials and exchange-rate movements. For example, the very large outflow from banks in the USA in 1978 recorded in Table 2.2, when there was a 40 per cent expansion in their foreign lending in dollars, largely reflected the weakness of the dollar on the foreign exchange markets. As speculators sold the dollar in the forward exchange market or borrowed Euro-dollars to sell in the spot market, this put upward pressure on Euro-dollar interest rates, making it profitable for US banks to supply funds to the Euro-dollar market. The role of the Euro-market as a channel for short-term capital movements is an interesting policy issue (Chapters 5 and 8). Some proportion of the continued rapid expansion of the Euro-currency market may also reflect the absence of direct monetary controls in the market and a process of money or credit creation (Chapters 9 and 10) or simply decisions by the banks themselves to continue to expand in an aggressive way their international loan portfolio (Chapter 7).

2.3.2   *Recycling and the OPEC surpluses*

One of the most important economic developments in the 1970s, which significantly increased the growth and international importance of international banking flows, was the succession of oil price rises in 1973–4 and again since the end of 1978. The immediate impact of these increases was to create unprecedented imbalances in countries' balances of payments. Between 1973 and 1974 the oil exporters' current-account surplus rose from around $6 billion to $68 billion and the counterpart of this was a massive increase in the current-account deficits of the oil-importing world, particularly among non-oil developing countries, smaller developed economies and some larger industrialised countries. These oil surpluses were so large in relation to the size of the oil-exporters' countries and economies that, despite ambitious development projects, a very considerable proportion

Table 2.2
International bank lending 1974–80

	Amounts out-standing end-1973	1974	1975	1976	1977	1978	1979	1980	1974/80	Amounts out-standing end-1980
		Changes, in billions of US dollars and in percentages								
Foreign currency lending by:										
(1) Banks in the narrowly defined Euro-currency market[1]										
$ billion	187.6	27.6	42.9	47.2	68.5	117.2	137.9	111.5	552.8[5]	751.2
percentage		14.7	19.9	18.3	22.4	30.5	27.5	17.4	294.7	
(2) Canadian and Japanese banks										
$ billion	28.2	4.6	− 0.6	4.2	− 0.5	11.7	11.5	24.4	55.3	83.5
percentage		16.3	− 1.8	13.0	− 1.4	32.6	24.2	41.2	196.1	
(3) Offshore branches of US banks[2]										
$ billion	23.8	9.4	17.9	23.8	16.2	15.4	21.2	14.4	118.3	142.1
percentage		39.5	53.9	46.6	21.6	16.9	19.9	11.3	497.1	
Lending in domestic currencies by:										
(4) Banks in the USA										
$ billion	26.7	19.5	13.6	21.3	11.5	36.7	17.1	40.9	150.6	176.9
percentage		73.0	29.4	35.6	14.2	39.6	14.4	30.1	564.0	
(5) Banks in reporting countries other than the USA[3]										
$ billion	23.0	10.3	7.9	9.1	13.4	32.5	36.2	21.1	130.5[5]	169.3
percentage		44.8	23.7	22.1	26.6	38.1	30.7	14.2	567.4	

Overall gross international lending [4]

(6) = (1) + (2) + (3) + (4) + (5)									
$ billion	289.3	71.4	81.7	105.6	109.1	214.6	218.1	212.3	1012.8[5]	1323.1
percentage		24.7	22.7	23.9	19.9	31.0	24.2	19.1	350.1

Overall net international bank lending [6]

(7)										
$ billion	170	50	40	70	75	110	130	145.0	620[5]	810
percentage		29.4	18.2	26.9	22.7	25.6	24.1	21.8	364.7

[1] Banks in Belgium—Luxembourg, France, West Germany, Italy, the Netherlands, Sweden, Switzerland, the United Kingdom and, since end-1977, in Austria, Denmark and Ireland.
[2] Branches of US banks in the Bahamas, Caymans and (since end-1974) in Panama and (since end-1975) in Hong Kong and Singapore.
[3] Banks in Belgium—Luxembourg, Canada, France, West Germany, Italy, Japan, the Netherlands, Sweden, Switzerland, the United Kingdom and, since end-1977, in Austria, Denmark and Ireland, as well as certain trade-related items for the United Kingdom and France, which had been formerly excluded from the statistics.
[4] External assets in domestic and foreign currency of banks in Group of Ten countries, Luxembourg and Switzerland, of the branches of US banks in the offshore centres listed in note 2 and, since end-1977, of banks in Austria, Denmark and Ireland.
[5] Owing to the inclusion, since end-1977, of data reported by banks in Austria, Denmark and Ireland and also slight changes in the coverage of the statistics, these totals do not always correspond to the differences between the amounts outstanding at end-1980 and end-1973.
[6] After making an adjustment for double-counting from redepositing of funds between banks in the interbank market.

Source: BIS Annual Reports.

could not be spent on imports of goods and services and therefore accrued in the form of foreign exchange reserves.

The counterpart of the current-account deficits in the oil-importing world was the need for balance-of-payments finance, if world output were not to decline dramatically under the burden of external payments constraints. In particular, this involved the channelling of capital flows from the surplus OPEC countries to the oil-consuming deficit countries. A large part of this 'recycling' of the OPEC surplus, as it became known, was taken up by the international banking system. Initially, the rise of the oil-induced cash surplus of the oil-exporting countries was so sudden that a very large proportion was placed in short-term bank deposits and other liquid securities and it thus fell largely to the banking system to recycle the funds to deficit countries. Table 2.3 shows that of the OPEC cash surplus of $58 billion in 1974, $30 billion or over 50 per cent was held in bank deposits. In later years this proportion tended to decline but, as the table shows, when the surplus expanded again in 1979 the largest burden again fell in the first instance on the banking system.

Table 2.3
Disposition of oil-exporting countries'
identified cash surplus 1974—80 (US dollars bn)

	1974	1975	1976	1977	1978	1979	1980
Identified cash surplus*	58	38	42	41	23	61	87
Disposition:							
Bank deposits	30	11	14	13	5	40	41
Other	28	27	28	28	18	21	46

* The cash surplus differs from OPEC's current-account surplus because of external borrowing and other capital transactions.

Sources: International Monetary Fund and Bank of England.

The role of international markets in the recycling process is examined in Chapter 6 and some of the reasons why the banking system was able to accommodate the increased external demand for loans, particularly through the market for syndicated medium-term Eurocredits, are discussed in Chapter 7. This market was particularly suited as it allowed large amounts of funds to be recycled, while the risks of lending to foreign borrowers were shared across the international banking system. During the latter half of the 1970s the syndicated loan market grew rapidly, and by end-1980, at about

$200 billion, it accounted for roughly one-third of the net total of outstanding Euro-currency claims of banks in Europe.

2.3.3 The International Monetary System

The impact of the oil price rises and the role of the international banking system in the recycling process had wider implications. In many ways the Euro-market had grown to become an integral and indispensable part of international monetary arrangements as regards the financing of international payments imbalances. In the 1960s the transfer of capital to developing countries and the smaller developed economies, which could be used to finance balance-of-payments deficits, was almost completely from official aid, direct investment flows and short-term trade-related credits. Responsibility for the administration and co-ordination of longer-term development needs and the balance-of-payments adjustment process predominantly fell to international agencies – the World Bank and regional aid agencies and the International Monetary Fund respectively. However, with the advent of private financial markets willing (on suitable lending terms) to transfer large amounts of funds to sovereign borrowers which could be used to finance balance-of-payments deficits, and which also avoided the conditionality attached to drawings and loans from the international agencies, dependence on the financing role of the IMF for bridging finance to cover cyclical payments deficits and to a smaller extent on the World Bank for development finance was eroded.

The evolution of the international monetary system from the Bretton Woods system of closely administered rules to one of looser international monetary arrangements was already well under way in the early 1970s. Under the Smithsonian Agreement of December 1971 the official link between the dollar and gold had been broken and official exchange-rate parities realigned. The failure of these and subsequent realignments to correct what some saw as a fundamental disequilibrium in the international monetary system led towards a generalised floating of exchange rates in 1973. Attempts were made at an all-embracing reform of the international monetary system in the Committee of Twenty negotiations. However, these became fundamentally unstuck with the quadrupling of oil prices in 1973. Specifically the size and structure of the oil-induced surpluses and deficits fell completely outside the normal rules and arrangements guiding the adjustment of national economies to external imbalances. They imposed on the oil-importing world an unprecedented deflationary shock at a time when the general rise in commodity prices and rapid economic expansion had led to a sharp acceleration of inflation in Western economies. There seemed little prospect that the oil surplus could be adjusted away except through a severe world recession, or in the long term through energy-saving policies. The only immediate response was to finance the deficits, but in this respect IMF resources were inadequate and ill-designed. Additional official sources of finance were made available, such as the IMF's Oil Facility established in 1974 and 1975, but these were generally too small to meet the problem; and with official balance-of-payments resources under strain official encouragement was given to a more active role for private markets in the recycling process. The traditional facilities of the IMF, designed to deal with cyclical balance-of-payments problems, could carry harsh conditionality when drawings were made in the upper credit tranches; and during the years 1974–6 credit tranche borrowing financed a much smaller share of countries' payments deficits compared with the previous seven years, and in 1974 only 19 per cent of credit tranche borrowing extended into the upper credit tranches, compared with 58 per cent in earlier periods. Drawings on the IMF's new facilities nevertheless expanded, but as these carried weaker conditionality they were closer to private market sources of finances. In effect countries became reluctant to use the IMF's traditional facilities except as a source of lender of last resort finance when private markets became unwilling to lend.

The emerging role of private markets in international monetary arrangements was also reflected by other international developments. The introduction of floating exchange rates meant that it was much more important than during a fixed-exchange-rate regime for exporters and importers of goods to obtain forward exchange cover against possible erratic movements in exchange rates when trading abroad, and a large proportion of these transactions were undertaken in the Euro-currency market. In the later 1970s, following large US balance-of-payments deficits, a number of central banks and private holders of dollars sought to diversify their foreign exchange reserves away from the dollar. Because of national restrictions on capital inflows and the absence in national money markets of suitable assets in alternative currencies which were desired by central banks – mainly the Deutsche Mark and yen – currency diversification occurred largely through the Euro-currency market expanding the non-dollar segments of the market. Between the years 1975–80 the proportion of dollars in official foreign exchange reserves held in the Euro-currency market fell by 10 per cent, while that of Deutsche Mark and yen holdings expanded by 7 and 3 per cent respectively. Similar patterns emerged for non-official Euro-currency placements where the proportion of dollar holdings declined by some 6 per cent, while those held in sterling, the Deutsche Mark, the Swiss franc and the yen all expanded. Not only did this impose on some countries, perhaps reluctantly, the role of new reserve currency centres (Chapter 8) but it also acted as a substitute to official schemes to meet the desire by countries to diversify their foreign exchange reserves.[7]

2.3.4   Banking crises

Herstatt and Franklin. In 1974 there were a series of banking losses and failures largely associated with imprudent foreign exchange dealing by several banks. Following the move to the generalised floating of exchange rates many banks were slow to realise that authorities would allow a significant movement in the level of exchange rates or the possibility of very rapid movements away from expected par exchange-rate values. Consequently many commercial banks had failed to establish the necessary mechanisms to restrict open foreign exchange positions, and some foreign exchange operators were caught by unanticipated depreciation in some currencies – for example, sterling – in 1973 and 1974. Under the fixed-exchange-rate system it had been less important to avoid large open currency positions as exchange-rate movements were limited by official parities and foreign exchange market intervention.

One of the most serious of the banking failures, because of its wider repercussions on the Euro-currency market, was the collapse of the Cologne bank I. D. Herstatt on 26 June 1974. Also notable were the losses of Franklin National Bank, reported on 13 May 1974 – at that time Franklin was New York's largest commercial bank and twenty-third largest in the USA. *The Times* of 28 June 1974 reported: 'At 4 o'clock on Wednesday afternoon, Bankhaus Herstatt in Cologne closed its doors for the last time . . . with over DM 2,000 million in deposits, it had been asked to go into liquidation by the West German Board for Credit after it had suffered heavy losses in its foreign exchange dealings.' These were finally put at DM 1,200 million. Subsequently, reports of foreign exchange losses by other major banks emerged at Lloyds Bank in Lugano (reported to have lost £33 million); at Belgium's third largest bank, the Bank of Belgium; and at Westdeutsche Landesbank (more than $100 million). Reports from this period provide a nearly unbelievable tale of 'frenzied speculative activity' as banks tried to recoup their losses and of undisclosed and unauthorised foreign exchange dealings by even relatively minor members of some banks' staff.

The foreign exchange losses of both Franklin and Herstatt

produced more general fears about banks' international exposure and operations and the solvency of banks in the Euro-currency market. Initially this caused a loss of confidence in the interbank market and erratic movements in the interest rates banks had to pay for deposits among themselves. A feature of this was the tendency for banks to discriminate sharply between the credit standing of different institutions when lending funds and a marked 'tiering' of interbank interest rates. Some banks, for example Japanese banks, and a number of smaller banks had to pay very high premia for interbank deposits which virtually excluded them from participating in the market.[8] Depositors moved funds out of the Euro-currency market into national markets, the overall size of the London market fell temporarily in the summer of 1974, and interest-rate differentials between the Euro- and the US domestic markets widened sharply.

Combined with the burden that the recycling of the OPEC surpluses was placing on the market and a deepening world recession there was, for a time, widespread concern for the stability of the international banking system. As a consequence, in September 1974 the central bank governors of the Group of Ten countries and Switzerland took the unusual step of issuing a press communiqué outlining their commitment to the continuing stability of the markets. In this they stated:

> At their regular meeting in Basle on 9th September the Governors also had an exchange of views on the problem of the lender of last resort in Euro-markets. They recognized that it would not be practical to lay down in advance detailed rules and procedures for the provision of temporary liquidity. But they were satisfied that means are available for that purpose and will be used if and when necessary.[9]

Following this move, which, though not committing central banks to automatic lender of last resort intervention, did indicate their willingness to intervene in a crisis and also the absence of any further banking failures, stability returned to the Euro-currency market by early 1975.

Iran. A second international banking crisis, which highlighted the potential sovereign risks in international lending, accompanied the revolution in Iran. Under the Shah large borrowings had been made by Iran on the international capital markets. Several Western, particularly US banks, had been highly aggressive in their lending strategies and Iran's total contracted syndicated loan debt had grown to some $5.5 billion. With the overthrow of the Shah relationships between the new revolutionary government in Iran and the West deteriorated and in the early months of 1979 concern grew among Western banks about the willingness of Iran to continue to service its debt commitments. In November 1979 developments took an abrupt turn for the worse following the seizure of American diplomats in Iran, who were to be held hostage for the next fourteen months. As a sanction against this action and a threat by Iran to withdraw its dollar foreign exchange reserves, President Carter enacted the order to freeze Iranian assets both in the USA and with US banks abroad. Thereafter followed a good deal of confusion. Chase Manhattan Bank declared that Iran had failed, apparently for largely technical reasons, to make a regular payment of interest on a $500 million loan for which it was acting as agent bank and that the loan was being called in default. Subsequently there were attempts to call other loans to Iran in default as cross-default clauses[10] took effect, and a number of American banks and other corporations with interests in Iran sought legal permission to claim Iranian assets in compensation for a default by Iran on its obligations. Confusion also surrounded the legal authority of the Presidential order to extend to the operations of the branches and subsidiaries of US banks in foreign countries, as up to that time it had normally been assumed that Euro-markets provided protection against action by national governments in other countries. The ensuing complex mesh of legal issues was largely avoided by the US–Iranian agreement of January 1981. In return for the unfreezing of Iranian assets, Iran agreed to repay $3.7 billion of its outstanding syndicated banking debt and to retain sufficient funds on deposit in the West to cover non-syndicated bank credits and other claims against it which were to be the subject of negotiation and international litigation.

The circumstances surrounding the Iranian crisis may have longer-term implications on the international markets. The attempt by the USA to extend sovereignty over the operation of its banks in other countries has raised complex legal questions which may now never be tested. It may nevertheless suggest that the Euro-market provides less protection against unilateral action by national governments than hitherto thought, which may make some countries, and perhaps particularly Arab depositors, more cautious when placing funds directly in Western banks. It has stimulated a faster expansion of Arab banks and a more direct role for Arab institutions in the international recycling process, which is desirable in any case. The calling of Iranian loans in default also highlighted a preponderance of cross-default clauses on syndicated loans which could have quickly generalised a default by a borrower with the implication that syndicated lending did not provide as much protection to lending banks as had been assumed. As a consequence there is much greater emphasis on the 'small print' in syndicated loan contracts. At the time of the Iranian crisis no sovereign borrower had defaulted on its borrowing from the Euro-market, though loans to some countries – for example, Zaire and Turkey – had been rescheduled to allow time for the repayment and servicing of the loans. However, the confusion surrounding the payments on Iranian loans led to concern that there would be a default by a major borrower. In the event this did not occur. Shortly after the Iranian crisis the banks were involved in rescheduling Poland's debts. This debt crisis was (and at the time of writing continued to be) potentially more serious, as Poland's private debts amount to some $16 billion but unlike Iran its deposits in Western banks were negligible in comparison, its short-term prospects of earning foreign exchange poor and political relationships between the West and the Eastern bloc at a low ebb following the Soviet invasion of Afghanistan. With a background of possible military intervention by the Soviet Union, mounting economic chaos in Poland and a very large number of banks involved in the Polish syndicates the rescheduling negotiations became protracted. For the first time in debt rescheduling negotiations the banks attempted to impose their own economic conditionality, and the proposed agreement to reschedule Poland's 1981 debts appears to have provisions for the bankers to work closely with Polish officials on the recovery programme.

The Herstatt, Iranian and Polish crises have all acted as testing grounds for the underlying stability of the international banking system. The system has survived and flourished, and indeed the experiences have led to greater knowledge and awareness of the risks involved in international markets. Most likely the system will be tested again in the coming decade. Countries' debts to private markets have grown very rapidly, while the economic prospects of many debtor countries have deteriorated. The issue of international banking stability is examined in Chapter 11.

2.4   SUMMARY

The growth of international banking during the past twenty years has been continuous and rapid. By end-1980 gross overall international bank lending exceeded $1,300 billion and external foreign currency lending of banks in the more narrowly defined Euro-currency market had reached \$750 billion. Over the years the Euro-currency market has widened geographically into a global market with many links to national banking systems; it has developed in its range and scope of financial services, and into one of the predominant channels for the flow of short- and longer-term capital between national economies.

Many and varied factors have influenced the growth of international banking and the expansion of international bank lending. At an early stage, the importance of the dollar as the dominant international currency, the internationalisation of manufacturing and the expansion of world trade gave an initial incentive to the growth of Euro-currency markets. In later years the existence of capital or exchange controls in the USA and the absence of regulations in the Euro-currency market stimulated the expansion of larger and increasingly sophisticated external capital and banking markets in Europe and elsewhere. The innovative and competitive nature of the banks themselves generally aided this process. By the time national controls on capital movements were lifted, the market was institutionally well established and continued to retain competitive advantages over national banking systems. The removal of capital controls, however, reduced the Euro-market's independent role. International banking flows expanded rapidly in national currencies and the Euro-currency system became much more closely integrated with national banking systems. The Euro-currency market remains, however, the most important channel for international banking flows in absolute terms.

In the 1970s the significance and importance of international banking flows were greatly enhanced by the succession of oil price rises. By imposing unprecedented balance-of-payments surpluses and deficits on the world, a much large 'recycling' of capital was required than the resources of the international agencies could hope to accomplish in the short term. The burden of financing balance-of-payments deficits was therefore, to a much greater extent than previously, taken up by the private banks, particularly in the Euro-market. This evolution in the role of private capital markets coincided with, indeed some might even say was a factor in, the breakdown in the rules of the international monetary system. International banking has played an integral, if not an indispensable, part in the subsequent development of looser international monetary arrangements.

NOTES

1. It was often quoted that over 40 per cent of the world's trade was still conducted in sterling in the immediate post-war years.

2. The collection of data by the Bank of England on external liabilities and claims of banks in the United Kingdom began earlier in 1962.
3. Belgium—Luxembourg, France, West Germany, Italy, the Netherlands, Sweden, Switzerland, the United Kingdom and Japan. Quarterly reporting of foreign currency banking statistics of these nine countries, plus Canada, was put on a regular basis at end-1964. In 1965 these ten countries also began to report to the Bank for International Settlements on external liabilities and claims of their banks in domestic currencies.
4. In subsequent years various technical changes were made. In particular, in 1971 all export credits were freed from the ceilings. For a description of the controls and their impact in the 1970s see McClam (1973).
5. A notable exception is the New York Free Banking Zone or International Banking Facility established in 1981. Under this facility the US authorities have effectively established an 'off-shore' market onshore as a way of competing for international business (see Chapter 4).
6. West German authorities continued to discriminate against non-resident deposits with domestic banks until August 1975, and did so again in 1978.
7. Among these is an SDR Substitution Account, administered by the IMF, which would allow the voluntary exchange of short-term foreign currency assets (mainly dollars) for SDR-dominated assets. There are, however, many other difficult problems involved in setting up such a scheme, in particular the interest rates paid on holdings with the account and coverage of possible losses of the account from movements in exchange rates, and this made it impossible to reach agreement on the scheme.
8. Bachman (1976) has suggested that up to ten tiers of banks could be identified in 1974, ranked from prime US banks, as the best, to Japanese banks as the worst. This contrasted with six tiers in 1976.
9. Bank for International Settlements, Basle, 10 September 1974.
10. These meant that if a bank were a member of two separate syndicates which lent to the one country, and if one of the syndicates (but not the other) were to call its loans to that country in default, then the bank would have an obligation to have the loans by the second syndicate called in default also.

3 Euro-currency Statistics: Interpretation and Implications

In Chapters 1 and 2 reference has been made to the size of the Euro-currency market without very much analysis of the underlying statistics. The incorrect interpretation of Euro-currency data is a source of considerable confusion about the market's economic implications. We therefore now examine two sets of Euro-currency data: the international banking statistics compiled by the Bank for International Settlements in Basle (section 3.1) and Bank of England data on the maturity structure of London banks' foreign currency assets and liabilities (section 3.2).

3.1 THE BIS STATISTICS

Official statistics on international banking flows and the size of the Euro-currency market have been compiled by the BIS since the early 1960s. They are reported annually in the Bank's annual report and, since 1974, quarterly in a regular press release. The main purpose of the exercise is to monitor the development of international and Euro-currency banking from a macroeconomic and balance-of-payments point of view.[1]

The data are collected via the central banks from banks in the Group of Ten countries[2] plus Switzerland, and since end-1977 from banks in Austria, Denmark and Ireland as well. They provide quarterly information on the reporting banks' assets and liabilities in individual foreign currencies *vis-à-vis* both residents and non-residents and also on external positions in domestic currency.[3] The figures are not only broken down geographically, i.e. according to country or area of residence of the suppliers or borrowers of the funds, but also provide a distinction between positions *vis-à-vis* banks and non-banks.

The USA itself was originally not a participant in this extremely complex statistical exercise, partly because the great bulk of the external assets and liabilities of banks in the USA are in domestic currency and are therefore not 'Euro'. In the early 1970s the Federal Reserve began to collect data on the foreign branches of US banks, and provided the BIS with the figures for assets and liabilities of US banks' branches located in the offshore centres of the Caribbean and the Far East (US banks' affiliates operating in the other reporting countries are covered by these countries' reporting systems). Later, the BIS also started to include the external assets and liabilities of banks in the USA in its statistical compilations. Unfortunately, no currency breakdown is available for banks in the USA and their foreign branches and only a very limited bank/non-bank breakdown for offshore branches.

The other main source for estimates of the overall size of the Euro-currency market is the data published by Morgan Guaranty in *World Financial Markets*. Originally the coverage of these estimates was geographically somewhat broader than the BIS reports, which were initially confined to the external activities and foreign currency positions of banks in eight European reporting countries — Belgium—Luxembourg, France, West Germany, Italy, the Netherlands, Sweden, Switzerland and the United Kingdom. Morgan, however, also included data on the activities of banks in Canada and Japan and certain offshore centres derived from national banking statistics. But with the increased geographical coverage by the BIS numbers, there is little to choose between the different estimates, which are anyway conceptually the same. As Morgan estimates are in any case based on BIS figures and give a much less detailed geographical breakdown, discussion here is confined to the official BIS statistics.

There are several statistical measures of the external and foreign currency activities of banks. One of the broadest is the estimate of 'international bank lending', defined as the external positions of banks in the Group of Ten countries plus Switzerland, Austria, Denmark, Ireland and the branches of US banks in certain offshore centres. Column 1 of Table 3.1 reports developments in this aggregate from 1970 and shows its extremely rapid expansion over the period. This measure includes domestic currency lending by reporting banks to non-residents which are not Euro-currency transactions. At end-1980 international lending by banks in domestic currencies amounted to about one-quarter of gross international bank lending (columns 2 and 3 of Table 3.1). However, the measure excludes foreign currency lending by reporting banks to residents in the countries in which the banks are located since these are not classified as external banking business, but nevertheless are Euro-currency transactions (at end-1980 foreign currency loans to residents amounted to $318.9 billion — column 4 of the table).

Over the years increasing emphasis has been placed on the growth of international banking rather than the narrower Euro-currency banking concept, as it is recognised from the viewpoint of a number of economic concerns that it is the overall external lending of the banking system which is important, rather than that simply denominated in foreign currency. For example, lending abroad in domestic currencies may equally have implications for the structure of national exchange rates, the interdependence of national monetary policies and overall balance-of-payments financing or for the lending exposure of the banking system to different borrowing countries. With the removal of capital controls in a number of countries it has become very difficult to distinguish the role of Euro-market lending from the more traditional bank lending overseas in domestic currencies. A main distinguishing feature of Euro-currency intermediation, however, remains − the different regulatory treatment of the Euro-currency bank deposit and loan market.

To move from the estimates of total international banking to the broadest measure of the Euro-currency market − the total foreign currency assets or liabilities of all reporting banks − it is necessary to subtract external lending by banks in domestic currencies and add in foreign currency lending to residents to the international banking aggregate. This statistical measure is known as the *broadly* defined gross measure of the Euro-currency market (BDGM):

$$
\text{BDGM} = \boxed{\begin{array}{l}\text{International}\\ \text{bank lending}\end{array}} - \boxed{\begin{array}{l}\text{External lending by banks}\\ \text{in domestic currencies}\end{array}}
$$

$$
+ \boxed{\begin{array}{l}\text{Lending by banks in}\\ \text{foreign currencies to}\\ \text{residents}\end{array}}
$$

Estimates are reported in column 5 of Table 3.1. It is known as a 'gross' measure because it includes interbank transactions between reporting banks, and broadly defined as it covers the widest geographical reporting area.

A second Euro-currency statistic is the *narrowly* defined gross measure of the Euro-currency market, NDGM. This differs from the BDGM in that coverage is confined to reporting banks in the European area only and excludes lending by the 'offshore' branches of US banks and the foreign currency lending by banks in Canada and Japan:

NDGM = BDGM −

$$
\boxed{\begin{array}{l}\text{Lending by offshore branches}\\ \text{of US banks}\end{array}} - \boxed{\begin{array}{l}\text{Foreign currency lending}\\ \text{by banks in}\\ \text{Canada and Japan}\end{array}}
$$

These estimates are reported in column 8 of Table 3.1.

Table 3.1
Estimates of international bank lending and the size of the Euro-currency market
(in billions of US dollars)

End-years	(1) International bank lending[1,2]	(2) International lending by banks in the USA	(3) Domestic currency lending by other reporting banks to non-residents	(4) Foreign currency lending by reporting banks to residents	(5) Broadly defined *gross* measures of the Euro-currency market (5) = (1) − (2) − (3) + (4)
1970	117.1	13.9	10.0	10.1	103.3
1971	142.7	16.9	11.9	10.6	124.5
1972	184.1	20.7	13.4	14.2	164.2
1973	289.4	26.7	23.0	24.5	264.2
1974	359.3	46.2	33.4	43.1	322.8
1975	442.4	59.8	41.2	109.3	450.7
1976	548.0	81.1	50.3	123.3	539.9
1977	698.7	92.6	85.2	151.2	663.1
1978	904.7	130.8	117.7	188.4	844.6
1979	1,110.7	136.0	148.2	242.1	1,068.6
1980	1,321.9	176.8	169.3	318.9	1,294.7

Table 3.1 continued

End-years	(6) Lending by offshore branches of US banks[2]	(7) Foreign currency lending by banks in Japan and Canada	(8) Narrowly defined (European area) gross measure of the Euro-currency market (8) = (5) – (6) – (7)	(9) Estimated net size of narrowly defined (European area) Euro-currency market	(10) Annual growth rate of the narrowly defined net size of the Euro-currency market
1970	—	19.0	84.3	57.0	29.5
1971	—	18.4	106.1	71.0	24.6
1972	—	24.2	140.0	92.0	29.6
1973	23.8	50.1	190.3	132.0	43.5
1974	31.7	51.2	239.9	177.0	34.1
1975	51.1	52.1	347.5	205.0	15.8
1976	74.9	58.1	406.9	247.0	20.5
1977	91.1	59.9	512.1	300.0	21.4
1978	106.5	82.6	655.5	375.0	25.0
1979	127.6	105.0	836.0	475.0	26.0
1980	141.0	147.5	1,006.2	575.0	21.0

[1] External assets of banks in the Group of Ten countries and Switzerland and from end-1977 of banks in Austria, Denmark and Ireland also.

[2] External positions of foreign branches of US banks are included for the Bahamas and Cayman Islands from 1973 and in Panama, Lebanon, Hong Kong and Singapore since 1975 as well.

Source: BIS quarterly press releases. (*Note*: columns (3) and (4) include estimates of lending by banks in Canada and Japan not included in the press releases.)

The NDGM was the original estimate of the size of the Euro-currency market made by the BIS, as initially the market was mainly confined to European countries. (Originally only eight reporting countries were included, extended to eleven at end-1977.) There is thus a historical precedent in reporting this figure. There are also other reasons for concentrating attention on this measure. As regards off-shore lending by US banks, much of this is entrepôt business, with the loans and deposits being contracted at the head offices of banks in the USA and then simply 'booked' through the offshore branch. The overwhelming volume of this business is also believed to be conducted in dollars – in the Bahamas and Cayman Islands, for example, 94 per cent of the assets of the branches of US banks were thus held – although there is not a complete breakdown by currency for all offshore centres. Offshore business of the branches of US banks is therefore not fundamentally different from international bank lending in dollars by banks in the USA and thus should be excluded from measures of Euro-currency banking proper. Also, for Canadian banks about 94 per cent of foreign currency assets are held in dollars, reflecting the particularly important links between the two North American economies. Much of this may be regarded as lending for traditional foreign exchange purposes. Finally, the omission of Japan from the figures, for it has not as yet emerged as a major Euro-currency centre, may not be too serious.

3.1.1   Double-counting

One of the most striking features about both the narrowly and broadly defined gross measures of the Euro-currency market is the predominance of interbank positions. As Table 3.2 shows, only 26 per cent of European reporting banks' foreign currency assets and 14 per cent of their Euro-currency liabilities were with non-bank entities.

These interbank flows are of course not without economic importance. Interbank 'churning' of funds is an important liquidity distribution feature of the Euro-currency market which may also have liquidity-creating effects if in this process there is a significant maturity transformation of deposits, i.e. short-term deposits placed at one bank are lent to another at a slightly longer term, etc. This aspect of interbank trading is considered in section 3.2. But based on an analogy with national money and credit stock definitions the various interbank positions can largely be netted out since they double-count the flow of credit from original non-bank depositors in the market to final non-bank borrowers. To give an example, say a non-bank wealth-holder in Country *A* places dollars in a bank in

Table 3.2
Narrowly defined gross measure of
the Euro-currency market:* end-1980
(in billions of dollars)

Vis-à-vis	Assets			Liabilities		
	Total	Non-banks	As % of total	Total	Non-banks	As % of total
Non-residents	751.2	193.5	25.7	800.5	111.4	13.9
Residents	255.0	72.1	28.3	214.7	30.7	14.3
Total	1,006.2	265.6	26.4	1,015.2	142.1	14.0

* Total foreign currency assets or liabilities of European area reporting banks.
Source: BIS quarterly press release.

country *B* (not the USA) which lends these to a bank in country *C* (also not the USA) which then uses the funds to make a loan to a non-bank borrower in country *D* (see Figure 3.1).

This set of transactions would be counted twice in the BIS statistics on banks' total foreign currency assets – once as an interbank asset ($B - C$) and once as a Euro-dollar loan to a non-bank ($C - D$). However, there has only been a single flow of credit through the banking system from original suppliers to final users of Euro-currency funds ($A - (B - C) - D$). Counting the interbank transactions is therefore unnecessary, and indeed, when there is a large amount of redepositing between banks in the Euro-market, would lead to a very significant overestimation of the amount of final credit intermediated through the Euro-banking system. To make allowance for such double-counting the BIS provides estimates of the 'net' size of the Euro-currency market. This measure, however, differs somewhat from the simple adjustment for double-counting described, as certain interbank transactions continue to be included. The development of

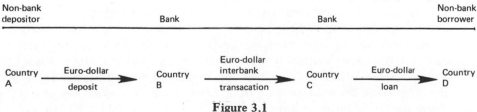

Figure 3.1

this aggregate over the 1970s and its rate of growth are shown in columns 9 and 10 respectively of Table 3.1.

3.1.2   *The BIS 'net' concept*

As with gross measures of the Euro-currency market, net estimates refer to the group of banks reporting within a specific geographical area. The most detailed reports are prepared for the narrowly defined (European) reporting area, but net estimates of the geographically more broadly defined market (and of international bank lending, row 7 of Table 2.2 on page 25) are also available. The methodology used to arrive at these various estimates is broadly similar (as before, for 'net' international bank lending foreign currency transactions with residents are excluded and lending abroad in domestic currencies included). The distinction between banks within the reporting area and those outside is one criterion used when deciding which inter-bank positions should be netted out, with interbank transactions with banks outside the reporting area being *included*. The logic is that the BIS concept attempts to show the *intermediary* role of the Euro-market in international banking or credit flows rather than only the volume of Euro-currency flows directly between non-bank suppliers and borrowers of Euro-currency funds. Part of the intermediary process involves interbank 'churning' of funds within the Euro-currency market, but that does not add to the stock of credit inter-mediated through the system which only increases when new funds are placed and borrowed from the Euro-currency banking system. When funds are placed in the market this is known, and counted on the liability side of the market, as a *source* of funds, and the counter-part, when funds eventually leave the Euro-currency system, as a *use* of Euro-currencies (counted on the asset side on the market). The process is illustrated in Figure 3.2, following the example above, but where A and D are now banks outside the reporting area and B and C are reporting area banks. When funds are borrowed by bank B from bank A this shows up as a 'source' of funds and when bank C lends to bank D as a 'use' of funds in the 'net' BIS statistics, while the transaction B to C is again netted out.

Outside reporting area banks are not considered part of the Euro-currency interbank 'churning' process as they predominantly represent a 'source' and 'use' of funds outside the Euro-market. One can imagine these 'outside' banks acting purely as depositors or bor-rowers of funds on the behalf of non-banks. Of course, to the extent that they do redeposit part of their Euro-currency borrowing in the Euro-market, double-counting will occur, but by including all the

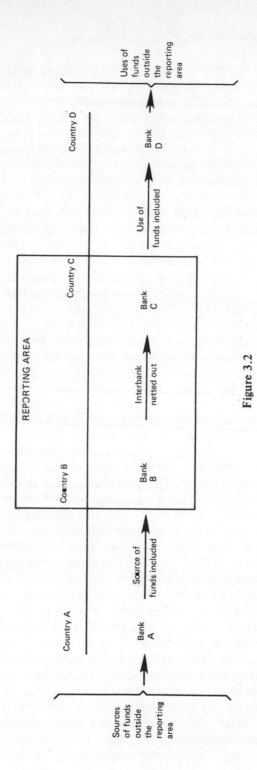

Figure 3.2

43

major Euro-currency centres actively trading with one another in interbank funds in the reporting area the amount of funds double-counted is thought to be reasonably small.

Within the reporting area certain interbank transactions are also included when reporting banks are themselves regarded as initial suppliers or final users of Euro-currency funds. There are essentially two ways in which this can occur (the logic is broadly the same as for including transactions with outside reporting area banks):

1. When reporting banks *switch* funds obtained in domestic currencies into foreign currencies, i.e. they use domestic currency to buy foreign currency to place in the Euro-market, they are considered as net suppliers of Euro-currencies, and when they switch foreign currency deposits into domestic currencies, i.e. they use foreign currency borrowed in the Euro-market to buy domestic currency, they are considered as net users of Euro-currency funds.
2. When a reporting bank lends domestic currency to a reporting bank in another country or borrows its domestic currency in the Euro-market. In the first case it is regarded as a source and in the second an end-use of Euro-currencies.

Some further examples illustrate why and how these flows are counted:

1.   *Switched positions.* Let us assume first of all that a bank located in West Germany (call it B_0) uses Deutsche Mark to buy dollars (i.e. it switches out, into dollars) and places these with a London bank, C, which uses them to fund its Euro-dollar lending to non-banks. Both B_0 and C are reporting area banks and thus this flow would show up as a Euro-currency interbank transaction in dollars between the reporting banks in London and Germany. However, as in the case of outside reporting area banks, the original source of funds is outside the Euro-currency market – in this case the German domestic market. Similarly, if another bank located in Germany (call it B_1) were to borrow dollars in London to buy Deutsche Mark (i.e. to switch in, out of dollars) to fund domestic lending, this would represent a use of Euro-currency funds outside the Euro-market. The German banks might then be viewed as intermediating purely on the behalf of domestic non-banks, illustrated in Figure 3.3.

To exclude the interbank transactions in dollars between the banks located in Germany (B_0, switching out, and B_1, switching in) and the London Euro-currency market (bank C) would be to underestimate the intermediary role of the Euro-market in international flows.

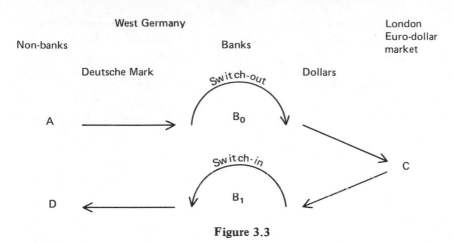

West Germany

Non-banks

London
Euro-dollar
market

Banks

Deutsche Mark

Dollars

Switch-out

A

B_0

Switch-in

C

D

B_1

Figure 3.3

Although the transactions between the German banks and non-banks ($A - B_0$ and $B_1 - D$) are purely domestic banking business they are dependent on the intermediary function of the Euro-currency system. To exclude them would underestimate the *net* size of credit flows through the Euro-market.

The situation is, however, slightly more complex if one also allows for the possibility of interbank trading between domestic banks in domestic currencies. Extending our example, let us assume that the London bank (call it now C_1) switches the dollars received from the bank in Germany (B_0) into sterling and lends these sterling funds to another London bank (call it C_2) which switches the sterling into dollars. This second London bank lends the dollars outside the Euro currency system. The process is illustrated in Figure 3.4.

Now to add in all the switched positions in the BIS figures would be to count the credit flow twice on both the sources and uses side of the market: on the sources side when the German bank B_0 and the British bank C_2 switch out; on the uses side when the British bank C_1 switches in and the British bank C_2 lends outside the Euro-currency market. However, there has only been one credit flow through the Euro-currency market – the original source of funds from the German bank B_0 and the end-use of funds by the British bank C_2. The UK interbank transaction in sterling ($C_1 - C_2$) has not added to the sources of funds to the Euro-market and therefore should be netted out of the figures in a similar way to an interbank transaction in dollars between the London banks. Instead of switching, bank C_1 could have lent the dollars directly to bank C_2, in which case it would have been netted out; there is no reason to count it just because it has taken place in sterling instead.

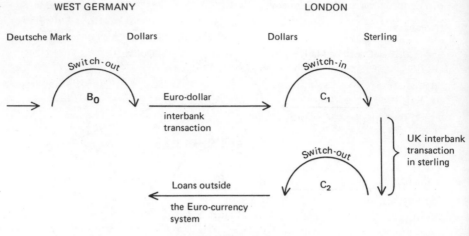

Figure 3.4

In assessing the volume of switched funds to be included in the estimates of the net sources and uses of funds in the Euro-market account has to be taken of these two sources and uses of switched funds – in the first case the switch is an intermediary function on behalf of non-banks, and in the second, part of the interbank 'churning' process. In practice, available data do not make this possible and the volume of switching to be included is based largely on informed guesswork with the allowance for the gross or net switched position of the banks varying from one centre to another depending on their particular operating characteristics. In fact, the BIS in arriving at its estimates tends to be conservative and nets out a large proportion of switched currency positions by banks in any one country.

2.   *Domestic currency lending and borrowing.* Very similar considerations apply to the treatment of banks' lending and borrowing abroad in domestic currencies with other reporting banks. To see this a bank located in Germany might lend and borrow Deutsche Mark in London purely on behalf of its domestic non-bank customers, in which case this would represent a 'real' source and use of Euro-Deutsche Mark. Alternatively it might use Deutsche Mark borrowed abroad to lend to another bank in Germany, which then relends Deutsche Mark in the Euro-market. Again, therefore, some allowance has to be made for double-counting of credit flows. In fact, the BIS includes most of the reporting banks' transactions in the Euro-market in their own currencies. The main exception is a substraction for 'traditional' working balances held by reporting banks in foreign

currencies which would exist without a Euro-currency market. An allowance is also made for trustee funds placed in the market by Swiss banks. These are recorded as liabilities of reporting banks *vis-à-vis* banks in Switzerland; however, an overwhelming proportion is owned and placed on behalf and at the risk of non-banks. They are therefore treated as a non-bank source of funds. The figures reported in Table 1.1 on page 5 show the changes in the net sources and use of Euro-currency funds and the geographical distribution of the flows.

3.1.3   *The net measure and world money stock*

An intriguing question about Euro-currency statistics is what part of them represents an addition to the stock of national monetary aggregates and therefore has been ignored in the formulation of national monetary policies. Some analysts have simply looked at the gross Euro-currency statistics and others at the net statistics as an indication of the volume of 'money' held in the Euro-market. Both are wrong because they include interbank transactions. Helmut Mayer of the BIS has broken down the net statistics in an attempt to indicate what fraction might be regarded as an addition to world money stock. His breakdown is reproduced in Table 3.3, which shows

Table 3.3
Sources of Euro-currency funds: end-1978

		In $ billion	In percentages
Private banks		173	46
Central banks		80	21
Funds from Eastern Europe		9	3
		262	70%
Non-bank funds		113	30%
of which:			
from non-residents	61		16
from residents	22		6
trustee funds (including some funds from non-bank financial institutions)	30		8
Total		375	100

Source: Mayer (1979a).

that in fact 46 per cent of the sources of Euro-currency funds at end-1978 was supplied by private banks. The ultimate liability counterpart of these funds, which is mainly in domestic currencies, is already included in countries' domestic monetary aggregates and thus to add them again would lead to double-counting. A further example illustrates why this is so and serves to revise the various statistical measures of the Euro-currency market.

Say *A* and *D* are again banks outside the reporting area and *B* and *C* reporting area banks, and that bank *A* has received a deposit of 100 in domestic currency from a domestic company which it places with bank *B* in the Euro-market. The source of the original deposit might be assumed to come from *A*'s monetary authorities by means of an open-market purchase of securities from *A*'s residents. Bank *B* lends the funds in the interbank market to bank *C*, which in turn lends them to bank *D* in another country. Bank *D* switches the funds into domestic currency and uses them to make loans to domestic non-banks. This set of transactions is illustrated, using some simple balance-sheets, in Figure 3.5.

The initial results for national and Euro-currency aggregates would then be as follows:

(1) *A*'s national money supply increases by 100.
(1)–(2) Net and gross *sources* of funds to the Euro-currency market rise by 100.
(2)–(3) Gross Euro-currency liabilities (and assets) rise by an additional 100 by the *B* to *C* interbank transaction.
(3)–(4) Net *uses* of Euro-currency funds rise by 100.
(4) *D*'s national money stock rises by 100 if foreign currency liabilities of *D*'s banks are included in *D*'s money stock definition; (otherwise no change).

Assuming that the foreign currency liabilities of *D*'s banks are excluded from *D*'s national monetary aggregates, then national monetary aggregates would rise initially by the 100 liability of *A*'s banks to non-banks, the net size of the Euro-market by 100 and the size of the gross Euro-currency market by 200. The increase in the holdings of 'money' by non-banks and the overall amount of funds intermediated between non-bank entities by the banking system as a whole has, however, only been 100 – the 100 deposit by *A*'s residents which results from the open-market purchase of securities by *A*'s monetary authorities, which is ultimately lent to non-banks in *D*. To add the net size of the Euro-currency market to national money stocks would clearly double-count the liquid or money holdings of non-banks. Exactly the same reasoning would apply if *A* and *D* were

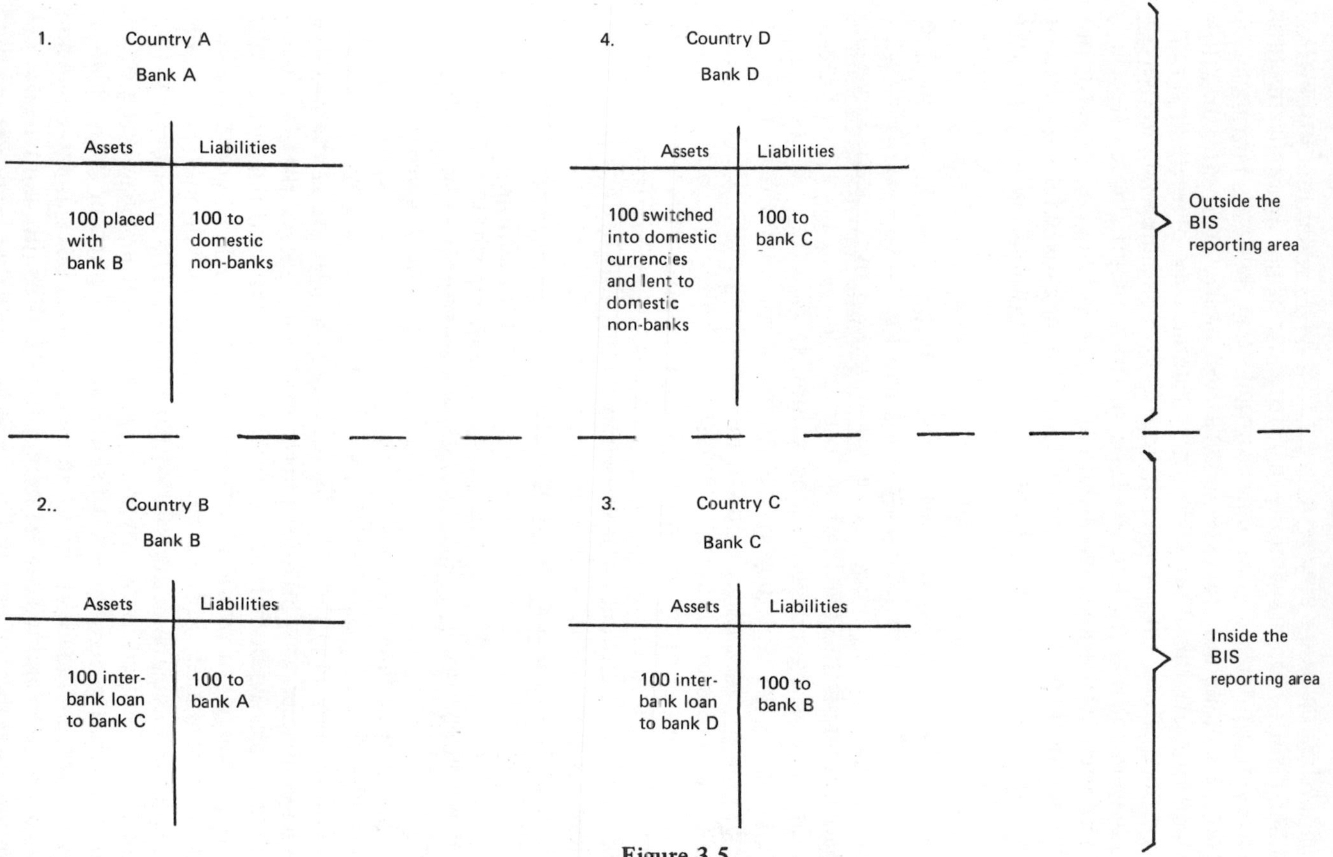

1. Country A
    Bank A

Assets	Liabilities
100 placed with bank B	100 to domestic non-banks

2. Country B
    Bank B

Assets	Liabilities
100 inter-bank loan to bank C	100 to bank A

4. Country D
    Bank D

Assets	Liabilities
100 switched into domestic currencies and lent to domestic non-banks	100 to bank C

3. Country C
    Bank C

Assets	Liabilities
100 inter-bank loan to bank D	100 to bank B

Outside the BIS reporting area

Inside the BIS reporting area

Figure 3.5

inside the reporting area and the funds placed in the Euro-market either resulted from switching into foreign currencies or placing (and borrowing) domestic currencies abroad. The redistribution of funds from A's non-bank lenders to D's non-bank borrowers from the operation of the Euro-currency system may nevertheless have economic effects on the overall liquidity of the non-banking sector. It may mean that a given stock of world money is more effectively distributed and can thus sustain a larger volume of expenditure. Ultimately the size of these effects will depend upon how the authorities in countries A and D react to outflows and inflows of funds (see Chapter 9).

Mayer's breakdown of the net sources of funds to the Euro-market also shows that central banks were important suppliers of funds to the market. These are not part of private money holdings – and in many cases already have a counterpart in domestic monetary statistics – and thus need not be counted, though they are a potential claim on world goods and services. Similarly Eastern European holdings are not part of the private money stock of the Western world. Taking out these three sources of funds – private banks, central banks and Eastern Europe – leaves $113 billion of non-bank funds which might roughly be regarded as a contribution of the Euro-market to world private money holdings. (Mayer (1976) also makes a number of other qualifications when adding this figure.) To obtain a more accurate measure it is necessary to examine the structure of national money stock definitions.

3.1.4   *Augmenting national money stocks*

In national economies there are usually several measure of 'money', typically referred to as the 'Ms'. M_1 is one of the narrowest including only currency plus the most liquid deposits with the banking system –demand deposits. Broader measures, such as M_2 or M_3, include a range of less liquid balances with banks, and, in some countries, with other financial institutions. Private non-bank Euro-currency holdings are predominantly in the form of fixed-term time deposits, or negotiable time deposits in the case of Euro-dollar CDs, and thus, if they are to be counted in money stock measures, would form part of the broader concept of 'money'. The question of whether these balances should be included at all in monetary aggregates is by no means clear and is examined in Chapters 8 and 10. For the moment we seek only to establish the type of statistical addition that might be required when augmenting national broad monetary aggregates with Euro-currency statistics in a systematic and rigorous fashion. The details are set out in the statistical annex to this chapter.

A proportion of private Euro-currency deposits do have a remaining maturity of one week or under and may be regarded as closer to the narrower M_1 concept of money. As we shall see in section 3.2, this proportion may amount to some 20 per cent of total private Euro-currency holdings. Some of this percentage represents balances which have been placed for a longer term and are nearing maturity. At a guess this might reduce the proportion of Euro-currency deposits with an original maturity of less than eight days to around 15 per cent, but no detailed information is available, which makes it impossible to use Euro-currency statistics to augment narrow money stocks except in a very rough and approximate fashion. Using the guess that these amount to 15 per cent of total private Euro-currency holdings would indicate that about $20 to $30 billion might have to be added to (although some are already included in) world narrow money stocks, which is not a very large amount in relation to the total.

The process involved in augmenting national broad monetary aggregates is itself complex since there are significant differences between countries' national money stock definitions. It is undertaken for ten major countries in the annex, which also describes the composition of different national definitions. The results of the exercise using end-1979 data show that when each country's money stock is augmented by the components of its own national definition about $160 billion would have to be added to national broad money stocks because of private holdings in the Euro-currency market (including offshore centres), representing 3.5 to 4 per cent of domestic broad monetary aggregates. On the broadest concept of money used by some countries – residents' holdings of domestic and foreign currency plus non-residents' holdings of the domestic currency – the maximum addition to world national monetary aggregates amounts to some $180 billion or about 4.5 per cent of the domestically defined money stock total. Of this total $50 billion are accounted for simply by the use of narrower money stock definitions in other countries, $30 billion by residents holding their domestic currency in the Euro-market and the remainder by non-residents' holdings of currencies outside the country of the currency concerned. The detailed estimates are reported in Table 3.8 and described in the annex. By themselves these figures do not indicate that the Euro-markets have added significantly to world money stock holdings. The striking feature is, if anything, how small they are compared with the gross measures of the Euro-currency market.

The average estimates obscure, however, some important inter-country differences. For seven of the ten countries — Canada, France, West Germany, Italy, Japan, Switzerland and the United Kingdom — the percentage by which national money stock definitions would need to be augmented to take account of Euro-currency holdings was less than 2 per cent — an insignificant proportion. In the case of two of the remaining countries — Belgium and the Netherlands — the larger addition to national aggregates largely reflected residents' holdings of foreign currency abroad which are included as these countries include residents' holdings of foreign currency in their national money stock definitions. Only for Belgium out of the ten countries were residents' holdings of domestic currency abroad larger than 2 per cent of domestic broad monetary aggregates, and indeed for seven of the countries they were less than 1 per cent.

The tenth country examined was the USA, and perhaps here the role of the Euro-currency market is most important because of the predominant position of the dollar in Euro-currency transactions. Adding together US residents' holdings of domestic and foreign currencies in the Euro-market and non-US residents' holdings of Euro-dollars, including a proportion held in certain offshore centres, gives a figure of about $141 billion, which represents 8 per cent of US M_3. Of this total $119 billion were held in the (broadly defined) Euro-currency market and $22 billion an estimated addition from offshore branches of US banks. Breaking down the $119 billion held in the Euro-currency reporting area shows that of this $25 billion were dollars and $4 billion foreign currencies held by US residents, while the remaining $90 billion were non-resident dollar holdings. In other words, the overwhelming proportion was held, not by the US public, but by the rest of the world. It is difficult to assess what the relevance of these holdings is for US monetary aggregates and policy. The USA does include in its money stock definitions non-residents' holdings of dollars with domestic banks and therefore arguably they should be counted under that definition — they represent, after all, a potential claim on the resources of the USA. However, because of the role of the dollar in international transactions (Chapter 4) a proportion, and perhaps a sizeable one, is undoubtedly held for third-country trade purposes and not for spending on US goods and services and thus may be totally irrelevant as regards US domestic economic activity. My own view is that they are not overly important in terms of US domestic monetary aggregate control designed to influence the aggregate level of spending in the USA but are more relevant for the value of the US currency on the foreign exchanges. There is a distinct possibility that, like other external dollar holdings, they will be sold when there are expectations that the dollar's exchange rate will weaken. That is also very relevant for US monetary policy but involves a much broader range of variables and cannot be causally related solely to the build-up of dollar balances in the Euro-market. In summary, the statistical exclusion of private Euro-currency holdings from national monetary aggregates is, at present, in stock terms a rather minor omission. Changes in the stock may nevertheless have implications for national monetary policy (see Chapter 10).

3.1.5 *Credit flows*

A somewhat different but related question concerns the role of the Euro-market as a source of credit outside national monetary control and whether an additional allowance, over and above that for 'money' holdings in the Euro-market, has to be made. Kessler (1980) has emphasised the importance of international banking as a 'credit circuit'.[4] He notes that credit flows through the Euro-currency system to the non-banking sector exceed their deposits with the system, and that this 'foreign credit expansion', as he calls it, is also relevant for national monetary and credit policy. Figure 3.6 gives a picture of the foreign asset and liability position of Euro-banks at end-1978 and of the changes that have occurred in that position in the five-year period 1974–8.

As this figure shows, outstanding credits to non-banks expanded by $130 billion during the five-year period to reach a total of $200 billion by end-1978. This was financed only partly by the placement of funds in the market by the non-banking sector (which rose by $95 billion to $135 billion), the remainder coming from monetary authorities and private banks. To the extent that non-banks have borrowed in the Euro-market rather than national money markets, the overall rate of world credit expansion has been greater than that recorded by national credit aggregates and apparently by as much as $200 billion.

In attempting to assess what is the contribution of the Euro-markets to global credit availability it is necessary again to examine the sources of Euro-currency deposits. Funds that are not placed in the market by the non-banking sector are from banks or monetary authorities. As discussed above, funds from private banks have already a counterpart in national monetary statistics – a domestic bank deposit. It may be very relevant for national policies that these funds are lent overseas, rather than at home, but from a global perspective

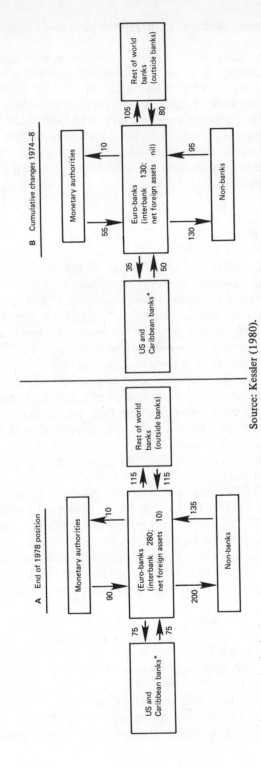

Source: Kessler (1980).

Fig. 3.6 Foreign assets and liabilities of Euro-banks (in billions of US dollars)

they are *not* an additional source of credit to the non-bank sector, having been counted in national monetary aggregates. When central banks place funds in the Euro-market they may be an additional source of bank credit. However, the overwhelming proportion of official foreign exchange reserves is held in dollars, and the USA has chosen to exclude deposits held by official institutions from their domestic monetary aggregates.[5] The placement of reserves in the Euro-market will therefore leave national monetary stocks largely unaffected and should not be counted as an addition to domestic money stocks. They could of course be used to finance lending to the non-banking sector but that is equally true when they are held in US domestic banks. From a macroeconomic viewpoint the important issue is whether central bank placements in the Euro-market have influenced the volume of Euro-market lending to the non-bank sector, i.e. whether a reduction in central bank deposits would have been fully offset by an increase in lending by, say, US banks to the Euro-market. We examine this question in later chapters, where it is suggested that although the offset would be large it is probably less than 100 per cent, in which case the development of Euro-market lending to the non-banking sector might have been somewhat, but not very, different from what actually occurred.

The conclusion from this assessment is that the additional element in the supply of credit to the non-banking sector, because of the operation of the Euro-market, amounts broadly to the placement of funds in the market by non-banks which are excluded from national money stock statistics – and that is the additional statistical element calculated in the previous section. A further adjustment for the volume of credit supplied by the Euro-market is therefore unnecessary when measuring the global availability of credit.

3.2   MATURITY TRANSFORMATION

A second set of data which is frequently discussed is the Bank of England data on the maturity structure of the foreign currency assets and liabilities of banks in the London Euro-currency market. The reports published regularly in the *Bank of England Quarterly Bulletin* provide a comprehensive breakdown of the remaining maturity of deposits and loans at different groups of banks to four categories of customers – other banks in London (the London interbank market), banks abroad, UK residents and other non-residents. Table 3.4 reproduces the summary statistics as at 21 November 1979 and Figure 3.7 graphs the net maturity mismatched position (i.e. claims

Table 3.4

Maturity structure of claims and liabilities in non-sterling currencies, all UK-based Euro-banks*
(21 November 1979)

Maturity	London interbank market		With banks abroad		Non-banks		Total		Certificates of deposit issued
	Claims†	Liabilities	Claims	Liabilities	Claims	Liabilities	Claims	Liabilities	
Less than 8 days	0.17	0.18	0.20	0.23	0.08	0.31	0.17	0.23	0.04
6 days – < 1 month	0.19	0.19	0.17	0.18	0.09	0.22	0.15	0.19	0.16
1 month – < 3 months	0.31	0.30	0.26	0.29	0.12	0.24	0.24	0.28	0.31
3 months – < 6 months	0.22	0.22	0.18	0.19	0.10	0.14	0.17	0.19	0.22
6 months – < 1 year	0.07	0.08	0.07	0.07	0.06	0.06	0.07	0.07	0.10
1 year – < 3 years	0.02	0.03	0.05	0.02	0.14	0.02	0.07	0.02	0.13
3 years and over	0.01	0.01	0.06	0.01	0.42	0.02	0.13	0.01	0.04
All maturities	1.00	1.00	1.00	1.00	1.00	1.00	1.00	1.00	1.00
Total all maturities ($ mn)	81,689	79,824	199,839	196,518	86,890	53,835	368,418	330,177	43,579
Net claims ($ mn)	+1,865		+3,321		+33,055		+38,241		

* Figures as proportions of the total unless otherwise stated.
† Includes holdings of certificates of deposit and other negotiable paper issued.

Source: *Bank of England Quarterly Bulletin*, September 1980, table 14.

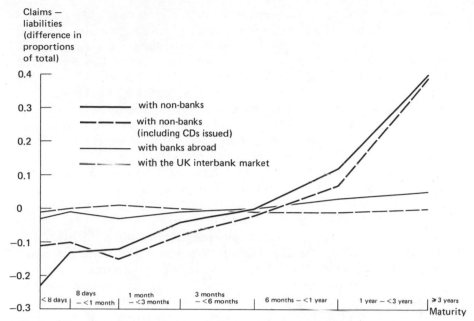

Claims —
liabilities
(difference in
proportions
of total)

- with non-banks
- with non-banks (including CDs issued)
- with banks abroad
- with the UK interbank market

Figure 3.7 **Maturity mismatch of all London banks with certain categories of customers**

minus liabilities) of the London market by category of customer. As a shorthand the UK resident and other non-resident categories have been combined as 'non-banks'.

These data are only a snapshot of the maturity structure of banks' assets and liabilities at the date of the report. Even so they show two features: first, the nearly perfectly maturity-matched position of London banks *vis-à vis* other banks in the London inter-bank market and, to a slightly lesser extent, with banks abroad; and second, a significant degree of mismatching between non-bank liabilities and claims. A conclusion is that interbank trading can indeed be netted out when attempting to measure the direct liquidity effects of the Euro-currency market since it does not appear to alter the liquidity structure of banks' assets and liabilities, but only the distri-bution of funds within the banking system. However, there is a dis-tinct problem in interpreting the maturity data on the London inter-bank market. *By definition*, the total assets and total liabilities of the London interbank market in each maturity category should sum to zero. When one London bank lends to another for one week, the first bank should record this as a claim at less than eight days and the second as a less-than-eight-day liability and thus no mis-matching should occur. The recorded mismatching, which is indeed very small, is a statistical error. A better picture of the maturity transformation in the London Euro-currency market can be obtained by examining the categories of banks individually, though this will still be somewhat distorted by borrowing and lending funds between banks within the category. When this is done (see Table 3.5) nothing startling happens. At 21 November 1979 American banks were the only group engaged in any significant interbank maturity transformation and even that was very limited, while British and consortium banks were actually borrowing interbank funds long to lend short. The aggregate conclusion is therefore not contradicted.

What interbank maturity mismatching was occurring is instructive. American banks had a large net claim position in the one- to six-month maturity categories reflecting their role as important net suppliers of liquidity to the Euro-currency system at these maturities. The counterpart was partly the borrowing by British and consortium banks, reflecting their position as net users of interbank funds when funding their Euro-currency loan portfolios. At very short maturities the position is reversed, which may be explained by the decision by these banks to place funds short term with American banks for liquidity reasons or as part of their precautionary reserve holdings. Chapter 4 analyses the reasons for this interbank trading.

3.2.1   *Yield curve arbitrage*

Much of the interbank trading also arises out of the continuous arbitrage operations of banks as they obtain interest-rate quotations from different banks, in different markets and on different currencies and move funds when a profitable margin or 'turn' is to be earned. The actual maturity profile of banks' liabilities and claims may then also reflect, *inter alia*, individual bank expectations about the future movement in Euro-currency interest rates. A bank might borrow short (overnight or seven days) and lend longer term when it believes interest rates may fall in the near future, or borrow six-month interbank deposits to lend at three months when it expects interest rates to rise by more than the market forecast of interest rates in three months' time. Using the current level of three- and six-month deposit rates it is possible to calculate the markets' 'implicit' forecast of the three-month rate in three months' time. This is done by assessing what rate of interest would have to prevail on three-month deposits, three months hence, to equalise the return on a current investment for six months in six-month deposits and an investment for six months in which the funds are originally placed only for three months

Table 3.5

**Maturity structure of London interbank liabilities and claims in
non-sterling currencies for specified categories of banks***

(21 November 1979)

Maturity	British banks		American banks		Japanese banks		Other overseas banks		Consortium banks	
	Claims	Liabilities	Claims	Liabilities	Claims	Liabilities	Claims	Liabilities	Claims	Liabilities
Less than 8 days	0.18	0.16	0.15	0.29	0.10	0.16	0.21	0.17	0.24	0.09
8 days – < 1 month	0.20	0.20	0.17	0.17	0.18	0.19	0.21	0.20	0.21	0.19
1 month – < 3 months	0.31	0.29	0.32	0.25	0.32	0.31	0.30	0.32	0.30	0.32
3 months – < 6 months	0.20	0.22	0.24	0.20	0.28	0.19	0.20	0.22	0.18	0.27
6 months – < 1 year	0.07	0.07	0.08	0.08	0.09	0.09	0.05	0.08	0.05	0.04
1 year – < 3 years	0.03	0.03	0.02	0.01	0.03	0.06	0.03	0.02	0.02	0.01
3 years and over	0.01	0.02	0.02	–	–	–	0.01	–	–	–
All maturities	1.0	1.00	1.00	1.00	1.00	1.00	1.00	1.00	1.00	1.00
Total all maturities ($ mn)	18,506	21,108	19,811	15,215	12,041	15,428	28,261	20,762	3,082	7,919

* Figures as proportions of the total unless otherwise stated.

Source: *Bank of England Quarterly Bulletin*, September 1980.

and then 'rolled over' for a further three months when the first three-month deposit matures. Algebraically this can be written:

$$\left(1 + \frac{1}{4} r_3\right)\left(1 + \frac{1}{4} r_3^F\right)$$

$$= \left(1 + \frac{1}{2} r_6\right)$$

where r_3 and r_6 are the current annual rates of return on three- and six-month deposits, respectively, and r_3^F is the market's three months forward forecast of the three-month deposit rate. Manipulating this equation yields the formulae for r_3^F:

$$r_3^F = 4\left[\left(\frac{1}{2} r_6 - \frac{1}{4} r_3\right) \bigg/ \left(1 + \frac{1}{4} r_3\right)\right]$$

When an investor expects interest rates to rise by more than the market forecast he would place funds short in the market. If, however, the investor's own forecast was close to the market forecast, he would be largely indifferent between holding a six-month investment as a six-month deposit or as two three-month placements.[6] As banks assess the outlook for short-term interest rates and compare this with the forecast for rates implicit in the market yield curve, they may borrow funds at one maturity and lend at another in the interbank market. The maturity profile of banks' interbank liabilities and claims may then move over time as they arbitrage along the interest-rate yield curve.

Figure 3.8 illustrates the term structure of interest rates prevailing in the London dollar interbank market on 21 November 1979 and one month (21 December 1979) and three months (19 February 1980) after that date. In fact, the November yield curve indicates that at that time the market was expecting the shortest-term interest rates to rise during the months towards the end of 1979 (indicated by the steep yield differential between the two-day, one-month and three-month deposits) and then to decline throughout the first months of 1980. At that time the market's implicit forecast of the three-month rate in three months' time was 14.10 per cent, which represented a decline of 1 per cent from the existing level of interest rates.[7] Similar expectations were still being held in December, when it seemed, from the shape of the yield curve, that the peak in short-term interest rates was just about to be reached. However, by February market expectations had been significantly revised. The

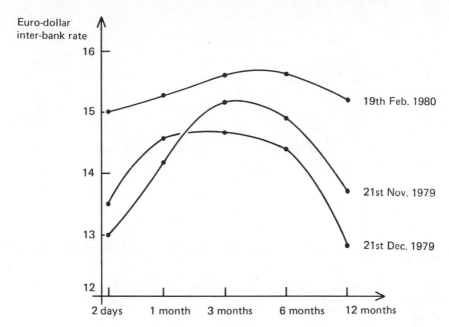

Figure 3.8   **Euro-dollar interbank yield curve**

implicit market forecast made in November underestimated by about 1.5 per cent the actual rise in interest rates that occurred and the yield curve had become very flat, indicating that the market was no longer expecting a drop in interest rates during 1980. Unfortunately, because interest-rate quotations in the Euro-dollar market are only made for specific maturities, it is impossible to obtain from market interest rates an implicit forecast of, say, the three-month rate in six or nine months' time. This would also require a nine-month interest-rate quotation as well as the current three-, six and twelve-month rates.

3.2.2   *Maturity transformation of non-bank deposits*

The second important feature of the data in Table 3.4 and in Figure 3.7 is the substantial degree of mismatching of London banks' non-bank liabilities and claims. The type of maturity profile which emerges is sketched in Figure 3.9. In an attempt to assess the significance of such maturity transformation for liquidity creation in the Euro-currency market, Niehans and Hewson (1976) have suggested that weights could be assigned to the maturity bands for banks'

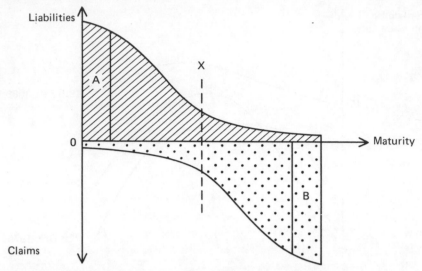

Figure 3.9   Maturity profile of London Euro-banks' liabilities and claims *vis-à-vis* non-banks'

liabilities and claims which reflect their degree of 'moneyness' and that these weights should be monotonically decreasing with the maturity of deposits and loans. A demand deposit with a bank might, for example, be given a weight of 1.0 and a short-term time deposit only 0.5, etc., along the maturity spectrum. The contribution of the banking system to the liquidity of the private sector could then be measured as:

$$\Delta M = \lambda_0 D_0 + \lambda_1 D_1 + \ldots + \lambda_n D_n = \Sigma_i \lambda_i D_i$$

where $D_0, D_1, \ldots, D_n$ represent the various maturities of deposits and λ_i, $i = 0\ 1, \ldots, n$, the liquidity weights. Assuming that the same weights also apply to the 'moneyness' of the loans made by the banking system, $L_0, L_1, \ldots, L_n$ the contribution to net liquidity from any maturity transformation is then:

$$Q = \Sigma_i \lambda_i D_i - \Sigma_i \lambda_i L_i = \Sigma_i \lambda_i (D_i - L_i)$$

with

$$\Sigma_i (D_i - L_i) = 0.$$

When banks have a perfectly matched book, $D_i = L_i$ for all i, there would be no liquidity creation ($Q = 0$). Liquidity creation requires that banks' assets and liabilities are mismatched (i.e. $D_i \neq L_i$ for some i) and that the banking system borrows short to lend long. Niehans and Hewson suggested the following weighting structure:

Maturity class	λ
Less than 8 days	0.9
8 days—1 month	0.8
1 month—3 months	0.7
3 months— 6 months	0.6
6 months—1 year	0.4
1 year—3 years	0.2
3 years and over	0.1

By applying this to the Bank of England maturity data at end-September 1973 they estimated that Euro-market intermediation between non-banks added only 16.49 cents of liquidity to every dollar deposited. Subsequently Jane Sneddon Little (1979) updated the study, investigated somewhat different weights and compared the amount of Euro-market 'liquidity' creation with that of US banks. She concluded that in recent years there had been a very substantial rise in the amount of liquidity provided by Euro-banks, which had reached 38.7 cents/dollar by 1977 (using Niehans—Hewson weights), and this was not very different from that provided by US banks (41.3 cents/dollar). However, about half of the increase observed by Little can be attributed to a change in Bank of England reporting procedures in May 1974. Before that date the maturity of roll-over loans was recorded by the period to the next roll-over date, and after by the time to the end of the commitment period, which significantly lengthened the recorded maturity of banks' Euro-currency claims. Another problem with these estimates is that they ignored the maturity structure of London banks' Euro-dollar CDs, which are predominantly purchased by non-banks and should be treated as a deposit with the banking system. Allowing for this and applying the Niehans—Hewson weights to the maturity data on 21 November 1979 yields the conclusion that banks were creating about 28 cents/dollar of liquidity for the non-bank sector.

A rather different problem with both the above estimates is the structure of the weights, which are rather arbitrary. More important is the assumption that bank liabilities of the shortest maturity (shown as *A* in Figure 3.9) obtain the largest positive weight, while the longest claims of the banking system (shown as *B*) are given the smallest negative weight in the calculations. The measurement of the contribution of the Euro-market to the liquidity of the public is obtained by treating the liquidity of bank claims in an exactly analogous way to the liquidity of non-bank liabilities. The liquidity created by the banks, Q, is equal to the liquidity of the public, ΔM_p, as measured by the weighting of liabilities by maturity, less the liquidity (or plus the illiquidity) of the banking system, ΔM_b, measured in a similar fashion:

$$Q = \Delta M_p - \Delta M_b$$

But what is relevant from the viewpoint of liquidity in the hands of the public is not the illiquidity of the banking system but the increase in the liquidity of the public due to bank lending. A five-year bank loan should add to non-bank liquidity, not reduce it, if even by a small amount; moreover, placing deposits with the banking system for three years would seem to actually reduce the liquidity of the non-banking sector, in a similar way to a domestic bond issue, not add to it, even by a small fraction. This suggests a somewhat radical alteration to the Niehans–Hewson weighting structure and that weights should be allowed to be both positive and negative for both liabilities and claims. One can imagine that there might be some cut-off point (shown as X in Figure 3.9), perhaps around the one-year mark, with deposits of a longer maturity than X having a negative weight, reducing non-bank liquidity, while loans longer than X have a positive weight and increase it. Maintaining the Niehans–Hewson properties that weights are monotonically decreasing and should indicate that no liquidity creation occurs when banks have a perfectly matched book, we can suggest the following alternative structure for the weights:

ALTERNATIVE WEIGHTING STRUCTURE

Maturity class	Liabilities	Claims
Less than 8 days	1.0	−1.0
8 days–< 1 month	0.5	−0.5
1 month–< 3 months	0.2	−0.2
3 months–<6 months	0.1	−0.1
6 months–< 1 year	–	–
1 year–< 3 years	−0.2	0.2
3 years and over	−0.6	0.6

Applying these alternative weights to the November 1979 maturity data shows that banks were adding about 50 cents/dollar to 'liquidity' in the hands of the public, higher than all previous estimates. However, when these weights are also applied to the available data on the maturity structure of US commercial banks' assets and liabilities in 1977 reported by Little, this reveals that US banks were adding around 80 cents/dollar in net 'liquidity'. Clearly any result depends on the weighting structure chosen; since this is arbitrary, so is the result. But these calculations underline some significant differences between the maturity structures of Euro- and US banks' liabilities. Taking Euro-dollar CDs into account, only 19 per cent of Euro-banks' liabilities *vis-à-vis* non-banks were at less than eight days, while, from Little's data, the corresponding figure for US commercial banks was 67 per cent. (Adding in maturities up to one month raises these percentages to 38 and 72 respectively.) This comparison provides a statistical basis for assumptions that the structure of Euro-banking is not like that of national commercial banks.

3.3   SUMMARY

There are several geographical and conceptual measures of the size of the Euro-currency market; as each statistic's coverage differs, careful interpretation is needed of the data. All estimates have grown at a rapid rate over the last decade. The broadest measures of the market include interbank trading within the Euro-currency market which significantly double-counts the flows of credit from original suppliers to final users of Euro-currency funds. 'Net' estimates prepared by the BIS are designed to make allowance for this double-counting and to show the intermediary role of the Euro-market in international financial flows. These estimates, however, also include sources and uses of funds by private banks and other entities and therefore do not measure the contribution of the Euro-market to liquidity in the hands of private wealth-holders. Using Euro-currency statistics to augment systematically broadly defined national monetary aggregates shows that this contribution is very small and on average of the order of some 4 per cent of national money stocks. There are nevertheless significant inter-country differences: for the majority of countries sampled non-bank Euro-currency holdings were negligible in comparison with domestic money stocks. In the case of the USA they amounted to as much as 8 per cent, but this predominantly represented holdings of dollars by non-US residents which may not be directly related to expenditures on US goods and services. An analysis of the sources of Euro-currency funds also suggests that private non-bank Euro-currency deposits are the main additional factor when assessing the flow of Euro-market credit to non-bank borrowers.

Bank of England data on the maturity structure of London banks' foreign currency assets and liabilities show that London banks maintained nearly perfect maturity matching in their interbank trading.

The significance of such trading is seen in terms of its role in the allocation rather than the creation of liquidity. For transactions with non-banks, the data show a good degree of mismatching between the maturity of banks' liabilities and claims, suggesting that the intermediary function of Euro-banking enhances the liquidity of the private sector. Some weighting structures are examined in an attempt to measure this. A comparison with US commercial banks indicates that there are significant differences in the maturity structure of assets and liabilities in the two markets.

3.4   STATISTICAL ANNEX: AUGMENTING NATIONAL MONEY STOCKS WITH EURO-CURRENCY STATISTICS

This annex provides the analytical background to the statistics of private holdings of Euro-currencies and their quantitative implications for nationally defined money stock statistics discussed in the chapter. It is assumed that non-bank Euro-currency deposits are most relevant for statistical measures of broad money holdings (M_2 or M_3). To illustrate the adjustment to the domestic statistics, both at a national and aggregate ('world') level, required to take account of Euro-currency deposits, ten major countries are examined. They are Belgium (B), Canada (C), France (F), West Germany (G), Italy (I), Japan (J), the Netherlands (N), Switzerland (S), the United Kingdom (UK) and the USA (US).

Among the group of countries there are sharp differences between what is included in and excluded from national money stock statistics. Table 3.6 summarises the country definitions and their composition. As the table shows, two countries – S and UK – include only residents' holdings of domestic currency at domestic banks, another four (B, G, I and N) add in residents' holdings of foreign currencies at home and Canada also includes non-residents' holdings of domestic currency at Canadian banks. The remaining three countries – F, J and US – augment these figures with non-resident holdings of foreign currencies at domestic banks to arrive at their broadly defined monetary aggregates. Because of the diversity in country definitions it is not possible to define a unique measure of 'money' which would be applicable in all countries. It will be assumed that each country has important institutional or economic reasons for adopting its own particular statistic. In the United Kingdom, for example, foreign currencies held by residents are excluded from sterling M_3, which is the monetary variable targeted by the authorities, because they are more closely related to trading abroad than to domestic economic developments; in other countries these balances are included because of their potential use for spending on domestic goods and services. The process of augmenting national money stock statistics with Euro-currency holdings should take account of the national differences in definitions. This, however, makes the procedure complex, especially when attempting to arrive at an aggretate measure of the ten countries' money stock which includes Euro-currency deposits.

The procedure adopted is as follows (it is summarised in Table 3.7). First, as regards *additions* to national money stocks, only those Euro-currency balances which, if they had been held with domestic banks of the country in question, would have been included in the national money stock are relevant. Thus in the case of the United Kingdom only UK residents' holdings of sterling abroad should be treated as potentially part of UK sterling M_3, while for the USA, US residents' holdings of dollars and other foreign currencies abroad plus non-resident dollar holdings in the Euro-market would all be included in US M_3 if held with banks in the USA. This is therefore the factor by which US national aggregates should be augmented by Euro-currency deposits, etc., for the other countries. For completeness, the additions to national money stocks that would be required to arrive at the broadest composition of national money stocks — residents' holdings of domestic and foreign currencies plus non-residents' holdings of domestic currencies — are also reported. This is anyway needed in the aggregation process.

Second, as regards the *aggregate* measure of the ten countries' money stock, the contribution of total Euro-currency holdings is built up in stages using the different national concepts of money. First of all, only the ten countries' residents' holdings of domestic currencies abroad are added to the total ten-country broad money stocks, as would be the case using S and UK definitions. At the second stage the ten countries' residents' holdings of foreign currencies abroad (and at home in the case of S and UK, as they are the only countries which do not already count them in domestic aggregates) are added to augment the aggregate using the B, G, I and N money stock concept. Next, non-residents' holdings of the ten countries' currencies are included as required under C, F, J and US definitions. Finally, some other components which have not already been added are taken into account (see below). Non-resident holdings of non-ten-country currencies are ignored as they are very small and unimportant.

This aggregation process, however, involves an amount of double-counting. Non-residents' holdings of domestic currencies at C, F, J and US banks are already included in these countries' broad money stocks, as are foreign currency holdings by non-residents at F, J and US banks, and so these have to be taken out of the aggregate measure to avoid counting them twice. Another double-counting adjustment has to be made at stage three. At the second stage the ten countries' residents' holdings of foreign currencies have been added but these include holdings of other ten-country currencies. These would be counted twice in the aggregate measure if all non-resident holdings of the ten countries' currencies are then also included. For example, a German resident's holdings of dollars in London are potentially relevant for the German definition of money stock and thus are an 'addition' to German M_3. They are also potentially relevant for the US money stock and thus also regarded as an 'addition' to US M_3. However, in an aggregate money stock measure these dollar holdings would be counted twice if we simply added the 'additions' — once as a contribution to German and once as a contribution to American 'money' holdings — and so a double-counting adjustment has to be made. This negative adjustment in fact turns out to be larger than the amount added in at the second stage because a correction has also to be made for foreign currency holdings that are already included in

Table 3.6
Composition of broadly defined monetary aggregates for ten major countries

Country	Money stock concept[1]	Composition				Monetary aggregate used as a target variable
		Domestic currency held by:		Foreign currency held by:		
		Residents	Non-residents	Residents	Non-residents	
Belgium	M_2 = financial assets up to one year held by the non-bank private sector	*	—	*	—	—
Canada	M_3 = currency plus total privately held chartered bank deposits	*	—	*	—	M_1
France	M_2 = currency plus sight deposits (M_1) plus savings deposits at certain financial institutions plus time deposits for a minimum of one month plus medium-term bank bonds with a maximum maturity of five years	*	*	*	*	M_2
West Germany	M_3 = currency plus sight deposits (M_1) plus bank time deposits (M_2) plus bank savings deposits	*	—	*	—	CBM^2
Italy	M_2 = currency plus sight deposits (M_1) plus time and savings deposits plus Post Office savings certificates.	*	—	*	—	Monetary base
Japan	M_2 = currency plus demand deposits (M_1) plus 'quasi-money' (other private and public deposits held with reporting institutions[3])	*	*	*	*	M_2 plus certificates of deposit

Country	Definition[1]					Target aggregate
Netherlands	M₂ = currency plus demand deposits (M₁) plus short-term Treasury paper plus time deposits of less than two years plus liquid savings deposits	*	—	—	—	M₂
Switzerland	M₂ = currency plus demand deposits (M₁) plus time deposits (resident foreign currency sight deposits also included in M₂ are not shown)	*	—	—	—	Monetary base
United Kingdom	Sterling M₃ = currency plus all deposits held with the UK banking sector	*	—	—	—	Sterling M₃
USA	M₃ = currency plus demand deposits at commercial banks (MIA)[4] plus other demand deposits (MIB)[5] plus savings and small denominated time deposits plus other overnight transactions (M₂)[6] plus large denominated time deposits and term repurchase agreements	*	*	*	*	MIA, MIB

Notes

* = Included.

— = Excluded.

1 For brevity the definitions given may not accord exactly with official definitions.

2 CBM = Central bank money stock; comprises currency plus banks' balances at the central bank in the amount of minimum reserve requirements against eligible deposit liabilities. To obtain a consistent series, which abstracts from changes in reserve requirements, reserve balances are weighted by the reserve ratio applying in January 1974.

3 Excludes branches of foreign banks.

4 Excludes demand deposits due to foreign banks, domestic banks, the US government and other official institutions.

5 Including negotiable orders of withdrawal and transfer service accounts.

6 Including overnight Euro-dollars held by US non-banks at Caribbean branches of member banks of the Federal Reserve System.

Table 3.7

Augmented national and aggregate broad money stock measures for ten major countries*

A. Money stock concept	B. Countries which apply the concept	C. Addition to national money stock measures for Euro-currency and other deposits not already counted	D. Addition to an aggregate money stock measure allowing for double-counting
1. Residents' holdings of domestic currency	S, UK	Residents' holdings of domestic currencies abroad	As in 1C *excluding* holdings with F, J and US banks
2. *Plus* residents' holdings of foreign currencies	B, G, I, N	S + UK residents' holdings of foreign currencies at home *plus* all ten countries' residents' holdings of foreign currency abroad	As in 2C *excluding* holdings with F, J and US banks and Canadian dollar holdings with Canadian banks
3. *Plus* non-residents' holdings of domestic currencies	C	Non-residents' holdings of the ten-country currencies *excluding* domestic currencies at C, F, J and US banks	As in 3C *excluding* other ten countries' currencies held by ten-country residents (as already counted in 2A or 2C) and by other non-residents at F, US and J banks
4. *Plus* non-residents' holdings of foreign currencies	F, J, US	Non-ten-country residents' holdings of non-ten-country currencies at banks other than F, J and US	As in 4C

* The countries are: B = Belgium, C = Canada, F = France, G = Germany, I = Italy, J = Japan, N = Netherlands, S = Switzerland, UK = United Kingdom, US = USA.

domestic monetary statistics. To see this suppose, following the example above, that the German resident held dollars with a domestic German bank rather than in London. Under German definitions these balances are already included in German money supply; however, they are still Euro-dollars and potentially relevant to the US monetary authorities. They are therefore also regarded as an 'addition' to US M_3. If this 'addition' were counted when aggregating the money stocks, it would double-count balances already included in the German money supply statistics and so has to be taken out. The stage-by-stage procedure is set out in Table 3.7.

3.4.1   *The estimates*

The results for this exercise of adding in and netting out are given in Table 3.8; they are reasonably self-explanatory and accord closely with the procedures outlined. Column I reports the size of the countries' broad domestic money stocks and column II residents' holdings of their country's domestic currency in the Euro-market. Column VII gives this as a percentage of domestic money stocks. Allowing for some double-counting, the aggregate addition to the ten countries' money stocks from these holdings amounts to $29.3 billion or only 0.7 per cent of total domestic money stocks (last row of the table). Residents' holdings of foreign currencies with banks abroad, and in the case of Switzerland and the United Kingdom at domestic banks, are shown in column III. After again making an allowance for double-counting this adds a further $45.7 billion to national aggregates, bringing the combined additions (column V) to $75.0 billion or 2 per cent (column VIII). The 'addition' to national monetary statistics from non-resident holdings of the ten-country currencies in the Euro-market totals $142.3 billion (column IV), but over half of this has already been counted, so the adjustment to the 'aggregate' measure of the ten countries' money stocks is only $64.4 billion. This brings total adjustment to $139.4 billion (column VI), which represents 3.4 per cent of the combined national money stocks (column IX).

This is not as yet the whole story. The figures in the table refer only to non-bank holdings of currencies with reporting banks in Europe, Canada and Japan. The omission of the USA is not a problem, since domestic and foreign currency deposits with US banks are already included in US money stock statistics, but the exclusion of other offshore centres is important. The only information available is for the branches of US banks in the Caribbean area, which shows that non-bank deposits amounted to $27 billion at end-1979 of which $17 billion was due to US residents. These deposits are also held predominantly in dollars. The USA, however, already includes overnight Euro-dollar balances in M_2 and M_3 with Caribbean branches and so the whole $27 billion need not be counted again. Making a guess I would say these amounted to some $5 billion, in which case a further $22 billion should be added to the aggregate measure of money stock and also introduced as an 'addition' to US M_3. Finally, allowance has to be made for trustee funds placed in the market by Swiss banks. As they are recorded as interbank transactions, they are not already counted as non-bank

Table 3.8
Augmented national and aggregate broad money stock measures for ten major countries:[1] end-1979 figures

	I		II	III	IV
				Non-bank holdings of Euro-currencies[2]	
	Domestic money stock definition	Domestic money stock	Residents' holdings of domestic currencies (1C)[3]	Residents' holdings of foreign currencies (2C)[3]	Non-resident holdings of ten countries' currencies by currency (3C)[3] (of which with banks of the currency concerned)
Belgium	M_2	28.7	0.9	3.5	3.1 (2.7)
Canada	M_3	117.7	–	1.0	– n.a.
France	M_2	320.3	0.4	3.1	1.5 n.a.
West Germany	M_3	403.4	1.9	2.5	24.5 (15.7)
Italy	M_2	369.8	0.05	2.4	1.0 (0.7)
Japan	M_2	808.3	0.05	0.4	0.5 n.a.
Netherlands	M_2	54.2	0.2	2.9	4.3 (3.4)
Switzerland	M_2	68.7	0.9	16.0 (of which 3.4 held with Swiss banks)	4.6[e] (2.5)[e]
United Kingdom	M_3	124.2	1.1	14.2 (of which 11.4 held with UK banks)	13.2 (11.0)
USA	M_3	1775.5	24.9	4.3	89.6 n.a.
					142.3
Totals		4070.8	30.4	50.3	(36.0)
Adjustment for double-counting[1]		–	−1.1	−4.6	−77.9
Addition to aggregate measure of money stock		4070.8	(1D)[3] 29.3	(2D)[3] 45.7	(3D)[3] 64.4

Notes: monetary magnitudes in US dollar billions; currency conversions at end-1979 exchange rates; e = estimate; n.a. = not applicable (figures already counted in domestic monetary aggregates).
[1] A description of the aggregation process is provided in the text and Table 3.7.
[2] With banks of Austria, Belgium–Luxembourg, Denmark, France, West Germany, Ireland, Italy, the Netherlands, Sweden, Switzerland, United Kingdom, Canada and Japan.

deposits. At end-1978 they amounted to some $30 billion, but part of these contain longer-term elements which should certainly not be included in monetary aggregates. If these long-term funds totalled about $10 billion, then the grand addition, on the broadest money stock concept, to the ten countries' aggregate money stocks would be $180 billion, or about 4.5 per cent. At the very most,

Table 3.8 contin.

			US Dollars (billions)				
V	VI	VII	VIII	IX	X	XI
II plus III	IV plus V	II as percentage of I	V as percentage of I	IV as percentage of I	National money stocks augmented by national definitions	X as percentage of I
4.4	7.5	3.1	15.3	26.1	33.1	115.3
1.0	1.0	–	0.9	0.9	118.1	100.9
3.5	5.0	0.1	1.1	1.6	325.3	101.6
4.4	28.9	0.5	1.1	7.2	407.8	101.1
2.4	3.4	–	0.7	0.9	372.2	100.7
0.5	1.0	–	0.1	0.1	809.3	100.1
3.1	7.4	0.4	5.7	13.7	57.3	105.7
16.9	21.5[e]	1.3	24.6	31.7	69.6	101.3
15.3	28.5	0.9	12.3	22.9	125.3	100.9
29.2	119.8 (141.0)[4]	1.4	1.7	6.7	1894.3 (1916.5)[4]	106.7 (108.0)[4]
80.7	223.0	0.7	2.0	5.5	4212.3 (4234.5)[4]	103.5 (104.0)[4]
−5.7	−83.6	–	–	–		
75.0	139.4 (180.0)[5]	0.7	1.8	3.4 (4.5)[5]		

[3] Headings in parentheses refer to entries in Table 3.7.
[4] After allowance for holdings with branches of US banks in the Caribbean area.
[5] Adjustment given in note 4 plus allowance for trustee funds placed in the market by Swiss banks.
Source: BIS data.

including all trustee funds and offshore deposits, it would not exceed $200 billion or 5 per cent of the broadly defined national money stocks.

This figure, however, results from an artificial aggregation of money stocks. It assumes that the United Kingdom, Switzerland, etc., adopt the same broad money concept as Japan, France and the USA. A somewhat better picture of the implications of the Euro-market for national monetary statistics may be given by examining the additions to each national measure under individual national definitions. Although this approach does not make any correction for double-counting, as the aggregate calculation does, it is perhaps more relevant as regards the operation of a country's monetary policy. It measures, in a sense, the amount of money-like balances which have been disintermediated out of domestic monetary statistics by the operation of the Euro-currency market. These nationally augmented broad money stocks are given in column X and as a percentage of official statistics in column XI. In fact, the overall result is not very different from the aggregate statistics. Including Euro-currency deposits in domestic broad monetary aggregates would have caused them to be on average 3.5 or 4 per cent higher than they actually were. This obscures, however, some rather important differences in the experience of different countries which are discussed in the chapter.

NOTES

1. A second set of statistical data on the maturity structure of banks' external assets is also compiled by the BIS. These data have been reported twice-yearly since end-1977. The purpose of these data is to monitor the maturity profile of banks' external lending. They differ in several respects from the Bank of England data discussed in section 3.2 and provide a much more detailed country-by-country breakdown of the maturity profile of banks' external assets, but give no information on the maturity structure of banks' Euro-currency liabilities.
2. The Group of Ten countries are Belgium–Luxembourg, Canada, France, Italy, Japan, the Netherlands, Sweden, the United Kingdom, the USA and West Germany.
3. 'Reporting banks' are simply banks supplying statistical returns to the central banks in the geographical reporting area. The definition of the geographical reporting area is an important one for the statistical measurement of the market, as will become clear later.
4. Kessler's paper is an extremely difficult one to follow. His credit circuit is a closed one in which flows pass around the banking system without regard to behavioural responses by any agents. It is thus a most unsatisfactory framework of analysis.
5. For a discussion of the composition of US monetary aggregates see 'The redefined monetary aggregates', *Federal Reserve Bulletin* (February 1980), 97–114.
6. The investor may, of course, have some liquidity preference for shorter-term deposits and he may require a marginally higher yield to entice him to hold six-month rather than three-month deposits. Comparing a long series of implicit forecasts with their actual out-turns, showed that the forecast errors were approximately normally distributed around a mean of 0.05. This mean error may reflect the average liquidity premium; it may also reflect, however,

the fact that interest is paid on three-month deposits every three months, while on six-month deposits it is paid every six months.

7. The calculation is:

$$r_3^F = 4\left[\left(\frac{1}{2} \times 0.1488 - \frac{1}{4} \times 0.1513\right)\middle/\left(1 + \frac{1}{4} \times 0.1513\right)\right]$$

$$= 0.1409$$

4 A Parallel Market

The Euro-currency system performs several economic functions. There is thus no unique framework which can explain its existence and rapid expansion. This chapter examines some of the general analytical reasons for Euro-currency markets, mainly from the side of depositors (Chapters 6 and 7 examine the borrowers and the banks in more detail).

The Euro-currency market is a parallel market in that it operates alongside and is interrelated with national money markets. Like other parallel markets, Euro-market activity involves some specialised intermediary functions such as the financing of international trade and intermediating between countries in balance-of-payments surplus and deficit (Chapter 6). These activities are closely related to the functions of internationally used currencies and these functions are reviewed briefly in section 4.1.

However, the roles of internationally used currencies do not in themselves explain why money markets should grow outside the countries of the currencies traded in the market. An investigation of the competitive reasons for Euro-markets thus begins in section 4.2 by examining a uniform asset world and the role of transaction costs. Section 4.3 extend the analysis into the more general world of imperfect substitutes. Numerically interbank transactions dominate the Euro-currency market. Section 4.4 examines the reasons for the large volume of interbank trading and the next chapter the interest-rate relationships which result from the interbank trading between domestic and Euro-markets.

4.1 INTERNATIONAL CURRENCIES

Euro-markets substitute both as a market to place and to borrow a transactor's home currency outside his or her own country and foreign currency outside the foreign country of the currency concerned. In the first case, the Euro-market competes with a resident's domestic money market for transactions in his domestic currency; in the second, with national money markets in other countries for transactions in foreign currencies. This second aspect of Euro-market competition dominates, and the overwhelming majority of Euro-currency transactions are in foreign currencies. At least three-quarters of deposits held in the market by non-bank wealth-holders are placed in currencies other than their own domestic currency, and as much as 90 per cent of Euro-market borrowing by non-bank entities is undertaken in foreign currencies, predominantly the US dollar. Figure 4.1 shows the currency composition of the total Euro-currency assets (bank and non-bank) of European reporting banks.

Currencies which are used internationally provide a very similar function for the international economy as they do at home: as a unit of account, a medium of exchange and a store of value. Taking account of these functions, the US dollar is used as the principal international currency, which also explains its predominant position in the Euro-currency market. As a *unit of account* the dollar is frequently used when invoicing international trade, particularly in primary commodities and especially oil exports. Trade between most industrialised countries is, however, usually invoiced in the currency of the importing or exporting country. Around forty countries also peg their foreign exchange rate to the dollar and a number of other countries peg to other currencies (such as the French franc) or currency units (such as the IMF's SDR). One approach to the growth of private Euro-currency examines the need to maintain working balances in foreign currencies, and particularly in the dollar for the financing of international trade. To analyse these trade influences Swoboda (1968) extended Baumol's (1952) inventory-theoretic approach to the optional holding of domestic cash balances, to show that transaction costs involved in moving between domestic and foreign currencies would encourage traders to hold balances denominated in foreign currencies.

An importer of goods required to meet a stream of foreign currency payments, M, has the option of either selling domestic interest-bearing assets and acquiring foreign exchange continuously as foreign payments have to be made, or making a lump-sum sale of domestic securities and lump-sum purchase of foreign currency. If r is the rate of interest on domestic securities, a the fixed cost per transaction of converting domestic currency into foreign currency and S the size of each purchase of foreign currency (assumed equal), the total cost of holding a foreign currency balance is:

$$C = \frac{aM}{S} + r\frac{S}{2}$$

where aM/S is the transactions cost (a times the number of transactions, M/S) and $\frac{1}{2}rS$ the domestic interest forgone on the average

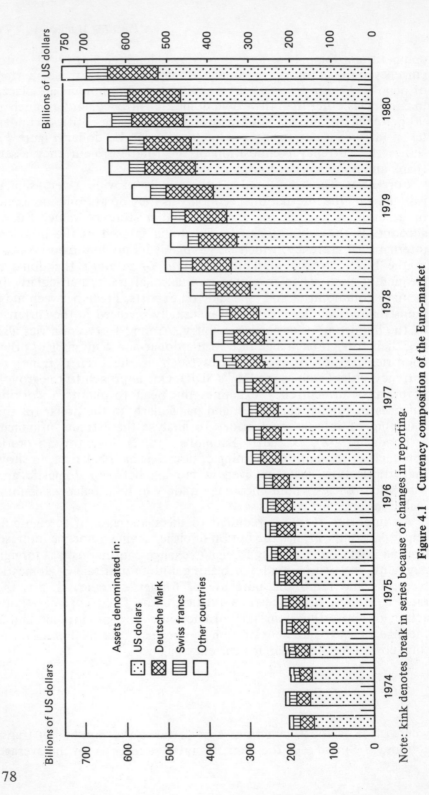

Figure 4.1 Currency composition of the Euro-market

Note: kink denotes break in series because of changes in reporting.

Billions of US dollars

Assets denominated in:

⬜ US dollars
▨ Deutsche Mark
▤ Swiss francs
⬜ Other countries

78

foreign currency balance (½S). Setting $dC/dS = 0$ gives the cost-minimising size of the lump-sum foreign currency purchase:

$$S^* = \sqrt{\frac{2aM}{r}}$$

and the optional average foreign currency balance as $½S^*$, which is directly related to the stream of foreign payments, M. This square-root formula suggests that foreign balances should grow at around half the rate of trade flows. Similar considerations also apply to an exporter of goods who would let foreign currency balances accumulate and only make infrequent lump-sum purchases of domestic currency.

Econometric work provides some evidence for a relationship between Euro-currency deposits and the growth of international trade. Makin (1972) found, for example, a significant relationship between the real stock of Euro-dollar deposits held by entities outside the USA, the volume of real trade flows between industrialised countries, the returns on Euro-dollar deposits and other external assets which could be regarded as close substitutes. In his equation the elasticity on the trade-flow variable was, however, larger than would have been predicted from the inventory-theoretic approach (which suggests an elasticity of around 0.5 instead of 2.3 which was actually found) and the dependent variable included interbank transactions, which might question the validity of the results. Cross-section regressions of non-bank holdings of different currencies on bilateral trade flows also revealed, however, significant relationships. The results for Deutsche Mark, sterling and the dollar are given in Table 4.1 (and section 4.3 reports supporting time-series evidence for foreign private holdings of Euro-dollar and sterling balances).

Table explanation. The regressions in Table 4.1 are of the form

$$D_{ij} = a_j + b_j E_{ij} + u_j \qquad (j = 1, 2, 3)$$

where D_{ij} is the holding of the currency of country j by non-banks in country i; and E_{ij} are the exports of country j to country i, on the assumption that exports are mainly invoiced in the currency of the exporting country. The countries i are the Group of Ten plus Austria, Denmark, Ireland and Switzerland. Since the dollar has a more general role in invoicing international trade, the final regression in the table examines the relationship between countries' total imports, adjusted for the approximate volume of imports invoiced in dollars, and non-bank Euro-dollar holdings. The results varied somewhat depending on the measure of non-banks' external currency holdings

Table 4.1
Cross-section regression of non-bank
foreign currency deposits on trade variables*
(end-December 1980)

| Dependent variable | Explanatory variable | | | $\bar{R}^2$ |
	Constant	Bilateral trade	Total imports	
Non-bank holding of				
Euro-Deutsche Mark	8.08 (0.05)	0.586 (3.36)		0.46
external sterling	48.1 (0.24)	0.619 (3.19)		0.43
Euro-dollars	1758.3 (1.26)	4.03 (2.98)		0.40
	2036.9 (1.33)		0.975 (2.45)	0.29

* *t*-ratios in parentheses.

used as the dependent variable. For the Deutsche Mark, the best relationship was for holdings in the Euro-currency market only; for
sterling the best relationship was for total external sterling holdings
(i.e. those held in London and the Euro-market); and while Euro-
dollar holdings were significantly related to both bilateral trade
flows with the USA and to countries' total imports, the coefficient
on the trade variable in the first equation seemed implausibly large,
while the fit of the second was not so good. These are the four
equations reported in the table.

Thus the evidence would suggest that the international holdings of
currencies are related to trade transactions. Frequently Euro-currency
deposits act, for example, as a substitute for forward exchange contracts where there are transaction cost advantages in making a large
spot purchase of foreign currency and investing it in the Euro-market
at different maturities to coincide with payments abroad rather than
making a number of forward contracts. The trade explanation seems,
however, to be better for less important currencies than for the dollar.

The *medium of exchange* function of a currency which is used
internationally is also related to a currency's role in international
trade and more generally to the settlement of international transactions. Residual financing of a country's balance-of-payments deficit

is normally accomplished through the transfer of foreign exchange reserves and the dollar is the main official intervention currency in the foreign exchange markets.

Finally, internationally used currencies also act as a *store of value* and are held for investment purposes by both private and official entities. About 75 per cent of official foreign exchange reserves are held in dollars, of which about one-third are held in the Euro-currency market. Unlike the unit of account and medium of exchange functions, the store of value function of international currencies need not be specifically transaction-related and the holding of Euro-currency deposits has therefore also to be seen as part of wealth-holders' broader portfolio decisions (section 4.3).

None of the functions of internationally used currencies automatically explains why currency balances have built up in the Euro-currency markets, as well as in the home countries of the currencies concerned. Even if the currency has an international role, this could be accommodated by the money markets in the country of the currency concerned. Indeed, the large number of domestic currency transactions carried out in the domestic economy should mean that domestic banks should have achieved economies of scale in financial intermediation. National financial intermediaries will also benefit from the range of domestic currency financial markets and from the willingness of central banks to provide lender of last resort facilities in the home country. Home-country financial intermediaries should therefore have a considerable advantage, if not an effective monopoly, when undertaking business in their own currency. Nevertheless, this monopoly has been broken by Euro-currency markets. There are two general reasons why this has been possible: the structure of transaction costs and national regulations, and the preferences of investors and wealth-holders.

4.2 PARALLEL MARKETS WITH UNIFORM ASSETS

Because of the existence of transaction costs it is generally observed that markets are spatially distributed. Prices of commonly required goods and services differ in one town from those in another because of the costs and inconvenience of arbitraging between them. Even when arbitrage costs are small, markets may be organised on a decentralised basis because of the inconvenience incurred by transactors in different market-places. The low cost of shifting funds through a nation's banking system usually means that money-market interest rates are uniform throughout a country and are determined by the supply and demand for funds in centralised markets in the country's main financial centre. Withdrawals or deposits of funds with the banking system are, however, more easily facilitated by a personal visit to a local bank than through a transaction with a centralised head office hundreds of miles away. Banks therefore set up branches throughout the country to service local customers' needs, to attract business and to monitor their borrowers. The existence of transaction costs therefore may give rise to distinguishable markets, when there are costs involved in arbitraging between them, or to more uniform markets being organised on a decentralised basis.

It is not difficult to show that, in a *uniform asset* world of free capital mobility, a necessary condition for the development of a Euro-currency market is that the sum of transaction costs incurred by at least some operators in the Euro-currency market should be less than those incurred in national money markets. The algebraic exposition which derives the result is provided as an annex to this chapter. This analysis is of interest since it shows that it is the *sum* of transaction costs incurred by depositors, borrowers and intermediaries, rather than those incurred by any individual set of transactors, which determines the location of a bank deposit and loan market. In the uniform asset world these must be less than or equal in the Euro-currency market, for at least some transactions, to those in the domestic currency market, for development of a Euro-currency market to take place. Thus, for example, even if the dollar transaction costs incurred by borrowers and depositors of funds were greater in London than New York, a Euro-dollar banking market could still develop if the transaction costs incurred by intermediaries were substantially greater in New York than in London. In such circumstances banks in London would be able to operate on narrower lending margins than those in New York and would be able to attract borrowers and depositors to London by offering higher nominal deposit rates and lower nominal loan rates than banks in New York. It is frequently suggested that the existence of narrower lending margins led to the development of a Euro-currency market. Alternatively, even if the costs of acting as an intermediary in the two markets were the same in both markets, a Euro-dollar market could still evolve because the costs incurred by some borrowers and lenders of dollars are greater when doing business in New York.

From this analysis of the necessary conditions it is not a large step to assert that the volume of foreign currency business passing through any particular Euro-currency centre will be closely related to the costs incurred by depositors, borrowers and intermediaries in that centre, relative to those in domestic currency markets and other Euro-currency centres. Niehans and Hewson (1976) have drawn an interesting linear programming analogy which the following discussons adapts slightly. Suppose there are $i = 1, \ldots, n$ ultimate borrowers and lenders of funds scattered all over the globe. Some are ultimate lenders of dollars, with $x_i > 0$ denoting the supply by agent i, while others are ultimate borrowers, with $x_i < 0$ denoting the amount demanded. There are also $j = 1, \ldots, k$ intermediaries scattered all over the globe and ultimate borrowers and lenders are assumed only to transact with these intermediaries. The actual amount agent i lends to intermediary j is denoted by x_{ij} (and his borrowing by x_{ji}). In transacting with intermediaries, ultimate borrowers and lenders incur transaction costs which may well differ from one intermediary to another, depending, for example, on their geographical location. The transaction costs on a loan from agent i to intermediary j is thus denoted as C_{ij} and on a borrowing as C_{ji}. Both transaction costs are simply in the form of a per unit dollar charge. What should then be minimised are the total transaction costs in the system:

$$\min T = \Sigma\Sigma_{ij} \ (C_{ij}x_{ij} + C_{ji}x_{ji})$$

The solution to this linear programming problem determines the whole network of credit flows. However, it does not need some imaginary planning agency as it is known from duality theory that the optimal solution to the problem is the only solution consistent with perfect competition in a system in which each agent maximises profit.[1] As Niehans and Hewson note, 'it is therefore plausible to assume that a highly competitive financial system [such as the international banking system], would tend to approximate the optimal solution at least in rough outline', and that flows will tend to pass through the lowest-cost transaction centres. (Niehans and Hewson's analysis is examined further in section 4.4.)

In the uniform asset world a transaction cost model would seem to be a valuable framework with which to analyse the location of banking business and the growth of Euro-currency markets. It provides necessary conditions for the emergence of Euro-currency markets and also indicates why some markets could expand more rapidly than others. The reasons for differing transaction costs remain, however, to be explained.

Perhaps one of the simplest explanations of differing transaction costs is the physical location of the market, relative to depositors and borrowers. It is usually easier to do business with a local bank than one thousands of miles away. Time differences with the foreign money market restrict the number of hours of trading and thus flexibility in conducting business. International telephone calls are more expensive than local ones and personal visits can be made to a local bank to smooth and discuss problems of operation. Local banks are also likely to be more in tune with the local needs of customers and therefore to be more helpful to local borrowers and lenders; and, as noted in Chapter 1, Euro-markets perform an important regional borrowing and investment function. However, in a world of increasingly sophisticated international communications these advantages are likely to be only marginal, particularly as concerns the wholesale nature of Euro-currency business. Nevertheless, it is usually the case that investors and borrowers have more information about market conditions and the standing of the institutions in the local market than those abroad. Euro-currency interest rates are quoted daily in the European press and compared with local domestic interest rates, and European journals regularly assess overall developments in the Euro-market. The local dissemination of information reduces uncertainty and the need for the investor or borrower to undertake his own costly search for the alternatives available.

It is also true that Euro-currency markets initially emerged in centres where there were already highly developed financial structures. In a sense the potential infrastructure for foreign currency markets was already in place and thus did not involve a large initial investment of new resources. The wholesale nature of business in Euro-markets, is, moreover, low cost in terms of the intermediaries' transaction costs; and because of the size of deposits the per unit transaction cost to depositors is small. Euro-markets do not, and most likely could not, compete for the type of retail deposit business undertaken by domestic banks, which involves a large number of transactions and turnover of business to be profitable. Wholesale business can, however, be profitably conducted using the existing arrangements for foreign exchange trading within most major banks.

Euro-currency markets are also highly competitive and, at least in the early years of the markets' development, this may have meant that lending rates were lower there than in domestic banking systems. In domestic markets the relatively small number of banks may lead to oligopolistic or monopolistic market structures. Domestic banks may implicitly follow certain conventions when setting domestic interest rates, banks' prime or base lending rates may be tied to officially administered bank rates rather than market interest rates, and deposit rates may be altered only infrequently. By these conventions, bank lending margins and profits may be kept above competitive market levels in the domestic market.

Relatively uncompetitive domestic banking structures may themselves be a factor encouraging markets which intermediate in foreign currencies and aggressive international banking activity. If domestic banks collude to set the domestic lending margin, they may, as in the classic model of a pure monopolist, equate marginal revenues and marginal costs. Figure 4.2 illustrates this and shows that the domestic intermediation charge (shown on the vertical axis) would be set at r_d by the domestic banking industry (which in aggregate faces a downward-sloping demand curve in the domestic market) and domestic banks would supply OA of domestic intermediation services. In the competitive international market the price of intermediation services is set at r_e. Providing the domestic banking system is small relative to the total international demand for credits, such that the demand for international intermediation services is nearly perfectly elastic at the price of r_e, and domestic banks can discriminate between domestic and international borrowers, domestic banks would increase their total supply of intermediation services to OB. They would supply OA of domestic intermediation services at the domestic monopolistic price of r_d and AB of services in the international market at the price of r_e. International markets may also be used by banks as a convenient and effective way of discriminating between large and small borrowers which they might otherwise be unable to do at home. When international business is marginal in nature, this may cause banks to be highly aggressive when intermediating in the Euro-currency market. Over time, however, aggressive international lending by other nationalities of banks has itself eroded domestic banks' monopoly positions when operating in their own currencies domestically, it has encouraged more competitive domestic banking structures and it has tended to bid down national lending margins to competitive international levels.

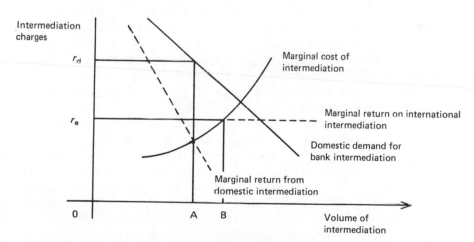

Figure 4.2

4.2.1   *The regulatory framework*

While these institutional characteristics of domestic and international banking are certainly important in explaining the existence of markets which intermediate in widely used international currencies, it is doubtful whether Euro-markets would have grown as rapidly if it had not been for the asymmetry in the regulation of domestic and Euro-currency banking. Table 4.2 summarises the regulations which seven countries apply to non-resident transactions with their banks in foreign currencies and the regulations which apply to non-resident transactions with their banks in domestic currencies. It also summarises exchange-control restrictions which affect resident transactions abroad.

At present (i.e. at end-1980) only one European country – West Germany – extends domestic monetary regulations to their domestic banks' foreign currency business with non-residents. No monetary controls have ever been imposed on banks' Euro-currency deposits in France and the United Kingdom; in Belgium–Luxembourg and the Netherlands the authorities have some power to restrict Euro-currency transactions but these are not implemented in practice; and although Switzerland had placed minimum reserve requirements on foreign currency deposits, they were removed in February 1977. In most countries, non-resident holdings of domestic currencies are either subject to the same regulations as residents' domestic currency deposits or to specific regulations designed to discourage non-resident deposits in domestic currencies. At times in West Germany, the Netherlands and Switzerland interest payments on non-resident domestic currency deposits have been banned, in Switzerland negative interest rates have been charged and in West Germany larger minimum reserve requirements have been imposed. One interesting exception is the International Banking Facility (IBF) established in the USA in December 1981. Under these facilities US domestic banks are able to accept deposits from and extend credit to foreigners in domestic and foreign currencies free of domestic monetary regulations. A stated reason for the establishment of these facilities is to 'enhance the international competitive position of banking institutions in the United States'[2] and to attract Euro-dollar business back to the USA. As well as the absence of direct monetary regulations, few countries impose any form of exchange control on non-resident transactions in foreign currencies. However, several countries' resident transactions abroad have at some time been subject to extensive regulations.[3]

The importance of the domestic regulatory framework is illustrated by the fact that West Germany, which imposes domestic monetary regulations on banks' foreign currency business, accounts for only 3 per cent of European banks' total Euro-currency liabilities. This compares with 47 per cent for the United Kingdom, 17 per cent for Belgium—Luxembourg and 15 per cent for France (see Table 4.3). At only 23 per cent, German banks had also the smallest share of their own residents' foreign currency balances and only 60 per cent of non-resident holdings of Deutsche Mark deposits were with German banks. This compares with 75 and 85 per cent respectively for the United Kingdom. The figures reported in Table 4.3 highlight another important feature of the Euro-currency market. Although the regulatory framework of Euro-currency liabilities is similar in the United Kingdom, Belgium—Luxembourg, France and the Netherlands – in none of these countries are non-resident foreign currency balances subject to monetary, tax or exchange control regulations – the share of the Euro-currency market accounted by each centre is quite different. Banks in the United Kingdom dominate the market and account for nearly one-half of total Euro-currency liabilities.

London had once been the world's most important financial centre and it is therefore not unnatural that it should remain a leading centre for international transactions. Sharing a common language with the USA it was the obvious location for a Euro-dollar market, and the proportion of Euro-dollar business conducted in London is larger than its share of total Euro-currency liabilities. The authorities in the United Kingdom have been relatively accommodating to the influx of foreign banks and have given official encouragement and support to London's international role.[4] The regulatory structure of banking activities in the United Kingdom is a flexible one and, although the Bank of England has moved to establish more formal guidelines for the supervision of banking activity, these continue to emphasise banks' own self-regulatory responsibilities. Few formal limits are imposed on the structure of banks' balance-sheets. This flexible environment, coupled with London's historical role, has generally endeared it as a centre of international business. Such qualitative aspects are important reasons for the development of Euro-currency markets independent of the asymmetrical nature of regulations.

4.3   IMPERFECT SUBSTITUTES

The assumption of uniform assets on which the transactions cost model is based is thus perhaps not a very good one when analysing the reasons for Euro-currency markets, as other qualitative factors

Table 4.2

Regulations affecting international banking operations*

	(1) Non-resident transactions in foreign currencies			(2) Non-resident holdings of domestic currencies in banks of the currency concerned	(3) Resident transactions
	(a) Monetary	(b) Tax	(c) Exchange control		
Belgium–Luxembourg	None presently implemented; however, the authorities have powers to restrict transactions	Interest on interbank transactions and non-bearer securities exempted	None, but the authorities have power to impose restrictions	The Belgium–Luxembourg Economic Union operates a two-tier foreign exchange market: a controlled market reserved for current-account transactions and a free market for capital movements. Transactions through the free market are normally unrestricted	Capital outflows are extensively restricted and authority is normally only granted for trade-related activities
France	None	None	None	No restrictions, but balances are subject to a reserve requirement of 5 per cent, and interest payments to withholding tax	
West Germany	Subject to minimum reserve requirements and other regulations on a nearly equal basis to domestic currency deposits (see 2). Exemption for interbank transactions	None	None other than the restrictions noted in 1(a) and 2	At various times extensive restrictions have been imposed, including the prohibition of interest payments, minimum reserve requirements and restrictions on the type of money-market instruments purchased. Most specific restrictions had been removed by end-1980, but deposits remain subject to domestic reserve requirements	No restrictions on capital outflows; from December 1980 to March 1981 German banks were, however, asked to refrain in their external Deutsche Mark lending

The Netherlands	Authorisation has to be granted for participation in syndicated medium-term Euro-credits and at present is freely permitted. Otherwise no restrictions	None	None	Restrictions on non-resident bank accounts from 1972–5, including the prohibition of interest payments	The purchase and issue of Euro-guilder securities is not permitted. There are no restrictions on the holding of foreign currency bank accounts
Switzerland	Minimum reserve requirements were imposed up to end-February 1977. None enforced at present	35 per cent withholding tax on interest received on deposits with maturities greater than one year	None	Up until end-1979 considerable restrictions were enforced, including a ban on interest-rate payments, negative interest rates and other special concession charges. No restrictions are presently enforced	Commercial banks require authorisation for certain capital transactions in excess of S.Fr. 10 million, otherwise no restrictions
United Kingdom	None	None	None	No discriminative restrictions, balances are subject to the same minimum reserve and special deposit requirements as sterling liabilities to residents	Until October 1979 exchange controls restricted capital outflows. Residents are now free to transact in domestic and foreign currencies at home and abroad
USA (a) Domestic banking	Similar regulations as apply to domestic bank deposits, including minimum reserve requirements and interest-rate ceilings	None	None	No discriminative restrictions, balances subject to the same minimum reserve requirements and interest-rate ceilings as dollar liabilities to residents	Restrictions on capital outflows through the US banking system were removed in January 1974. No restrictions are presently enforced
(b) International banking facility (IBF) (effective 3 December 1981)	None on deposits associated with international banking activity (minimum size of transaction $100,000)	Exemption from state and local taxes	None	None on deposits associated with international banking activity (minimum size of transaction $100,000). Exemption from state and local taxes	Resident transactions with IBFs are not permitted

* Status as at end-1980 unless otherwise stated.

Sources: OECD, *Regulations affecting International Banking Operations* (Paris, 1981); Federal Reserve Board, Press Release (July 1981).

Table 4.3

Indicators of different centres' competitiveness: end-1980 (percentages)

Country	United Kingdom	Belgium–Luxembourg	France	Netherlands	West Germany
Share of total Euro-currency liabilities[1]	47	17	15	6	3
Share of resident foreign currency balances	75	54	47	47	23
Share of private non-resident domestic currency balances[2]	85	87[3]	70	82	61

[1] Banks in Europe reporting to the BIS. (See Chapter 3 for a description of Euro-currency data.)
[2] For example, the share of private non-resident sterling balances held in London rather than the Euro-sterling market.
[3] Belgian francs only.
Source: BIS data.

have to be taken into account. There are different sovereign, institutional, regulatory and interest-rate risks. The physical location of the market will determine the type of regulations and the legal jurisdiction to which deposits may become subject. The possibility that sovereign governments may take political action against a foreign country by freezing its deposits introduces a considerable risk, which the Iranian crisis has made very evident. This crisis has also shown that the Euro-market, and particularly US banks abroad, are not immune from the political influence of the US authorities and the legal issues surrounding the jurisdiction over the Iranian deposits have not been resolved. Nevertheless, the political authority of the USA is certainly less in Europe than at home and most European-owned banks did not actively co-operate in the freeze of Iranian assets. Euro-currency markets may therefore give some groups of depositors a greater degree of protection against political intervention. On the other hand, the absence of a well-defined lender of last resort in the Euro-market may lead investors to believe that Euro-currency deposits are on average somewhat more risky than domestic bank deposits. Table 4.4 summarises the regulatory and risk factors which may influence the allocation of funds between domestic, Euro- and foreign money markets.

Decisions to place or borrow currencies in one market rather than another are therefore likely to be the outcome of more general portfolio decisions. The portfolio approach notes that risk-averse wealth-holders will tend to diversify their investments among a range of assets. What is relevant for the investors' overall portfolio is the holdings of the stock of any asset and its risks and returns relative to other investments in the portfolio. The equilibrium demand for the stock of an asset would then be expressed in terms of its own rate of return, that on other assets available for holding in the portfolio, total wealth and a variety of other variables. The demand for Euro-dollar deposits could be specified as:

$$D_{ed} = D_{ed}(r_e, \bar{r}, N, W)$$

where $\bar{r}_e$ is the rate of interest on Euro-dollar deposits, $\bar{r}$ the vector of expected returns on other assets, including the domestic dollar interest rate and expected exchange-rate movements, N some non-interest-rate factors which may well include transaction costs, risk variables and the type of different attributes outlined in Table 4.4, and W the wealth of the investor. Rises in the Euro-dollar rate and investors' wealth should increase, while rises in the expected return on other assets should tend to decrease the stock of Euro-dollar holdings. Portfolio model frameworks have been frequently used to

Table 4.4
Factors influencing portfolio allocations

	Domestic	Euro-currency			Foreign*
Type of placement →	Domestic currency	Domestic currency	Foreign currency		Foreign currency
Currency of denomination of asset →	Home	Abroad	Home	Abroad	Abroad
Where held →					
Subject to:					
1. Political or sovereign risks	No	Yes	No	Yes	Yes
2. National monetary regulations	Yes	No	No	No	Yes
3. Domestic capital controls (outflows)	No	Yes	Yes	Yes	Yes
4. Foreign capital controls (inflows)	No	No	No	No	Yes
5. Protection by central banks†	Yes	No	Yes	No	Yes

* 'Foreign' refers, for example, to a dollar placement in New York by a British resident.
† See Chapter 11.

analyse short-term international capital movements between national economies, and many studies explicitly include a Euro-currency interest rate (usually the Euro-dollar interest rate) as an explanatory variable in the capital-flow equation. The rationale is that, for many investors, the closest substitute for a domestic asset is a Euro-currency deposit. Euro-dollars and sterling deposits can, for example, be held at the same London bank, which reduces political risks and the possibility that the foreign currency balance will become subject to foreign capital or exchange controls.

Thus to the extent that domestic and Euro-currency deposits are imperfect substitutes the portfolio model would be the more appropriate analytical framework and it may well explain why Euro-markets originally emerged and expanded, as investors took advantage of the different constellation of interest rates and risks available there. Because of the lack of data on private Euro-currency deposits. there have been few opportunities to examine the approach empirically, however, and most analysis has been concerned with portfolio explanations of the movements in Euro-currency interest rates. As is discussed in the next chapter, efficient bank arbitrage may dominate private wealth-holders' portfolio adjustments in the determination of short-term Euro-currency interest rates, so that the conclusion from portfolio-model explanations of Euro-currency interest-rate movements may be flawed. Some econometric estimates of non-bank holdings of Euro-currencies are, however, reported below. There is, moreover, a second difficulty with the portfolio model explanation (and the transactions cost model explanation) of the growth of Euro-currency deposits. *to explain why in many cases private Euro-currency deposits have expanded at a faster rate than deposits in national currency markets*.

By focusing on the allocation of the stock of wealth, portfolio models emphasise that changes in the equilibrium structure of a wealth-holder's portfolio only occur when the rate of return or the attributes of different assets change, or when the overall size of the portfolio varies because of a rise or fall in the investor's wealth. When the *differential* between the rates of return on domestic and foreign investments widens in favour of foreign securities, investors will adjust their portfolio, reducing their stock of domestic and increasing their stock of foreign assets. But these adjustments are finite, being constrained by the overall size and requirements of the portfolio. Moreover, the existence of international interest-rate differentials — say between US domestic and Euro-dollar interest rates – is not necessarily evidence of portfolio disequilibrium or that there is a continuous incentive for wealth-holders to move funds between one money market and another. Thus, for these reasons, if portfolio models are to explain the relatively rapid expansion of Euro-currency deposits, the portfolio-adjustment process must be more complex.

4.3.1   *Stock adjustments*

Some models hypothesise that, because of rigidities, market imperfections or slow behavioural responses, investors will take time to alter their portfolio composition to a change in circumstances — these models are usually known as stock-adjustment models. Very gradual stock adjustments may even lead to the observation of a continuous flow of funds between markets over extended periods of time.

In explaining Euro-market growth it may well be reasonable to expect that investors take time to adjust their portfolios to the emergence of a new market in bank deposits and loans: there will be a learning period as information about the market and the institutions involved is disseminated and assessed. New agents may be continuously becoming aware of the advantages, costs and risks of placing and borrowing funds offshore. However, a glance at the data suggests that if this process is to explain the continued expansion of the market, it must be occurring very slowly and cannot be easily explained by some distributed-lag hypothesis in which the influence of a portfolio disturbance diminishes over time. In a comparatively early study of the determination of Euro-dollar interest rates using a stock-adjustment model Hendershott (1967) found, for the period 1957–64, that the adjustment in Euro-dollar rates to a change in the US Treasury bill rate was fairly rapid and completed within one year.[5] Moreover, most econometric studies of short-term capital flows do not indicate that the adjustment lags in capital-flow equations are excessively lengthy.[6] One should not therefore expect that they should be any greater when placing funds in the Euro-market, which is, after all, no longer a new phenomenon. In a more recent study Knight (1977) found a rather slow adjustment in non-US residents' holdings of Euro-dollars. His estimates suggest that less than 1 per cent of the adjustment occurs in the first period following a disturbance to desired Euro-dollar holdings, and tends to diminish thereafter. The dampening period is estimated at over six years. However, his estimates relate to a period when UK exchange controls were in force and they failed to take account of the impact of Regulation Q ceilings. On simple *a priori* grounds the result appears implausible, as Knight himself comments. It is very difficult to explain the expansion of the Euro-currency market solely in terms of lags in adjustment in portfolios. But other factors may influence the stock-adjustment process.

4.3.2   *Stock-flow adjustments*

An alternative explanation is based on a portfolio framework which incorporates flow adjustments through factors which expand the overall size of the portfolio. Specifically, to explain the comparatively rapid expansion of Euro-currency holdings, wealth-holders must have a higher propensity to hold additions to net worth in the Euro-currency market than in other types of assets. Knight's (1977) estimates indicated, for example, that a 1 per cent rise in a proxy for world wealth caused investors to increase their demand for Euro-dollar deposits by just over 2 per cent.[7] An examination of data on *US resident* non-bank Euro-dollar holdings over the period 1974IV—1980I revealed a similar conclusion. Regressing in log linear terms the real stock of US non-bank Euro-dollar holdings, ED_{US}, on the differential between the three-month Euro-dollar and US domestic CD rate $(r_e - r_d)$, real US wealth, W_{US}, and a lagged dependent variable gave:

$$ED_{US} = -15.820 + 0.355(r_e - r_d) + 2.899W_{US} + 0.244ED_{US-1}$$
$$(4.00) \quad (5.38) \qquad\qquad (5.01) \qquad\quad (2.86)$$

$\bar{R}^2 = 0.99$, Durbin—Watson statistic $= 1.68$, t-ratios in
    parentheses

This equation exhibits three noteworthy properties. First, the coefficient on the lagged dependent variable indicates that the speed of adjustment of US non-bank Euro-dollar holdings to changes in wealth or interest rates is indeed rapid, with around three-quarters of the adjustment occurring in the first quarter. Second, US non-bank entities are highly interest-rate sensitive to movements in the Euro-dollar/US domestic CD interest-rate differential. The estimates suggest that the final impact of a small rise in the differential by 0.1 percentage points from 0.5 to 0.6 percentage points (i.e. by 20 per cent) causes US non-banks to increase their real stock of Euro-dollars by about 9 per cent. Third, the coefficient on the wealth term indicates that, in the long run, a 1 per cent rise in real US wealth leads to nearly a 4 per cent increase in US non-banks' real Euro-dollar holdings. The conclusion from these estimates is therefore that Euro-dollar holdings appear as superior assets in the portfolios of wealth-holders and increase more than proportionally with wealth.

This result is not perhaps implausible. Diversification of investments internationally may simply be a function of higher levels of wealth. At lower levels priority is given to a diversification of domestic asset holdings within the domestic economy, as these are seen as the first line of defence to variations in domestic income streams. However, because 5 Euro-currency assets may involve an unfamiliar set of markets and institutions, and different sovereign and political risks, they are seen as inherently more risky and investors are only willing to take on such risks at higher levels of wealth. In other words, over the relevant range, risk aversion in investment strategy is a function of income and wealth levels. This effect might not be as important if depositors could hold small Euro-currency balances in proportion to their wealth-holdings, but various transaction costs have prevented this development and there are effectively quantitative limits to entry into the competitive Euro-currency deposit market. Indeed, the notional *desired* demand for Euro-currency deposits might well exceed the actual demand because of these quantitative limits to entry. As wealth increases, stock-flow adjustments occur and investors can move towards their desired portfolio positions.

Stock-flow adjustments and trade influences. Recalling the discussion in section 4.1, internationally used currencies perform several functions and act as a unit of account as well as a store of value. In explaining *non-US resident* non-bank holdings of Euro-dollars — which, in practice, account for 80 per cent of non-bank Euro-dollar deposits — it seems likely that trade and portfolio effects are both important. Euro-dollars could be held as an alternative investment to domestic currency and to finance trade transactions normally conducted in dollars. Johnston (1982) has attempted to examine these factors by pooling together cross-section and time-series data on non-bank holdings of Euro-dollars from six countries[8] and has estimated the demand for Euro-dollars within the framework of a three-equation model.[9] The demand for non-US private Euro-dollars, ED_{NUS}, was written in terms of a set of country dummy variables, which allow for different average responses in each country, reflecting, for example, the structure of national controls on capital movements;[10] the level of imports in each country, adjusted for the approximate volume invoiced in dollars, Im_c; the rate of growth of GNP in each country, $G\dot{N}P$, to proxy the growth of national wealth; the three-month Euro-dollar rate r_{ed}; the three-month Euro-currency rate of the country, r_{ec}, to proxy the return on assets in the domestic currency; the rate of change of the spot rate of the country's domestic currency against the dollar, $\dot{e}$ (currency units per dollar) to catch possible exchange-rate expectational effects; and a lagged dependent variable. In addition, a variable which attempted to measure shocks to domestic wealth-holders' portfolios — the ratio of national broad money stocks to a trend estimate of money demand, M^s/M^d − was also entered in the equation. The result of the pooled regression for the period 1977IV−1980IV, where Ln denotes that the variable was entered in natural logarithms, were:

$$Ln ED_{NUS} = 1.18 + 0.44 Dum_{UK1} + 0.52 Dum_{UK2} + 0.42 Dum_{CA}$$
$$(2.03)\ (3.28)\qquad\quad (3.55)\qquad\qquad (3.01)$$

$$+\ 0.32 Dum_{JP} + 0.12 Ln Im_c + 0.60 Ln M^s/M^d$$
$$(2.50)\qquad\quad (1.62)\qquad\quad (1.58)$$

$$+\ 0.43\, G\dot{N}P + 0.0086 r_{ed} - 0.00674 r_{ec} + 0.27 \dot{e}$$
$$(1.58)\qquad (1.25)\qquad\quad (2.00)\qquad\quad (0.81)$$

$$+\ 0.72 Ln ED_{NUS-1}$$
$$(8.84)$$

$\bar{R}^2$ = 0.987, Durbin−Watson statistic = 2.00, t-ratios in parentheses

Although some of the t-ratios in this equation are low, all variables enter with the correct sign giving support to a mixed trade financing/ portfolio-adjustment explanation of non-US non-banks' holdings of Euro-dollars. It is interesting that the long-run coefficient on the rate of growth of national GNP, 1.5, again implies that Euro-dollar deposits are superior assets and that, unlike the simple cross-section results reported in Table 4.1, the long-run coefficient on the trade variable, 0.42, is now in line with the inventory-theoretic approach.

Turning to non bank holdings of other Euro-currencies, data on sterling holdings, both in London and in the Euro-sterling market, by residents in France, West Germany, the Netherlands and Belgium showed that these were all closely correlated with UK exports to these countries in the time-series data, supporting the cross-section analysis in Table 4.1. There was also some evidence that proxies for investors' wealth had a positive influence on their sterling holdings but this relationship was dominated by the trade variable. It seems that during the period (1974−80) the unit of account function was much more important than the store of value function in explaining private holdings of sterling balances. Because of the weakness of sterling during the estimation period this seems a reasonable con- clusion. For some countries the location of sterling holdings − whether held in London or the Euro-sterling market − was found to be sensitive to relative domestic and Euro-sterling interest rates; and there was evidence that total sterling holdings were sensitive to exchange-rate movements and to the differential between the country's domestic interest rate and sterling interest rates. None of the equations seemed particularly satisfactory, however.[11] Much research remains to be done to explain the international holding of Euro-currencies. For weaker currencies it seems likely that the unit of account function may prove to be the more fruitful line of investigation, while holdings of stronger currencies should be responsive to more general portfolio considerations.

4.4   INTERBANK TRADING

One of the largest numerical functions of banks in the Euro-currency market is interbank business. Within the Euro-currency system the volume of business accounted for by interbank transactions is much larger than in any national money market. In the USA, for example, the Federal funds market amounts to only about one-eighth of the aggregate liabilities of US banks, and the position is broadly similar in European national markets. In the Euro-currency market between two-thirds and three-quarters of banks' total external liabilities and claims are with other banks.

All interbank trading in the Euro-currency system is not, however, analogous with that in national markets. Interbank trading in the Euro-markets might be said to perform four functions: those of 'liquidity smoothing', 'liquidity transfer', 'currency transfer', and 'global liquidity distribution'. To describe these functions it is useful to draw a distinction between interbank trading within an individual Euro-currency centre – for example, the London interbank market – and interbank trading which takes place between spatially distributed markets – for example, between London and Singapore or the USA. The first three functions of interbank trading will be described as activities within the Euro-currency centre, while the fourth is an activity of trading between centres. Although this distinction is only abstract – all aspects of interbank trading may occur within and between centres – it is analytically useful.

For any individual bank the inflow and outflow of funds from deposits and loans will not always – or even usually – be matching. The bank can maintain a stock of liquidity assets, cash or precautionary balances to act as a buffer between the inflows and outflows of funds. Alternatively it can borrow or lend funds with other banks. Thus, for example, if an individual Euro-bank receives new deposits unexpectedly it will usually be able to lend these temporarily to other banks in the London interbank market, earning a small return of some 1/32 per cent. When an individual bank finds itself temporarily short of deposits, it will usually be able to borrow from other banks to meet its lending commitments. This *liquidity-smoothing* function involves the bank managing at the margin the structure of its assets and liabilities and is most often associated with interbank trading within national banking systems. It reduces intermediaries' transaction costs by economising on the volume of precautionary balances that the bank has to hold.

The *liquidity-transfer* function of interbank trading refers to intra-marginal transfers of liquidity from one bank to another in the Euro-currency centre. Not all banks in the Euro-market are equally able to attract funds from primary depositors or from other banks outside the Euro-currency centre, and the initial allocation of funds to the centre depends very much on the name, size, nationality and credit standing of different banks. Corporations and other non-bank wealth-holders are often reluctant to place funds in smaller banks – although, because of their lower status, the smaller banks usually offer marginally higher yields than larger competitors – and deposits are frequently only channelled to the best-named banks in the market. In the London market, for example, the proportion of banks' foreign currency liabilities due to non-banks varies from around 40 per cent for American banks to only some 10 to 15 per cent for consortium banks. Similarly, banks peripheral to the centre usually channel funds to the market via their own branches or subsidiaries in the centre or to banks with which they have well-established correspondent relationships. Banks which are primary recipients of funds then frequently pass these on to other banks in the centre via the interbank market. Some smaller banks indeed show a very heavy dependence on interbank borrowing when funding their lending.

One feature of Euro-market lending encourages the liquidity-transfer function of interbank trading. Many loans are in the form of syndicated medium-term credits. The larger banks, which are the prime recipients of funds in the market, also act as the lead managers of loans, while smaller banks participate for small amounts in the syndicate. By providing funds to smaller banks through the interbank market, larger banks effectively fund a larger proportion of the loan than they take on to their own books. The advantage of this syndication process to the larger banks is that the credit risks of the loan are spread more widely across a group of banks. The liquidity-transfer function may also involve two-way trading between banks. Banks are reluctant to be seen only as borrowers of funds in the market as this may harm their credit standing and their ability to borrow funds from other banks at competitive market rates. They therefore lend some interbank borrowed funds so as to be seen as suppliers of funds and also to disguise their net indebtedness to the interbank market. When the point of contact between peripheral banks and the centre is via certain nationalities of banks, this will also lead to two-way trading in the market.

Since the Euro-currency market is an international market and accepts deposits and makes loans in a range of currencies, there is no necessary reason why the currency composition of deposits should match that of loans. I term *currency transfer* the process by which banks match the currency composition of their assets and liabilities through interbank trading. A bank may receive a Deutsche Mark deposit but wish to make a dollar loan. To avoid the risks involved in holding an open foreign exchange position the bank can borrow or lend funds in the interbank market, for example matching its Deutsche Mark deposit with a Deutsche Mark placement in the interbank market and borrowing dollars to meet its loan commitment. In a large Euro-currency centre, banks' individual currency positions may be offsetting to a considerable degree. Some banks may be 'short' in dollars and 'long' in Deutsche Mark, while the position of other banks may be reversed, and by trading together through the interbank market banks may be able to match their individual currency positions. The alternative matching process is to trade through the foreign exchange markets. The bank could sell its Deutsche Mark deposits for dollars in the spot foreign exchange market and simultaneously contract to buy back the Deutsche Mark for dollars in the forward exchange market. When its dollar loan matures it can use the dollars to unwind the forward contract, paying over dollars for Deutsche Mark and can use the Deutsche Mark to repay its original depositor. These alternative processes are analytically similar and, indeed, because of the efficiency of arbitrage between different currencies (see Chapter 5), banks in the Euro-currency market determine interest rates on non-dollar currencies as the Euro-dollar rate plus or minus the forward discount or premium of the particular currency against the dollar. There is therefore rarely an interest-rate advantage when trading through the forward exchange market rather than the interbank market. The interbank process, by pooling together a large group of transactors, will, however, tend to reduce the amount of residual trading through the forward exchange market when the overall supply of and demand for different currencies in the Euro-centre are not matching. Banks also place and borrow funds in the Euro-market to cover their open forward exchange positions. The process is described in Chapter 8.

In interbank trading between peripheral banks and the Euro-centre, the interbank functions of liquidity smoothing, transfer and currency transfer are also very relevant. Efficient interbank arbitrage usually ensures that Euro-currency interest rates are fairly uniform between Euro-currency centres. Banks in Singapore borrow dollars in London to fund their Asian-dollar business and banks in London borrow in New York to fund their Euro-dollar lending when this is profitable. Niehans and Hewson (1976) have suggested that a Euro-centre such as London plays a more important function in the interbank relationship between banks in different countries: that of *global liquidity distribution*. Certain assumptions generate a network model in which this would occur:

1. There are large excess demands and supplies of funds in individual local markets.
2. Transaction costs between non-banks are very high (otherwise non-banks would contract directly).
3. Transaction costs between non-banks and banks vary widely, being lower between parties in the same area (if this were not so, each bank would balance its own non-bank business).
4. Transaction costs between peripheral banks in different countries are higher than between peripheral banks and the Euro-currency centre (otherwise funds would flow directly between peripheral banks and not through the Euro-currency centre).

Figure 4.3 illustrates the type of network system that is envisaged. Peripheral banks contract with their own branches and subsidiaries in the Euro-centre and funds are passed from one peripheral bank to another by way of interbank transactions between banks in the market. Banks in the centre bring together resources from outside banks and from primary depositors to fund loans to final borrowers and other peripheral banks. The centre's function of liquidity and currency transfer eases the distribution of liquidity around the world's banking systems and integrates peripheral banking centres – the centre acts as a form of global clearing system for currency flows.

Bank of England data on the foreign currency assets and liabilities of UK banks illustrate these types of processes. These data provide a breakdown into five categories of liabilities and claims – the London interbank market, other UK residents, bank overseas, other overseas residents, and certificates of deposit outstanding – for five groups of UK banks – British, American, Japanese, other overseas and consortium banks (see Table 4.5). The following observations can be made about the data in Table 4.5. First, the proportion of the total balance-sheet accounted for by trading with banks overseas is some 10 per cent larger for foreign banks – the American, Japanese and other overseas banking groups – than for British banks. As might be expected, foreign banks are more involved in trading with peripheral area banks than British banks. British banks, on the other hand, conduct the largest proportion of business with residents in the local area (the other UK residents category). Second, in the foreign

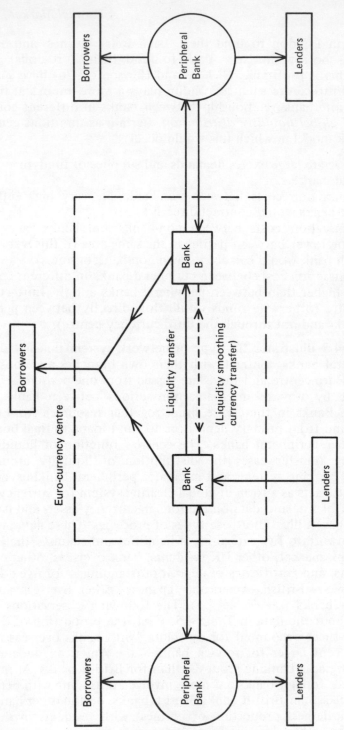

Figure 4.3 Liquidity distribution through the interbank market

banking group the net claims of other overseas banks on the London interbank market exceed their net liabilities to banks overseas by a similar margin. This position is roughly reversed for Japanese banks and suggests that foreign banks use the London interbank market as an outlet or source of funds for peripheral area banks. In this respect London interbank trading and interbank transactions with banks overseas are complementary. Third, only for American banks are liabilities to the London interbank market a relatively small fraction of the total balance-sheet. These banks also raise the largest proportion of funds from non-banks (roughly proxied as the sum of the other UK and overseas resident plus the certificate of deposit (CD) categories – this result is due solely to the volume of CDs). For these banks, London interbank trading will most closely reflect the function of liquidity smoothing (and currency transfer) and in this respect it is not very much larger than within national markets. The American banks are also using their strong liquidity position to fund other UK banks and banks overseas – the liquidity-transfer function of interbank trading. Fourth, consortium banks seem to accord most closely with small banks in the market. They fund over 85 per cent of their business through the interbank market but hold the smallest proportion of claims on the London market (reflecting liquidity smoothing and currency transfer) but make proportionally the largest volume of loans to primary borrowers. These general observations seem consistent with the description of the functions of interbank trading in the Euro-currency market. They also indicate that a Euro-centre, such as London, plays an important role in the global liquidity distribution process and one that complements the intermediation function of national banking systems.

4.5 SUMMARY

The largest volume of transactions by non-banks in the Euro-market is in currencies other than their own domestic currency, and the US dollar is overwhelmingly the most important. Internationally used currencies provide a very similar function for the international economy as a unit of account, a medium of exchange and as store of value as they do at home. There is evidence that private Euro-currency balances are related to trade flows and Euro-dollar holdings to international portfolio allocations more generally.

The reasons why business is contracted outside the countries of the currencies traded in the market reflects transaction costs and the structure of regulations in the uniform asset world, as well as the different attributes of markets when assets are imperfect substitutes.

Table 4.5

Sectoral analysis of foreign currency assets*
and liabilities of UK banks (November 1980)

	British banks	American banks	Japanese banks	Other overseas banks	Consortium banks
Liabilities to (percentage of total):					
The London interbank market	26	12	28	21	39
Other UK residents	6	3	–	2	1
Banks overseas	48	50	56	57	48
Other overseas residents	15	12	5	14	9
Certificates of deposit (CDs)	5	23	11	6	3
Total ($ billion)	101.8	119.0	90.4	122.1	23.4
Claims on (percentage of total):					
The London interbank market	26	18	24	27	14
Other UK residents	10	5	3	4	3
Banks overseas	42	59	58	51	39
Other overseas residents	20	17	14	17	43
Certificates of deposit (CDs) held	2	1	1	1	1
Total ($ billion)	102.7	117.4	89.0	121.1	23.6

* Trustee funds and central bank deposits are included as 'interbank' transactions.

Source: *Bank of England Quarterly Bulletin* (March 1980).

The empirical evidence indicates two conclusions. First, private Euro-currency deposits are interest-rate sensitive, and factors which tend to widen the differential between domestic and Euro-currency interest rates will cause the Euro-currency market to expand. In itself this may have important monetary policy implications (see Chapter 10). Second, some underlying trends, be they wealth effects or trade factors, have given the Euro-market an apparent expansionary momentum and have tended to cause a larger proportion of business to be conducted 'offshore'. Coupled with the regulatory asymmetry of domestic and Euro-currency banking, there is concern for the macroeconomic implications of this expansion (see Chapter 8).

One of the largest activities of Euro-markets is interbank trading. Such activity can be said to perform four functions: those of liquidity smoothing, liquidity transfer, currency transfer and global liquidity distribution. The general efficiency of Euro-currency centres such as London will tend to mean that a very large volume of interbank flows will pass through the centre, which acts as a type of global clearing system for currency flows. The liquidity distribution process integrates peripheral banking centres and leads to important interest links between national economies: a subject examined in the next chapter.

4.6 ANNEX: TRANSACTION COSTS AND EURO-CURRENCY MARKETS

In a one-currency uniform asset world of free capital mobility, decisions by investors or borrowers to place or borrow funds in one market rather than another will depend on the relative returns and costs from doing so. These could be divided into market interest rates and non-market transaction costs. When financial intermediaries are also involved in intermediating between depositors and borrowers of funds, the returns which they earn and the transaction costs they incur in one market rather than another will also be relevant in explaining the location of business.

Consider, for example, European residents seeking to borrow or lend dollars. They have the choice of doing this in New York or the local Euro-dollar market, say in London. The net cost of borrowing and the net return from depositing dollars can be expressed in terms of the nominal interest rates in the two markets and, for illustrative purposes, as a per unit dollar transaction charge. The cost of borrowing will be greater and the return on deposits smaller by the amount of these transaction costs. This is written:

New York domestic market

Net borrowing costs $\qquad \bar{r}_d^b = r_d^b + c_d^b$ $\qquad\qquad$ (1)

Net returns $\qquad\qquad \bar{r}_d^d = r_d^d - c_d^d$ $\qquad\qquad$ (2)

London Euro-dollar market

Net borrowing costs $\qquad \bar{r}_e^b = r_e^b + c_e^b$ $\qquad\qquad$ (1a)

Net returns $\qquad\qquad\quad \bar{r}_e^d = r_e^d - c_e^d$ $\qquad\qquad$ (2a)

where r_d^b and r_d^d are the nominal interest rates on borrowing and depositing dollars in New York and c_d^b and c_d^d the associated transaction costs, r_e^b and r_e^d the nominal interest rates on borrowing and depositing dollars in the Euro-dollar market in London, and c_e^b and c_e^d the associated transaction costs.

Necessary conditions for placing or borrowing dollars in London rather than New York would be that net borrowing costs should be less than or equal and net returns on deposits should be greater than or equal in London than in New York for at least some transactors. If these conditions did not hold, all business would be done in New York and none in London – in this uniform asset world there would be no incentive for a Euro-dollar market. These conditions can be written as:

$$\bar{r}_e^b \leqslant \bar{r}_d^b \qquad\qquad (3)$$

$$\bar{r}_e^d \geqslant \bar{r}_d^d \qquad\qquad (4)$$

and from equations (1), (2), (1a) and (2a) they can be expressed as:

$$r_e^b + c_e^b \leqslant r_d^b + c_d^b \qquad\qquad (3a)$$

$$r_e^d - c_e^d \geqslant r_d^d - c_d^d \qquad\qquad (4a)$$

Abstracting for the moment from the role of intermediaries, there is only one *market* rate of interest for dollars in New York:

$$r_d^b = r_d^d \qquad\qquad (5)$$

and similarly in London:

$$r_e^b = r_e^d \qquad\qquad (5a)$$

These might, for example, be the interest rates available in the primary security markets – the dollar bond markets – in New York and London. Rearranging equations (3a) and (4a) as:

$$r_e^b - r_d^b \leqslant c_d^b - c_e^b \qquad\qquad (3b)$$

$$r_e^d - r_d^d \geqslant c_e^d - c_d^d \qquad\qquad (4b)$$

using the conditions (5) and (5a) and substituting (3b) into (4b) reveals:

$$c_d^b + c_d^d \geqslant c_e^d + c_d^d \qquad\qquad (6)$$

Equation (6) states that, when assets are uniform and there is free capital mobility, a necessary condition for the development of a primary dollar security market in London is that the sum of transaction costs faced by at least some depositors and borrowers in the New York market exceed those in London. Notice that this result is independent of the actual nominal level of interest rates, which may be higher than, lower than, or the same in London as in New York and depends only on relative transaction costs. To the extent that these are lower in London than in New York for some transactions, there will be an incentive for some primary dollar security business to be conducted in London, i.e. for the development of, for example, a Euro-dollar bond market.

Let us now introduce into the picture financial intermediaries which are in the business of taking deposits and making loans. We will now assume that all business in New York and London passes through these intermediaries and that again there is free capital mobility. Instead of equilibrium conditions (5) and (5a) we now have equations defining the relationship between intermediaries' deposit and loan rates in New York and London:

$$r_d^b = s_d + r_d^d \tag{7}$$

$$r_e^b = s_e + r_e^d \tag{7a}$$

where s_d and s_e are the lending margins or spreads which the intermediaries charge over the nominal deposit rates when making dollar loans in New York and London. The spreads will contain a profit element and will cover the costs to the intermediary when doing business in New York and London.

Say these costs are c_{db} in the domestic dollar market in New York and c_{eb} in the Euro-dollar market in London. A necessary condition for the growth of intermediaries in each market is that lending margins or spreads cover these costs, otherwise private-sector intermediaries at least would not exist. The condition is written:

$$s_d \geqslant c_{db} \text{ or } r_d^b - r_d^d \geqslant c_{db} \tag{8}$$

$$s_e \geqslant c_{eb} \text{ or } r_e^b - r_e^d \geqslant c_{eb} \tag{8a}$$

Combining these conditions with equations (3b) and (4b), the conditions that some borrowers and lenders do business in London rather than New York, reveals the following necessary conditions for the emergence of a Euro-dollar market:[12]

$$c_d^b + c_d^d + c_{db} \geqslant c_e^b + c_e^d + c_{eb} \tag{9}$$

Equation (9) states that the necessary conditions for the development of a London market for Euro-dollar bank deposits and loans is that the sum of borrowers', depositors' and intermediaries' transaction costs should be less for at least some transactors in London than in New York. Note again that this result is independent of nominal dollar interest rates in the US domestic and Euro-dollar markets. This comparatively simple and plausible result is of some interest. In particular, it shows that it is the sum of transaction costs which matters rather than those incurred by any individual set of transactors.

NOTES

1. For a discussion of duality theory see, for example, Baumol (1977, ch. 6).
2. Federal Reserve Board, Press Release, 18 June 1981.
3. When banks conduct entrepôt business there is, of course, little reason why the authorities in the countries of the banks concerned need to regulate these transactions. Nevertheless, foreign currency transactions by non-residents may be relevant to the monetary authorities in the countries of the currencies concerned, which is one reason for the debate over the need to regulate the Euro-market (see Chapters 8 and 10).
4. For an interesting and lively discussion of the development of international banking in London, with specific reference to American banks, see Kelly (1977).
5. See also Kwack (1971) for an extension of Hendershott's tests and which came to the same conclusion.
6. See, for example, Herring and Marston (1977) and Branson and Hill (1971).
7. These estimates may, however, be biased upwards by the very low stock-adjustment coefficient discussed above.
8. The countries are Canada, France, West Germany, Italy, Japan and the United Kingdom.
9. This model allowed for the simultaneous determination of the demand for Euro-dollar loans and deposits and the Euro-currency interest rate. We report here only a single-equation estimate of the demand for deposits equation.
10. Significant dummy variables were found for the United Kingdom (before and after the lifting of UK exchange controls in October 1979), Canada and Japan. These are written Dum_{UK1}, Dum_{UK2}, Dum_{CA}, and Dum_{JP} respectively.
11. The results for private French holdings of sterling in London (L£) and at banks in France (F£) were:

$$L£ = -98.59 + 0.37 UKXF + 9.37 Ex£/FF$$
$$\quad\quad (2.84)(24.01) \quad\quad\quad (2.46)$$

$$\bar{R}^2 = 0.96, DW = 2.59$$

$$F£ = 68.68 + 0.15 UKXF + 2.91 (r_{E£} - r_{FF}) + 7.52 Ex£/FF$$
$$\quad\quad (1.31) (6.62) \quad\quad\quad (2.02) \quad\quad\quad\quad (1.32)$$

$$\bar{R}^2 = 0.70, DW = 2.74$$

$$F£/L£ = 0.47 + 0.069 (r_{E£} - r_{D£})$$
$$\quad\quad\quad (2.5) \quad (2.03)$$

$$\bar{R}^2 = 0.12, DW = 1.85$$

where UKXF = UK exports to France

Ex£/FF = sterling/French franc exchange rate

$r_{E£}$ = three-month Euro-sterling interest

r_{FF} = a representative short-term domestic French interest rate

$r_{D£}$ = three-month domestic sterling interbank rate

t-ratios in parentheses

There was no evidence of interest sensitivity in the L£ equation. Estimation period was 1974IV–1980II.

12. Equation (8) and (8a) can be rewritten as:

$$(r_e^d - r_d^d) + (r_d^b - r_e^d) \geqslant c_{db}$$

$$(r_e^b - r_d^b) + (r_d^b - r_e^d) \geqslant c_{eb}$$

subtracting one from the other gives:

$$(r_e^b - r_d^b) - (r_e^d - r_d^d) \geqslant c_{eb} - c_{db}$$

substituting equations (3b) and (4b) yields:

$$(c_d^b - c_e^b) - (c_e^d - c_d^d) \geqslant c_{eb} - c_{db}$$

or

$$c_d^b + c_d^d + c_{db} \geqslant c_e^b + c_e^d + c_{eb}$$

5 Short-term Interest-rate Determination*

Because of the close substitutability between assets in domestic and in external money markets, it is clear that, in the absence of restrictions on the free flow of capital, interest rates in the two markets should be closely related. Also, because of the availability of forward cover in the foreign exchange market and the close association of the Euro-currency market with the foreign exchange market, there should clearly be a very close relationship between the interest rates offered, on different currency deposits, in the Euro-currency market, and the costs of forward cover. Analysis of the movement of Euro-currency interest rates, however, within this general framework has revealed more specific and systematic relationships between domestic and Euro-currency deposit rates; indeed, some of the observed margins between interest rates in the domestic and external money markets have been so stable as to be termed a technical differential.

This chapter attempts to rationalise some of the observed relationships within a fairly general framework of the supply of, and demand for, individual Euro-currencies. The first section considers a simple model of a single Euro-currency deposit market and recent empirical experience which illustrates how restrictions and imperfections can cause systematic deviations from the model. The model is then extended, in the second section, to discuss how two Euro-currency deposit markets and the spot and forward exchange markets interact. This section also considers why interest-rate parity appears to hold between Euro-currency interest rates but not between nominal interest rates in different domestic markets, and also the role of the Euro-market in channelling short-term capital flows. Empirical experience is reported in support of the model. An additional section examines the more recent empirical relationship between US domestic and Euro-dollar interest rates, and concludes that this is also consistent with the model.

* This chapter was initially prepared for and published in the *Bank of England Quarterly Bulletin* (March 1979). It is reproduced here with the Bank's permission; it has been amended slightly, and an additional section has been included updating the empirical analysis shown in the original article.

5.1 A MODEL OF THE RELATIONSHIP BETWEEN THE EURO-CURRENCY AND DOMESTIC MARKETS

The initial assumptions of the model are that:

1. Euro-currency deposits and domestic deposits are, in terms of the number of settlement days and marketability, perfect substitutes.
2. There are no capital controls on the movement of funds between the domestic money market and the Euro-currency market.
3. Domestic banks are required to hold non-interest-bearing reserve balances against domestic currency deposits.[1]
4. Institutions which take deposits and make loans in a currency other than that of the country in which they are operating — hereafter termed 'Euro-banks'[2] — are not legally obliged to hold reserves against such foreign currency deposits.[3]
5. Private non-bank holders of funds may have strong, non-pecuniary preferences for holding either a domestic or a Euro-currency deposit.
6. For domestic banks, loans to Euro-banks are no more risky than loans made in the domestic interbank market.

The first four assumptions are factual in nature, and therefore may be easily verified. In general, assumptions (3) and (4) hold for most currencies in the Euro-currency market; the validity of assumption (2) varies as between currencies and over time; assumption (1) need not strictly hold, but it does not seem an unreasonable simplification.[4]

Private non-bank holders of funds are assumed to have non-pecuniary preferences for depositing in one market rather than the other — assumption (5). This may reflect different perceived degrees of political or financial risk in the two markets.

The validity of assumption (6) is likely to depend on domestic banks' perceived degree of risk in lending to the Euro-currency market. This may vary over time. One reason for expecting this risk to be small is that Euro-banks have very close links with domestic banks — in many cases Euro-banks are the wholly or partly owned subsidiaries or branches of domestic banks in a foreign country — which may, as a matter of routine, make loans to or take deposits from their overseas affiliates. Whether, in fact, domestic banks' perceived degree of risk in lending to the Euro-currency market is small is an empirical question investigated below. For the purposes of exposition, it is assumed here to be zero.

It is now possible to derive the supply and demand curves for Euro-currency deposits under this set of assumptions and four simple propositions about the behaviour of non-bank holders of funds, domestic or parent banks, and Euro-banks:

1. Non-banks' supply of funds to the Euro-currency market will depend, among other things, on the relative return on deposits in the two markets, and it is likely that, *ceteris paribus*, for a given domestic deposit rate, the supply of currency to (demand for deposits from) the Euro-market will be positively related to the Euro-currency deposit rate. This may be simply written as:

$$S_{cc}^{nb} = f_1(i_{ec} - i_d) \tag{1}$$

with

$$\frac{\delta S_{ec}^{nb}}{\delta i_{ec}} > 0$$

where i_{ec} and i_d are respectively the Euro-currency and domestic currency deposit rates; and S_{ec}^{nb} is the supply of Euro-currency by non-banks.[5] This supply schedule is illustrated as segment 1 in Figure 5.1. It is drawn so that even when the Euro-currency deposit rate is below the domestic deposit rate there is a positive supply of currency to the Euro-market, on the assumption that there exist investors

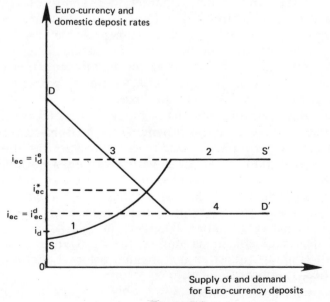

Figure 5.1

who, even in these circumstances, would prefer a Euro-currency holding to a domestic currency deposit.

2. The supply of currency to the Euro-market by domestic banks will depend on the cost to banks of raising deposits domestically and on the returns they receive from lending these in the Euro-currency market. To a domestic bank, the effective cost it pays for loanable funds at the margin is not just the nominal deposit rate but this nominal cost adjusted for the extra costs it incurs from holding (non-interest-bearing) reserves against these deposits plus any extra costs, such as the cost of Federal Deposit Insurance in the USA. The effective cost per unit of loanable funds to a domestic bank is therefore:

$$i_d^e = \frac{i_d + x_d}{1 - r_d} \tag{2}$$

where r_d is the domestic reserve requirement on resident deposits and x_d is any extra cost of domestic currency borrowing to domestic banks.

Given this effective cost to banks of raising funds in the domestic market, they would only on-lend funds to the Euro-market if the rate they would obtain on Euro-currency deposits exceeds this cost.

This gives the supply condition for domestic banks:

$$S_{ec}^b = f_2(i_{ec} - i_d^e) \tag{3}$$

with

$$S_{ec}^b = 0 \text{ when } i_{ec} \leqslant i_d^e$$

$$= f_2 \text{ when } i_{ec} > i_d^e$$

It might also be expected that this schedule would be highly elastic with respect to the Euro-currency deposit rate: if this rate exceeded the effective cost to domestic banks of raising loanable funds, any domestic bank could obtain a profit simply by borrowing domestically and lending the proceeds in the Euro-currency market. In the absence of capital controls and other imperfections in the market, arbitrage by banks between the domestic and Euro-currency markets should therefore be such as to place an upper ceiling on the Euro-currency deposit rate.[6] The supply schedule is therefore illustrated as being perfectly elastic at the effective cost of loanable funds to domestic banks — segment 2 of Figure 5.1.

3. The demand for funds (supply of deposits) by Euro-banks will depend on the demand for loans from Euro-banks by final users. We

might expect, *ceteris paribus*, that this demand for loans, and the Euro-banks' derived demand for funds, would be inversely related to the Euro-currency deposit rate.[7] This demand curve for funds is therefore drawn downward-sloping (segment 3 of Figure 5.1). The determinants of the relative position of this curve are likely to be fairly complex, but would be expected to depend upon the relative costs to final users of borrowing from banks in the Euro-currency rather than the domestic market – this latter cost would depend, *inter alia*, on the cost of loanable funds to domestic banks (i_d^e) – and on the relative ability to borrow in the two markets. This might be expressed algebraically as:

$$D_{ec}^{nb} = f_3(i_{ec} - i_d^e) + X \tag{4}$$

with

$$\frac{\delta D_{ec}^{nb}}{\delta i_{ec}} < 0$$

which shows the derived demand for funds by Euro-banks as a function of the relative effective cost of loanable funds in the two markets plus exogenous factors (X) such as relative lending margins.

4. A domestic bank would only borrow its own currency from the Euro-currency market if the effective cost of raising loanable funds from the Euro-currency market were less than the effective cost of loanable funds in the domestic market. The Euro-currency interest rate at which this becomes profitable will depend on relative interest rates in the two markets and on the relative reserve requirements on resident and non-resident deposits. The effective cost per unit to a domestic bank of raising loanable funds in the Euro-currency market is:

$$i_{ec}^e = \frac{i_{ec}}{1 - r_e} \tag{5}$$

where r_e is the domestic reserve requirement on non-resident deposits, on the assumption that domestic banks do not pay any extra costs on their Euro-currency borrowing. Combining equations (2) and (5), the Euro-currency interest rate at which it will become profitable for domestic banks to borrow Euro-currency is given at:

$$i_{ec}^e = i_d^e \tag{6}$$

or where

$$i_{ec} = i_{ec}^d = \frac{(i_d + x_d)(1 - r_e)}{(1 - r_d)}.$$

At this rate the demand for funds from the Euro-currency market by domestic banks should become nearly perfectly elastic with respect to the Euro-currency deposit rate. This might be expressed algebraically as:

$$D_{ec}^b = f_4 (i_{ec}^d - i_{ec}) \tag{7}$$

with

$$D_{ec}^b = 0 \text{ when } i_{ec} \geqslant i_{ec}^d$$

$$= f_4 \text{ when } i_{ec} < i_{ec}^d$$

This is illustrated as segment 4 in Figure 5.1.

This completes the simple analysis of the supply of, and demand for, a single Euro-currency in isolation from the rest of the Euro-currency market.

The equilibrium Euro-currency deposit rate is then determined by the intersection of the demand and supply schedules at i_{ec}^* in Figure 5.1. The figure also shows that the equilibrium Euro-currency deposit rate is constrained within narrow limits by the arbitrage activity of domestic banks, the upper arbitrage limit (segment 2) depending on the nominal cost to domestic banks of raising deposits in the domestic market and the level of reserve requirements on resident deposits, and the lower arbitrage limit (segment 4) depending on the domestic deposit rate and the relative level of reserve requirements on resident and non-resident deposits.

5.1.1 *A test of the model*

As a test of this analysis, Figure 5.2 compares, from January 1973 to end-March 1978, the three-month Euro-dollar bid rate[8] and the US secondary market three-month certificate of deposit (CD) rate, corrected for US domestic reserve requirements and the costs of Federal Deposit Insurance,[9] i.e. the effective cost to US banks of raising loanable funds in the domestic market.

The figure shows that the relationship between the two rates has been particularly close since end-1975, suggesting that, in this period,

116

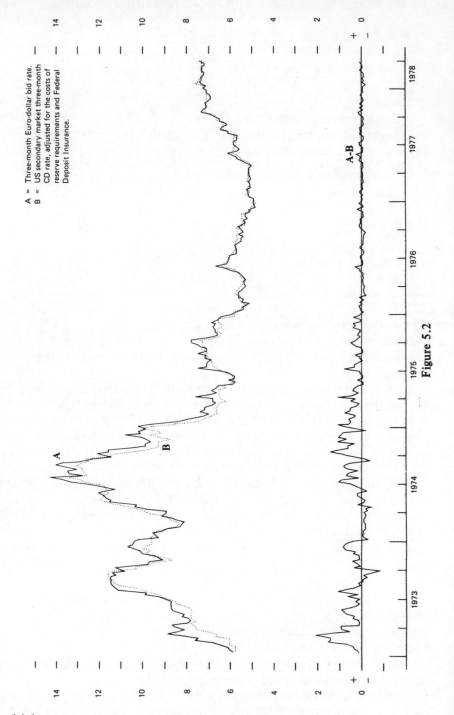

A = Three-month Euro-dollar bid rate.
B = US secondary market three-month
    CD rate, adjusted for the costs of
    reserve requirements and Federal
    Deposit Insurance.

Figure 5.2

Table 5.1
Three-month Euro-dollar rate less effective cost to
US banks of loanable funds in the domestic market*

	Mean	Variance	Number of observations
1 January 1973– end-December 1973	0.48	0.26	52
Mid-June 1974– end-December 1974	0.64	0.18	28
Mid-June 1974– mid–June 1975	0.53	0.16	52
1 January 1975– end-March 1978	0.07	0.05	169
Total sample	0.22	0.16	249

* Calculated as the US secondary market three-month CD rate corrected for the cost of reserve requirements and Federal Deposit Insurance.

the three-month Euro-dollar rate has been determined by the rate at which it was profitable for US domestic banks to supply funds to the Euro-dollar market (i.e. at an intersection of the demand curve with segment 2 of the supply curve in Figure 5.1). Indeed, the mean differential between the two rates after 1 January 1975 was only 0.07 percentage points, with a variance of only 0.05 percentage points (see Table 5.1).[10] Not surprisingly, published BIS statistics on the size of the Euro-market also show US banks as large net suppliers of funds to the Euro-market during this period (see Table 5.2).

Table 5.2
External assets and liabilities of US banks

$ billion		Assets	Liabilities*
1974	December	46.2	60.4
1975	December	59.8	58.7
1976	December	81.1	70.7
1977	December	92.6	78.1
1978	March	98.8	79.3

* Excluding US Treasury bills and certificates held in custody on behalf of non-residents.

Source: Bank for International Settlements statistics on international banking developments.

This in itself might be accepted as sufficient evidence to support the model in terms of the efficiency of arbitrage flows from the US domestic market to the Euro-dollar market.[11]

It is, however, worth considering why during 1973 and 1974 the differential between the two rates fluctuated sharply. One reason may be that during this period US domestic banks were either unable or unwilling to arbitrage between two markets.

Until 1974 the USA enforced a capital-restraint programme which included ceilings on US domestic bank lending to non-residents. This had the effect of making the upper arbitrage limit (segment 2 of Figure 5.1) ineffective, allowing the Euro-dollar rate to rise above the effective cost to US banks of domestic dollar borrowing.[12] After the removal of the controls in January 1974, the differential between the rates narrowed temporarily; however, during the summer of 1974 a crisis of confidence developed in the Euro-currency market after the closure of the Cologne bank, Herstatt, on 26 June. Although this banking failure was due to heavy losses sustained in foreign exchange dealings, it produced more general fears about the solvency of banks in the Euro-currency market. In these circumstances it would not have been unusual for depositors to require a significant risk premium for depositing in the Euro-currency market or, as a consequence, for Euro-dollar rates to move erratically and above the effective cost to US banks of borrowing domestically. In September 1974 the central bank governors from countries of the Group of Ten and Switzerland stated that they were satisfied that means were available for the purpose of the provision of temporary liquidity to the Euro-markets and would be used if and when necessary. Subsequently worries about the solvency of Euro-banks appear to have largely evaporated, and by mid-1975 the differential between the rates had returned to its technical level.

In the year before the removal of capital controls, the mean and variance of the differential between the rates were respectively 0.48 and 0.26 percentage points, while, during the Herstatt crisis (mid-June to end-December 1974) the mean and variance of the differential were 0.64 and 0.18 percentage points respectively. For both these periods, the means and variances of the differential were significantly different from those found for the period after January 1975, thus tending to confirm the visual evidence (see Table 5.3).

The movement in Euro-dollar interest rates in recent years tends to give strong support for the simple model developed above and suggests that, in the absence of market imperfections such as capital controls, there is at the margin a very close relationship between the effective cost of loanable funds to banks in the Euro-dollar and US domestic markets. This analysis also confirms that, in the absence of

Table 5.3
Analysis of variance: Euro-dollar/domestic CD
differential

	1 January 1973– end-December 1973	Mid-June 1974– end-December 1974
Mid-June 1974– end-December 1974	$F_{51,27}$ = 1.4	
1 January 1975– end-March 1978	$F_{51,168}$ = 5.3*	$F_{27,168}$ = 3.7*

* Indicates that the variances are significantly different at a 1 per cent level of significance.

serious crises of confidence, domestic banks do not generally regard the risks of depositing in the Euro-currency market as significantly greater than those of depositing in the domestic market.

The analysis also tends to suggest that the Euro-dollar rate is determined largely independently of both the forward exchange market and the interest rates on other Euro-currencies. While this might not be unreasonable for the Euro-dollar, which is the dominant currency in the Euro-market, making up about three-quarters of its gross size, and which also acts as the *numéraire* in the foreign exchange market, it is certainly not the case for other currencies in the Euro-market.[13] The question of the interrelationship between Euro-currency interest rates and the foreign exchange market is considered in the next section.

5.2   AN EXTENSION OF THE MODEL

In fact, the supply of, and demand for, a Euro-currency are not independent of the rate of interest on alternative currencies in the Euro-market, as assumed above. Euro-currency interest rates are instead directly related through the forward market, since an investor holding, say, Euro-dollars could sell the dollars spot for, say, Deutsche Mark, invest the Deutsche Mark in the Euro-Deutsche Mark market and cover forward. Indeed, arbitrageurs would shift funds between currencies as long as it was profitable to do so. For equilibrium, the Euro-currency rate should equal the Euro-dollar rate less the forward discount on dollars *vis-à-vis* the currency – the familiar interest-rate parity theorem. To explain the determination of Euro-currency interest rates, it is therefore necessary to discuss the forward exchange market and its relationship with the Euro-currency market.

Before proceeding to this, it should be noted that it is usual practice in the Euro-market for banks to determine a non-dollar Euro-currency rate as simply the Euro-dollar rate less the forward discount or plus the forward premium on dollars against that currency, implying that interest-rate parity holds between currencies in the Euro-market. However, even in the absence of restrictions on capital flows, arbitrage flows between domestic money markets do not seem to bring national interest rates into interest-rate parity. Indeed, to the extent that Euro-currency interest rates are different from nominal domestic interest rates, interest-rate parity between Euro-currency rates (and the forward exchange market) may be inconsistent with interest-rate parity between nominal domestic interest rates – and there has been considerable discussion among economists on the reasons for a less than perfectly elastic arbitrage demand schedule for forward exchange.[14]

To simplify the analysis, no discussion is made of the spot exchange market. The justification for this is that, following Walras's Law, the excess demand in the four markets (the spot and forward exchange market and two Euro-currency markets) must sum to zero and therefore one market (here taken as the spot exchange market) is redundant.

5.2.1   *An integrated model*

In diagrams 1 and 2 of Figure 5.3 the supply and demand curves for two individual Euro-currencies – the Euro-dollar market and the one other Euro-currency market (for example, the Euro-Deutsche Mark market) – have been redrawn under the assumptions described previously. These show the supply of, and demand for, the Euro-currency, given the level of interest rates and reserve requirements in the two domestic markets.[15] For illustrative purposes it is assumed that West German domestic interest rates are less than US domestic rates.[16] The equilibrium Euro-dollar and Euro-Deutsche Mark rates are assumed, initially, to be $i^*_{e\$}$ and i^*_{ec} respectively.

Diagram 3 of the figure illustrates the supply and demand for forward cover in the foreign exchange market.

The speculators' supply of forward exchange,[17] which is illustrated as $S''S''$ in diagram 3 of Figure 5.3, will depend, *inter alia*, on their expectations about the future spot dollar/Deutsche Mark exchange rate and on the forward discount on dollars. The shape of the supply schedule will reflect the aggregation of individual speculators' supplies, which may themselves depend on the size of individuals' outstanding forward contracts; the effect of one speculator's supply on another's;

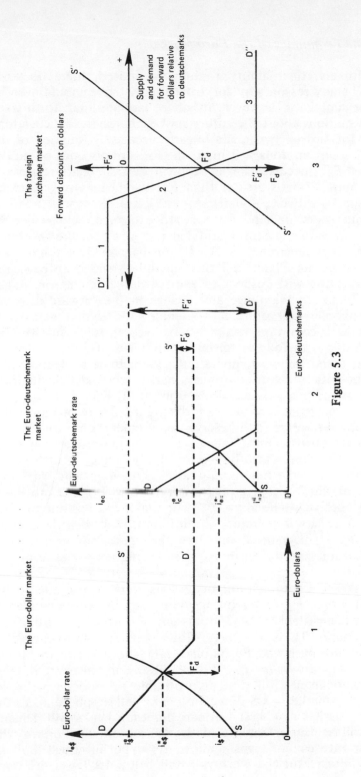

Figure 5.3

their wealth and their ability to borrow. Indeed, there does not appear to be any reason why the total supply curve should even be stable. For simplicity, however, it is here assumed that, for a given set of expectations about the future spot exchange rate, speculators' supply of forward exchange is a linearly decreasing function of the forward discount on dollars. Thus if the forward discount on dollars is less that F_d^*, speculators will supply forward dollars relative to Deutsche Mark; if it is greater than F_d^*, they will supply forward Deutsche Mark relative to dollars.

The arbitrageurs' demand for forward exchange may be derived from an analysis of the supply and demand curves for the two Euro-currencies – it is illustrated as $D''D''$ in diagram 3 of Figure 5.3. Between the points F_d' and F_d'' this schedule is shown to be nearly perfectly inelastic with respect to the forward discount on dollars (segment 2), i.e. in this range any change in the forward discount will produce only small capital movements, while beyond these points the schedule becomes perfectly elastic (segments 1 and 3). The reason for this is as follows: given US and West German domestic interest rates and reserve requirements, then domestic banks' arbitrage limits with the Euro-currency market are fixed – and these are shown as the perfectly elastic sections of the demand and supply schedules in diagrams 1 and 2 of the figure. Therefore, provided domestic interest rates (and reserve requirements) are unchanged, the maximum possible Euro-dollar rate is $i_\$^e$, the rate at which US domestic banks find it profitable to supply dollars to the Euro-dollar market, and the minimum possible Euro-Deutsche Mark rate is the rate at which West German domestic banks find it profitable to borrow Euro-Deutsche Mark, i_{ec}^d. The maximum possible forward discount on dollars is therefore the difference between these rates, shown as F_d'' in diagrams 2 and 3 of the figure, and arbitrageurs' demand for forward dollars must become perfectly elastic at this foward discount.

For if the forward discount on dollars were to rise and to become greater than F_d'', then arbitrageurs in the Euro-currency market would find it profitable to shift funds out of Euro-dollars into Euro-Deutsche Mark. These arbitrage flows between Euro-currencies would tend to push the Euro-dollar rate above $i_\$^e$, or the Euro-Deutsche Mark rate below i_{ec}^d. But at these Euro-currency interest rates, domestic banks will find it profitable to arbitrage with the Euro-currency market – US domestic banks will supply funds to the Euro-dollar market and West German domestic banks will demand funds from the Euro-Deutsche Mark market. In equilibrium, the Euro-dollar rate cannot remain above its upper arbitrage limit of $i_\$^e$ nor the Euro-Deutsche Mark rate fall below its lower arbitrage limit of i_{ec}^d, and the forward discount on dollars cannot exceed F_d''. The demand for forward dollars will therefore become perfectly elastic at this rate.

Similarly, the equilibrium forward discount on Deutsche Mark cannot exceed F_d' – the difference between US banks' lower arbitrage limit and West German banks' upper arbitrage limit. The demand for forward Deutsche Mark therefore must also become perfectly elastic at F'_d.

Between the forward discounts, F_d' and F_d'', movements in Euro-currency interest rates are unconstrained by the arbitrage activity of domestic banks, and within this range Euro-currency interest rates should adjust rapidly to a change in the forward discount. If the forward discount of dollars were to increase from its equilibrium level F_d^* (say to F_d'' in diagram 3 of Figure 5.4), suppliers of funds to the Euro-dollar market would find it profitable, at the initial rates of interest on Euro-dollars and Euro-Deutsche Mark, to transfer these funds to the Euro-Deutsche Mark market and cover forward; and arbitrageurs would find it profitable to borrow Euro-dollars to lend on a covered basis as Euro-Deutsche Mark. The combined effect is therefore to shift the supply curve for Euro-dollars to the left (from SS, to SS' (see diagram 1 of Figure 5.4) and the demand curve for Euro-dollars to the right (from DD to DD' in diagram 1 of Figure 5.4), sharply increasing the Euro-dollar rate from $i_{e\$}^*$ to $i_{e\$}^{**}$ (see diagram 1 of Figure 5.4), while shifting the supply curve for Euro-Deutsche Mark to the right (from SS to SS' in diagram 2 of the chart) and the demand curve for Euro-Deutsche Mark to the left (from DD to DD' in diagram 2), as banks which had previously borrowed Euro-Deutsche Mark would now find it profitable to borrow Euro-dollars instead and switch these into Deutsche Mark and cover forward. These shifts in the supply and demand schedules for Euro-Deutsche Mark will sharply decrease the Euro-Deutsche Mark rate from i_{ec}^* to i_{ec}^{**} (see diagram 2 of Figure 5.4). The movements in the Euro-dollar and Euro-Deutsche Mark rates, combined with some subsequent narrowing in the forward discount on dollars (from F_d'' to F_d^{**} in diagram 3 of Figure 5.4), would re-establish equilibrium between the markets. At the new equilibrium, as Figure 5.4 shows, the Euro-dollar rate is higher, the Euro-Deutsche Mark rate lower, and the forward discount on dollars somewhat wider.

Because both the supply and the demand curves shift in both Euro-currency markets, however, the actual movement of funds between the markets need only be small to re-establish equilibrium – the shift out of Euro-dollars is illustrated in the figure as d_0 to d_1;[18] the shift into Euro-Deutsche Mark as c_0 and c_1 – and therefore the arbitrageurs' demand curve for forward dollars is likely to

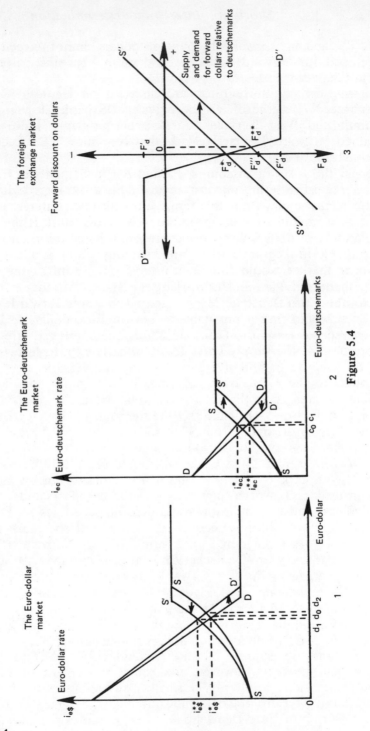

Figure 5.4

appear to be nearly perfectly inelastic with respect to the forward
discount on dollars between the points F'_d and F''_d. It is the mobility
of capital between Euro-currencies, and the adjustment in Euro-
currency interest rates, which allows dealers to determine a Euro-
currency rate simply as the Euro-dollar rate less the forward discount
on dollars. If arbitrage between Euro-currency markets were not
perfect, and it took considerable time and movement of funds to
remove disequilibrium between Euro-currency interest rates, then
other influences – the demand for the Euro-currency by final
users and the supply of the Euro-currency by holders of funds –
could determine a rate of interest on the Euro-currency which was
different from the Euro-dollar rate less the forward discount on
dollars, and covered differentials between Euro-currency interest
rates could emerge.

However, this model also shows that the range over which the
demand schedule for forward dollars is inelastic is a limited one, and
therefore only over a rather narrow range can the Euro-currency
rate be determined independently of other influences. If, for example, the speculators' supply curve of forward exchange were to
shift from SS to $S'S'$ (see Figure 5.5), this would widen, initially, the

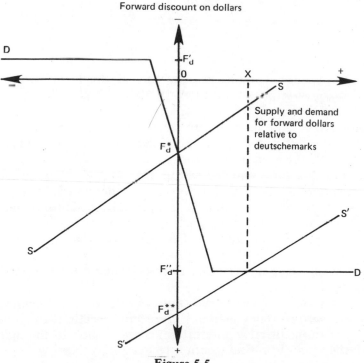

Figure 5.5

forward discount on dollars from F_d^* to F_d^{**}. If Euro-banks determine
the Euro-currency rate as the Euro-dollar rate less this forward discount, F_d^{**}, then Euro-currency markets remain in equilibrium –
there is no arbitrage flow between Euro-currencies – but Euro-
currency markets are now out of equilibrium with domestic currency
markets. A forward discount of F_d^{**} forces the quoted Euro-currency
rate below the rate at which domestic banks find it profitable to borrow the Euro-currency. Domestic banks would therefore find it
profitable to borrow their domestic currency in the Euro-market
rather than in the domestic market, or to borrow Euro-dollars, swap
these into the domestic currency and cover themselves forward; and
they would continue to do so until the forward discount on dollars
narrowed to F_d'' (see Figure 5.5) – the rate at which they no longer
find it profitable to borrow Euro-currency rather than domestic
currency – or until domestic interest rates fell into line with the
Euro-currency rate. The net result would be that X forward contracts
would have been made and that there would have been an inflow of
X from Euro-dollars into the domestic currency (see Figure 5.5).
This inflow would continue until either the forward rate or domestic
interest rates adjusted. The main determinants of the Euro-currency
rate then comprise a wider set of variables than just the Euro-dollar
rate and the forward discount on dollars.

5.2.2 *The Euro-markets and short-term capital flows*

An interesting question concerns the role of the Euro-market as a
channel for short-term capital flows. Some observers have suggested
that, because there are no restrictions on flows between currencies in
the Euro-market and because arbitrage is nearly perfect between
Euro-currences but not between domestic currencies, Euro-markets
have increased the volume of short-term capital flows, aggravating
exchange-rate pressures and decreasing the effectiveness of countries'
domestic monetary policies. However, to the extent that Euro-
banks determine Euro-currency rates as simply the Euro-dollar rate
less the forward discount on dollars, there is never any incentive for
covered arbitrage flows between Euro-currencies within the Euro-
market. Indeed, even if there were, the above framework suggests
that very small flows would bring Euro-currency interest rates back
into equilibrium.

The main reason for short-term capital flows which are channelled
through the Euro-currency market is the arbitrage activity of domestic
banks when Euro-currency interest rates are pushed to the margins
at which they find it profitable either to lend to, or borrow from, the
Euro-currency market. These margins are exclusively a function of

domestic interest rates, reserve requirements or other domestic capital controls and independent of the existence of the Euro-currency market. The role that Euro-banks play is one of inter-mediating between currencies, e.g. matching demands for Deutsche Mark with dollar deposits (see Chapter 8 for a further discussion of this point).

One further question is why, even in the absence of restrictions on capital flows, interest-rate parity appears to hold between Euro-currency interest rates but not between nominal domestic interest rates. One reason may be that whereas country and default risk may be quite different between domestic markets they need not differ between Euro-currencies.[19]

An alternative way of answering the question is to consider why, given that interest-rate parity does hold between Euro-currencies, the supply of currency to the Euro-market is not perfectly elastic at the nominal domestic interest rate. This may simply reflect the imperfect substitutability between domestic and Euro-currency (or external) deposits for non-banks: while the supply and demand curves for external deposits by domestic banks become perfectly elastic at certain Euro-currency interest rates, the supply of currency to the Euro-market by non-banks is not perfectly elastic at the nominal domestic rate of interest. Rather, it appears upward-sloping (as illustrated in *SS'* in diagram 1 of Figure 5.3), first because non-bank holders of funds are likely to have strong preferences, other than pecuniary ones, for holding domestic currency rather than Euro-currency, and second because they may have limited sources of funds with which to arbitrage. In other words, while it seems appropriate to view banks as flow-adjusters freely borrowing funds on competitive terms, it seems more appropriate to view non-banks in general as stock-adjusters allocating a given portfolio between domestic and external assets of varying risk and return.

5.2.3 *A simple test of the integrated model*

As a test of this integrated model, it would be instructive to see whether the Euro-currency interest rate on a strong currency, such as the Deutsche Mark, has been determined, in the absence of controls on the free flow of capital to the domestic market, at the rate at which it would have been profitable for domestic banks to borrow from the Euro-currency market. To investigate this, the nominal three-month Euro-Deutsche Mark rate and the nominal West German domestic three-month interbank rate have been plotted,[20] in Figure 5.6, together with the differential between the rates, for the period January 1973 to end-March 1978.

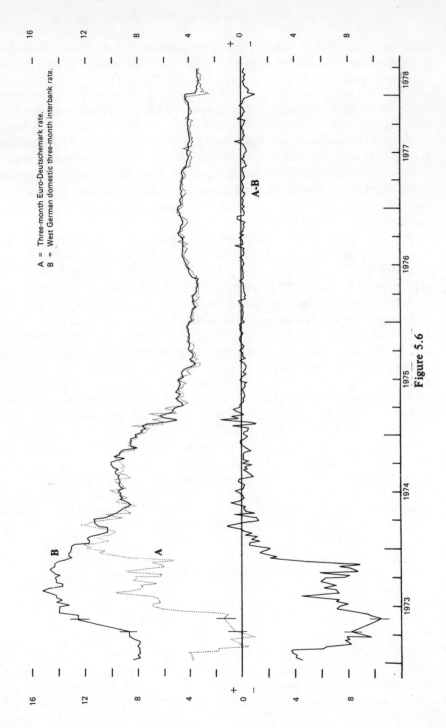

A = Three-month Euro-Deutschemark rate.
B = West German domestic three-month interbank rate.

Figure 5.6

128

While this figure suggests that there was a very close relationship between the rates from mid-1975 to end-1977, there were also considerable deviations, particularly in 1973 and 1974, and again in 1978. However, at different times during this period the West German authorities have imposed controls, of varying severity, in an attempt to reduce capital flows into West Germany, and only between August 1975 and December 1977 were West German domestic reserve requirements the same on West German banks' domestic and foreign-owned Deutsche Mark liabilities (see Table 5.4). Only for this period would

Table 5.4
Minimum reserve ratios on time liabilities of
West German banks*

	Liabilities to residents	Liabilities to non-residents	On growth of liabilities to non-residents
Applicable from the first day of			
1972 July	10.70	35.00	60
August	11.75		
1973 March	13.55		
July		35.00	60
October		35.00	60
November	13.95		
1974 January	13.25	30.00	0
September	11.90		
October	10.95	27.60	0
1975 June	10.40		
July	9.35	24.85	0
August		9.35	0
1976 May	9.85	9.85	0
June	10.35	10.35	0
1977 March	10.45	10.45	0
June	9.95	9.95	0
September	8.95	8.95	0
1978 January	8.95	15.00	80
March	9.65		
June	9.00	9.00	0

* Reserve class DM 1,000 million and over from December 1970 to February 1977; thereafter DM 100 million and over.

Source: *Monthly Report of the Deutsche Bundesbank*, table on reserve ratios.

the extra costs of raising loanable funds to West German banks have been the same in the domestic and Euro-market, and therefore only for this period would the model suggest that there should be a close relationship between nominal domestic and Euro-Deutsche Mark rates. For this period, the calculated mean and variance of the differential (see Table 5.5) were, respectively, −0.15 and 0.03 percentage points, suggesting that the relationship between the rates was in fact very close.[21]

Table 5.5
Three-month Euro-Deutsche Mark rate less West German three-month interbank rate*

	Mean	Variance	Number of observations
1 January 1973– end-December 1973	−6.42	5.89	46
1 January 1974– end-July 1975:			
Unadjusted for reserve changes	−0.23	0.27	87
Adjusted for reserve changes	−0.21	0.24	87
1 August 1975– end-December 1977	−0.15	0.03	120
Total sample	−1.32	6.97	253

*The interest rates used were Monday middle closing rates (where available).

Between January 1973 and January 1974 West German reserve requirements were discriminatory as between banks' domestic range of reserve requirements (11.75–13.95 per cent) and foreign-owned (35 per cent) Deutsche Mark liabilities. Further, a 60 per cent reserve requirement was imposed on the growth of West German banks' time liabilities in Deutsche Mark to non-residents. Together these imposed a 95 per cent reserve requirement on any increase in West German banks' time liabilities to non-residents and effectively discouraged West German domestic banks from borrowing Deutsche Mark from the Euro-currency market. In terms of the model, these measures would remove the perfectly elastic segment of both the demand schedule for Euro-Deutsche Mark and the demand schedule for forward dollars, which would now become *DD′* rather than *DD* (see Figure 5.7). This latter schedule is now inelastic over a much larger range, which allows the forward discount on dollars to widen in equilibrium, beyond F_d''. The net effect is that the Euro-Deutsche Mark rate will fall below the rate at which domestic banks would have begun to find it profitable to borrow Euro-Deutsche Mark in the absence of the discriminatory reserve requirement; the forward discount on dollars will widen to F_d^{**}; and there will be a smaller flow out of dollars into Deutsche Mark — X_0 rather than X_1 in the absence of the discriminatory reserve requirement (see Figure 5.7).

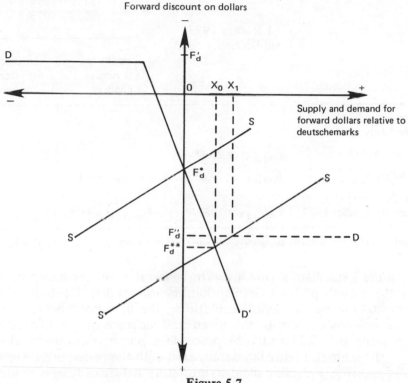

Figure 5.7

Further, during the period July 1972 to February 1974 the West German government, under the Bardepot Law, imposed a 50 per cent minimum reserve requirement (initially 40 per cent in July 1972; subsequently reduced to 20 per cent in February 1974; removed in September 1974) against foreign loans contracted by West German companies, making it unprofitable for them to borrow externally. Together these measures appear to have effectively insulated the West German domestic market from short-term capital inflows during 1973, and there were very sharp deviations between the level of domestic and Euro-Deutsche Mark rates. The mean and variance of the differential during this period, −6.42 and 5.89 percentage points respectively, are sharply different from those in the 1975−7 period (see Table 5.6).

Table 5.6
Analysis of variance: Euro-Deutsche Mark/
domestic Deutsche Mark differential

	1 January 1973− end-December 1973	1 January 1974− end-July 1975	
		Unadjusted for reserve changes	Adjusted for reserve changes
1 January 1974− end-July 1975:			
Unadjusted	$F_{45,86} = 22.3^*$		
Adjusted	$F_{45,86} = 24.8^*$	$F_{86,86} = 1.1$	
1 August 1975− end-December 1977	$F_{45,119} = 198.7^*$	$F_{86,119} = 9.0^*$	$F_{86,119} = 8.0^*$

* Indicates that the variances are significantly different at a 1 per cent level of significance.

In the immediate period after the removal of reserve requirements on the growth of West German banks' non-resident Deutsche Mark deposits and the Bardepot regulations, the deviations between the rates were reduced, with the mean and variance of the differential narrowing to −0.23 and 0.27 percentage points respectively. However, these are still fairly large compared with the period after August 1975, possibly reflecting the discriminatory nature of reserve requirements on West German banks' foreign-owned liabilities.

In January 1978, when again faced with large capital inflows, the West German authorities once more imposed discriminatory reserve requirements on the level and growth of the Deutsche Mark liabilities of West German banks to non-residents. A reserve requirement of 95 per cent was once more effectively placed on any increase in West German banks' foreign-owned time liabilities. Following this, the Euro-Deutsche Mark rate dropped below the domestic interbank rate. However, it subsequently returned to a more 'normal' level. One possible reason may be that, in the absence of restrictions on foreign borrowing by West German companies, corporations may themselves have arbitraged between the domestic and Euro-markets. The discriminatory reserve requirements were rescinded in June 1978.

These movements in the differentials between the West German domestic and Euro-Deutsche Mark interest rates are broadly consistent with the model developed above. They suggest first that, in the absence of restrictions or discriminatory reserve requirements on foreign inflows, domestic banks will arbitrage with the Euro-market to equalise the costs of borrowing in the two markets and consequently to place a lower limit on the Euro-Deutsche Mark rate and, when combined with the arbitrage activity of US banks, an upper arbitrage limit on the forward discount on dollars; and second that discriminatory domestic currency reserve requirements – particularly those which impose large penalties – are effective in reducing flows to the domestic market, even though they may be, to some extent, circumvented by the arbitrage activities of corporations.

5.3 EURO-DOLLAR RATES AND US DOMESTIC CD RATES: RECENT EXPERIENCE

More recent fluctuations in Euro-dollar and US domestic three-month interest rates provide the opportunity to make a further test of the close links between the US domestic and Euro-dollar markets and to examine the appropriate US domestic interest rate for comparison with Euro-dollar interest rates. At times, during the years 1979–81, US domestic banks were net lenders and net borrowers of funds in the Euro currency market. This period therefore allows a test to be made of the efficiency of both inward arbitrage to the USA and outward arbitrage to the Euro-market by US domestic banks in placing limits on the movement in Euro-dollar interest rates.

The nominal cost to US domestic banks of raising marginal funds in the USA is the cost of issuing new certificates of deposit in the primary market – primary CDs. The primary CD rate adjusted for reserve requirements (using equation (6) on page 114) would therefore be the appropriate rate for comparison with the Euro-dollar (offer) rate when US banks are arbitraging into the USA – i.e. borrowing funds in the Euro-dollar market to lend domestically. Usually this primary CD rate is some 0.10–0.15 percentage points below the interest rate on CDs in the secondary market. However, at certain times the quoted primary and secondary market CD rates have tended to diverge by larger margins. This is usually the case when US domestic banks have little need to raise new funds and the rate quoted in the primary market may simply be a notional rate which is posted at a low level. This may be especially true when US domestic banks are able to borrow more cheaply in the Euro-currency market.

When arbitraging out of the USA to the Euro-market, the appropriate interest rate for the calculation of the effective cost of funds in the USA may also be the primary CD rate. However, it appears to be the practice among large US banks to use the secondary market three-month CD rate as a reference rate when lending funds. The funding department of a US bank will provide funds to its lending department at the secondary market rate on certificates of deposit adjusted for domestic reserve requirements. The three-month secondary market rate would therefore appear to represent more accurately the opportunity cost of short-term funds in the US domestic market and therefore, adjusted as in equation (2) on page 113, it would be the more relevant interest rate for comparison with the three-month Euro-dollar (bid) rate when US domestic banks are arbitraging out to the Euro-dollar market.

Using the three-month primary and secondary US CD rates adjusted for US domestic reserve requirements (equations (6) and (2) respectively) allows an arbitrage 'tunnel' to be constructed. The ceiling of this 'tunnel' is the effective US secondary market three-month CD rate at which US domestic banks would find it profitable to supply funds to the Euro-dollar market; the floor of the tunnel is the adjusted US primary market three-month CD rate at which US domestic banks would find it profitable to borrow in the Euro-dollar market. The three-month Euro-dollar rate should fluctuate within or closely around the arbitrage 'tunnel' if US domestic bank arbitrage is effective.

5.3.1 *Reserve requirement changes*

The US authorities altered the level of reserve requirements on large denominated domestic CDs and the Euro-currency liabilities of US banks on several occasions in 1979 and 1980, and this influences the shape and size of the arbitrage tunnel. Table 5.7 records the changes in US reserve requirements. Throughout the period a basic reserve requirement of 6 per cent was imposed on large denominated certificates of deposit; in November 1978 a 2 per cent supplementary reserve requirement was introduced and was in force until July 1980; and between October 1979 and July 1980 US banks were also subject to varying marginal reserve requirements on any increase in their managed liabilities over a given base. All of these reserve requirements raise the effective marginal cost of domestic CDs to US domestic

Table 5.7
US reserve requirements 1 January 1978 and
changes 1978–81

Effective date	Large denomination domestic certificates of deposit			Euro-currency liabilities	
	Basic rate	Supplementary rate	Marginal rate	Basic rate	Marginal rate
1 January 1978	6	0	0	4	0
24 August 1978				0	
2 November 1978		2			
25 October 1979			8		8
3 April 1980			10		10
12 June 1980			5		5
24 July 1980		0	0		0
13 November 1980				3	

Source: *Federal Reserve Bulletin*, table 'Depository institutions' reserve requirements'.

banks and thus the upper margin at which US domestic banks would find it profitable to supply funds to the Euro-dollar market.

In August 1978 the US authorities removed reserve requirements on US domestic banks' Euro-market borrowing. As US domestic banks were no longer required to hold reserve requirements against Euro-currency liabilities, this had the effect of moving the lower arbitrage margin up to the upper arbitrage limit. The arbitrage tunnel would then disappear except to the extent that primary and secondary market three-month CD rates diverged and there are bid/offer margins in the Euro-currency market. When placing funds in the Euro-market, banks receive the bid rate, which is typically 1/8 per cent below the offer rate at which banks can borrow funds in the interbank market.

Like domestic certificates of deposit, US banks' Euro-currency liabilities were also subject to marginal reserve requirements between October 1979 and July 1980. However, since the marginal reserve requirements applied equally to both types of managed liabilities they did not affect the relative Euro-dollar interest rate at which US banks would find it profitable to borrow in the Euro-currency market. Relative to nominal US domestic interest rates the lower arbitrage margin therefore remained largely the same. But because the marginal reserve requirements added to the effective cost of the funds raised by US banks when lending to the Euro-dollar market, this raised the upper arbitrage margin above the lower arbitrage limit and widened the arbitrage tunnel. An example illustrates why this is so. On 25 October 1979 the marginal effective cost to a US domestic bank of raising domestic CDs to lend in the Euro-currency market amounted to the nominal interest rate plus the cost of holding a total 16 per cent reserve requirement (the 6 per cent basic rate, the 2 per cent supplementary rate and an 8 per cent marginal reserve requirement). If the nominal US domestic interest rate were 10 per cent, then from the equation (2), after allowing for Federal Deposit Insurance, the effective rate is 11.95 per cent. This is the rate at which US domestic banks would be willing to supply funds to the Euro-dollar market. If instead the US bank were to borrow in the Euro-dollar market, it would only have to pay the marginal rate of 8 per cent on its Euro-currency liabilities. But the US bank has to hold the same marginal reserve requirement against any increase in managed liabilities, including domestic liabilities, and so the *saving* in reserve requirements in borrowing Euro-dollars rather than domestic dollars remains the basic 6 per cent and 2 per cent supplementary reserve requirements. The Euro-dollar interest rate at which this becomes profitable using equation (6) is 10.95 per cent and an arbitrage tunnel of 1 per cent has opened up. With the subsequent removal of marginal reserve requirements in July 1980 the arbitrage tunnel narrowed again.

The final reserve requirement change which affects the arbitrage tunnel occurred in November 1980 when a basic 3 per cent reserve requirement was imposed on US banks' Euro-currency liabilities. This had the effect of returning the shape of the arbitrage tunnel to that which existed before August 1978 by reopening a margin between the rates at which US domestic banks would find it profitable to borrow or lend in the Euro-currency market.

5.3.2   *Empirical experience*

To show the effects of the reserve changes, the US secondary market three-month CD rate has been adjusted for all reserve requirements affecting outward arbitrage and the US primary market three-month CD rate for all reserve requirements affecting inward arbitrage by US banks. In addition, as these schedules will be compared with the three-month Euro-dollar bid rate, 1/8 per cent has been subtracted from the adjusted primary CD series to allow for the bid/offer spread in the Euro-currency market. In borrowing funds US domestic banks

would have to pay 1/8 per cent over the bid rate and thus the effective primary CD rate for comparison with the Euro-dollar bid rate is
less by 1/8 per cent. Figure 5.8 compares the corrected series with the
three-month Euro-dollar bid rate.

The shape of the arbitrage tunnel can be shown more clearly by
subtracting the adjusted primary CD rate from the adjusted secondary
market three-month CD rate. This is shown in Figure 5.9, which also
plots the difference between the three-month Euro-dollar bid rate
and the adjusted primary CD rate. The zero line in this chart can be
viewed as the floor of the arbitrage tunnel and the heavy line $(A-B)$
as the ceiling. The dashed line $(C-B)$ shows fluctuations in the Euro-
dollar rate relative to the floor of the tunnel.

Up to about March 1980 the three-month Euro-dollar rate fluctuated around the floor of the tunnel, after which it moved towards
the ceiling. For a short period at the beginning of 1979, the Euro-
dollar rate fell below the floor, but generally it has fluctuated around
the arbitrage margins. In the period from the beginning of 1979 to
mid-April 1980, when the Euro-dollar rate was at the floor of the
tunnel, the mean differential between the adjusted US primary
market three-month CD rate and the Euro-dollar rate was only -0.09
percentage points. Comparing this with the mean differential of 0.07
observed over the earlier period January 1975 to March 1978, and
using the estimates of the variance derived for two periods of 0.03
for the later period and 0.05 for the earlier period, show that the
absolute difference in these means is statistically non-significant. The
efficiency of US bank arbitrage which was observed on the outward
arbitrage schedule is not significantly different from the efficiency of
US banks when arbitraging into the USA from the Euro-dollar market.
The existence of these mean differentials in both the outward and
inward arbitrage schedules, which are both statistically different
from zero, may mean that there are some additional transaction
costs when US banks arbitrage with the Euro-currency market. On
neither arbitrage schedule do these appear to amount to more than
0.10 percentage points.

This statistical evidence therefore again supports the hypothesis
that to US domestic banks the US domestic and Euro-dollar interbank markets are nearly perfect substitutes in terms of raising funds
or lending deposits. It also suggests that the correct US domestic
interest rates for comparison with Euro-dollar interest rates will
vary depending on whether the US domestic banks are borrowers
or lenders of funds in the Euro-currency market. When US banks
are arbitraging out, secondary market three-month CD rates seem
to be the appropriate interest rate; primary CD rates, however,
reflect the marginal cost of raising new funds in the USA and are

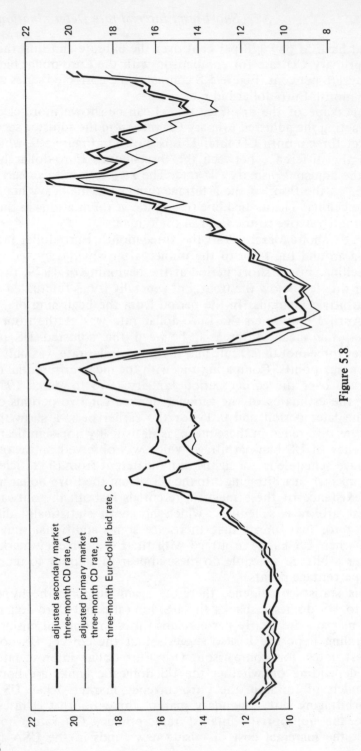

Figure 5.8

adjusted secondary market
three-month CD rate, A

adjusted primary market
three-month CD rate, B

three-month Euro-dollar bid rate, C

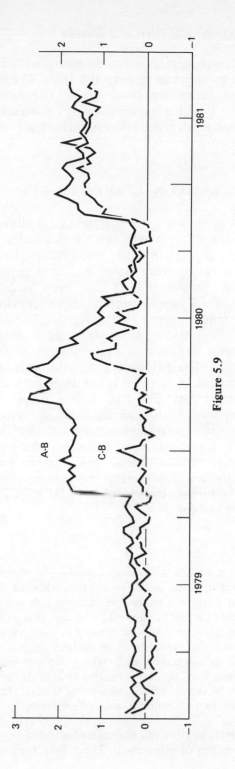

Figure 5.9

the appropriate interest rate for comparison with Euro-dollar rates when US banks are arbitraging into the USA. The margins between the primary and secondary three-month CD rates may diverge, depending on the liquidity position of US domestic banks and the relative cost of other deposit sources including Euro-currency borrowing.

5.4   SUMMARY AND CONCLUSIONS

This chapter has discussed some systematic relationships which have been observed between domestic and Euro-currency interest rates. It described a model to explain these relationships, based on the extra costs which banks incur from holding reserve requirements against domestic deposits. Statistical tests have been used to compare the marginal cost of three-month money (after allowing for the extra cost of reserve requirements) in the Euro-dollar and domestic US markets, and in the Euro-Deutsche Mark and domestic West German markets. These tests confirm that, in the absence of disruptions to the free flow of capital, the differences in these costs are virtually zero and that domestic banks effectively arbitrage between the Euro- and domestic money markets. The Euro-currency system appears to be very highly integrated with national banking systems. Changes in domestic interest rates and reserve requirements will directly influence the level of Euro-currency interest rates, and the role of the market as a channel for short-term capital flows appears to be very closely linked to the activities of domestic banks. It is completely inappropriate to treat the Euro-currency market as if it were an autonomous or closed banking system.

NOTES

1. The conclusions from the model would be unchanged if an uncompetitive rate of interest were paid on reserve balances held with the central bank, though this would have to be allowed for in the subsequent analysis.
2. The distinction between domestic banks and Euro-banks is of course artificial but is made for convenience of analysis. In practice, an institution which is primarily concerned with taking deposits and making loans in foreign currencies may also be permitted to take deposits and make loans in the currency of the country in which it is resident. However, such transactions may be viewed, without loss of generality, as domestic banking operations.
3. It might, however, be expected that some margin of reserves would be held against the possibility of withdrawals. The analysis requires only the assump-

tion that this margin is less than the legal domestic reserve requirement, or that these reserves can be employed at a rate of interest greater than the domestic interest rate payable on obligatory reserves.

4. A deposit between Euro-banks in London is normally for the delivery of funds on the second business day after the deal has been made, and may therefore be somewhat longer than for a domestic agreement, which is usually for the delivery of funds on the same day as the deal or the day after.

5. Under the assumption that domestic and external deposits are imperfect substitutes to private non-bank wealth-holders, equation (1) is viewed as a stock relationship, in line with the portfolio-selection theory of capital flows.

6. This formulation of the supply schedule for domestic banks suggests a flow rather than a stock-adjustment model of capital movements. The justification for this is that it is assumed that domestic banks, unlike non-banks, are largely indifferent between lending to Euro-banks and lending in the domestic money market, and therefore, while it might be appropriate to formulate equation (1), for non-bank wealth-holders, as a stock-adjustment relationship, it would seem more appropriate to view equation (3) as a flow relationship. For a model which analyses the supply of Euro-dollar deposits by financial intermediaries in terms of a flow relationship, see Hendershott (1967).

7. Euro-bank loans are usually in the form of bank credits of a specified term. The interest rate on these credits is normally a fixed spread over LIBOR (London interbank offered rate) — the rate at which major banks are prepared to lend funds in the London interbank market. The above formulation of the demand curve for loans suggests that this demand is responsive to the total cost of borrowing, i.e. the Euro-currency interest rate plus the spread (see Chapter 7).

8. The bid rate is taken to approximate the rate which US banks would receive on their lending to the market. This is the rate at which a selection of large banks in the Euro-market are prepared to borrow funds in the London interbank market. In practice, the bid rate would be the subject of negotiation between the individual banks.

9. The US domestic reserve requirement on large denominated CDs was, from 1 October 1970 to 12 December 1974, 5 per cent, and thereafter, until 2 November 1978, 6 per cent. The cost of Federal Deposit Insurance is approximately 0.036 per cent. The formula used to calculate the effective cost to US banks of raising loanable funds in the domestic market was therefore:

$$i_d^e = \frac{i_d + 0.036}{1 - r_d}$$

where r_d equals 0.05 from 1 October 1970 to 12 December 1974, and equals 0.06 after 12 December 1974, and i_d was the dealers' offer rate in the secondary market for large denominated CDs in New York. The calculation is updated in section 5.3.1.

10. While these statistics indicate that the population mean is significantly different from zero, this may only reflect measurement error or transaction costs in the markets. For example, the difference between the rates offered by dealers in the secondary market and the actual cost to US banks of borrowing high-denomination CDs, although subject to variations, might, in normal circumstances, amount to some 0.10–0.15 percentage points. Allowing for this difference could completely eliminate the mean differential observed between the rates during the period. For a further discussion of this point see section 5.3.

11. This analysis does not test the efficiency of arbitrage flows from the Euro-market to domestic markets. This is, however, considered in the next section.

12. Such restraints may have also increased US corporations' external borrowing, since the capital controls restricted their raising capital domestically, for use overseas. By increasing the demand for funds from the Euro-currency market, this would also have tended to widen the differential between domestic and Euro-dollar interest rates.

13. Domestic and Euro-market interest rates, and forward and spot exchange rates, are jointly determined. While the size of the US domestic money market suggests that a causal chain from events there to the Euro-dollar market, and thence to the forward exchange market, will often explain changes in all markets, this will not always, nor even generally, be the case. Euro-markets may at times affect US money markets: for example, if New York banks borrow domestically in order to lend in the Euro-markets, this would tend to push up US CD rates.

14. See, for example, Officer and Willett (1970). Of particular interest is the paper by Branson (1969), in which it is suggested that transaction costs will produce a discontinuity in the arbitrageurs' demand schedule for forward exchange. This proposition is considered further later in the chapter.

15. For the purposes of simplifying the analysis, it is assumed that the level of domestic interest rates is given exogenously of short-term capital flows. In fact, it has already been observed (note 13 above) that capital flows can affect domestic money markets, but this assumption may not be unreasonable in the short term if domestic monetary authorities set (interim) targets for the level of domestic short-term interest rates.

16. This does not necessarily imply that the equilibrium Euro-dollar rate need be greater than the Euro-Deutsche Mark rate. Instead it will depend on the relative interest rates at which US domestic banks find it profitable to borrow from the Euro-dollar market (the perfectly elastic segment of *DD* in diagram 1 of the figure) and West German domestic banks find it profitable to supply funds to the Euro-Deutsche Mark market (the perfectly elastic segment of *SS* in diagram 2 of the figure). This model would therefore suggest that, even when there is a free flow of capital, perverse relationships could develop between domestic and Euro-currency interest rates.

17. The term 'speculators' refers to any market operators taking an open position in the forward exchange market.

18. If, as is likely, banks are the main arbitrageurs between Euro-currencies, then there need be no decrease in the size of the Euro-dollar market when the

forward discount on dollars increases above its equilibrium level. If banks only arbitrage in the Euro-dollar market, only the demand curve for Euro-dollars will shift and the size of the Euro-dollar market would increase as banks borrow dollars covered as Deutsche Mark for lending. In segment 1 of Figure 5.4 the size of the Euro-dollar market would increase from d_0 to at least d_2.

19. For example, Euro-dollar and Euro-Deutsche Mark deposits could both be made with the same London bank.

20. The interest rates used were the middle closing rates on Mondays (where available).

21. However, these statistics again indicate, contrary to that expected from the model, that the population mean was statistically different from zero. This may only reflect the fact that no allowance has been made for bid/offer spreads in either of the markets. These would be expected to increase the mean differential, i.e. to make it less negative, by about 0.13 percentage points depending on the spread margin in the West German interbank market.

6 Payments Imbalances and Financial Intermediation

It is frequently observed that the Euro-markets have come to play an indispensable role in the recycling of the oil-exporting countries' financial surplus. The willingness of private banks to intermediate between countries in balance-of-payments surplus and those in deficit has important implications for the world economy and for the process by which countries adjust their domestic economies to external payments deficits and surpluses. If international capital markets functioned perfectly, countries might even be able to avoid the need to adjust their external payments positions, as they would be able to attract finance, or lend funds, relatively easily. Section 6.1 reviews the role of the banking system in providing international balance-of-payments finance. Section 6.2 considers a somewhat different question: the role of payments imbalances run by the reserve currency country – the USA – in Euro-market expansion.

6.1 RECYCLING AND FINANCIAL INTERMEDIATION

The channelling of the cash surplus of OPEC, associated with the rise in the price of oil, to countries experiencing balance-of-payments deficits induced by their oil imports has become known as *recycling*. In principle, since the world is a closed economy, the sum of individual countries' actual balance-of–payments surpluses and deficits must always add to zero. It will always be true that *ex post* balance-of-payments surpluses and deficits will have been financed. The central issue in recycling is therefore not so much that financing of balance-of-payments surplus and deficits has taken and will take place in an *ex post* sense, but rather what level of deficits is sustainable by the financing process: can the recycling of funds from surplus to deficit countries permit the actual (*ex post*) structure of balance-of-payments deficits to approximate to some set of current-account deficits that would be required to meet some 'desired' (*ex ante*) level of economic activity in deficit countries, or to put it another way can the recycling process avoid the need for deflationary adjustments by oil-importing countries?

6.1.1 *International versus interregional financing*

Within national economies residents in one region of a country dis-
charge their debts to residents in another region simply by trans-
ferring ownership of a bank deposit. So efficient is the interregional
payments and adjustment process that one rarely if ever hears of an
interregional recycling problem. The interregional adjustment process
may be easier than the international adjustment process because the
elasticity of demand for imports and exports of goods may be larger
between regions or the degree of labour and capital mobility may be
greater within a country (Meade, 1951). Frequently it is also suggested that the existence of a common money and banking system
and the higher degree of substitutability between claims in different
regions of one country allow regional current-account surpluses and
deficits to go virtually unnoticed. For example, in a branch banking
system, a current-account imbalance between the residents of Manchester and London will simply be met by a transfer of the ownership
of the assets and liabilities of the banking system at a centralised
head office.[1] Secondary effects may occur as the residents of the
different regions seek to adjust their portfolios to a change in current
expenditures and receipts. The residents of Manchester, who are in
deficit, may sell assets or borrow from local banks to maintain their
monetary positions, while those in London, who are in surplus, may
build up balances with the banking system or purchase new assets.
The operation of the branch banking system, however, ensures
that these transactions are absorbed smoothly by head offices
allowing some regions to become deficit areas financed in effect by
other areas becoming surplus regions. The requirements of channelling
capital from surplus to deficit units is automatically accomplished by
a simple reallocation of credit by domestic banks.[2]

The ease with which interregional financing occurs is contrasted
with the problems encountered in international balance-of-payments
adjustment. Goodhart (1975), for example, comments:

> The ease of interregional financial adjustment results from the
> high degree of substitution between financial claims issued in the
> different regions. This may be contrasted with a significantly
> lower degree of substitution between financial claims issued in dif-
> ferent countries, e.g. because of unfamiliarity with each other's
> laws and customs, because of the possibility of conflict between
> autonomous governments, because of concern over exchange rates,
> etc.

He continues:

> In reality, however, this contrast between international and inter-

regional adjustment processes is much too stark, precisely because the assumption that there is little substitution between the financial assets of the different countries (though there is — it will be noted — substitution between their goods) may often be invalid. The higher the degree of substitution between countries' financial assets (e.g. *via an integration of capital markets*), the greater the ease of financing current-account imbalances.[3]

Chacholiades (1978) comments that the failure of international financial intermediation is at 'the heart of the international balance-of-payments problem'. He notes that a balance-of-payments surplus in one country (an excess of domestic savings over investment) is exactly matched by a balance-of-payments deficit somewhere else (an excess of domestic investment over savings). The payments problem arises because units in the surplus economy, although in the market to buy securities, do not wish to buy them from the deficit country. As a result, central banks must, in a fixed-exchange-rate world, intervene in the foreign exchange market and use their own reserves to finance the deficit — i.e. they act themselves as a form of international financial intermediary — which is at most a temporary solution. Corrective action in the form of national monetary or fiscal policy will then have to be used to remove the deficit. If, however, surplus units did wish to purchase the securities of deficit units, as in the interregional case — perhaps because some kind of international financial intermediary converts the securities of the deficit country into a form acceptable to the surplus country — the balance-of-payments problem would disappear.

In the international economy, international banks and, more narrowly, the Euro-currency markets can, however, be regarded as just such an international financial intermediary: they take deposits from surplus economies and lend them to deficit countries; they specialise in evaluating international lending risks; they are largely outside direct interference by national governments; and, because international banking is based on global networks of branches and subsidiaries, it might be viewed as a world branch banking system. Moreover, since the overwhelming majority of deposits and loans are denominated in the main international reserve currency — the dollar — international intermediation need not involve the taking of exchange risks. One therefore wonders whether the development of international bank lending has fundamentally altered the international balance-of-payments adjustment process. To elaborate on this, it is instructive to return briefly to the interregional financing case and to examine an (albeit extreme) example.

Say the inhabitants of Belfast experience a sudden rise in the cost of a major item of their consumption – Scotch whisky – which leads them to run down their cash balances and to borrow from Northern Irish banks in an attempt to maintain consumption. They may also substitute locally produced whiskey, but we shall assume, naturally, that these are imperfect substitutes and anyway Northern Irish distillers could only supply the total new demands from the local market after a long investment and gestation period. The current deficit which results between Northern Ireland and Scotland is financed by Belfast banks running up net liabilities to head offices in London matched by the net assets of head offices to their Scottish branches. If, however, Belfast people persist in drinking Scotch, it is very unlikely that the banks will be willing to finance the habit indefinitely by providing new loans. Head offices in London may observe that it is not adding to the productive potential of Northern Irish industry and that the surplus funds they are receiving from Scottish banks could be put to better use elsewhere. They might, for example, willingly accommodate a request by distillers in Northern Ireland for funds to expand their bonded warehouse space or even from gin distillers in London who are also seeking to expand their production because some whisky drinkers have turned to gin. Northern Irish residents will simply not be able to run a flow deficit indefinitely; the cost of loans will either rise, cutting off demand, or banks will place quantitative limits on their exposure to whisky drinkers. The interregional financing process will come to a halt because of the prudential limits imposed by the banking system.

Now substitute oil, less developed countries (LDCs) and oil-producing countries for whisky, Northern Ireland and Scottish residents and we have an analogy with the international balance-of-payments problem associated with recycling the oil surplus. The major difference between this and the somewhat frivolous example above is the difference in the nationalities of borrowers and lenders (as well as, of course, the importance of the commodity).

Unlike an individual, a government enjoys national sovereignty. Ruling out forceful intervention by other nations, a government can refuse to pay its creditors and maintain control of its domestic assets. An individual by contrast would be stripped of his assets in bankruptcy proceedings.[4] Even so, failure by sovereign entities to repay debts involves penalties, and specifically that they will be unable to borrow again, or at least in the foreseeable future, from private markets. They may also be stripped of their foreign assets. Loans to sovereign borrowers may then even be regarded by the banking system as better risks than loans to private individuals because of the damage of a debt default to a country's international standing. Bank loss experience tends on the whole to be better on international than domestic loans. However, even if international lending risks are less, international loans are certainly not riskless and banks will therefore be unwilling to extend indefinitely their exposure. The important question is how much the operation of efficient international capital markets has eased the international adjustment problem. The next sub-section therefore examines the historical role of international banking flows. But even the operation of perfect capital markets would not necessarily allow countries' (*ex ante*) desired balance-of-payments deficits to be realised (*ex post*). The way in which capital markets adjust to surpluses and deficits of funds from different sectors, including, *inter alia*, the assessment of credit risks, will also be very relevant.

6.1.2   *Balance-of-payments finance and international banking flows*[5]

The first oil price shock in 1974 had a dramatic effect on the pattern of current-account payments balances. This is illustrated in section A of Table 6.1. The counterpart of the massive OPEC surplus in 1974 was a move into substantial balance-of-payments deficit by all groups of countries, though a few individual countries – the USA and West Germany in particular – were able to run small current-account surpluses. In the subsequent years up to 1978 the large, if diminishing, OPEC surpluses continued to impose very large financing requirements on the rest of the world and particularly on the smaller developed and non-oil developing countries. With the further substantial oil price rises since end-1978 OPEC once again moved into massive current-account surplus and the rest of the world into very heavy deficit.

The way in which the balance-of-payments deficits were financed was not in any way systematic. Initially, many countries ran down their foreign exchange reserves either to pay directly for oil imports or to protect their exchange rates against excessive depreciation resulting from their external payments deficits, and in the two years 1974–5 the smaller developed and non-oil developing countries lost net around $10 billion of foreign exchange reserves (see section B of Table 6.1). Capital-market finance, however, also expanded rapidly and these countries were able to borrow $19 billion in 1974–5 from banks in the Euro-currency market. While this represented a very major contribution, it amounted to only about one-quarter of their total financing requirement, the remainder coming from other capital-market finance, direct investment and concessionary loans (again, see Table 6.1). It was in fact only in 1977 that bank finance from the Euro-currency markets became the

Indicators of international payments imbalances and their financing
(in billions of US dollars)

	1973	1974	1975	1976	1977	1978	1979	1980
A *Current-account balance of payments*								
1 OPEC	6	67	31	34	26	-2	65	110
2 Group of Ten countries plus Switzerland	12	-13	17	2	4	20	-22	-53
2a (of which the USA)	(7)	(2)	(18)	(5)	(-14)	(-14)	(-1)	(-)
3 Smaller developed economies	-	-16	-19	-23	-24	-9	-10	-24
4 Non-oil developing countries	-6	-23	-32	-19	-13	-24	-39	-66
B *Financing the current-account deficits: smaller developed and developing countries*								
5 Sum of current-account deficits in 3 and 4	-6	-39	-51	-42	-37	-33	-49	-90
6 Capital-market finance	11	27	31	34	33	45	35	62
6a (of which new borrowing from banks in the Euro-currency market)	n.a.	(10)	(9)	(12)	(17)	(16)	(26)	(32)
7 Other capital flows *	6	8	14	12	16	10	24	28
8 Change in reserves (increase = -)	-11	4	6	-4	-12	-23	-10	-
C *International capital markets*								
9 Announced volume of syndicated medium-term Euro-credits	6	28	20	22	37	(51)† 58	(64)† 71	(55)† 73
10 Average Euro-market spread (per cent)	0.9	1.0	1.7	1.6	1.2	1.0	0.7	0.7
11 Net new international bank lending	n.a.	n.a	40	70	75	110	130	145
12 Net new international bond market finance	n.a.	n.a.	20	30	31	29	28	29

* Includes direct investment and concessionary loans
† Adjusted for approximate refinancing and pre- and repayments

n.a. = not available

Sources: IMF, BIS and Bank of England publications.

most important channel for external finance, and up to 1979 new Euro-market borrowing from banks by the smaller developed and developing countries amounted to about one-half of their combined current-account deficits. During this latter period, as well as financing the balance-of-payments deficits, Euro-market borrowing allowed these countries to add significantly to their foreign exchange reserve holdings.

The aggregate contribution of the Euro-markets to financing payments imbalances has been very considerable; however, the precise timing of the increased availability of international banking financing has not always coincided with the periods of greatest need. In 1975, for example, when the sum of the smaller developed and non-oil developing countries' current-account deficits grew to $51 billion, new Euro-market bank lending to these countries fell slightly from $10 to $9 billion and expanded in later years when the size of countries' balance-of-payments deficits was declining. In the market for syndicated medium-term Euro-credits, which was one of the primary channels through which countries raised funds for balance-of-payments finance, the volume of newly announced credits, after expanding rapidly in 1974, fell in 1975–6 before surging ahead in

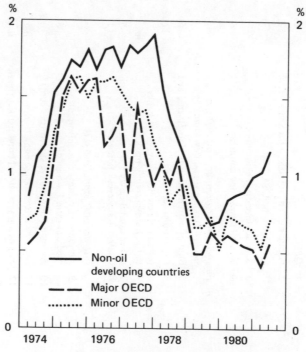

Figure 6.1   Average spreads on syndicated medium-term Euro-credits

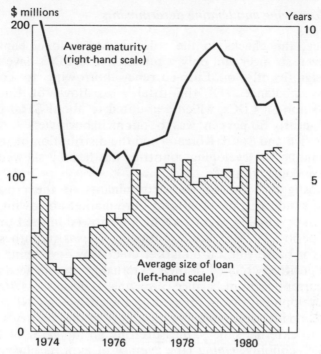

Figure 6.2   Other indicators of borrowing conditions

subsequent years (Table 6.1, section C). The oil-induced increase in countries' financing requirements coincided with a sharp tightening of terms. Spreads rose for all categories of borrowers (Figure 6.1), while maturity of loans and their average size fell (Figure 6.2). This tightening in Euro-market lending margins, despite the large amount of funds placed in the market by OPEC, generally discouraged borrowers from increasing rapidly their new Euro-market borrowing until lending conditions eased in 1977–9.

There are several reasons why the average level of Euro-banks' lending margins widened in 1974–5 (Chapter 7) but perhaps most obvious was the deterioration in countries' external positions. To the extent that a country's balance-of-payments deficit influences its ability to service debt payments, enlarged balance-of-payments deficits will be associated with a decline in a country's credit standing and banks will seek larger lending margins for accepting increased credit risks. International lending risks are likely to be greatest exactly at the times when international financing requirements are largest and this limits the role of the banking system in the international recycling process.

6.1.3   *Borrowing and lending determinants*

In practice, the checks to the role of international bank lending may be even stronger and only a relatively few LDCs have been able to rely significantly on Euro-currency borrowing to cover large payments imbalances. Of the total gross flows of Euro-market lending to non-oil LDCs, which amounted to about $160 billion by end-1979, nearly 60 per cent was to four main borrowers – Argentina, Brazil, Mexico and South Korea – and the distribution of total Euro-market lending to developing countries was heavily skewed towards the upper-income groups.[6]

To investigate some of the determinants of the cross-country volume of syndicated medium-term Euro-market borrowing a sample of nineteen developing countries which borrowed in the Euro-market over the period 1974–8 was examined.[7] It was hypothesised that demands for borrowing Euro-market credits by developing countries would be positively related to their external payments needs, proxied by their current-account balance-of-payments deficit, *CABOP*, and to overall development needs, proxied by the change in GNP *per capita*, $\Delta GNP/N$; and inversely related to the ability of the country's economy to adjust to external shocks, measured by an indicator of the openness of the economy, *Opind* (the average of exports plus imports to GNP in 1974), the cost of borrowing funds, S_p, the spread charged to each borrower on syndicated medium-term Euro-credits, and a scale factor for the level of a country's development, *GNPD*. This latter variable, which was set equal to 1.0 when GNP *per capita* was less than $1,000 and at zero otherwise, was used in an attempt to catch factors which restrict lower-income country access to the syndicated medium-term Euro-currency market. The results for the pooled cross-section/time-series regression using annual observations when the dependent variable was the new volume of syndicated Euro-currency borrowing by each country, ΔL, were:

$$\Delta L = 1.07 + 0.302 \; CABOP + 0.0013 \, \Delta GNP/N - 1.895 \; Opind$$
$$\;\;\;\; (4.51) \;\; (6.06) \;\;\;\;\;\;\;\;\;\;\;\; (1.30) \;\;\;\;\;\;\;\;\;\;\;\;\;\;\;\; (3.41)$$

$$\;\;\;\;\; - 0.221 \; S_p - 0.536 \; GNPD$$
$$\;\;\;\;\;\; (0.95) \;\;\;\; (4.51)$$

$\bar{R}^2 = 0.498$, *t*-ratios in parentheses

All coefficients accord with *a priori* expectations, and the highly significant coefficient on the GNP *per capita* dummy variable provided strong evidence of restrictions to entry into the syndicated loan market by lower-income LDCs. The conclusion from this equation is that the largest borrowers of syndicated medium-term Euro-credits appear as the comparatively closed, high-income and fast-growing economies which seem to be financing about one-third of current-account balance-of-payments deficits through medium-term syndicated Euro-currency borrowing. A disappointing feature of the equation was the non-significance of the spread term. This single-equation 'explanation' of the flow of syndicated medium-term Euro-credit borrowing does not allow, except through the GNP *per capita* dummy, for supply restrictions, which may be highly important in determining the flow of new funds to developing countries and which may explain this result.

Supply restrictions. Rational economic behaviour on the part of lenders suggests that they would be concerned with maximising some joint function of risks and return in their overall portfolios. In an uncompetitive market, where a lender can discriminate on the basis of the price of loans, he is likely to alter the interest rates charged in line with the varying credit risks attached to each borrower (given the overall requirements of the portfolio). In a competitive market, the rate of return to an individual lender will, however, be determined largely exogenously by market forces, and a lender's optimal portfolio decision will be one of allocating funds between different risky assets in an attempt to minimise (overall) default risk; this is done through rationing the quantity of loans made to any borrower. The Euro-currency market exhibits many of the properties of a highly competitive market, most especially because of the large number of banks involved in international lending. Discrimination in the interest rates or spreads charged to borrowers does of course occur, but this is frequently the outcome of an overall market or syndication group assessment of the risks involved in lending to different borrowers. The market assessment, which places a ceiling on lending margins to each borrower, may well vary from one bank to another, depending, for example, on their existing credit exposure to different countries and any particular links between the bank and the borrower. Individual banks will ration their commitment to borrowers by limiting the participation in market-negotiated syndicated medium-term credits, where the spread is determined by the overall decisions of the syndicate or by negotiation between the lead managing banks and the borrower. Institutional factors may also prevent the market as a whole from discriminating perfectly between borrowers on the basis of price factors, or other lending terms, alone. Credit ceilings may be imposed on borrowers specifically to avoid the possibility of default, i.e. to limit the borrower's debt service payments and to ensure that the cost to the borrower from defaulting on his debt, associated with exclusion from borrowing in the market in the future, never becomes smaller than the costs of servicing it. Some borrowers are completely excluded from the market at any price because of their poor credit standing. Because the level of lending spreads is seen as an indicator of a country's credit standing, which may affect the future cost of borrowing, countries tend to be sensitive to and to resist a rise in spreads they are charged compared with other borrowers; and banks themselves may have a limited basis for trading off the spreads charged and risks accepted using any rigorous optimising criteria. The efficiency of relative interest-rate movements as a means of allocating credit tends therefore to be limited.

Many factors may nevertheless influence banks' commercial judgements and credit assessments of and lending limits to different countries. These might include measures of:[8] the ability of a borrower to meet immediate debt servicing commitments; the future capacity of the country to cover its debt burden; the vulnerability of the economy to external shocks; the overall debt financing burden placed on the country; and the bank's individual loan exposure to the borrower. Kapur (1977) examined the arguments in a quantity-rationed supply equation of Euro-currency finance. Based on a sample of twenty-five developing countries which borrowed in the Euro-currency market during the period 1972–4 he found that 'risk' variables (the projected debt service ratio and the gross claims outstanding of banks on individual countries) had a significant negative influence on the flow of Euro-market credits to borrowing countries, while variables which measured the ability of the country to service its debts (the ratio of gross international reserves to imports of goods and services, the average annual rate of growth in real GNP, and the volume of the country's exports of goods and services) had a positive influence on the volume of Euro-market lending. Since many of these variables also enter a country's demand for external borrowing, they are likely to be highly important in determining the balance between a country's ability to borrow or to adjust to its payments deficit. A simultaneous study by Eaton and Gersovitz (1980) of the demand and supply of international bank lending also indicated that quantity rationing by banks was important.[9] Using the criterion that the debt ceiling would be set by lenders such that the utility to the borrower from defaulting would be less than the disutility (because of future exclusion from the markets) by a certain probability, they estimated that of forty-five LDCs sampled in 1970 and 1974, in fifty-six out of eighty-one observations a country was classified as constrained in its borrowing with a probability greater than 0.5. The overall conclusion from the existing empirical work is thus that there are numerous restrictions to the volume of international bank borrowing which is available to countries and which may be used to finance balance-of-payments deficits. The availability of private banking flows has not removed countries' external constraints or their need to adjust their balance of payments.

6.1.4 Benefits and costs

With the initial appearance of the OPEC surpluses, three interrelated questions were at the forefront of policy discussions: how could the world economy sustain output, how should the structure of current-account deficits be distributed between countries, and how could the resulting pattern of deficits be financed? The role of international banks in recycling the surpluses, however, significantly eased these concerns and removed the need for some supranational agency to dictate the pattern of deficits and financial flows, which were instead determined by a free-market mechanism. Many countries were able to meet their payments deficits without resorting to restrictions on trade flows or by an excessive deflation of domestic demand. World trade volumes and world industrial production, after declining temporarily following the first oil shock, continued to expand in the 1970s despite very large global payments imbalances (see Table 6.2). The benefits of private markets and international banks in promoting world development and sustaining free international trade have been

Table 6.2
World trade, industrial production and payments imbalances

	Volume of world exports*	Industrial production*	World payments imbalances†
1970	76	80	1.2
1971	82	83	1.4
1972	89	90	1.2
1973	100	98	1.3
1974	105	102	3.6
1975	100	100	2.7
1976	112	108	2.4
1977	116	113	2.2
1978	112	118	2.1
1979	130	123	2.2

* 1975 = 100.
† Absolute sum of world current-account surpluses and deficits as a percentage of the gross product of market economies.

Sources: *United Nations Monthly Bulletin of Statistics*; Stanyer and Whitley (1981).

very substantial. In this sense international banking flows have played an indispensable role in the transfer of real resources from surplus to deficit countries.

These benefits are not, however, without their costs. Most obviously, financing rather than adjusting to payments imbalances has led to a large increase of international debt by deficit countries. The total private- and public-sector debt of developing countries quadrupled in the ten years to 1979 to reach $370 billion (see Table 6.3). Even more rapid was the increase in debt to private creditors, which grew at the rate of 28 per cent a year and to financial institutions at 41 per cent a year; and the proportion of outstanding debt to private financial institutions expanded from 12 per cent in 1970 to 43 per cent in 1980. As a percentage of GNP, debt outstanding rose in the same period from 16 to 22 per cent. The direct cost of this debt is that future external earnings have to be used to service it, i.e. to pay the interest charges and to meet debt repayments, which imposes a burden on the future export earnings of developing countries in particular. The indirect cost of such enlarged external debts is that banks may be less willing to lend and deficit countries less able to borrow to meet future payments deficits or indeed to cover the cost of servicing outstanding debt. On both scores there is, however, room for some optimism. Because of the relatively strong export performance of developing countries, the aggregate debt service as a percentage of exports of goods and services of developing countries – the debt service ratio – has risen more modestly from 15 to 18 per cent (see Table 6.3); and although the debt service ratio is considerably higher for some individual countries and a source of

Table 6.3
Developing country debt indicators

	Disbursed debt outstanding* ($ billion)	Debt service as a percentage of exports of goods and services	Disbursed debt as a percentage of GNP
1971	90e	14.6	16.4
1974	139	12.1	16.4
1977	253	14.4	21.6
1978	316	17.9	23.3
1979	368	17.8	22.4

* Total public and private disbursed debt.
e = estimate.

Source: World Bank, *World Debt Tables*.

concern, the aggregate figures do not suggest that there is reason for general alarm. On the side of the banks, lending to developing countries remains at present a small fraction of total bank loan portfolios, so that the overall portfolio constraint on lending by the banking system is less than the nominal debt figures might indicate. Nevertheless, the expansion of nominal lending, the possibility of a debt default by individual country borrowers or by developing countries as a group, and the more active involvement of private banks in the official balance-of-payments financing process, all have implications for the overall stability and supervision of the international banking system (Chapter 11).

The increased role of international banks in intermediating between surplus and deficit countries also raises broader issues for the operation of the international monetary system. Effectively the role of private markets has caused a considerable 'privatisation' of the sources of balance-of-payments finance and international reserve growth. Countries no longer depend exclusively on 'outside' increases in the supply of reserve assets from, for example, allocations of reserve assets by the IMF (SDRs) or balance-of-payments deficits run by the reserve currency country (section 6.2); nor do individual countries have to run a payments surplus themselves to gain international reserves. At the cost of increased indebtedness, reserve gains can result simply from expanded borrowing by countries on the international capital markets. As Crockett (1978) has pointed out, the role of private markets has led to a situation where balance-of-payments disequilibrium can generate, endogenously, increases in international reserves. If countries in surplus place their reserve holdings in international banks and these are lent to countries in balance-of-payments deficit, the deficit country will be able to finance its deficit without experiencing any decline in its gross reserve holdings. This lack of centralised control over the stock of international liquidity has implications for the process of international balance-of-payments adjustment, which comes to depend rather crucially on how private markets allocate funds between countries and how countries react to the private sources of finance and the signals given by private markets.

As discussed above, the availability of private sources of balance-of-payments finance does not remove the need for countries to remain creditworthy or to adjust their balance of payments. However, private market flows may have allowed countries to avoid for a time taking the type of abrupt domestic economic measures that their payments situations might have called for. In this sense, private banking flows have certainly eased countries' external payments constraints, and may have led to an important structural shift in the international adjustment process. If countries trade off the various costs and benefits of running payments deficits in terms of the burden of servicing external debt, the loss of foreign exchange reserves and the utilisation of domestic resources, it is likely that the easier availability of private balance-of-payments finance will mean that payments adjustments will occur more slowly and that world payments imbalances may remain historically large. Even with the sharp decline in the OPEC surpluses between the years 1974 and 1978 (see Table 6.1) world payments imbalances remained at very high levels, being nearly twice as great in 1978 (when OPEC registered a small balance-of-payments deficit) as in 1970 (see Table 6.3). An important reason for this was the availability of balance-of-payments finance and the ability of countries to use resources productively at home.

These developments are not 'bad' *per se*. They have been a considerable benefit to the world economy when the banking system was recycling the OPEC surpluses. Easier payments financing may also have removed the type of deflationary bias that tended to be associated with adjustments under the Bretton Woods fixed-exchange-rate system when effective balance-of-payments surveillance was confined to deficit countries, and it may well imply a faster pace of world economic development. The developments do, however, raise other questions. It is true that the interest rates charged in private markets will provide signals about the market's assessment of countries' economic prospects, and, in trading off the costs and benefits of running payments deficits, market interest rates will influence the extent of adjustment undertaken by individual countries. This process may, however, contain several inefficiencies for the overall working of the international monetary system. First, the free-market 'signals' may not accord with what might be regarded as optimal for the world economic system as a whole. The relative ease of payments finance may lead to too little payments adjustment and in this respect the term 'over-recycling' has been coined. Second, the signals given by private banks may have only a small influence on countries' international adjustment policies. Unlike the IMF, private banks are not able to make recommendations on countries' economic policies. In some cases they may refuse to lend unless countries agree a recovery programme with the IMF; and in the case of Poland's debt rescheduling, the banks have sought the development of a domestic stabilisation programme. But these approaches have been confined to situations where the country is already facing national bankruptcy. Third, the process of allocating credit through the private market may lead to discontinuities and inequities in the distribution of balance-of-payments finance. As noted above, the availability of funds is not always rationed through a price mechanism. The quantity rationing of loans means that some poorer countries are completely excluded from private markets; and when banks determine their lending policies on the basis of a few short-run economic indicators, which do not correctly reflect countries' longer-term prospects, there may be discontinuities in the flow of private market finance to particular borrowers. The availability of private market finance may not always coincide with the periods of greatest need, being less when there are large payments deficits and greater when there is less need for private financial flows. The role of the markets in offsetting the deflationary effects of oil deficits and facilitating more inflationary domestic policies may not be symmetrical.

Because of these considerations private markets cannot and should not substitute for overall surveillance of the working of the adjustment process. Firm surveillance over the adjustment process and the availability of global liquidity can be regarded as complementary, as surveillance is designed to influence the size of deficits, and liquidity exists to finance them. They may, however, substitute for one another, as effective surveillance of countries' balance-of-payments policies would do away with the need to be concerned with an excess supply of liquidity. Willett (1980) comments that failures in the adjustment process exist because of inadequacies in the surveillance process and not because of the supply of international liquidity. Attempts to regulate the amount of payments adjustment by exercising centralised control over the supply of liquidity is an attempt to exercise more control by 'the back door' than could be achieved directly. In his view such an approach is not very promising To reduce the deficiencies which result from private market finance is to try to improve the operation of international surveillance of the adjustment process, and not to attempt to exert greater control over international liquidity aggregates.[10] Nevertheless, private market borrowing does reduce leverage by the IMF, as countries frequently only turn to it as a lender of last resort when private markets become unwilling to lend. As long as countries remain creditworthy, which means that they will have to satisfy the commercial judgements of bankers and accept the perhaps volatile nature of private market flows, they will be able to avoid firm international surveillance – the imposition of conditionality – on their policies. This is an inescapable cost of the very real benefits of international banking flows. However, this development is not perhaps that different from the situation which has always applied to the reserve currency country.

6.2   THE ROLE OF THE US BALANCE OF PAYMENTS

Unlike other countries, the domestic currency of a reserve currency country is an acceptable international means of payment. Reserve currency countries do not therefore face the same immediate problems as other countries when financing payments deficits. With the removal of US capital controls in 1974 the USA in fact became a large net exporter of capital through its domestic banking system and thus assisted other countries to finance their balance-of-payments deficits. It is also sometimes suggested that the US balance of payments has been a major factor explaining the expansion of Euro-currency lending – and also the movement in the spreads charged on Euro-market loans.

The argument is based on the proposition that balance-of-payments deficits, or surpluses, run by a reserve currency centre have asymmetrical effects on world and Euro-market liquidity. The paradigm runs as follows: Trade imbalances between two non-reserve currency countries are settled in terms of a third reserve currency – the dollar. Reserve flows from the deficit to the surplus country will, in a fixed-exchange-rate world, tend to have net monetary expansionary effects in the surplus country and monetary contractionary effects in the deficit country when these are not sterilised by central banks. These effects are, however, largely offsetting and thus there will be no net monetary expansion in the world. The reserve flow may even be equilibrating, acting to expand expenditures in the surplus country and to reduce expenditures in the deficit country. The analogy is with the specie-flow mechanism operating under the 'Gold Standard'. Moreover, since by assumption only the reserve currency is held and counted as foreign exchange reserves, the transfer of reserves from the deficit to the surplus country has not added to global liquidity. The situation is different, however, if one of the countries is the reserve centre. When the reserve country – the USA – runs a balance-of-payments deficit it settles in its domestic currency, which is acceptable to the surplus country as reserves. This again leads to net monetary expansionary effects in the surplus country (when exchange rates are fixed and inflows are unsterilised); however, because the surplus country willingly holds the reserve currency and, moreover, invests these in the currency of the reserve centre, there are no corresponding contractionary effects in the reserve currency country. Thus the deficit by the reserve centre is self-financing and leads to monetary and liquidity expansion abroad without any corresponding contraction at home. International liquidity – as measured by global reserve holdings – increases with the size of reserve country deficit.[11] There are, of course, many qualifications to be made: exchange rates may float, central banks may sterilise inflows, and foreigners may only willingly hold reserve currencies up to a certain amount after which they will diversify into other 'quasi' reserve currencies. Resulting exchange-rate pressure may then cause the reserve centre to alter its monetary policy.

In its 1978 Annual Report the BIS commented extensively on the influence of the large US deficit (which on the current account amounted to some $14 billion in both 1977 and 1978) on Euro-market conditions, and suggested that 'under the liquidity-creating effects of the US external payments deficit the market has become increasingly supply determined'.[12] The specific mechanism was seen in both the supply and demand for funds from the Euro-market. On the supply side, a US balance-of-payments deficit places dollars in the hands of non-residents who have a higher propensity to hold these in the Euro-currency rather than the US domestic market, or to convert them into foreign currencies for use in markets outside the USA. In the former case there will be a direct liquidity inflow to the Euro-market; in the latter foreign exchange intervention by central banks will tend to ease national monetary conditions and encourage secondary reflows of funds into Euro-dollars. On the demand side, a large US balance-of-payments deficit eases the balance-of-payments financing requirements of other countries, which in turn reduces their need for Euro-market borrowing for external purposes, and may also raise their credit standing with international banks. The combined effect of the liquidity inflow into the market and the improvement in countries' creditworthiness causes the supply curve of Euro-market loans to shift out (from S_0 to S_1 in Figure 6.3), while the decline in external financing requirements causes the demand for loans to decline somewhat (the demand curve shifts from D_0 to D_1), or perhaps not at all if borrowers were originally constrained by credit rationing. The Euro-market expands (from L_0 to L_1 in Figure 6.3) and lending rates decline (from r_0 to r_1). Casual observations also suggests a link between, for example, the US current-account balance of payments and the level of spreads on syndicated medium-term Euro-credits (comparing rows 2a and 10 of Table 6.1 shows that spreads rose sharply in 1975 when the USA was in large current-account surplus, and fell in 1977 when the USA moved into deficit).

Other commentators, however, reject any direct link between Euro-market expansion and the US balance of payments. Dufey and Giddy (1978) conclude a discussion of the question thus:

A continuing US balance-of-payments deficit neither provides an assurance of, nor constitutes a necessary condition for, the growth

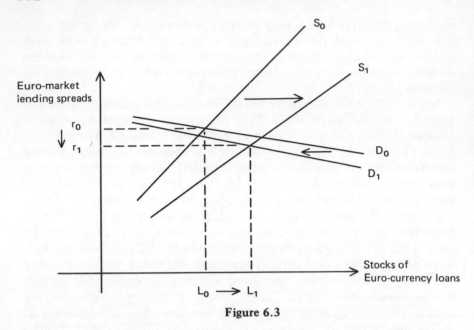

Figure 6.3

in the availability of Euro-dollars. Although a US deficit certainly does increase the volume of dollars held by non-residents, there is no reason to suppose that those particular foreigners would want to place their surplus funds in the Euro-dollar market. The relevant questions are (1) whether economic entities have funds that they wish to invest temporarily, (2) whether they wish to invest them in US dollar-denominated assets, and (3) whether they wish to invest them in the domestic or the external dollar market. The status of the US balance of payments has little bearing on the answers to any of these questions.[13]

Over long runs of data there is, for example, no visible correlation between the US balance of payments measured on an official settlements basis or a net liquidity basis and the rate of growth of the Euro-dollar market. Moreover, it is observed that the Euro-Deutsche Mark segment of the market has grown in line with the Euro-dollar portion despite large German balance-of-payments surpluses. However, there are other reasons why this has been so, and particularly the inability of wealth-holders to diversify into Deutsche Mark except through the Euro-currency market. Freedman (1977b) also notes that the argument that the US balance of payments leads to a rapid expansion in the Euro-dollar market because the rest of the world has a higher propensity to hold marginal additions to wealth there than US residents leads to a rather tenuous relationship between the two.

Is it possible to reconcile these apparently diametrically opposed positions? The view that there is no link between a US deficit and Euro-market growth is founded on the assertion that none *need* exist, i.e. the dollars accruing to the rest of the world can be placed in any number of assets and therefore do not automatically flow to the Euro-dollar market. One can readily agree with this proposition. A range of behavioural and portfolio responses will ultimately determine the location of funds between different money markets. However, such a view does not preclude the possibility that, *de facto*, a link *can* exist, though it seems an improbable outcome on this view. The alternative opinion is, however, that not only does a relationship exist but, *de facto*, it is highly important in explaining developments in the market. It might be observed that non-Group of Ten countries have a high propensity to hold their dollar foreign exchange reserves in the Euro-currency market rather than the USA, and that private investors in European countries also hold a large proportion of their dollar placements there. It will be recalled that Euro-markets perform a regional borrowing and investment function for non-banks in their local area. Over some periods simple regressions of the change in the net size of the Euro-currency market on the US current-account balance of payments and some other plausible explanatory variables do indeed show that there was a statistically significant correlation,[14] though this may not necessarily be a causal one. It was over such a period that the BIS made their commentary on the role of the US balance of payments. Perhaps these differing views may be reconciled by saying that because of various portfolio adjustments and preferences on behalf of rest of the world wealth-holders, the *proportion* of a US deficit which finds its way into the Euro-market will be rather small; but depending on the size of the US deficit the increase in *absolute* terms may be quite significant in determining the aggregate volume of international bank lending. A US deficit of $10 billion amounts to nearly 10 per cent of the existing *stock* of non-bank Euro-dollar holdings. If only a quarter of that deficit were placed in the Euro-market, it may still be important in terms of the rate of growth of the Euro-market.

6.3 SUMMARY

Within national economies financial intermediaries play a highly important role in channelling funds from surplus to deficit units. They issue liabilities which, because of their liquidity and credit standing, are acceptable to investors of funds, and by pooling to-gether resources they can diversify their loan portfolio and provide longer-term loans which are desired by borrowers of funds. So efficient is the national banking system that problems of recycling funds between different regions with the national economy rarely arise. In the international economy international banks provide a similar intermediary function as domestic intermediaries in the domestic economy: they take deposits from surplus countries and agents in the main international currencies and make loans to deficit countries and agents. This international financing process has lessened and delayed the need for countries to take severe action to adjust their balance-of-payments deficits; it has not, however, removed countries' external payments constraints, and indeed the timing of the avail-ability of Euro-market finance has not always coincided with the periods of largest payments imbalances. Banks are commercial enterprises seeking profits. They may raise their lending margins to cover the possible risks involved when providing international loans or strictly ration the amount of funds available to any par-ticular borrower. The distribution of international lending is skewed towards more creditworthy countries, and the general worsening of countries' external positions in 1974 coincided with a sharp increase in Euro-market lending margins – spreads. These factors acted to limit the initial flow of balance-of-payments finance to countries through the international banking system. A subsequent easing of Euro-market lending margins allowed borrowers to attract very large amounts of funds and countries to rebuild substantially their gross foreign exchange reserves.

The growth of private banks willing to intermediate in the inter-national medium of exchange brings with it several benefits but also potential costs. World output and trade growth continued in the 1970s, and countries were able to delay adjustments to the unprece-dented balance-of-payments deficits. The cost of this has been a con-siderable 'privatisation' of the international monetary system and a greater role for private markets in determining the timing and the size of balance-of-payments adjustments. Market signals may, how-ever, be inefficient in achieving the overall pattern of payments adjustment considered optimal from the point of view of the inter-national monetary system. Private market flows have certainly not removed the need for international surveillance of the adjustment process; indeed, the increased availability of international liquidity through private markets has increased it.

Several commentators have suggested that the balance-of-payments position of the reserve currency centre – the USA – can have asymmetrical effects on liquidity conditions in the Euro-currency market. Others are, however, unconvinced. Casual empiricism does suggest some link between the two. A reconciliation of the differing views may be that while the behavioural responses of agents are likely to mean that the proportion of a US balance-of-payments deficit placed in the Euro-markets will be small, in absolute terms this may at times be quite important for the volume of Euro-market lending and conditions in the market.

NOTES

1. This example is taken from Goodhart (1975).
2. In a branch banking system no monetary or reserve flows need even occur, with payments imbalances being accommodated by book-keeping entries. Even in a unit banking system, such as in the USA, banks in a 'deficit' region will be able to borrow from 'surplus' area banks to meet payment requirements relatively easily by bidding for funds in the interbank market. The good name of the institution ensures that funds will be forthcoming at little extra cost.
3. Goodhart (1975, pp. 265–6), italics added.
4. Eaton and Gersovitz (1980).
5. For an authoritative analysis of the financing of global payments imbalances see Stanyer and Whitley (1981).
6. Killick (1981).
7. The countries were: Brazil, Argentina, Colombia, Ecuador, Mexico, Peru, Panama, Costa Rica, Egypt, Gabon, Ivory Coast, Morocco, South Korea, Algeria, Taiwan, Philippines, Thailand, Malaysia and Hong Kong. Data for the equation were taken from various World Bank and IMF publications.
8. See also Chapter 11 for a discussion of the techniques involved in assessing the creditworthiness of borrowers.
9. The demand for debt equation in this study was specified in terms of the percentage variability of exports, the share of imports in GNP, the average rate of growth of *per capita* income, GNP *per capita* and total population.
10. Willett (1980, p. 69).
11. Mayer (1979b), for example, discusses at some length the asymmetrical influences of flows out of the USA.
12. See also Kessler (1980). Inoue (1980) provides an analytical basis for a link between the US balance of payments and spread movements in the Euro-currency market.
13. Dufey and Giddy (1978, pp. 112–16).
14. For example, regressing the quarterly change in the net size of the Euro-currency market, ΔE, on an average index of Euro-market spreads, S_p, the US current-account balance of payments in the current, $USCB$, and previous quarter, $USCB_{-1}$, and the size of the OPEC current-account balance of pay-

ments, *OPECCB*, reveals for the period 1974II–78II:

$$\Delta E = 0.06 \, S_p - 0.65 \, USCB - 0.66 \, USCB_{-1} + 0.51 \, OPECCB$$
$$\quad (4.18) \qquad (1.80) \qquad\quad (2.02) \qquad\qquad (3.31)$$

$\bar{R}^2 = 0.94$, Durbin–Watson statistic = 2.62, *t*-ratios in parentheses

While all coefficients are significant and of the right sign in the equation and the fit seems satisfactory, the coefficients on *USCB* and *USCB*$_{-1}$ seem implausibly large — they indicate that a rise in the US current deficit of \$1 billion would lead to an eventual increase in the size of the Euro-market of \$1.3 billion. This might, however, reflect an influence of the US balance of payments on short-term capital flows included in the BIS net measure of the market.

7 Lending Decisions and Spreads: The Syndicated Loan Market*

Syndicated medium-term Euro-credits are 'roll-over' bank credits (denominated predominantly in dollars) which have been syndicated typically amongst an international group of banks. The term 'roll-over' reflects the fact that the cost of the loan is altered every three, six or twelve months, depending on the original loan agreement, in line with reigning interbank rates — typically the London interbank offered rate (LIBOR). The loan agreement may also give an option to alter, at roll-over dates, the length of the next roll-over period. The 'spread' over LIBOR — which is a premium charged by banks — is normally fixed[1] for the life of the loan. Over time, as described in the previous chapter (Figure 6.1), there have been large fluctuations in level of spreads charged to all groups of borrowers in the syndicated medium-term Euro-credit market.

In examining the movement in Euro-market spreads we emphasise in this chapter some micro aspects of the intermediation process in the Euro-market, i.e. the determination of banks' lending decisions. The emphasis on the supply side of the market is, of course, only a partial approach since the demand factors associated with the OPEC surpluses discussed in the previous chapter are also very important. An analysis of the supply of funds does, however, seem to explain much of the observed movement in Euromarket spreads during the 1970s. We begin in section 7.1 by discussing the relevance of the spread, section 7.2 analyses some of the factors which may be im-

* This chapter is based on the results of a research project conducted in the Bank of England. The results are reported in detail in Johnston (1980) and discussed in Fleming and Howson (1980). Many other of our colleagues were involved in the work, especially Chris Davies and John Ellis. The work benefited from the comments of John Flemming and Richard Portes. None of these people, that is apart from myself, is necessarily implicated in this revised and simplified version.

portant in explaining the level of lending spreads set in the Euro-market and section 7.3 reports the results of empirical work. The analysis is extended and a simple conceptual framework of the intermediation process in the Euro-currency system is discussed in section 7.4.

7.1   THE RELEVANCE OF THE SPREAD

The 'price' of syndicated medium-term Euro-credits comprises several elements: the floating interest rate, LIBOR, the spread, and a range of fees. Loans, for example, usually carry a commitment fee payable on undrawn funds, a front-end fee payable to lead and co-managers of the loan, and participation fees. In addition, the effective cost of the loan may also vary with its maturity, with a longer maturity, at a given level of spreads, indicating easier borrowing conditions. Why therefore emphasise the spread?

It is useful first to distinguish between the components of the loan which are fixed at the outset – size, fees, spreads and maturity – known as the terms on the loan, and the component which varies during the life of the loan, at roll-over dates – LIBOR. The latter, as a short-term interest rate, is determined largely outside the market for syndicated loans, in the global market for dollars (Chapter 5) and may be viewed as the clearing price in the market for 'finance'. Fluctuations in this rate are beyond the control of the banking system and individual market borrowers, which have to accept the rate quoted in the market at roll-over dates. The terms on the loan are, however, set in the syndicated loan market and subject to direct negotiation between borrowers and lenders when the loan is arranged. They can be seen as the return to the banks for acting as financial intermediaries, covering the costs and risks involved in funding loans, accepting the risk of default by borrowers on their debts and a profit element to the banking system. To borrowers, the terms are the additional margins over short-term interest rates which they pay for the availability and advantages of syndicated medium-term loans. Governments might alternatively obtain balance-of-payments finance by raising domestic interest rates to attract short-term capital inflows, by issuing bonds on the international capital markets or by approaching international agencies. But these involve varying costs, and for less creditworthy borrowers the alternatives of attracting short-term private capital flows or of issuing bonds are frequently unavailable. Even for industrialised countries, the option of raising domestic interest rates to protect their exchange rates is not always desirable because of the consequences for their domestic economies.

7.1.1   *Fees*

Among the terms charged in the syndicated credit market, the spread is signalled out as the most important. It is usually numerically the largest component, varying from as little as 3/8 of 1 per cent on some loans to over 2 per cent on others. These spreads are charged over the life of the loan. By contrast, *fees* are normally paid at the 'front end' when the loan is contracted and drawn down.

Participation fees are paid to each bank in the syndicate in relation to the size of its contribution to the loan. These might vary from 1/4 per cent on a participation of $2 million to 1/2 per cent for over $5 million. Commitment fees may also be arranged, especially if the credit is not expected to be drawn down immediately. Commonly amounting to 1/2 per cent of the committed amount, they are paid to banks who agree to provide funds if they are required, and are replaced by participation fees (and the spread) if the credit is actually used. Banks who make larger contributions to the syndicate are classed as managers or co-managers and will normally receive additional management or co-management fees. The lead manager which organises the credit receives a further front-end fee or praecipium, typically about 1/8 of 1 per cent. In some loan agreements, prepayment penalty clauses are also included, usually involving a penalty of around 1 per cent on the amount prepaid. The borrower will also have to pay the legal and other administrative costs of arranging the loan. While this structure of fees is fairly common, they vary from one loan to another, and may be described by different labels. Over the life of the loan, the total cost of the fees is much smaller than that of the spread. On a seven-year credit, for example, even adding front-end fees of 7/8 per cent would only provide a comparable return equivalent to adding about 1/8 per cent to the spread. Nevertheless, fee payments boost banks' current revenue and thus encourage participation in loans. The praecipium earned by lead managing banks, which is calculated as a percentage of the total credit, also allows successful lead managers to earn a significant extra return.[2]

A second, more practical, reason for emphasising the spread rather than the level of fees is that while information on the spread is frequently reported, data on the fee structure of loans is more difficult to obtain. What evidence is available tends to suggest that the level of fees moves in line with the level of spreads, and thus an observed decline in the level of spreads is not offset by a significant rise in the level of fees. The spread is therefore a reasonable indicator of the price of the loan. Of a sample of nine borrowers which obtained lower spreads in 1978, relative to 1977, fees were unchanged in five and lower in four of the cases in 1978 (see Table 7.1). The

Table 7.1
A sample of fees and spreads in 1977 and 1978

Borrower	Spreads		Commitment fees		Participation fees	
	1977	1978	1977	1978	1977	1978
Banco Nacional de Desarrollo	$1\frac{3}{4}$	$1\frac{3}{8}-1\frac{1}{2}$	$\frac{3}{4}$	$\frac{1}{2}$	$\frac{1}{2}-\frac{3}{4}$	$\frac{1}{4}-\frac{1}{2}$
Central Bank of Chile	$2-2\frac{1}{8}$	$1\frac{1}{8}-2\frac{1}{8}$	$\frac{3}{4}$	$\frac{3}{8}-\frac{1}{2}$	$\frac{3}{8}-\frac{7}{8}$	$\frac{1}{4}-\frac{5}{8}$
Cyprus	$1\frac{3}{4}$	$\frac{7}{8}-1$	$\frac{1}{2}$	$\frac{1}{2}$	$\frac{1}{4}$	$\frac{1}{8}-\frac{3}{8}$
Ivory Coast	2	$1\frac{3}{4}$	$\frac{3}{4}$	$\frac{1}{2}$	$1-1\frac{1}{4}$	n.a.
Morocco	$1\frac{1}{8}-1\frac{1}{4}$	1	$\frac{1}{2}$	$\frac{1}{2}$	$\frac{1}{16}-\frac{1}{4}$	n.a.
Office Cherifien des Phosphates	$1\frac{1}{2}$	$\frac{7}{8}$	$\frac{1}{2}$	$\frac{3}{8}$	$\frac{1}{8}-\frac{3}{8}$	$\frac{1}{8}-\frac{3}{8}$
Panama	2	$1\frac{7}{8}$	$\frac{3}{4}$	$\frac{3}{4}$	$\frac{3}{8}-\frac{3}{4}$	$\frac{1}{8}-\frac{5}{8}$
Electrobras	$1\frac{7}{8}-2\frac{1}{8}$	$1\frac{7}{8}$	$\frac{1}{2}$	$\frac{1}{2}$	$\frac{1}{2}-\frac{3}{4}$	$\frac{3}{8}-\frac{3}{4}$
Pemex	$1\frac{1}{2}-1\frac{5}{8}$	$1\frac{1}{4}$	$\frac{1}{2}$	$\frac{1}{2}$	$\frac{1}{8}-\frac{7}{8}$	$\frac{3}{8}-\frac{5}{8}$

n.a. = not available.

majority of participation fees in the sample were also lower on 1978 loans.

7.1.2 *Maturities*

Over time, the final maturity of banks' sydicated medium-term Euro-credit lending has also varied (Figure 6.2, p. 151), falling as spreads have risen and increasing as spreads have fallen. If, as might be expected, banks would require a larger spread for lending for longer maturities, i.e. there is a positive yield curve in the syndicated loan market in a similar way to a nominal yield curve in a domestic money or bond market, then a fall in spreads which was also accompanied by a rise in maturities would suggest that borrowing conditions had become easier than the spread alone would indicate. Consider, for example, observations on spreads and maturities at two points in time, t_0 and t_1, at A and B in Figure 7.1. Between t_0 and t_1 spreads have fallen from S_0 to S_1 and maturities lengthened from M_0 to M_1 along some observed inverse trade-off curve, L. Assuming some direct trade-off between spreads and maturities at any one point in time, i.e. a positive spread maturity yield curve, shown by the curves t_0 and t_1, then it should be possible to correct the movement in spreads from S_0 to S_1 for the lengthening in the maturity of loans. The corrected spread is shown as S_1^c in Figure 7.1. When there is a positive yield curve, $S_1^c < S_1$ and the corrected spread shows a larger fall than the uncorrected one.

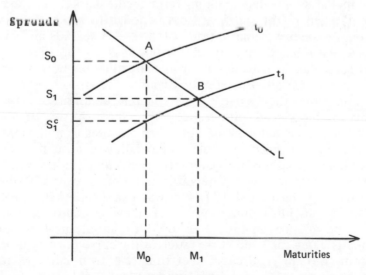

Figure 7.1

Commentators on the Euro-credit market have tried to compensate for this by constructing indexes which combine spread and maturity movements to measure changes in market conditions. The index published by *Euro-money*, which is perhaps the most widely known, is the ratio of weighted spreads to weighted maturities.[3]

$$\text{Overall index} = \frac{\sum_i w_i \dfrac{\Sigma sv}{\Sigma v}}{\sum_i w_i \dfrac{\Sigma mv}{\Sigma v}}$$

$$\text{Individual group index} = \frac{\Sigma sv}{\Sigma mv}$$

where i = the group of borrowers (the index identifies five separate
       borrowing groups)
  w_i = the weight given to each borrowing group
  Σ = the summation of the borrowings in each group
  s = spread on the loan
  v = volume of the loan
  m = maturity of the loan

There are, however, significant problems when comparing spreads and maturities in this way, particularly if the index is designed to give some accurate impression of the movement in borrowing conditions in the syndicated medium-term credit market. The assumptions embodied in the index are easy enough to make: that is, the existence of some systematic trade-off between spreads and maturities such that a lengthening of maturities at given spreads is equivalent to some fall in spreads at given maturities on borrowing conditions in the market. But simply dividing the spread by maturity would imply that the trade-off is a stable one, and moreover that the elasticity of the spread with respect to maturity in this trade-off is unity in the syndicated loan market: both the spread and the maturity of loan have equal weight in explaining conditions in the market.

To establish whether any systematic yield curve trade-off between spreads and maturities was observable, a sample of over 550 observations, covering the period 1974–9, was examined. After grouping the observations into four groups of borrowing countries and into quarters, covariance analysis was used in an attempt to isolate movements along the yield curve (such as the curve t_0 or t_1 in Figure 7.1) from shifts in yield curve over time (e.g. from curve t_0 to t_1). This analysis revealed very little independent yield curve trade-off between spreads and maturities. Practically all the variation in spreads and maturities was accounted for by shifts in the yield curve over time, making it impossible to identify any stable yield curve trade-off at a single point in time. The conclusion is that, on empirical grounds, it is not possible to make any rigorous correction to spreads for changes in the maturity of loans, and moreover indexes which combine spread and maturity movements add very little information to what can be observed directly from the movement in spreads themselves. Indeed, sometimes the indexes may give misleading impressions about how conditions are changing in the market because of the large weight given to maturity movements. *A priori* observation suggests that the yield curve trade-off is significantly less than unity. The general conclusion is therefore: since lower spreads are systematically accompanied by lower or unchanged fees and longer maturities, the spread itself can be taken as a reliable indicator of conditions in the syndicated loan market.

7.2 LENDING DECISIONS AND SPREADS

Since the spread is a market-determined rate it should contain the market's assessment of country or credit risks, and as expected there have been persistent differentials between the spreads which different groups of borrowers have had to pay: major OECD borrowers have consistently obtained lower spreads than non-oil developing countries (Figure 6.1, p. 150). Over time, however, there have also been fairly large movements in the spreads charged to all groups of borrowers. After falling to historically low levels in 1973 and 1974, spreads rose in 1975 and 1976 and then fell back in 1977 and 1978 and to pre-1974 levels in 1979 and 1980. These overall fluctuations suggest that more general factors have been important in explaining conditions in the syndicated loan market.

As has been noted elsewhere, the Euro-currency market is not an independent system but one that has rather close institutional and economic links with national banking systems. Seen as part of banks' overall activities the volume of syndicated medium-term Euro-credit lending indeed amounts to only a very small, if increasing, fraction of the banking system's total loan portfolio. At end-1979 the outstanding volume of syndicated medium-term Euro-credits amounted to only 3 per cent of the total assets of banks in six major countries (France, West Germany, Japan, Switzerland, the United Kingdom and the USA). Because of the institutional links between domestic and Euro-market banks and the relative size of the two segments of banks' overall portfolios, it seems plausible to hypothesise that factors within domestic markets would have an influence on banks' lending policy in the Euro-currency market. There are nevertheless important differences between domestic and international banking, most especially as regards the sources of lending and funding risks. An analysis of the intermediation process in the Euro-currency market should examine both the links and differences between domestic and Euro-markets.

7.2.1 *Internationalisation trends and parental resources*

Like other risk-averse investors, banks seek to diversify their asset holdings and to trade off risks and returns in their portfolios. The search by banks for effective ways of diversifying portfolio risks may be an important determinant of the growth of Euro-currency bank lending. As discussed in Chapter 2, an early reason for the internationalisation of banking was to service customers' increasing external needs. More generally, if domestic economic activity and the risks of domestic borrower defaults are cyclical, so that the risks in lending to domestic borrowers are positively correlated, the scope for hedging risks in purely domestic loan portfolios will be limited. The risks involved in international lending and particularly lending to sovereign borrowers may appear to banks to be quite different and perhaps even independent from those normally encountered in domestic economies – in which case the enhanced range of investment opportunities provided by international loans could present banks with an attractive means of increasing their lending activity and reducing overall portfolio risks.

In seeking to 'internationalise' their portfolios, banks have a number of investment options. They may directly increase their international lending out of the domestic market in domestic currencies or through their branches in the Euro-currency market, or they may establish legally independent subsidiaries and consortium banks which specialise in international lending. The shares the parent bank owns in international subsidiaries represent a diversification of parent-bank portfolios. The importance of the syndicated Euro-currency market is that it has facilitated the internationalisaton process. The introduction of floating-rate bank credits and the development of the technique of syndicating loans between banks allows risk-sharing, and permits participation by relatively small banks whose involvement in international lending might otherwise be limited by size or expertise. The development of the wholesale and interbank markets in Euro-currencies allows the entry of non-US-based banks into lending in the main international currency – the dollar – and also reduces banks' funding risks in foreign currencies. These various innovations have reduced constraints on banks' international lending behaviour.

The way in which banks seek to internationalise their lending will have implications for the links between the lending policies of banks in national and Euro-currency markets. If banks set up foreign branches to conduct their international business, Euro-market lending decisions may be closely integrated with the overall portfolio decisions of the parent organisation, and may reflect part of the global management of the combined balance-sheet of the whole organisation.[4] For foreign subsidiaries and consortium banks, the direct linkages with parent organisations may be much weaker; nevertheless, portfolio decisions of parent banks will be reflected in the original and subsequent allocations of capital to foreign subsidiaries which are used to support their operations. Parental interest in foreign subsidiaries may also extend beyond that simply of shareholders in a company. Parent banks may have a moral responsibility for the activities of their foreign affiliates. The diverse nature of banks in the Euro-currency market and their institutional relationships with parent banks make it difficult to analyse the economic links between the domestic and Euro-markets in a consistent fashion. One common link is that to a greater or lesser extent Euro-market banks are dependent on resources supplied by their parent organisations. This link provides the basis for a conceptually simple – if analytically more complex – model in which parent banks' portfolio decisions determine the allocation of capital resources which support their branches' and subsidiaries' international operations.

As an analytical framework, it could be assumed that the management of the parent is not itself concerned with the detailed business of banking – for example, with managing the level of deposits and loans which is left to parts of its organisation 'on the ground' – but reacts to profit and risk signals received from its domestic and foreign branches and subsidiaries. The former make loans to domestic customers and the latter loans to international borrowers. The way the management of the parent bank reacts to these signals is determined by its desire to maximise a (subjective) utility function which, following general portfolio theory, has arguments in both the expected level and risk of return. It achieves its optimum utility by allocating varying proportions of its given total capital stock to its domestic and offshore subsidiaries and branches.

A more rigorous analysis which illustrates this decision process using Tobin–Markowitz mean-variance analysis[5] is described in Johnston (1980). This approach restricts the variables in the parent banks' utility function to the ratio of expected returns to the capital base of the bank and the variance of return to the square of the capital base of the bank, on the assumption that the bank's capital places two constraints on management behaviour: the management of the bank seeks to earn a return on shareholders' capital; while the bank's capital provides the cushion to the bank against unexpected loan losses.[6]

After imposing a number of simplifying assumptions, it can be shown that the optimal allocation of capital by an individual bank to its international activities can be derived a linear function of the difference between the ratio of expected returns to risk (as measured by the standard deviation of returns) on the bank's international and domestic lending.

Now the total supply of capital to banks engaged in international lendings is the outcome of aggregating over individual banks, within and across a number of countries. Under the reasonably plausible assumption that the stock of international lending is small relative to global bank credit aggregates (see above), i.e. domestic markets dominate the international one in size, the analysis can be extended to show that the aggregation over individual banks implies that in equilibrium the ratio of expected returns to risks on international loans approximates to a weighted average of the ratio of expected returns to risks on different banks' domestic lending. The exact equation is written:

$$\frac{E(\pi_e)}{\sigma_e} = A + \frac{\Sigma_j B_j K_j \left[\dfrac{E(\pi_d)}{\sigma_d} \right]_j}{\Sigma_j B_j K_j} \tag{1}$$

where $j = 1, 2, \ldots, n$, $E(\pi_e)$ and $E(\pi_d)$ are respectively the expected returns on international and domestic lending, σ_e and σ_d are the standard deviations of returns on international and domestic portfolios, K is the total capital base of bank j, and A is a constant term. The weights B_j depend on the covariance of returns on individual banks' domestic lending and international lending, and the ratio of the marginal utilities of expected returns to risks in individual banks' utility functions.

As more nationalities of banks become involved in international lending the aggregation process could thus imply a number of constraints on international banking margins and specifically that the ratio of profits to risks on international lending would tend over time to some weighted average of the ratio of profits to risks in domestic markets. If lending risks are perceived on average to be lower in the international market, the margins on international lending may be expected to decline below those on domestic lending. The increasing number of banks involved in international lending may be one reason why spreads rose by a much smaller amount following the second oil shock. Portfolio analysis may also explain why at times banks of certain nationalities tend to be very aggressive in their international lending strategies, as this could reflect a relative decline in the expected returns these banks earn on their domestic loans. Indeed, even if international competition pushes returns on loans below those obtainable by some banks on their domestic lending, those banks may continue to lend because of the gains that portfolio diversification itself gives to the overall structure of the banks' portfolio. Another reason for aggressive lending is the attempt by banks to adjust their loan portfolios following the removal of restrictions on their international lending. This phenomenon explains, for example, the expanding activity of Japanese banks in 1978 and 1979 in the market for syndicated Euro-loans, following the easing by the Japanese Ministry of Finance of the guidelines on the foreign currency lending of their banks. Llewellyn (1979a) has also argued that this was the reason for a rapid expansion of external lending by US banks following the removal of US capital controls in January 1974.

7.2.2   Own and borrowed resources

While portfolio analysis provides a framework for examining the links between domestic and Euro-market lending decisions, more specific Euro-currency factors have also to be taken into account to explain the movement in Euro-market spreads. As well as parental resources, banks in the Euro-market take deposits from non-bank depositors and in the interbank market. As a reasonable approximation, the balance-sheet of a Euro-bank could thus be written as:

$$L_e = D_{nb} + D_b + k_e \tag{2}$$

where L_e is the volume of the Euro-bank's loans, D_{nb} and D_b are respectively the supply of deposits by non-banks to the individual Euro-bank and the volume of deposits which the Euro-bank takes (or lends, in which case $D_b < 0$) from other banks in the interbank market, and k_e is the capital allocated to the Euro-bank by its parent. The capital allocation is determined by the arguments in the portfolio model described above. We also distinguish between the two sources of deposits by calling primary non-bank deposits the bank's 'own' resources — those which it obtains directly from wealthholders — and interbank deposits as 'borrowed' resources, for reasons now described.

The existence of highly developed interbank markets in Euro-currencies enables Euro-banks to manage relatively easily and at low cost their total liabilities by borrowing (or lending) funds. That is, they can manage their liabilities through the interbank market. A number of factors influence, however, the actual cost of the funds at which an individual bank can borrow from other banks in the Euro-currency market – for example, its size, existing indebtedness to other banks and whether it regularly places funds in the interbank market. These various factors, which influence the bank's credit standing with other banks in the market, lead to some tiering of the interest rates which different banks pay for funds in the interbank market and may mean that banks may not always be able to manage at *fixed costs* the total size of their balance-sheets through the interbank market. In a balance-sheet of a given size the volume of deposits taken from non-banks will determine the amount of residual funding through the interbank market, and if interbank interest rates are variable and uncertain the supply of non-bank deposits may have an important influence on the costs and risks involved when funding the portfolio and thus the rates of interest at which the bank is willing to lend. This effect may be most important when interbank conditions are highly volatile (e.g. during the Herstatt crisis of 1974; see pp. 29–30) but it may also have a more general influence on the movement in Euro-market spreads.

Whether in fact this type of 'endowment' effect from the supply of 'own' resources exists and international bank lending policy reflects the primary supply of deposits by non-bank wealth-holders, or whether it is possible to regard Euro-banks as perfect liability managers who treat deposits from non-banks as perfect substitutes for those taken in the interbank market, is a very interesting empirical question with important implications for the development of the Euro-currency market. If non-bank deposits and interbank deposits taken by a Euro-bank are perfect substitutes and if, in addition, the supply of deposits to the interbank market by domestic banks can be assumed to be nearly perfectly elastic (Chapter 5), then *international bank lending would be independent of the international portfolio decisions of non-banks*. The analysis of the reasons for depositing in the Euro-currency market (Chapter 4) would be largely irrelevant in explaining developments in lending conditions in the Euro-market. Alternatively, and perhaps more realistically, if they are not perfect substitutes, then factors which influence the supply of non-bank deposits to the Euro-currency market will be important determinants of the volumes and terms of international lending.

Additionally some other funding risks, such as the amount of maturity transformation undertaken by the banking system, may also have to be taken into account when explaining banks' funding costs, but these have not been examined separately in the empirical work discussed below; and in setting the level of spreads charged to each borrower allowance has to be made for some proxies of the riskiness of the loan. Combining the various arguments from sections 7.2.1 and 7.2.2 the empirical model of the determination of spreads examines the influence of:[7]

1. Credit risks associated with the risks of default by borrowers.
2. Funding risks associated with the source of the supply of deposits to the banking system and the volatility of interest rates in the interbank market.
3. The opportunity cost to parent banks of allocating resources to international rather than national lending.

A summary of the main empirical findings is given at the end of the next section.

7.3   THE EMPIRICAL RESULTS

There is a general data problem when investigating an empirical model of the movement in Euro-market spreads: that is, a short and perhaps even unrepresentative sample. Reliable information on spreads has only been collected since about 1974 and these data show only one 'cycle' in spreads (Figure 6.1, p. 150). The succession of banking failures in 1974 (Chapter 2) produced general fears about the solvency of banks in the Euro-currency market, caused sharp movements in Euro-dollar interest rates (Chapter 5) and led banks to withdraw at least temporarily from expanding their Euro-currency business. In those circumstances, even though the main effects of the banking crisis in 1974 was to influence confidence in certain banks and the banking system and not the risk of default by borrowers, it would not have been surprising if banks had sought sharply higher spreads on their syndicated medium-term Euro-loans to compensate for the increased risks involved in funding loans, with the implication that the decline between 1976 and 1979 reflected only a recovery in confidence. Specific allowance has therefore to be made to test the significance of this event. The short sample and the presence of shocks to the Euro-market obviously mean that the empirical estimates have to be treated as tentative.

After examining a number of possible proxies for the explanatory variables and different equation specifications, the final empirically tested spread determination equation was written as:[8]

$$S = a_0 + a_1 S_{US} + a_2 S_{DM} + a_3 (r_{ed} - r_{cda}) + a_4 \frac{D_{nb}}{L_e} + a_5 def$$
$$+ a_6 ML_e + a_7 D_1 + \epsilon \tag{3}$$

where the variables and their expected impact are described as follows:

S, the dependent variable, is the average spread on syndicated medium-term Euro-credits for each group of borrowing countries investigated.

S_{US} and S_{DM} are calculated 'implicit' spreads on US and West German domestic medium-term lending. These variables are used to proxy the opportunity cost of allocating resources to banks' international rather than domestic lending, i.e. the links between returns on domestic and international lending described by equation (1). They should have a positive influence on Euro-market spreads.[9]

$r_{ed} - r_{cda}$ is the differential between the three-month Euro-dollar rate and the reserve-adjusted cost of US three-month CDs. This variable is used to measure possible interbank funding risks and acts as a proxy for the effect of the Herstatt bank collapse. As increased funding risks will increase the cost of intermediation in the Euro-market, the variable should enter the equation with a positive sign.

D_{nb}/L_e is the ratio of non-bank deposits to total Euro-market loans in the London Euro-currency market. This variable is used to proxy the proportion of banks' 'own' resources to total resources. If banks are not perfect liability managers, an increase in this variable should reduce bank funding risks and have a significant negative impact on Euro-market spreads.

def proxies the risk of default by borrowers, and in the equations reported is the ratio of aggregate reserves to imports of the borrowing group. Increased risks of default should raise the level of Euro-market spreads.

ML_e is the volume of syndicated medium-term Euro-credits, which is used to test whether the spread is responsive to the volume of syndicated lending. If the supply curve is upward sloping, this variable will have a positive sign.

D_1 is a first-quarter dummy variable.

Equation (3) was estimated for three groups of sovereign borrowers in the syndicated medium-term credit market: major OECD, minor OECD and non-oil LDCs. (It would be reasonable to suspect that these individual country group equations would not be independent of one another, and moreover that certain of the explanatory variables – funding risks, the implicit domestic spreads and the non-bank deposit variable – would have a similar influence in each of the equations. To allow for these factors, the equations were estimated by a restricted joint generalised least squares (GLS) procedure (see Theil, 1971). When tested the across-equation restrictions were found non-significant and imposed on the equations.) The results are reported in Table 7.2. These provided a reasonable statistical fit. The coefficients on the implicit domestic spread variables and the non-bank supply of deposits variable were significant and took the right signs. Evaluated at period means the coefficients on the implicit

Table 7.2
Estimates of the spread determination equation*

RESTRICTED COEFFICIENTS

S_{US}	S_{DM}	$r_{ed} - r_{cda}$	D_{nb}/L_e
0.111	0.097	0.081	−10.380
(3.10)	(3.55)	(1.18)	(4.07)

UNRESTRICTED COEFFICIENTS

	Major OECD	*Minor OECD*	*Non-oil LDC*
Constant	2.364	3.197	4.867
	(5.02)	(6.55)	(8.50)
def	0.274	−0.584	−2.539
	(0.67)	(2.93)	(6.45)
ML_e	−0.0017	−0.0019	−0.0017
	(1.71)	(3.58)	(5.01)
D_1	−0.117	−0.070	−0.090
	(1.26)	(1.06)	(1.33)
$\bar{R}^2$	0.733	0.881	0.887
D–W	1.97	1.89	1.81

F-test for restrictions $F_{(8,42)} = 1.28$

t-ratios in parentheses

* Restricted GLS estimates: period 1974–1979II.

US and West German domestic spreads imply that a 1 per cent change in these domestic spreads would lead to a 0.16 per cent and 0.09 per cent change respectively in the average level of Euro-dollar spreads, and that an increase of 1 per cent in the proportion of Euro-banks' total liabilities due to non-banks (i.e. D_{nb}/L_e) would cause a 1.17 per cent fall in the average level of spreads on syndicated medium-term Euro-credits.

The elasticity on the implicit level of US domestic spreads seems somewhat low but is not inconsistent with the observation that the lending policy of US banks in the Euro-currency market does not continuously dominate the level of Euro-market spreads. It might also suggest that the speed of response of Euro-market spreads to those in national markets might be rather slow. For a number of reasons – the period between lending policy decisions by parent banks and the time involved in meeting policy objectives – such a conclusion and result may not seem unreasonable. Thus, while the level of lending margins in national markets are important, they do not dominate the movement in Euro-market spreads. This conclusion is also consistent with the highly significant and negative coefficient found on D_{nb}/L_e: 'own' resources of banks in the Euro-market bear a close relationship with spread movements, and by implication banks are not perfect liability managers. Inflows and outflows of non-bank deposits have an important influence on banks' willingness to intermediate and the movement in spreads. This variable may also be picking up part of the impact of Herstatt on the market as this caused non-banks to withdraw deposits. Indeed, the other funding risk variable – the Euro-dollar rate and reserve-adjusted US CD rate differential – had only a small and insignificant impact on the level of Euro-market spreads. The coefficient on the proxy for default risk – the ratio of aggregate reserves to imports, *def* – enters the minor OECD and non-oil LDC group equations with a correct and significant negative sign (i.e. a rise in reserves relative to imports reduces banks' perception that countries will default on their loans) but is, not surprisingly, non-significant in the major OECD equation. The result would indicate that banks do take risk factors into account when setting the level of spreads and it supports the type of limitations to the intermediation process suggested in Chapter 6.

A feature of the results is the negative and significant coefficient on the stock of syndicated medium-term Euro-credits (ML_e). *A priori*, it would be expected that this variable would at least have entered the supply equation with a positive sign. One plausible explanation for this result may be that the use of implicit domestic spread variables in the US and West German domestic markets, as the only proxies for returns on lending in national markets, has failed to capture the competitive influence of banks of other nationalities on spreads in the Euro-currency market. It would be expected that these competitive pressures would manifest themselves both in a fall in Euro-market spreads and in an increase in the volume of syndicated medium-term lending, causing a significant negative correlation. Alternatively, the stock of loans variable might be picking up a longer-run downward trend in spreads as more nationalities of banks sought to internationalise their business.

An alternative explanation for the result is that the spread on syndicated medium-term Euro-credits is the outcome of an interaction between the supply of and demand for credits and that the negative coefficient on the volume of loans in the supply equation reflects simultaneous-equation bias. To investigate this possibility, a fairly *ad hoc* demand equation was estimated. The main findings from these results, which have not been reported in detail here,[10] were that on the demand side borrowers were responsive both to the level of spreads and LIBOR, but the average elasticity of the demand for syndicated medium-term Euro-credits with respect to the spread (-1.3) was larger than with respect to LIBOR (-0.8). The demand for syndicated medium-term credits by non-oil LDCs and minor OECD countries was also significantly related to their balance-of-payments deficits and to the ratio of aggregate reserves to imports for the country grouping. This latter variable was introduced on the assumption that countries would seek to achieve some optimal ratio for the level of reserves to imports by borrowing in the Euro-currency market. Allowing for simultaneous effects had, however, very little impact on the coefficients or the significance of variables in the spread-determination equation. The coefficient on the volume of syndicated loans remained negative and significant.

Another explanation for this result follows from the finding (also not reported in detail) that the stock of syndicated medium-term Euro-credits became non-significant when the absolute volume of non-bank deposits (D_{nb}) was entered into the equation instead of D_{nb}/L_e. This suggests a collinearity between D_{nb} and ML_e and hence that perhaps D_{nb} may act both as a factor determining Euro-banks' funding costs, as in Table 7.2, and also a factor explaining the longer-term internationalisation of banking which was otherwise picked up by the volume of loans term. If, indeed, this is the case, it suggests, together with the highly significant value of the coefficient found on D_{nb}/L_e, that non-bank portfolio decisions and factors which influence these are of considerable importance in explaining the movement in spreads and the general internationalisation of banking.

7.3.1   *A summary of the results*

The main empirical findings are summarised as follows:

1. The average level of Euro-market spreads responds to relative returns on banks' domestic lending. Elasticities are, however, low, which suggests that national lending policies do not dominate the movement in Euro-market spreads, at least in the short term.
2. The source of funds to banks in the Euro-currency markets is highly significant in explaining spread movements. This suggests that banks are not perfect liability managers and that the supply of 'own' resources is an important determinant of banks' lending decisions.
3. Spreads are responsive to a proxy for credit risks.
4. There appears to have been a trend decline in spreads during the 1970s which may reflect an aggressive policy by banks to internationalise their loan portfolios or a trend by non-banks to internationalise their portfolios which has encouraged banks to expand their own international lending.
5. On the demand side, borrowers appear to be responsive both to the level of Euro-market spreads and to movements in LIBOR. The elasticity of response with respect to the spread is, however, greater than that with respect to LIBOR.

7.4   A CONCEPTUAL FRAMEWORK

The results of this analysis and that in earlier chapters provide a framework for analysing developments in the Euro-currency market. It is described by the following four equations and illustrated in Figure 7.2:

Supply of Euro-currency deposits by
non-banks $\qquad\qquad\qquad\qquad D_{nb}^{s} = D_{nb}^{s}\ (r_e, r_d, W)$ (4)

Residual supply of deposits by banks
(bank arbitrage schedule) $\qquad\qquad D_{b}^{s} = L^{s} - D_{nb}^{s}$ (5)

Demand for Euro-currency loans $\qquad L^{d} = L^{d}(S_p, r_e, BOP)$ (6)

Euro-bank intermediation function $\qquad S_p = S_p\,(L^{s}, D_{nb}^{s}, S_d, R)$ (7)

Equation (6) describes the demand for Euro-currency loans, L^{d}, and this schedule is drawn downward-sloping in Figure 7.2, being negatively related to the Euro-currency spread, S_p, and LIBOR, r_e,

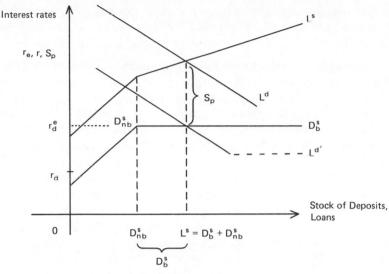

Figure 7.2

and a function of the structure of borrowing countries' balance of payments, *BOP* (Chapter 6). The derived demand for Euro-currency deposits implied by this curve is shown by $L^{d'}$, which is vertically lower than L^d by the size of the spread over LIBOR. (The demand for deposits curve, $L^{d'}$, may also become highly elastic at some point — shown on the dashed section in Figure 7.2 — when domestic banks find it profitable to borrow from the Euro-currency market.) The supply of deposits to the market is derived in two segments. First, the supply of funds by non-banks, D_{nb}^s (equation (4)), is drawn positively related to the Euro-currency deposit rate in Figure 7.2 and, as described by equation (4), may be assumed to be negatively related to the domestic rate, r_d, and a function of wealth, W (Chapter 4). Second, the residual supply of funds to the Euro-market by domestic banks, D_b^s (equation (5)), is shown perfectly elastic at the effective cost of raising funds in the domestic market, r_d^e (Chapter 5). The supply of loans by Euro-banks, L^s, is derived from the banks' intermediation schedule (equation (7)) and is shown positively related to the Euro-currency spread, which can be read off as the difference between deposit and loan supply schedules. It is drawn upward-sloping, even after the supply of deposits to the market becomes perfectly elastic, to allow for the influence of a changing balance of bank and non-bank deposits on bank-lending behaviour. Other arguments in the banks' intermediation equation (7) include the level of domestic spreads, S_d, and lending risk factors, R.

Within this conceptual framework the expansion of the Euro-currency market can be explained by any or all of the following developments which shift the loan supply and demand schedules:

1. An increase in the demand for Euro-currency loans, reflecting balance-of-payments developments or some other exogenous factors which shifts the L^d schedule to the right,
2. An increase in the supply of funds to the market by non-banks, which shifts the L^s schedule to the right as Euro-banks become more willing to supply intermediary services in the Euro-currency market,
3. An exogenous change in the supply of intermediary services to the Euro-market, which shifts the L^s schedule vertically downwards as the spread banks require for external intermediation is reduced, *ceteris paribus*. This would occur if there were a fall in the return on banks' domestic lending or if there were a decline in the relative risks of international lending. The trend effects noted in the empirical analysis also suggest that this schedule has been shifting down over time as more nationalities of banks become involved in the Euro-currency market.

7.4.1   *An example*

The system of equations (4)–(7) may be used to analyse the effect of some exogenous shocks on the level of Euro-market spreads and the growth of the Euro-currency market. An interesting example concerns the influence of the location of OPEC funds on the recycling process, and specifically whether OPEC placements in national markets – such as the US domestic bond market – would have a detrimental effect on the ability of the Euro-market to recycle funds to countries in balance-of-payments deficit. We investigate a hypothetical process below. It is described in its simplest form and the analysis does not examine certain indirect effects, for example on national money stocks and the reactions of national authorities.

The assumptions of the system are that there is free capital mobility and efficient interbank arbitrage between domestic and offshore markets. A rise in the OPEC surplus initially raises its cash surplus by a similar amount and this is borne by countries other than reserve-currency centres (for a discussion of a possibly different result when one country happens to be the USA, see Chapter 6). The immediate impact of the payments imbalance leads deficit countries to run down their foreign exchange reserves and OPEC to increase theirs. These reserve transactions occur through the Euro-currency market, after which OPEC may reallocate their reserves to national markets. The influence of reserve losses on deficit countries causes them to increase their demand for borrowing in the Euro-currency market. The banking system is initially in portfolio equilibrium; the type of competitive trend effects observed in the 1970s, which may sustain the supply of balance-of-payments finance at a higher level, are assumed not to occur.

The transfer of foreign currency reserves from deficit countries to OPEC through the Euro-currency system will not initially affect the liquidity position of Euro-banks or the volume of their 'own' resources. An increase in the demand for Euro-market loans by deficit countries will thus have to be met by banks increasing their borrowing from national markets through the interbank market and also perhaps by an allocation of parental resources to banks in the Euro-market. Spreads on Euro-market loans will rise because of the risks of taking funds in the interbank market, and by a sufficient margin to cover any increased credit risks — associated perhaps with the worsening external position of borrowing countries — and to attract any parental resources that may be needed. Short-term domestic and Euro-currency interest rates will also tend to rise somewhat because of the increased international demand for funds, unless authorities intervene to fix domestic interest rates. The rise in Euro-market spreads and short-term interest rates will reduce borrowing demands by deficit countries. OPEC, which have a cash surplus, may decide to repay some outstanding loans and this will reduce the need for Euro-banks to seek new resources. Assuming, however, that new borrowing demands exceed the amount of loans repaid by OPEC, the demand curve for loans will shift to the right (say from L_0^d to L_1^d; see figure 7.3) along the supply curve (L_0^s) and spreads will rise (from S_0 to S_1 in Figure 7.3).[11]

Second-round effects on Euro-market liquidity may occur if deficit countries redeposit some of their borrowing proceeds in the Euro-market. The redepositing of funds will increase the supply of 'own' resources to banks in the market and shift the loan supply curve to the right (from L_0^s to L_1^s in Figure 7.3). Spreads may therefore fall back and the Euro-market will endogenously expand from a shift in both the supply of and demand for funds. The final outcome for the level of spreads will then depend on the elasticities of and the relative shifts in the loan supply and demand curves. The elasticity of the loan supply curve will reflect the additional intermediation costs associated with increased lending risks and the opportunity cost of the allocation of parental resources to the Euro-market when these are needed to support the enlarged volume of lending. These factors will tend unequivocally to raise Euro-market spreads. The

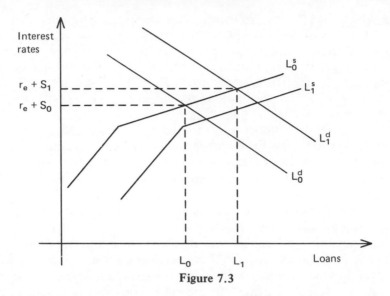

Figure 7.3

shift in the supply curve from the redepositing of funds will, however, tend to lower the spread so that the final outcome is uncertain. If only a small fraction of funds are redeposited (see Chapter 9), some rise in spreads would be expected.

Say OPEC now shift some of their deposits out of the Euro-currency market and buy US domestic bonds; what are the effects on Euro-market spreads? Two factors will be important: first, the direct influence of the deposit shift on the liquidity of banks in the Euro-market; and second, the indirect effect of the shift by OPEC from short-term bank deposits to bonds on the liquidity of the financial system. The direct effect on Euro-banks is that they will be short of deposits and will have to bid to replace them. This bidding for funds may attract some primary non-bank deposits from the US market, where average interest rates may have fallen somewhat because of the deposit shift by OPEC, but more generally it would be accom-modated mainly by an interbank arbitrage flow from the US market to the Euro-market. The increased use of interbank funds by Euro-banks will tend to raise their costs of intermediation and put upward pressure on Euro-market spreads.

In the US market the purchase of bonds by OPEC will tend, how-ever, to alter the structure of US domestic interest rates. Bond rates will tend to fall relative to short-term domestic interest rates. This relative movement in interest rates may encourage US domestic borrowers to shift from bank to bond finance, squeezing US domestic banks' lending margins. In this case US banks may be willing to increase their supply of resources to their branches and subsidiaries in the Euro-market, and this will tend to lower the level of Euro-market spreads.[12] From the empirical analysis it appears that Euro-market spreads are more responsive to funding risks than to relative returns in national money markets – at least in the short term – and the shift of funds by OPEC would therefore tend to exert some upward pressure on Euro-market spreads.

7.5   SUMMARY AND CONCLUSIONS

The importance of the spread derives from its role as an indicator of conditions in the syndicated medium-term credit market and the importance of this market as a source of balance-of-payments finance and a channel for the internationalisation of bank loan portfolios. Risk/return portfolio analysis provides a theoretical framework for examining the links between banks' domestic and international lending decisions. Within this framework consideration has to be given to the sources of risk and return in the international market to explain the movement in Euro-market spreads. An important question is whether the source of the supply of funds to banks in the Euro-market has an influence on banks' lending decisions.

Empirical analysis suggests that Euro-market spreads are responsive to relative returns in national money markets, the supply of funds to the market by non-bank wealth holders, and to specific borrower risk variables. There is also evidence that there has been a trend decline in spreads during the 1970s which may reflect competitive pressures, as the number of banks involved in the market increased, or a trend by wealth-holders to internationalise their portfolios. It is possible that, because of these trends, the flow of balance-of-payments finance to deficit countries through the banking system has expanded at a faster pace than is sustainable in the longer term. The portfolio model framework suggests that once banks have adjusted the overall size of their portfolios to the new international lending opportunities, international loans would not grow at a significantly faster rate than domestic loans. Euro-market spreads would have to rise or the role of the banking system in the international financing process would contract.

The sharp decline in spreads which occurred in the later 1970s has been a source of concern for the overall stability of the banking system. What matters, however, is whether the returns to banks generated by any level of spreads are commensurate with the risks – both lending and funding risks – involved in international banking; and the fall in spreads seems to have been accompanied by some improvement in both sources of risk. Because of the medium-term nature of the lending, concern may, however, remain as to whether spreads adequately reflected future sources of risk to the banking system.

NOTES

1. In practice, loans have sometimes, when the general level of spreads has fallen, been renegotiated in order to reduce the spread.
2. As the praecipium is calculated as a percentage of the total credit, but is received in its entirety by the lead manager, the larger the proportion of the credit that the lead manager is able to sell down, the larger is this praecipium sum as a percentage of the remaining funds which he has to provide from his own books. If after arranging the syndicate the lead manager is left to provide 25 per cent of the credit from his own resources, a praecipium of 1/8 per cent of the total credit is equivalent to an additional front-end fee of 1/2 per cent on the money supplied by the lead manager himself.
3. See 'The launch of the Euro-money index', *Euro-money*, October 1980.
4. On the issues involved in global management, see Moscowitz (1979).
5. See Markowitz (1957) and Tobin (1965).
6. In practice, banks will tend to make provisions out of their profits to cover expected loan losses.
7. For a more rigorous derivation of the empirical equation and the links between the arguments in sections 7.2.1 and 7.2.2 the interested reader is referred to Johnston (1980).
8. See Johnston (1980).
9. It was impossible to arrive at satisfactory estimates of 'implicit' spreads in other national markets whose banks are important participants in the Euro-currency market; and the use of only US and West German domestic spreads may therefore fail to catch the influence of the lending policy of banks of other nationalities on Euro-market spreads.
10. Johnston (1980) gives the detailed estimates.
11. If instead the transfer of resources from deficit countries to OPEC occurs only in national markets — for example, from sales of US Treasury bills by deficit countries matched by purchases of US Treasury bills by OPEC — the effects on Euro-market spreads will be very similar.
12. The relative fall in bond rates may also encourage international borrowers of funds to shift from bank to bond finance, tending to squeeze Euro-market lending margins and spreads.

8 Macroeconomic Concerns

Hitherto the analysis has been preoccupied with explaining the parameters and responses by agents which affect the operations of the Euro-currency system, and little has been said about the implications of the system for the rest of the world. Chapter 6 examined some of the beneficial consequences (and costs) of credit intermediation by the market for the world economy. In fact, ever since the Euro-market emerged there has been considerable debate about its impact on world economic stability. The concerns raised in this debate derive largely from the following observations:

1. The market is not subject to *direct* regulation for monetary control purposes.
2. The institutions involved in the market are mainly branches and subsidiaries of banks. In their own domestic markets banks are normally regulated for monetary control purposes and are regarded as playing an especially important role in national monetary systems.
3. The rather visible and efficient nature of the Euro-market as a channel for international capital and banking flows.

There are many shades to the debate, and indeed the views expressed about the macroeconomic implications of the Euro-market are frequently so conflicting that two extreme positions are readily identifiable. At one are those who see the market as an autonomous or independent source of disequilibrium to the world economy, which is 'out of control'. At the other extreme are those who view the Euro-markets as only one, albeit efficient, channel for monetary and capital flows which derive from more fundamental disequilibrium in the world economy.[1] To characterise these extreme positions I will call them respectively the 'autonomists' and the 'channelists'.

Macroeconomic concerns about the Euro-market refer to their implications for the stability of the price level — inflationary concerns — and for the stability of exchange rates. Specific worries about the rate of growth of an external market in bank deposits are not perhaps surprising given the emphasis in domestic economies on relationships between monetary aggregates and inflation. Some might extend these relationships to a measure of the global money stock, which aggregates national money stocks with private Euro-currency deposits, and world inflation; and combined with the role of the Euro-market as an intermediary of capital flows there is also concern for the impact of the market on the *relative* price of different currencies, i.e. exchange rates. But, as regards the world money stock, we have already seen in Chapter 3 that the addition from Euro-currency holdings is still very small.

The important question for the macroeconomic issues is to what extent the Euro-currency market has caused national authorities to lose control over national or international policy variables. Or to put it another way, how much more difficult do unregulated external markets make policy formulation? There is of course an overlap between the macroeconomic concerns within the policy framework. A policy to stabilise exchange rates by varying national interest rates or intervening on the foreign exchange markets will influence the anti-inflationary stance of monetary policy. It is therefore useful to examine three more general influences of the Euro-market: its impact on (a) the rate of growth of the world money or credit stock; on (b) the currency composition and distribution of the money and credit stock; and on (c) the volume of capital flows between national economies. This chapter examines the latter two influences, but to give an overall feel for the debate the first is also discussed briefly.

8.1   MONEY AND CREDIT STOCKS

Money is an asset in the hands of the public which has certain specified characteristics. The actual choice of assets can be made on a variety of grounds, but usually those which act as a means of payment or a medium of exchange, such as currency and demand deposits, are automatically counted. In many countries broader definitions of money include a variety of less liquid assets, which primarily act as a store of value. Large negotiable certificates of deposit (CDs) are, for example, included in US M_3; however, Treasury and commercial bills are excluded. The choice of the definition of money is therefore sometimes rather arbitrary and may depend on the relationship between holdings of the assets and developments in the economy, i.e. a stable demand for money function. As we have seen in Chapter 3, most countries exclude residents' foreign currency and domestic currency deposits held in banks abroad, including Euro-currency deposits, from their national money stock definitions – although a number of countries include foreign currencies held by residents, and sometimes non-residents, at domestic banks in broader monetary aggregates. There are several possible reasons for this. First, the information only became available comparatively recently when the BIS began to collect and make available detailed Euro-currency statistics to central banks, and their coverage remains incomplete and reporting usually lags behind two or three months that of domestically held bank deposits; second, the magnitude of externally held deposits by non-banks, as opposed to those held by banks and central banks, is still relatively small (Chapter 3). Third, a typical Euro-currency deposit may have less 'monetary' characteristics then domestic assets included in monetary aggregates: being usually a large denomination time deposit of a fixed term, it is not compatible with a domestic demand deposit held by private individuals. Only a small proportion of Euro-currency deposits are very short term — overnight or seven days.

The counterpart of financial asset holding is the extension of *credit*. Credit can be extended in the form of money holdings — when an individual holds currency he extends credit to the government, and credit to the banking system when he holds bank deposits. It can also be extended without the creation of money, for example when an individual buys a bond, or when a trader defers payment for goods. The creation of credit thus involves a much broader range of assets than those narrowly defined as money.

A feature of the relationship between money and credit which is frequently commented on is the ability of the banking system to expand the money and credit stock. When a domestic bank lends out funds deposited with it, it issues claims upon itself. If these claims are in the form of newly created bank deposits — they may be simply in the form of lines of credit — which are counted as money, when a bank extends credit it can also add to the stock of money. Providing deposits with the banking system are not withdrawn — for example, for the purchase of government bonds — the process of extending credit by issuing new bank deposits, and, more generally, of the redepositing of funds lent out by a bank with itself and other banks in the system, may lead to money and credit multiplier effects. Similar credit-creating effects can occur through other groups of financial intermediaries. However, because of the role of the banking system in providing a means of payment, it is normally warranted particular attention. This attention may simply reflect the importance of the banking system in the settlement of payments within the domestic economy and the adverse effects that a banking collapse would have on the financial system. It may also reflect the view that direct regulation of the banking system is necessary for efficient monetary control because other techniques are less effective. In some countries, the USA for example, domestic banks are required to hold non-interest-bearing reserve balances at the central bank against their deposits. By sterilising a proportion of bank deposits as reserve holdings, the legal reserve requirements limit a bank's ability to extend credit, and by acting on the supply of reserves to the banking system, or the price at which they are supplied, the Federal Reserve has an instrument to control the money stock. In some other countries control by means of legal reserve requirements is not a feature of monetary policy. It is not presently (1982) the case in the United Kingdom, where the Bank of England has chosen, through its open-market operations, to concentrate on influencing short-term interest rates.

Two general points can thus be made about the role of the Euro-market in relation to the control of money and credit stocks:

1. The extent to which the Euro-market creates money and adds to the world money stock will be rather arbitrary depending on the actual definition of money employed. But if the type of deposits held in the Euro-currency market are close substitutes to money-like assets in domestic economies, this may be rather important to *some* national authorities as regards the mechanism which is used to control them. The absence of direct Euro-market regulations may imply some loss in the efficiency of domestic monetary control.
2. Regardless of whether Euro-banks issue money-like assets, in their role as financial intermediaries, they still extend credit, and this may have implications for the conduct of national monetary policies and for global variables such as the level of world income and inflation.

8.1.1   *Multiple credit creation*

The absence of direct monetary regulations on Euro-currency deposits has led to concern that the Euro-market can autonomously expand the global stock of money or credit. Unlike some national markets no reserve requirements restrict banks in the Euro-market expanding the volume of credit, and money, by a multiple of their initial deposits in an analogous way to a 'fractional reserve' multiplier process in a domestic banking system.[2] To some – the 'autonomists' – this theory suggests that the redepositing of funds lent out by Euro-banks in the Euro-currency system can proceed virtually without limit, causing national authorities to lose complete control over money and credit creation, with obvious inflationary implications. Other propositions also follow. If the Euro-market enlarges the global volume of money and credit stocks, then the amount of funds which can flow between national economies will also be greater and the markets may have an autonomous influence on the volume of capital movements; they may encourage speculative attacks on currencies and undermine the independent stance of national monetary policies. Others – the 'channelists' – are impressed by the scope for leakages from the Euro-currency system, which limits any multiplier process and many doubt the usefulness of applying fractional reserve multiplier models to the Euro-currency market. When the Euro-markets have a limited multiplier potential, their role must be seen as essentially that of efficient allocators of the stock of money or credit determined within national economies. The issue of credit creation is thus a central one to the debate (Chapter 9).

8.1.2 *Disintermediation*

The reallocation – or 'disintermediation' – of a given volume of credit flows between residents to intermediaries outside the domestic banking system may have an influence on national money and credit policies. Such 'disintermediation' causes the nationally defined money and credit stocks, which do not include Euro-market deposits, to understate the total amount of money or credit available for spending by residents, reducing the reliability of domestically defined monetary and credit aggregates as indicators of domestic monetary conditions. Disintermediation of flows through the Euro-currency system, and indeed other unregulated domestic non-bank financial intermediaries (NBFIs), may be particularly acute during periods of credit restraint, when the structure of domestic monetary regulations severely dis-criminates against the operations of domestic banks, and this has led the 'autonomists' to argue that offshore markets in a country's domestic currency undermine the restrictive stance of monetary policy.

There is also a broader concern about the equity of treatment of banks in some national markets and the Euro-currency market. The presence of legal reserve requirements on regulated banks in the USA has disadvantaged them relative to banks in the Euro-market and led to some fears of a gradual erosion of the US banking system as banks and non-bank wealth-holders move an increasing proportion of their business to offshore markets. As a reflection of these fears, the US authorities have allowed the establishment of International Banking Facilities (IBFs) in the USA (Chapter 4). By removing a regulatory inequity in the treatment of US domestic foreign lending compared with their branches in offshore centres, the International Banking Facilities are designed to attract more foreign business to the USA, bringing it within the purview of the domestic authorities. The presence of inequalities in treatment between Federal Reserve member banks and other banks in the USA had also caused a number of US domestic banks to leave the Federal Reserve system. The intro-duction of the Monetary Control Act in the USA in March 1980 is, however, designed to remove many of the domestic inequalities.[3]

While 'channelists' recognise these concerns, they observe that in sophisticated financial markets a 'disintermediation' of funds out of the domestic banking system can occur through many channels; and that the Euro-currency market is not always the most important. They also observe that the incentive for 'disintermediation' reflects the structure of national monetary regulations and will depend on the particular type of policies being pursued by national authorities, i.e. whether they adversely discriminate against the domestic banking system. The aggregate money and credit stock is anyway controllable by altering the level of domestic interest rates since interest-rate arbitrage ensures that this will affect credit conditions in the Euro-currency market. The domestic monetary policy effects remain, however, an important reason for the calls for more direct control of the Euro-market (Chapter 10).

8.1.3   *Credit distribution*

Even if the authorities can control the total stock of money or credit by restraining their domestic banking systems, this may have adverse distributional affects. It is argued that larger institutions will be more able to avoid the restraining affects of policy than smaller entities by turning to the Euro-currency market. Wallich (1979) comments:

> Perhaps an even more serious problem in carrying out a monetary policy that takes explicit account of the Euro-currency market would arise because of the uneven effects of restrictive policy on the domestic and Euro-currency markets. Those smaller domestic banks and their customers that have less access to the Euro-currency market than the large international banks and their US and foreign customers would absorb a disproportionate share of the burden of a restrictive policy.

Again, however, 'channelists' might argue that this is not a particularly new phenomenon. Larger entities have always had a better access to credit facilities than smaller ones. They can tap non-bank financial intermediary channels, such as the market in commercial paper or bankers' acceptances when there are direct restraints on domestic bank lending. During periods of high interest rates, some of the worst-hit institutions are the building societies and savings and loan institutions which cater for small borrowers.

Another argument has to do with the distribution of expenditures associated with international borrowing and the complicating effect this has for the formulation of national monetary policy.[4] Thus, for example, if Brazil borrows dollars in New York or London to pay for oil imports from the Middle East, initially this has nothing to do with the purchase of goods and services in the USA. Secondary effects may occur if the oil exporters make direct purchases from the USA, or even if they make purchases from West Germany the Deutsche Mark may appreciate, displacing some demand back to the USA. The relationship between borrowing in dollars and expenditures on US goods and services is, however, loose and difficult to gauge. International borrowing in dollars may, nevertheless, have implications for the level of dollar interest rates and the domestic availability of credit. It may make US domestic credit conditions tighter or crowd out US domestic borrowers. But as this borrowing is only loosely related to expenditures on US goods and services, US credit conditions may become more restrictive than warranted by the development of final expenditures in the USA.

'Channelists' respond that this problem has always been associated with the use of currencies internationally to finance third-country trade or to settle transactions. The reserve-currency country also receives a number of benefits from the use of its currency internationally (Chapter 6) and these have to be offset against any costs. Moreover, there is little evidence that international borrowers crowd out domestic ones. On the contrary, international lending has expanded most rapidly during periods of slack domestic loan demand and the concern is, if anything, that domestic borrowers will crowd out international ones and hamper the international recycling process.

8.2   ASSET SHIFTS AND EXCHANGE RATES

Following the collapse of the Bretton Woods system of fixed exchange rates, currency movements showed a much greater degree of volatility. The average absolute monthly change in the exchange rates of the major industrialised countries increased from around 0.5 per cent in the six years prior to the Smithsonian Agreement of December 1971 to nearly 2 per cent in the three years following the move to the generalised floating of exchange rates in 1973. This increased exchange-rate volatility has coincided with the expansion of Euro-currency markets and the much-increased international mobility of short-term capital flows. The Euro-markets provide a highly efficient channel for short-term capital movements and some observers suggest that the Euro-markets therefore constitute a fundamental source of exchange-rate instability. One vivid description has termed the markets an 'atomic cloud' of 'footloose funds' which are suddenly and arbitrarily shifted from one currency to another, destabilising exchange rates.

In recent years there has also been a trend by private and public agencies to diversify the currency composition of their assets and liabilities away from the main international currency – the dollar. The desire by transactors to use a currency to make or receive payments, hold assets denominated in and to borrow in the currency in question is ultimately determined by a broad range of considerations. The currency composition of official foreign exchange reserves appears, for example, to be significantly related to a country's exchange-rate regime, i.e. whether it is pegging its exchange rate to one major currency or a basket of currencies, and its pattern of international trade with reserve-currency centres (Heller and Knight, 1978) – the composition of foreign exchange reserves being determined by the need to intervene in foreign exchange markets to defend the value of the currency or to settle residual trade transactions. But perhaps the most important reason for currency diversification has been the highly unstable nature of the value of currencies and national interest rates. Rational risk-averse investment and borrowing behaviour requires a greater portfolio diversification of currency risks. The facilities for diversification have been provided by the Euro-currency market.

Since about 1974 about one-fifth of syndicated medium-term Euro-dollar credit agreements have included multicurrency loan options, which allow the borrower to switch part of the loan out of dollars into a specified alternative currency or currencies at one of the roll-over dates. These options, however, involve the borrower carrying the risk that the exchange rate in the stronger currencies will appreciate against the dollar, and have not been very widely utilised – but their use has been increasing. A small fraction of credits are also in non-dollar currencies; in most years it is around 2–4 per cent of the total volume. The volume of foreign and international bond issues in non-dollar currencies has grown rapidly. In 1978, at a time of high dollar interest rates and dollar depreciation, the proportion of issues in non-dollar currencies accounted for 70 per cent of total issues of around $30 billion equivalent. Central banks have also sought to diversify the currency composition of their foreign exchange reserves through the Euro-currency market. The use of the Euro-currency market was largely because of restrictions on asset holdings in the national markets of the currencies concerned.[5] Of identified total foreign exchange reserves held in Deutsche Mark about 60 per cent are held in the Euro-currency market (see Table 8.1), and this total grew rapidly in the years 1976–9.

An enlarged Euro-Deutsche Mark market, which was associated with an increased international role for the currency, might act to complicate policy formulation. Short-term fluctuations in a country's monetary policy or economic performance might lead to sudden shifts in the volume of externally held claims in the

Table 8.1
Diversification of official foreign exchange reserves ($ bn)

	1976	1977	1978	1979	1980
US dollars					
Claims on the USA	92	159	157	143	157
Euro-dollar deposits	47	53	62	73	78
(As percentage of total)	(34)	(25)	(28)	(34)	(33)
Deutsche Mark					
Claims on West Germany	5	7	11	14	20
Euro-Deutsche Mark deposits	8	12	17	24	24
(As percentage of total)	(62)	(63)	(60)	(63)	(54)

Source: BIS and IMF Annual Reports.

currency, which aggravate exchange-rate movements. Countries whose currencies are used widely internationally or are held as international reserves have to sustain a satisfactory economic performance if investors are not to lose confidence in the value of the currency, and this may place constraints on national economic policy. For these reasons, some strong currency countries have been for a time reluctant to see a greater international role for their currencies. However, it has become increasingly accepted that currencies should play an international role which reflects the relative economic position of the countries of the currencies concerned. Evidence of this is the official easing of restrictions on the international use of the Deutsche Mark and the yen, and the effective opening of the West German and Japanese domestic markets to foreign investors of short-term capital. This easing also reflected a turnaround in these countries' balance-of-payments positions and their need to attract capital inflows. The Euro-market may have acted to speed up the internationalisation process, but the figures in Table 8.1 do not suggest that its influence has been overwhelming.

8.2.1 *Theoretical considerations*

Without an active Euro-currency market speculative and arbitrage activity would be confined to operations in domestic markets and

the foreign exchange markets. A market operator wishing to speculate – i.e. to hold an open position in a currency – could sell a
depreciation-prone currency *forward* – e.g. for delivery three months
hence – in the expectation that, when the forward contract matured,
he would be able to make a profit by purchasing the currency in the
spot market at a price less than that at which he had contracted to
supply it in the forward market. Alternatively, a speculator could sell
spot either existing funds he held in the depreciation-prone currency
or currency borrowed in the domestic currency market, in the expectation of making a profit by repurchasing the domestic currency at a
later date (for example, when the domestic loan matured) at a price
less than he had previously sold it for. The difference in the current
and expected future spot rates is assumed to be more than sufficient
to cover any interest-rate costs of the transaction.

Speculation in the spot market is, however, partly conditional on
the absence of capital controls on flows of short-term capital between national money markets. These can restrict residents' holdings
of foreign currencies or non-residents' purchases of domestic currencies, and the ability of speculators to borrow a depreciation-prone
currency to sell spot. These restrictions would tend to concentrate
speculative activity in the forward market, though they might not
prevent speculative runs on currencies where there already exist large
external holdings of the currency in the domestic market, which was
a feature of sterling's problems and those of the dollar in 1978 and
1979. Nor do such restrictions prevent the type of currency speculation that results from the timing of trade payments abroad which is
an important element during periods of pressure on exchange rates.
When the domestic exchange rate is expected to depreciate, for
example, domestic importers of goods will speed up their payments
abroad in the depreciation-prone currency ('leading'), while domestic
exports will delay receiving payment in foreign currencies expected
to appreciate ('lagging').

The basic principles of speculation still apply to market operators
in the Euro-currency market: operators will tend to 'go short' in
currencies they expect to depreciate by selling them spot and forward, and to 'go long' in currencies expected to appreciate by
buying them spot and forward. In the Euro-markets there are,
however, no restrictions on moving between currencies. Thus when there
are restrictions on capital movements between national economies,
speculators may find it easier to borrow a depreciation-prone currency
and to hold assets denominated in an appreciation-prone currency. The
constellation of geographical, political and institutional risks and
transaction costs are different (Chapter 4), and this may encourage
a different structure of foreign asset holding which has implications

for exchange-rate movements; and the possibility that a currency can be borrowed and lent outside national capital controls may increase its international role. The type of process involved can be traced by examining the effects of an asset shift out of Euro-dollars into Euro-Deutsche Mark. Initially it is assumed that the German authorities are operating controls on capital inflows into West Germany.

Assuming that banks in the Euro-market are matching the currency composition of their assets and liabilities, the asset shift out of Euro-dollars into Euro-Deutsche Mark will lead initially to an excess supply of Deutsche Mark and excess demand for dollars in the Euro-market and will tend to appreciate the Deutsche Mark exchange rate as investors sell dollars for Deutsche Mark in the spot exchange market. To match these excess supplies and demands, banks in the Euro-market can sell Deutsche Mark spot for dollars, and cover, by buying Deutsche Mark in the forward market. The spot sales of Deutsche Mark will tend to offset the initial upward pressure on the Deutsche Mark exchange rate, while the forward purchases will bid up the forward premium on Deutsche Mark in the forward market.[6] At this stage the effect of asset diversification through the Euro-market is thus similar to taking a speculative position in the forward market; however, a statistical increase in Euro-Deutsche Mark liabilities would be recorded.

A rise in the forward premium on the Deutsche Mark will lower Euro-Deutsche Mark interest rates relative to Euro-dollar rates (recall that banks determine non-dollar Euro-currency rates as the Euro-dollar rate plus or minus the forward discount or premium of the currency against the dollar). This relative fall in Euro-Deutsche Mark rates may encourage some non German entities to shift from borrowing dollars to borrowing Deutsche Mark. The fall in Euro-Deutsche Mark interest rates might also discourage further asset diversification into Deutsche Marck. A shift by borrowers would mean, in effect, that the excess supplies and demands for each currency would be less and that banks would be required to undertake smaller matching spot sales and forward purchases of Deutsche Mark. The Deutsche Mark exchange rate would thus be somewhat higher than before the asset shift and Euro-Deutsche Mark interest rates would fall by a smaller amount. (This assumes that borrowers of Deutsche Mark do not sell all their new Deutsche Mark borrowing for dollars. If they did, the impact on the exchange rate would be similar to that described in the previous paragraph.) When the German authorities are fixing their exchange rate they would intervene to supply Deutsche Mark in the foreign exchange market. The official supply would meet the *net* new demand for Deutsche Mark by borrowers in the Euro-market and expand the overall stock of Deutsche Mark liquidity. Providing that German controls on capital inflows are effective, liquidity in the German domestic market should remain largely insulated, however, from the direct affects of diversification through the Euro-currency market.

When the authorities do not intervene to fix the exchange rate the *overall* stock of Deutsche Mark liquidity will initially be unaffected; however, its distribution may change. The rise in the Deutsche Mark exchange rate may entice some German residents to sell Deutsche Mark for dollars, increasing the internationally held stock of Deutsche Mark at the expense of domestically held stock. The fall in Euro-Deutsche Mark interest rates and the appreciation of the Deutsche Mark exchange rate may also encourage some international holders of Deutsche Mark to sell these for dollars. However, if there is some *net* new demand for Deutsche Mark by international borrowers, this would have to be met by sales of Deutsche Mark by German domestic holders. Thus, even if the authorities do not intervene in the foreign exchange markets, the international stock of the currency may increase.

Hence, when there are controls on capital inflows into West Germany, this analysis suggests that there are two possible outcomes for the international role of the Deutsche Mark. If international borrowers are insensitive to the fall in Euro-Deutsche Mark interest rates (or if they sell all their borrowing in Deutsche Mark for dollars), the diversification into Euro-Deutsche Mark may have little impact on the spot Deutsche Mark/dollar exchange rate or international Deutsche Mark liquidity. If, following the asset shift, there are net new borrowing demands for Euro-Deutsche Mark, these will either be met by official or German private sales of Deutsche Mark. International Deutsche Mark liquidity will tend to increase and the international role of the currency may expand. In both cases an increase in Euro-Deutsche Mark liabilities would be recorded. The reasons why international borrowers might be interest-rate sensitive or insensitive would of course involve a broad range of factors such as the currency's acceptability in international transactions, its future availability and the overall cost of borrowing including, *inter alia*, expected exchange-rate movements.

When there are no controls on capital inflows into West Germany the domestic and Euro-Deutsche Mark markets will become integrated (Chapter 5) and falls in Euro-Deutsche Mark interest rates relative to German domestic interest rates will bring forth arbitrage by German domestic banks. In these circumstances the effects of diversification through the Euro-market will be similar to those of diversification into the German domestic market directly. The Deutsche Mark would tend to appreciate, or unsterilised foreign exchange intervention by the German authorities would ease Deutsche Mark liquidity, including German domestic liquidity. The German authorities may, of course, seek to sterilise the effects of foreign exchange market intervention by selling securities from their own portfolio on the open market. In this case the Euro-market acts as a channel for inflows into the domestic market.

Diversification through the Euro-market may circumvent selective controls on capital inflows. For example, controls which prohibited foreign purchases of short-term domestic money market instruments, but which do not prevent foreign inflows through borrowing abroad by the domestic banking system, would be largely ineffective in insulating the domestic market from the liquidity effects of diversification through the Euro-market. In this respect the selective restrictions on non-resident purchases of short-term German domestic securities, enforced up to February 1981, may have been made ineffective by diversification into Euro-Deutsche Mark. Even when there are no controls on capital movements it is conceivable that Euro-Deutsche Mark and Euro-dollar deposits would be closer substitutes than assets in the German and US domestic markets, and thus that the amount of currency diversification would be larger and shifts between currencies more frequent. It is interesting, however, that with the easing from four years to one year in 1980 of the restrictions on the maturity of German domestic securities purchased by non-residents, all the increases in official holdings of Deutsche Mark took place in the German domestic market (see Table 8.1). There were similar large foreign inflows into Japan in 1980 following the relaxation of restrictions on non-resident purchases of domestic securities.

8.2.2   *Bank forward cover and spot exchange pressure*

With the advent of floating exchange rates it became much more important for traders to be able to obtain forward exchange market cover against possible erratic fluctuations in exchange rates. Banks are the main operators in the forward exchange market and their activity as 'market makers' and their willingness to take small open positions in currencies has greatly added to the depth and sophistication of the foreign exchange markets. Banks may, for example, run what is known as a 'jobber's book' and refrain from trading off small open currency positions until they have built up a position which is large enough to trade off in the wholesale market at more favourable rates of exchange. They may also take currency positions on their own account when they expect one currency to appreciate relative to another, i.e. they may speculate. Usually, however, these open currency positions are quite small and are not a major source of speculative pressure on exchange rates. (There are, of course, exceptions, for example the Herstatt crisis of 1974; see Chapter 2.)

The mechanism by which banks provide forward exchange cover for their customers may shift exchange-rate pressure from the forward to the spot market. Say a trader buys Japanese yen three months forward against the dollar from its bank in the Euro-currency market. The trader might be an American importer who has to meet a payment for goods from Japan in three months' time and wishes to protect himself against an unexpected appreciation in the yen. Initially, the bank will find itself with an open forward position in yen, as it has agreed to supply yen at a specified rate three months hence. To cover this position, the bank can (a) borrow the currency being sold forward by the trader – dollars – in the Euro-currency market; (b) sell the dollars spot for the currency being purchased forward – yen; and (c) invest the proceeds from the spot sale in the Euro-yen market in deposits of a maturity to coincide with the maturing forward contract – three months. In this way the bank can avoid the foreign exchange risk of the transaction: when the forward contract matures in three months' time the bank can exchange the maturing Euro-yen deposits, which the trader has contracted to buy, for the dollars the trader has contracted to sell and the bank can use the dollars to repay the initial Euro-dollar loan. The cost of the transaction to the trader – the three-month forward rate for yen against the dollar – is determined by the bank as the difference between the interest rates on the three-month Euro-dollar and Euro-yen deposits it initially borrows and lends respectively, plus a margin to cover the inconvenience of the operation to the bank. The implication of these transactions on the dollar/yen exchange rate is that the trader's need to meet a payment of goods from Japan in three months' time is transferred immediately to the spot exchange market, rather than being delayed until the payment falls due. If, however, there is a continuous flow of payments abroad, the pressures on the spot exchange rate need not be any greater than otherwise; and the action may lead to compensating capital movements depending on how other market operators react to the immediate fall in the spot dollar/yen exchange rate.

8.3   INTERDEPENDENT MONETARY POLICIES

'Autonomists' observe that a very large volume of capital movements indeed occurs through the Euro-currency market and they argue that this has placed additional constraints on national monetary policies by increasing the integration of national economies. They also argue that short-term capital flows are destabilising causing exchange rates to overshoot their long-run equilibrium values, aggravating domestic economic conditions; and that these effects cannot be dealt with solely by using exchange controls to restrict capital movements, as in the longer term these will be eroded and circumvented by the discovery of loopholes. To avoid the domestic policy implications the Euro-markets would have to be regulated directly: indeed, they would probably have to be regulated out of existence.

'Channelists' observe, however, that the problem of interdependent monetary policies derives mainly from the freedom of capital movements, and the Euro-market mechanism does not add to the linkages between economies. Because of the efficiency of arbitrage, Euro-currency interest rates are tied to those in domestic markets (Chapter 5). Short-term flows through the Euro-market occur mainly at the instigation of domestic banks and these would continue even if there were no Euro-currency market: they are a function of international banking and not just Euro-banking. To inhibit the Euro-currency channel would simply shift flows into others which might be even more difficult to monitor. They argue, moreover, that the worst short-term effects of capital flows can be avoided by controls on capital movements. Some also observe that the largest short-term capital movements result when countries' national economic performances and exchange-rate levels are out of line and require a fundamental correction, and that capital flows will tend to be stabilising rather than destabilising.

Any autonomous influence of the Euro-currency markets on international capital movements is extremely difficult to quantify as there are many channels for capital flows between national economies. The mechanisms in the market illustrate some of the problems and processes involved.

8.3.1   *Restricted capital movements*

Prior to the removal of controls on capital outflows from the USA the main concern about the Euro-currency market was that it autonomously added to the volume of capital flows outside these restrictions. It was argued that domestic corporations could borrow dollars in the Euro-dollar market and, by swapping these into their own currency, they were able to circumvent domestic credit policies designed to limit the domestic availability of credit. The problem is illustrated in Figure 8.1. The total supply of credit to domestic borrowers is shown as S_{e+d}, which is the sum of domestic currency loans supplied in the domestic market, S_d, and from dollar swaps

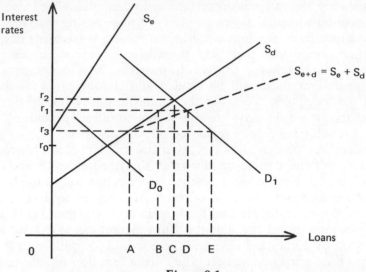

Figure 8.1

in the Euro-currency market, S_e. As domestic credit demands rise from D_0 to D_1 the domestic loan rate would increase towards r_2, and the cost of domestic borrowing would rise above the comparative interest rate in the Euro-currency market. The cost of borrowing in the Euro-currency market is determined mainly by the Euro-dollar rate and the forward rate of the domestic currency *vis-à-vis* the dollar in the foreign exchange market. Domestic borrowers may therefore turn to the Euro-currency market for the funds, and in equilibrium the loan rate in the two markets would be determined at the intersection of demand curve, D_1, and aggregate supply curve, S_{e+d}, at r_1. *OB* loans would be supplied in the domestic market and *BD* from the Euro-currency market, which increases the total availability of credit in the domestic economy to *OD*.

In 1970 under tight domestic monetary conditions the German corporate sector turned abroad and to the Euro-dollar market for credit totalling some DM 19.8 billion, which amounted to about 30 per cent of the sector's total borrowing (i.e. *BD/OD* = 0.3). This was generally believed to produce an expansion of credit much greater than the German authorities would otherwise have made available. McClam (1972) noted, however, that a large proportion of the credits from abroad would in any case have been provided by the domestic credit system. Figure 8.1 illustrates the process. In the absence of the Euro-currency credit market, domestic interest rates would have risen to r_2 and domestic credit supply would have increased to *OC*. The additional volume of Euro-market credit is thus only *CD* which McClam estimated to be only 35 per cent of the total external borrowing (i.e. *CD/BD* = 0.35). The additional contribution of the Euro-currency markets therefore amounted to only some 10 per cent of the German domestic sector's total borrowing (i.e. *CD/OD* = *BD/OD* x *CD/BD* = 0.10). The influence of external borrowing had therefore mainly been to keep domestic interest rates somewhat lower. The German authorities, by imposing domestic capital controls in 1972, appeared able to insulate their domestic market from the effects of external inflows in 1973.

Using these figures to obtain an estimate of the autonomous contribution of the Euro-currency market is not, however, as easy as this. The estimates clearly depend on assumptions about the elasticity of the supply curves. If the external interest rate had been fixed at r_3 (see Figure 8.1), total external borrowing would have been much greater and would have amounted to *AE*, of which *CE* would have been an additional flow of credit to domestic borrowers. Since there were restrictions on capital flows out of the USA it is quite possible that the costs of borrowing would have adjusted fairly rapidly, cutting off the external loan supply. When there are no restrictions the external credit supply is much more elastic (Chapter 5) and it is extremely difficult to isolate the specific influence of the Euro-market from the more general problem of the closer integration of national money markets.

This observation leads, however, to a second problem. Would the external supply of funds have been any different if there had been no Euro-currency market, even when there were restrictions on capital outflows from the USA? There was still scope for capital movements out of the USA – although this was less than perfect – and Euro-dollar rates, while not tied within an arbitrage band by the activities of US domestic banks, were fairly closely related to US domestic interest rates. The Euro-market may still have been performing the role of a channel for imperfect capital movements between national economies. The most likely answer is that the Euro-market probably did increase the elasticity of the external supply of funds to the German market, as a larger volume of dollar balances escaped the US restrictions, and the Euro market thus exposed the German domestic economy to a greater extent to international developments. However, the *autonomous* contribution of the Euro-market was probably even less than the 10 per cent estimated above.

Some other autonomous credit or money supply effects have also been attributed to the Euro-currency market. Money holdings might be shifted out of the Euro-market into the domestic market, which eases domestic liquidity and may add to the monetary base of the domestic banking system. But the specific influence on the domestic market is similar to that of the credit supply case: the main effect of the Euro-currency market was probably to expose the domestic economy to a greater extent to international monetary developments and to reduce somewhat the rise in national interest rates for a given restrictive policy stance.

On a more general point, several empirical studies have been made to test whether international capital mobility has made independent monetary policy impossible in a fixed-exchange-rate world.[7] Most of these in fact cover the period prior to the removal of capital controls in the USA in 1974 and therefore are more representative of a world of restricted capital mobility. The results showed that national authorities could partly offset the influence of capital inflows through domestic sterilisation policies. In examining empirically German experience over the years 1960–71 Herring and Marston (1977) concluded that the Bundesbank *was capable* of sterilising the impact of enormous flows of foreign exchange reserves, though the costs were ultimately too high and led to the abandonment of a fixed exchange rate.[8] Even in a fixed-exchange-rate world of less than perfect freedom of capital mobility authorities had therefore some scope for independent monetary policy.

8.3.2   *Free capital mobility*

Consequences for the independence of national monetary policy become much more acute where there is free international capital mobility. The closer integration of national money markets through capital flows has meant that the influence of one country's monetary policy is felt much more rapidly on another's, which reduces the freedom for independent policy action on interest rates or exchange rates by an individual country. The growth of the Euro-currency markets, it is said, by increasing the efficiency of international capital flows, has added to this financial integration. In particular, it is suggested, the existence of a market for dollar deposits in Europe has caused the effects of US monetary policy to influence European monetary policy to a greater extent by adding to the channels for international dollar flows.

Fixed exchange rates.   Consider what happens if the British authorities seek to raise domestic interest rates by selling Treasury bills. At the initial level of Euro-sterling interest rates the rise in domestic sterling interest rates will make it profitable for UK banks to borrow Euro-sterling and place it in the UK market. This they can do by borrowing

Euro-dollars, selling the dollars for sterling in the spot exchange market, while covering any foreign exchange risks of the transaction in the forward exchange market, i.e. UK banks 'switch' out of dollars into sterling. Under the fixed-exchange-rate regime two results follow. The switch out of Euro-dollars into domestic sterling will raise the supply of liquidity in the UK economy, as the UK authorities buy the dollars sold spot for sterling by banks. This increase in liquidity will tend to push UK rates back towards their previous level, defeating the initial restrictive action, unless the British authorities sterilise the inflow. At the same time, borrowing of Euro-dollars by banks in the Euro-currency market will tend to raise Euro-dollar interest rates and to widen interest-rate differentials with US domestic interest rates. This encourages banks and wealth-holders in the USA to shift deposits to the Euro-dollar market, avoiding any exchange risk, tending to offset the rise in Euro-dollar interest rates. Without further action by the UK authorities, UK and Euro-dollar interest rates will return to near their previous levels, the restrictive effects of the UK sale of Treasury bills having been met by an arbitrage flow of funds out of the USA to the UK market via the Euro-currency market.

If the British authorities now attempt to sterilise the effects of the inflow by selling more Treasury bills, this will encourage an additional round of inflows into the United Kingdom from the Euro-dollar market, and outflows from the USA, which will frustrate the policy and, in the extreme, make it ineffective. The domestic sterling interest rate, $r_£^d$, is constrained to equal the Euro-dollar rate, $r_\$^e$, minus the forward discount of the dollar against sterling in the forward exchange market, F, within some transaction margins, α, which reflect bank arbitrage costs and other market imperfections:

$$r_£^d = r_\$^e - F + \alpha \qquad (1)$$

Given that efficient international bank arbitrage limits the fluctuations in the arbitrage margins, α, the ability of the UK authorities to raise domestic interest rates then depends on movements in the Euro-dollar rate or the forward exchange rate. US domestic interest rates might rise as banks bid for funds to arbitrage with the Euro-dollar market, leading to some upward movement in $r_\$^e$. But usually, because of the size of the US economy, US domestic interest rates are dominated by US domestic monetary conditions and the compensating movement in Euro-dollar rates is therefore likely to be small. In the forward market UK banks will be selling sterling (demanding forward dollars) to cover their spot sterling purchases and this will tend to narrow F and Euro-sterling interest rates will tend to rise towards the level set by the authorities in the UK market. What then becomes crucial are the expectations of speculators in the forward exchange market.

Writing the forward dollar/sterling discount as $F = (s^f - s)/s$, where s is the spot dollar/sterling exchange rate (dollars per pound) and s^f the forward spot rate, equation (1) is rewritten as:

$$s^f = s(r_\$^e - r_\pounds^d + \alpha + 1) \tag{1a}$$

Now the expectation to speculators of making a profit on a forward transaction is the difference between s^f and their expected future spot rate, s^e. Equilibrium between the speculative supply of forward exchange and the interest arbitrage schedule thus requires:

$$s^e = s(r_\$^e - r_\pounds^d + \alpha + 1)$$

Under the fixed-exchange-rate regime, and the assumptions of exogenous US interest rates and efficient international bank arbitrage, s, $r_\$^e$ and α are given. There is therefore a direct trade-off between the speculative supply of forward exchange – which depends on speculative expectation about the future spot rate, s^e – and the domestic sterling interest rate (determined by the sales of Treasury bills by the UK authorities). The more elastic the speculative supply schedule, the more difficult it will be for the authorities to run an independent interest-rate policy.[9]

This conclusion is not substantially different from the one in the world of less than perfect capital mobility. The effect of international bank arbitrage when there is free capital mobility is to limit the deviation of interest rates from interest-rate parity, i.e. to reduce the transaction margins α within which interest-rate parity holds. The smaller the value of α, the larger is the necessary adjustment in the forward exchange rate and thus speculative expectations about the future spot rate, s^e, which is required to validate the national interest-rate policy. *Ceteris paribus*, such adjustments will involve larger capital inflows. One policy option which authorities may use is to place reserve requirements on domestic banks' foreign borrowing, as this will affect the transaction margins, α, at which domestic banks find it profitable to arbitrage with the Euro-currency market (see Chapter 5).

The effects of bank arbitrage on capital flows are shown diagrammatically in Figure 8.2 using the analysis developed in Chapter 5. As before, *DD* represents the arbitrage demand for forward cover and *SS* the speculative supply in the forward exchange market. Initially, without interbank arbitrage the demand schedule *DD* is elastic but

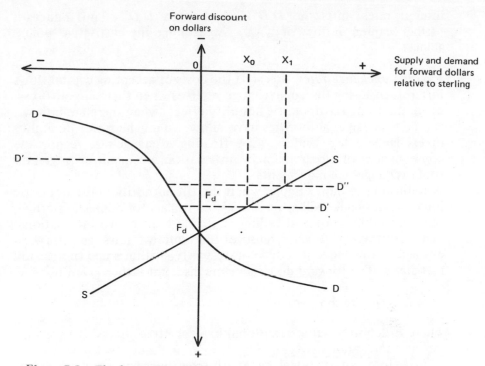

Figure 8.2   The forward exchange market with and without banking arbitrage

not perfectly so because non-bank wealth-holders do not treat domestic and foreign assets as perfectly substitutable. Non-banks may, for example, face a number of transaction costs when arbitraging between domestic and foreign assets; the risks of domestic and foreign assets will differ slightly even when held in covered form and the portfolio approach to asset selection implies that there will be diminishing returns to the international diversification of wealth-holders' portfolios. The borrowing costs to non-banks in the Euro-market will also differ from the interbank rates by the lending margins demanded by intermediaries. Introducing interbank arbitrage causes the demand for forward cover to shift to $D'D'$, as banks treat domestic and Euro-currency assets and liabilities as much closer substitutes (Chapter 5) and can also command the finest terms in the interbank market. At an original forward discount on dollars of F_d, banks therefore find it profitable to borrow dollars and swap them into sterling, and they would continue to do so until the forward discount on dollars narrows to F_d'. This action induces a net capital flow into the UK domestic market of OX_0 greater than the inflow under the non-bank arbitrage schedule. An attempt by UK authorities to raise domestic interest rates shifts the $D'D'$ schedule to $D'D''$ and induces a further capital inflow of X_0X_1, weakening the restrictive policy stance.

Floating exchange rates. Because the costs of accepting capital flows in terms of losing foreign exchange reserves when there are outflows, or of sterilising the domestic liquidity effects when there are inflows, can be very large, authorities have allowed a much greater flexibility in exchange rates. Under a free floating exchange-rate regime the consequences of closer financial integration are manifest in greater spot exchange-rate movements.

Returning to our example, when the UK authorities raise domestic interest rates banks will again swap Euro-dollars for domestic sterling, buying sterling spot and selling it forward. Effective international bank arbitrage will again ensure that interest rates and forward exchange rates move to interest-rate parity, within some transaction margins, α. The forward dollar/sterling discount is then given by:

$$\bar{F} = r_{\$}^e - r_{£}^d + \alpha$$

where $\bar{F}$ denotes that international bank arbitrage 'fixes' the forward rate at interest-rate parity.

As before, international bank arbitrage limits the movements in the forward exchange rate and equilibrium between speculators and arbitrators requires that, from equation (2),

$$s^e = s(\bar{F} + 1) \tag{2a}$$

Now, if $\bar{F}$ is set by national interest-rate policy and bank arbitrage, the spot rate, s, will be determined only by the expectations of speculators.[10] With $\bar{F}$ given, in the fixed-exchange-rate world speculative expectations determine the size of capital inflows, and in the free-floating world they determine the size of the movements in the spot exchange rate. If the authorities alter national interest rates, and thus $\bar{F}$, the spot rate will respond both to the change in interest rates and speculative expectations. When the speculative supply schedule is elastic, so that s^e is invariant to movements in the forward discount, then the whole influence of changing national interest rates will fall on the spot rate. International bank arbitrage, by reducing the margins for fluctuations in forward rates away from interest-rate parity, i.e. the transaction margins, α, and increasing the depth and sophistication of the forward market, will then increase speculative and arbitrage influences on the spot rate. Spot exchange rates may therefore become more volatile as they fluctuate directly with relative interest-rate movements and changing speculative expectations.[11] If, however, interest rates are not constrained to be at interest-rate parity by international bank arbitrage, perhaps because there are controls on capital movements, the arbitrage margin, α, may fluctuate to offset partly movements in national and Euro-currency interest rates, and the influence of interest-rate movements and speculative expectations on the spot rate will be reduced.

8.3.3   *An assessment*

Thus when international arbitrage is efficient it will tend to mean that the domestic economy is exposed to a greater extent to international developments. In the fixed-exchange-rate world the authorities will have to accept a larger volume of capital inflows (or outflows) for any given interest-rate policy; in the floating-exchange-rate world arbitrageurs will dominate speculators in the forward market and the spot rate will fluctuate by larger amounts. These effects are not necessarily adverse since the efficiency of arbitrage will also tend to mean that authorities will be better able to attract larger capital inflows to finance international payments imbalances or use interest rates to protect the level of their exchange rates. The mechanism of the process is, however, of interest and this has been described using the links between domestic and Euro-currency markets. The important question is whether the intermediary link provided by the Euro-market is essential for the processes described.

We can note first of all that arbitrage is only one side of the market. In both examples speculative expectations play an especially important role: arbitrageurs are setting the parameters of the system and speculators are determining the volume of capital flows. Speculative expectations are based on factors largely outside the Euro-currency market, within national economies. Banks may take small open foreign exchange positions themselves, but they are not a major source of speculative activity. It is therefore correct to conclude that a very large volume of capital flows will be caused by factors which have nothing at all to do with the Euro-market.

Second, we have observed (Chapter 5) that the major factor determining flows through the Euro-market is the level of national interest rates (and reserve requirements). If no Euro-market existed, it is quite plausible that international arbitrage between different domestic markets would be as efficient. In the example UK banks could have borrowed funds directly from banks in the USA at the same interest rates as in the Euro-currency market. The Euro-market would be acting purely as a channel for flows and would have absolutely no autonomous influence on the integration of national economies.

Third, however, there are reasons for the existence of Euro-currency markets (Chapter 4). One is the efficiency of the market as a global clearing system for international capital flows and its role as a low-cost transactions centre. Causes normally do have some effect and the intermediary function of the Euro-market is unlikely to be a solely neutral one. Institutional links between peripheral-area banks and the Euro-currency centre will tend to mean that flows are passed more efficiently through the Euro-market than directly between peripheral-area banks. The Euro-currency system will thus tend to increase somewhat the interest elasticity of capital movements by reducing the transaction margins, α in our equations.

To return to the original question posed at the beginning of the chapter — how much more difficult do Euro-markets make national policy formulation? — in the context of the integration of national economies, the answer is that they may make economies more open and expose them to a greater extent to international monetary and interest-rate developments. That has its benefits and costs. When there are controls on capital movements, the Euro-markets may add to the volume of currency flows outside the controls; when there are no controls, the Euro-market may add somewhat to capital mobility. However, the Euro-market is not some uncontrolled autonomous force, but essentially a rather efficient intermediary, or if you prefer a channel, for international capital movements between national economies. This conclusion will have to be revised, however, if the market has an autonomous ability to expand the volume of the world money stock and which could add to the global volume of capital flows — a question to which we turn in the next chapter.

NOTES

1. For a cross-section of the various views expressed in the debate see the statements by Bryant, Heller, Weatherstone and Wallich (US House of Representatives, 1979), Kessler (1980), McMahon (1976), Richardson (1979) and Savona (1974).
2. The classic reference is Friedman (1969); see, however, Klopstock's (1970) reply.
3 The Act, which became effective in September 1980, allows, however, for an eight-year phase-in of reserve requirements for non-member depository institutions. For a discussion of the Act and its theoretical effects, which are also relevant for an analysis of the influence of the Euro-market, see Klein (1981).

4. This argument has been made by Crockett and Knight (1978).
5. In *West Germany*, in December 1977, the authorities imposed restrictions on the acquisition by non-residents of domestic securities of maturities under four years. The maturity was shortened to two years in March 1980, to one year in November of that year and removed altogether in February 1981. In September 1979 the Bundesbank also sought to dissuade domestic banks from offering floating rate time deposits because of their attraction to foreign investors. In *Japan*, numerous restrictions were also enforced, but these were relaxed in 1979 and 1980. From November 1977 to February 1979 marginal reserve requirements were imposed on non-resident yen deposits (initially introduced at 50 per cent, the marginal reserve requirements were raised to 100 per cent in March 1978, then lowered to 50 per cent in January 1979 and to 0 per cent in February 1979). The outstanding maturity of yen securities purchased by non-residents was lowered from over five to over one year in January 1979 and removed in February 1979. In May 1979 restrictions on non-resident purchases of yen stocks were relaxed and non-residents were given free access to the Gensaki market; in March 1980 holdings of yen deposits by foreign official bodies were exempted from interest-rate ceilings and in December 1980 all external transactions were in principle freed from controls. There remain, however, interest-rate ceilings on bank deposit rates and quantitative limits on the volume of CDs issued.
6. This assumes, of course, that the forward rate can move, i.e. there is not a perfectly elastic supply of forward Deutsche Mark at the previous expected future Deutsche Mark/dollar spot rate. When the general principles of portfolio theory apply to speculators in the foreign exchange market, speculators should require some increase in expected returns to be willing to accept larger open forward positions, which would imply some rise in the forward exchange rate at which speculators are willing to deal. It is possible that there would be some combination of spot and forward rate movements which would leave the forward premium on Deutsche Mark unchanged. All that can be said is that the larger the offsetting spot sales of Deutsche Mark by banks and the larger their demand for forward Deutsche Mark, the greater will be the pressure on the Deutsche Mark's forward premium.
7. For a survey of the empirical work and a comprehensive analysis of the process of financial integration the reader is referred to Llewellyn (1980).
8. Other studies which indicate evidence of partly effective sterilisation policies are Argy and Kouri (1974), Porter (1972) and Kouri and Porter (1974).
9. The statistical work of Herring and Marston (1977) and Beenstock (1978) indicated that the speculative supply was reasonably inelastic and that movements in the forward exchange rate would limit the volume of capital flows.
10. Beenstock (1978) and McKinnon (1979, ch. 7) make a similar point.
11. To see this effect in more detail equation (2a) can be rewritten as:

$$s = \frac{s^e}{(\overline{F} + 1)}$$

and in rates of change as:

$$\dot{s} = \dot{s}^e - (\bar{F} \overset{\cdot}{+} 1) \tag{3}$$

$$= \dot{s}^e - \frac{1}{(\bar{F} + 1)} \frac{d}{dt} (r_\$^e - r_\pounds^d + \alpha)$$

The rate of change in the spot dollar/sterling exchange rate is decomposed into the rate of change in speculative expectations $\dot{s}^e$ and the rate of change in the forward dollar/sterling discount. As the forward discount narrows from a rise in domestic sterling interest rates, which causes banks to buy sterling spot and sell it forward, the spot number of dollars per pound rises, the dollar weakens and sterling strengthens. If $\dot{s}^e = 0$, the speculative supply schedule is perfectly elastic — i.e. speculative expectations are perfectly inelastic to movements in international interest-rate differentials — and if α is constant because of international arbitrage, the spot exchange rate will fluctuate directly with interest-rate differentials.

9 The Euro-currency Multiplier*

One of the most controversial issues surrounding the development of Euro-currency banking concerns the ability of Euro-markets to expand autonomously the stock of money and credit outside the control of national authorities. The rapid expansion of international banking aggregates, which have grown by around 25 per cent per annum, is said itself to provide evidence of monetary expansion in the Euro-market. A short-hand name frequently used to describe this process is the Euro-currency credit or deposit multiplier. This chapter reviews the models that have been used to estimate and explain the size of these 'multiplier' effects, and their implications for the rate of expansion of the Euro-currency market. Two distinct approaches have been adopted: one characterises the depositing and redepositing process by fixed coefficients (discussed in section 9.1), the other suggests that the size of any multiplier is variable and reflects general portfolio considerations and interest-rate adjustments (section 9.2). Both depend on making plausible guesses of the likely size of the coefficients and interest-rate adjustments to estimate the size of the multiplier. Some new approaches have therefore evolved to explain the growth and influence of the Euro-market in terms of empirically observed institutional links with national banking systems (section 9.3).

9.1 FIXED-COEFFICIENT MODELS

There is widespread agreement that financial intermediation can add to the stock of liabilities of financial intermediaries. Only two conditions are required for this to happen: that financial intermediation should have some net expansionary effect on the nominal levels of income and wealth, and that wealth-holders should have a propensity to hold part of nominal additions to wealth or income in the form of deposits with intermediaries. Multiplier theory, however, takes the

---

* This chapter is a shortened and revised version of R. B. Johnston, 'Theories of the growth of the Euro-currency market: a review of the Euro-currency deposit multiplier', *BIS Economic Paper No. 4*, May 1981.

view that the liquidity effects of groups of financial intermediaries and the redepositing of funds lent out by them with themselves can be characterised by fixed or predictable ratios, and that multiplier effects will generally tend to be positive and large. The underlying hypothesis is that some automatic process causes the loans of the banking system or group of intermediaries to be returned to it as new deposits. These models are most often applied to domestic banking systems where the liabilities of the intermediary act predominantly as a means of payment, deposits are subject to legally determined (or institutionally predictable) reserve ratios and the stock of bank reserves is exogenously determined by national monetary authorities. The automatic process which returns the loans of the banking system to it as new deposits is seen as the need to use the bank liabilities as a means of payment.

Some factors suggest that these multiplier models could be extended to the Euro-currency market. A proportion of Euro-currency deposits may substitute for domestic means of payment, for example when Euro-currency balances are used to make foreign trade payments and held instead of making spot purchases of foreign currencies. There are close institutional links between Euro-banks and domestic commercial banks, more so perhaps than between banks and other types of financial intermediaries; and although not subject to legal reserve ratios, Euro-banks hold some precautionary reserve balances, which might even be viewed by some as the reserve base of the Euro-currency system, to cover operating needs and the risk of withdrawal of deposits. However, the wholesale nature of Euro-banking is not at all similar to domestic retail banking, and Euro-currency deposits are, most likely, closer substitutes for less liquid assets in the portfolios of wealth-holders than for balances normally held for use as a means of payment. The reflow of private funds to the Euro-market must therefore involve a range of factors and not just their use in making payments.

9.1.1   *The analytical framework*

Multiplier theory is concerned with dynamic processes; there are initial inputs in the form of non-bank deposits and final outputs in the form of bank credits and new bank deposits. At least two agents are involved in this process — the banking system, and the non-bank public — and they interact one with another to produce the final outcome for credits and deposits. A third agent, which is also important, is the domestic central bank, but in these simple multiplier models central bank activities can usually be assumed to be exogenous.

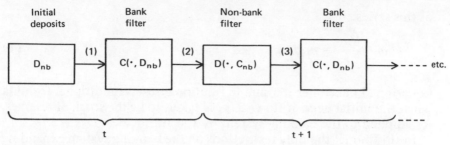

| Initial deposits | | Bank filter | | Non-bank filter | | Bank filter | |

Figure 9.1

Each agent may be viewed as a filtering system through which the stocks of deposits and credits are passed. This is illustrated in Figure 9.1.

This diagram shows an initial stock of non-bank deposits, D_{nb}, at time t; this is passed to the banking system (flow 1), which makes loans to the public. The size of the loans depends on the filter, $C(.,D_{nb})$, a function of the supply of bank deposits and other, as yet unspecified, factors. The action of making loans adds to non-bank liquidity (flow 2) and this additional liquidity is passed through the non-banking sector and its filter, $D(.,C_{nb})$, a function of the size of bank loans, C_{nb}, and other factors, and a proportion is then returned to the banking system (flow 3). The process can then begin again until some final equilibrium is established, which depends on the values of the various filters, i.e. whether they dampen or amplify the deposit and loan flows.

The simplest approach to these filters is the fractional reserve or deposit multiplier. This specifies

$$C(. , D_{nb}) = 1 - r,$$

where r is the fraction of deposits sterilised as holdings of reserves by the banking system, and

$$D(. , C_{nb}) = 1,$$

all additions to non-bank liquidity being returned to the banking system.

The redepositing chain from the initial stock of non-bank deposits is then:

$$D_{nb}^{F} = D_{nb} + (1 - r)D_{nb} + \ldots$$

and the final stock of bank deposits held by non-banks, D_{nb}^{F}, the sum of this series:

$$D_{nb}^F = \frac{D_{nb}}{r} = m_1 D_{nb} \tag{1}$$

Equation (1) becomes the simple fractional reserve multiplier formula when the initial deposit flow, D_{nb}, is taken to be the stock of reserves, R, supplied to the banking system by the authorities, $D_{nb}^F = R/r$.

In this model the only restrictions on the banking system expanding the stock of its deposits by a multiple of any initial flow is the sterilisation of deposits as reserve holdings, or the size of the exogenous supply of initial deposits or reserves to the banking system. The filtering system is therefore a very simple one.

A slightly more sophisticated approach is the leakage model, which allows the non-bank sector to redeposit some net additions to liquidity outside the banking system. In terms of the filtering model:

$$C(. , D_{nb}) = 1 - r$$

$$D(. , C_{nb}) = 1 - b,$$

where b, the leakage coefficient, represents the fixed proportion of additions to non-bank liquidity held outside the Euro-market.

The redepositing chain is

$$D_{nb}^F = D_{nb} + (1 - r)(1 - b) D_{nb} + \ldots$$

giving the familiar multiplier formula:

$$D_{nb}^F = \frac{1}{1 - (1 - r)(1 - b)} D_{nb} = m_2 D_{nb} \tag{2}$$

When $D_{nb} = R$, equation (2) can be interpreted as a reserve-base multiplier. The size of the redepositing multiplier, m_2, now depends on the sterilisation of deposits as reserves and non-bank leakages to other assets. The larger these leakages, the smaller the multiplier.

A third type of model, the multi-stage banking model, views the Euro-currency market as part of a larger financial system made up of Euro-banks and domestic banks. Non-banks disperse their deposits between the two markets, depending on some decision rule, and Euro-banks hold their reserves with the domestic banking system. This model recognises somewhat more explicitly than the previous leakage model that the Euro-currency market is an open banking system and that the precautionary reserve balances of Euro-banks are held with domestic commercial banks rather than central banks. There is therefore a feedback from expanding Euro-banking activity to the size of domestic bank deposits, which reduces the overall reserve leakage from the banking system. An assumption of the analysis is that if deposits were not held in the Euro-market they would be held automatically in the same currency with domestic banks, and subject to domestic reserve requirement regulations. Such an assumption will be unwarranted if Euro-markets change the currency preference of depositors. The process is illustrated in Figure 9.2.

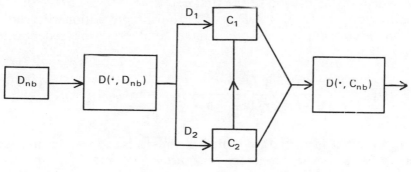

Figure 9.2

Non-banks have an initial stock of deposits, D_{nb}; the holding of these in the domestic market, D_1, or the Euro-currency market, D_2, is determined by the dispersion filter, $D(.,D_{nb})$, which depends on the amount of deposits and some other factors. This is normally specified simply as:

$$D(.,D_{nb}):D_2 = (1 - b)D_{nb}$$

a fixed portion $(1 - b)$ of initial deposits, D_{nb}, being held in Euro-banks. These two deposit flows pass through different banking filters, C_1 and C_2, which depend on the different reserve ratios held by each banking system:

$$C_1 = 1 - r_1$$

where r_1 is the proportion of deposits placed with the domestic banking system which is sterilised by legally imposed domestic reserve requirements; and

$$C_2 = 1 - r_2$$

where r_2 is the precautionary reserve ratio held by Euro-banks, against their deposits, with domestic banks.

The redepositing chain for the combined non-bank holdings of deposits in the domestic and Euro-currency market then becomes:

$$D_{nb}^F = D_{nb} + \{[bD_{nb} + r_2 (1 - b) D_{nb}] (1 - r_1)$$

$$+ (1 - b) D_{nb} (1 - r_2)\} + \ldots$$

where the first square-bracketed term shows the amount of domestic bank deposits at the end of the first depositing stage — bD_{nb} of non-bank deposits and $r_2(1 - b)D_{nb}$ of Euro-bank precautionary reserves.

Simplifying this formula gives the total non-bank redepositing multiplier as:

$$D_{nb}^F = \frac{1}{r_1 [1 - (1 - r_2)(1 - b)]} D_{nb} = m_3 D_{nb} \qquad (3)$$

If the initial deposits, D_{nb}, reflect the reserves supplied to domestic banks by domestic monetary authorities, R, and D_{nb}^F, the total money stock, then formula (3) can also be taken to explain the impact of a change in national bank reserves on the total money stock and the influence of the Euro-market on this process. It is immediately apparent from equation (3) that the larger the proportion of total deposits held in the Euro-currency market $(1 - b)$, then the the multiplier (m_3).

All three fixed-coefficient models have been used to estimate the liquidity-creating effect of the Euro-market by making guesses at the size of the various coefficients, r, b, etc. Certain assumptions are, however, needed before this is possible.

First, none of the models say anything about the *demand* for loans from the banking system, which may limit the ability of the banks to expand their balance-sheets. The state of the world must therefore be such either that there is very buoyant loan demand or that the supply of loans, perhaps by depressing the level of loan rates and expanding the level of nominal incomes, creates its own demand. Indeed, it is through such nominal income effects that multiplier theorists might see the dynamics of the feedback process working as expanding bank credit adds to inflation or real-income levels and thus to a demand for new bank deposits. To isolate the multiplier it is necessary, however, to be able to distinguish between such bank lending induced depositing from other sources of funds to the Euro-market which have nothing to do with credit expansion in the market.

In practice this is not easily done and therefore the analysis has to make *a priori* guesses about the size of leakages from the market. Rapid growth of Euro-currency deposits does not necessarily imply multiple credit creation.

A second assumption is that banks are willing to *supply* loans by the amount of new deposits and thus take on new lending risks, possibly at lower rates of return. There are other constraints on banking activity — the supply of equity and risk capital and management services — which must be assumed not to be binding.

Third, the various reserve and redepositing ratios, i.e. the filters, must be assumed to be reasonably stable or predictable. If this is not so, the economic value of the estimated multipliers is limited and can at most be taken as an explanation of *ex post* behaviour. It is quite likely, however, that the various filters will be highly unstable. Certainly, it seems most unlikely that the $C(.,D_{nb})$ filter will be characterised by a simple sterilisation of deposits through reserve holdings. The willingness of non-banks to redeposit funds in the Euro-currency banking system, the $D(.,C_{nb})$ filter, will also vary sharply over time, depending on the structure of national controls on capital movements, banking regulations, the varying degree of risk of Euro-currency deposits, relative Euro-currency and domestic interest rates and whether any liquidity effects that occur in the Euro-market are sterilised by national central banks. The assumption of a fixed leakage coefficient is at most an average approximation to reality; and even the average multiplier will be impossible to identify without knowledge of or assumption about the underlying structural relationships.

Finally, initial deposit flows or the stock of reserves made available to the banking system must be assumed exogenous, if they are to impose an effective constraint on the lending activity of banks.

With these qualifications in mind, we proceed to discuss the various estimates of the multiplier that have been made.

9.1.2 *Multiplier estimates*

Fractional reserve estimates. The simplest, but intellectually most unsatisfactory, approach is to attempt to estimate the reserve stock held by Euro-banks, R_E, and then to use equation (1) to calculate the multiplier as the *ex post* ratio of Euro-currency deposits, D_{nb}^F, to the reserve stock, under the assumptions that the only restriction on Euro-banks' balance-sheets is the exogenously given reserve base, and that there is a stable relationship between the final volume of lending and the reserves held by Euro-banks. The multiplier, m_1, is then:

$$m_1 = \frac{1}{r} = \frac{D_{nb}^F}{R_E}$$

A fundamental problem with this approach is, however, the assumption that the reserve base of the Euro-currency system is an exogenous variable and that causality runs from the supply of reserves to the stock of bank liabilities and assets. As balances with domestic commercial banks, which make up only a small fraction of domestic banks' total deposit liabilities, there is no reason why the reserves of the Euro-currency market should be exogenously determined. It is much more likely that causality runs from the supply of deposits to the Euro-currency market to their holdings of precautionary balances, and not the other way around. Thus there is no reason why the supply of reserves to the Euro-market should impose *any* constraint on Euro-banks expanding their balance-sheets, as fractional reserve theory suggests. Consequently, if a simple fractional redepositing multiplier exists, it should be able to proceed virtually without limit (or until Euro-banks had absorbed the complete stock of liabilities of the US and indeed other national banking systems as precautionary balances). The fact that it has not must imply that the re-depositing multiplier is limited by factors other than the reserve holdings of Euro-banks, which should be seen as only one of a number of leakages of deposits from the Euro-currency banking system.

There is also a major statistical difficulty with this approach: how can one measure D_{nb}^F and R_E? Indeed, several attempts have been made at this; most assume that D_{nb}^F, the stock of non-bank deposits, can be approximated by the net size of the Euro-dollar market, and R_E by some aggregate of the liquid liabilities of US domestic banks to foreign commercial banks. Any estimates derived from this approach, however, tend to be very diverse depending on the exact definition of the reserve base, ranging from 3.7[1] to 18.5.[2] Willms (1976) has undertaken several simulations to show in fact how diverse and unstable these multiplier estimates can be, ending with the conclusion that 'this type of multiplier approach is not a very meaningful concept'. Makin (1973) has attempted to estimate a model to explain the precautionary reserve holdings of Euro-banks which may explain some of the instability in reserve holdings. He does this in terms of the opportunity cost of holding precautionary reserves (measured as the three-month Euro-dollar rate), the cost of running out of reserves (measured by the US three-month certificate of deposit rate), the variance of the change in Euro-banks' total assets, Euro-banks' total assets and a time trend. The variables with the largest explanatory power in his equation were trend variables – the time trend and Euro-banks' total assets – which suggest to him that there have been large economies of scale in the management of precautionary balances as the volume of receipts and disbursements of the financial intermediaries rose over time.

Even these statistical estimates raise problems. All studies have used the BIS measure of the net size of the Euro-currency market, or some variant of it, as the proxy for Euro-banks' liabilities for the calculation of the multiplier. However, this includes not only sources of funds from non-banks but also sources from banks (see Chapter 3). What is relevant, however, is the amount of funds sterilised as reserves by the *banking system* in intermediating directly between non-banks. Interbank trading is part of and not an addition to this process and should be completely netted out of the estimates. Moreover, to the extent that banks are themselves net suppliers of Euro-currency funds, these presumably will have been caught within national money stocks and subject to national reserve requirements. They need not be counted again. The estimates of the multiplier based on the BIS net measure of the Euro-currency market therefore exaggerate the fractional reserve multiplier as applied to non-bank deposits.

Leakage model estimates. The second approach to estimating the Euro-currency multiplier is to use the leakage model, equation (2), and make guesses at the size of the reserve ratio, r, and the leakage coefficient, b. The redepositing multiplier is then derived as:

$$m_2 = \frac{1}{1 - (1 - r)(1 - b)} = \frac{1}{r + b - rb}$$

Clearly the larger is b, the leakage of additions to non-bank liquidity out of Euro-currency deposits to other assets, the smaller will be the multiplier. Indeed, for a reasonably large value of b it does not really matter what size r is, as the multiplier will still be small. Table 9.1 provides the calculations. The interesting question is: what determines the size of b?

Analysts usually proceed by defining a group of Euro-currency, or more usually Euro-dollar, assets or asset holders and they use the *ex post* ratio of Euro-currency (or Euro-dollar) holdings to the total (or dollar) assets of the group as the estimate of $1 - b$. The assumption is that average holdings of assets are a good proxy for marginal disbursements. Lee (1973), for example, defines the asset group as the short-term dollar claims of foreigners including central banks and derives the Euro-currency multiplier as 1.27 in 1963 and 1.92 in

Table 9.1
**Leakage model multipliers for various leakage
and reserve ratios**

Leakage coefficient (b)	Reserve ratio (r)			
	0.2	0.1	0.05	0.0
	EURO-DEPOSIT MULTIPLIER			
1.0	1.00	1.00	1.00	1.00
0.8	1.19	1.22	1.23	1.25
0.6	1.47	1.56	1.61	1.67
0.4	1.92	2.17	2.33	2.50
0.2	2.78	3.57	4.17	5.00
0.0	5.00	10.00	20.00	∞

Note: Calculations based on equation (2), p. 220.

1969. However, the fact that his estimate of the multiplier has risen suggests that average behaviour is not a good proxy for marginal behaviour and that the multiplier has been understated. But it is impossible to judge how much of the increase reflects bank lending induced redepositing rather than an exogenous change in preferences for Euro-currency deposits. Swoboda (1980) compares total Euro-dollar holdings of non-banks with different definitions of US money supply. This gives very high leakage coefficients of between 92 and 98 per cent. Assuming a Euro-currency reserve ratio of $r = 0.01$ gives a multiplier in the range of 1.02 to 1.09. Similar estimates about the size of the multiplier have been derived by Mayer (1979b). The conclusion from these models is therefore that any Euro-currency multiplier is very small indeed. Clearly, however, these estimates depend on the choice of asset stock for comparison with Euro-currency holdings, and Swoboda's comparison between non-bank Euro-dollar holdings and US monetary aggregates is not a very good one when 80 per cent of non-bank Euro-dollar deposits are held by non-US residents. Euro-dollars will also substitute for broad money holdings in the countries of the investors concerned and the leakage out of Euro-dollars would be divided into a leakage to the USA, b_1, and to other national markets, b_2. The revised formula for the multiplier is then:

$$m_2 = \frac{1}{1 - (1 - r)[1 - b_1 - b_2]}$$

When these alternative leakages are allowed for (see Table 9.2) the non-bank Euro-dollar multiplier is even smaller and comes out at only 1.03.

The role of central bank deposits. Somewhat different conclusions are, however, said to occur when consideration is given to the asset-holding behaviour of one particular group of investors – central banks. Lee (1973) attributes 69 per cent of the rise in his estimated multipliers to the increasing preference of central banks to hold dollars in the Euro-currency market. The story runs as follows. Say all non-bank leakages out of the Euro-dollar market, b, are to national money markets other than the USA, and that central banks fix their exchange rates against the dollar such that these leakages result in international reserve gains. If central banks re-invest a proportion, say c, of their dollar reserves in the Euro-market, the overall leakage of funds out of the market, taking non-banks and central banks together, is reduced and the multiplier will then be larger. The formula is

$$m_2' = \frac{1}{1 - (1 - r)\,[1 - b + cb]}$$

When $c = 1$, i.e. central banks hold all marginal increases in reserves as Euro-currencies, this formula collapses to the simple fractional reserve multiplier, m_1 (equation (1)) and the fractional reserve multiplier estimates become relevant. More generally we would expect leakages out of the Euro-dollar market both to the USA and to other national markets, and the revised multiplier formula is then:

$$m_2'' = \frac{1}{1 - (1 - r)\,[1 - b_1 - b_2\,(1 - c)]}$$

Only leakages to national markets, other than the USA, b_2, will add to central bank reserves and can be re-invested in the market. The figures in Table 9.2 permit us to make the revised estimate, reported in Table 9.3. This shows that allowing central banks to re-deposit about one-third of their foreign exchange reserves in the Euro-market raises the multiplier to 1.39 – still not a very large number. If in the extreme $c = 1$, the only leakages out of the Euro-dollar market would be by non-banks to the US domestic market – this leakage is estimated in Table 9.3 at 22 per cent – and the multiplier rises to 4.39. Thus under the extreme assumptions that central banks re-invest all international reserve gains in the Euro-dollar

Table 9.2

Multiplier estimate allowing for leakages to the USA and other national money markets (end-1979 figures)

(1) US non-bank holdings of domestic dollars (proxied by US M_3)	$1,775 bn
(2) US non-bank holdings of Euro-dollars	$25 bn
(3) Non-US non-bank holdings of domestic dollars	$18 bn
(4) Non-US non-bank holdings of their domestic currency (proxied by broad monetary aggregates in nine countries)*	$2,295 bn
(5) Non-US non-bank holdings of Euro-dollars	$90 bn
(6) US non-bank leakage ratio to the USA: (1)/[(1) + (2)]	0.986
(7) Overall non-US non-bank leakage ratio: [(3) + (4)]/[(3) + (4) + (5)]	0.963
(8) Non-US non-bank leakage ratio to the USA: [(7) × (3)]/[(3) + (4)]	0.007
(9) Average leakage ratio to the USA and other national markets: [(6) × (2) + (7) × (5)]/[(2) + (5)]	0.968
(10) Multiplier based on (9), assuming $r = 0.01$	1.03

* For the countries see the annex to Chapter 3.

Sources: data taken from the *US Treasury Bulletin*, national sources and BIS data.

Table 9.3
Multiplier estimate allowing for
central bank redepositing*
(end-1979 figures)

(a)	Central bank holdings of domestic dollars	$143 bn
(b)	Central bank holdings of Euro-dollars	$73 bn
(c)	Central bank redepositing ratio, c: $(b)/[(a)+(b)]$	0.338
(d)	Average leakage ratio to the USA: $[(6) \times (2) + (8) \times (5)]/[(2)+(5)]$	0.220
(e)	Average leakage ratio to other national markets: $(9) - (d)$	0.748
(f)	Multiplier, m_2'', based on (c), (d) and (e) assuming $r = 0.01$	1.393
(g)	Multiplier, m_2'', based on (d) assuming $c = 1$ and $r = 0.01$	4.39

* Numbers in parentheses refer to entries in Table 9.2.

Source: data on central bank holdings taken from the BIS *Fiftieth Annual Report*, 1980, p. 155.

market there could be a sizeable (but since there are still leakages directly to the US domestic market, not by any means huge) Euro-currency multiplier.

In addition to the various qualifications that have already been made, a further problem with this approach is the assumption that central banks rigidly fix their exchange rates against the dollar. If exchange rates are freely floating, international reserves will be unaffected by any switches by non-banks out of dollars into domestic currencies and no secondary reflow of funds to the Euro-market will occur from central banks. Similarly, flexibility in exchange-rate policy will also reduce the impact of inflows from the Euro-dollar market on domestic liquidity and thus reflows to the market from non-banks. Moreover, if non-banks outside the USA borrow Euro-dollars to finance international trade, initially official reserves will be unaffected and there will be secondary leakages to the US market when there is trade with the USA or with countries which hold their reserves in the USA. Interest-rate adjustments and other effects described later in section 9.3 may also limit the potential influence of central bank deposits on the Euro-currency multiplier. When there are very high interest-rate responses, central bank depositing may have a very limited influence on Euro-market liquidity. More generally, it would be expected that they have some influence on overall Euro-market expansion and this could be significant when governments encourage active borrowing in the Euro-market to increase their official reserves.

Multi-stage banking system estimates. Multi-stage banking system estimates are concerned with a somewhat different question from the previous two and specifically with the contribution of the Euro-currency market to the total – domestic and Euro-currency – liquidity or money holdings of the non-banking sector in a particular currency. The overall redepositing multiplier, m_3, is derived as (equation (3)):

$$m_3 = \frac{1}{r_1 [1 - (1 - r_2)(1 - b)]}$$

To isolate more clearly the influence of the Euro-currency market this can be written simply as:

$$m_3 = m_d m_2$$

where m_d is the size the domestic fractional reserve multiplier would be in the absence of a Euro-currency market, $1/r_1$, and m_2 is the Euro-currency multiplier obtained from the leakage model. The contribution of the Euro-market to overall credit availability is then:

$$\Delta m_3 = m_d m_2 - m_d$$
$$= (m_2 - 1) m_d$$
$$= (1 - r_2)(1 - b) m_2 m_d$$

which is the product of the Euro-currency multiplier derived from the leakage model, the domestic fractional reserve multiplier in the absence of the Euro-currency market, and the factors $(1 - r_2)(1 - b)$, which represent the proportion of funds not leaked out of the Euro-market to the national banking system.

Estimating the contribution of the Euro-market to credit growth in any particular currency is, however, complicated. Euro-dollars also substitute for money stocks outside the USA so that if there were no Euro-dollar market the US monetary aggregates would not necessarily be larger by the full size of non-bank Euro-dollar deposits. Perhaps the appropriate figure would be the Euro-dollar deposits of US non-banks only. We shall, however, take the most extreme case and assume now that all non-bank Euro-dollars would otherwise have been held in the USA and the only leakage out of Euro-dollars is to the US domestic market. (Note that under these assumptions the central bank redepositing argument is irrelevant since there are no leakages to markets outside the USA.) Swoboda's (1980) estimates can now be used and would yield approximately:

$$\Delta m_3 = 0.07 \, m_d$$

i.e. the Euro-dollar market has increased the overall dollar redepositing multiplier by about 7 per cent.

This model can be simplified even further by assuming that Eurobank reserve holdings are zero. The change in the domestic multiplier is then:

$$\Delta m_3 = \frac{(1 - b)}{b} \, m_d$$

This is illustrated in Figure 9.3, which plots $\Delta m_3 / m_d$, the rate of increase of the overall multiplier, against $1 - b$, the volume of deposits held in the Euro-dollar market. When dollar deposits are shifted to the Euro-currency market the overall rate of liquidity creation of the banking system and the velocity of circulation of domestically defined monetary aggregates will increase. This may tend to complicate somewhat the conduct of national monetary policy unless the authorities take offsetting action to reduce the domestic stock of reserves available to the banking system (see Chapter 10). But for this to have a major impact there have to be rather large shifts of funds between the domestic and the Euro-currency market. Comparing the stock of Euro-dollars held by non-banks with US M_2 gives a value of 0.07 for $1 - b$, and an increase in the overall multiplier, Δm_3, of 7.5 per cent. To double this value to 15 per cent

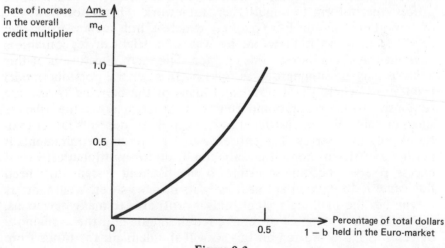

Figure 9.3

would involve a further shift out of the US market to the Euro-dollar market of nearly $100 billion!

9.2   PORTFOLIO APPROACHES

The main critique of fixed-coefficient multiplier models is provided by the portfolio or 'new' view of money.[3] According to this approach, the function of intermediaries is to satisfy simultaneously the preferences of borrowers and lenders by issuing direct claims upon themselves in the form of deposits, which can be held in the portfolios of wealth-holders, and purchasing claims directly from borrowers. It observes that financial intermediaries, be they commercial banks or other non-bank financial intermediaries, expand the overall size of their balance-sheets in a market environment in which there is competition between different types of financial intermediaries and primary security markets for both deposits and loans; and that the increase in the stock of assets or liabilities of any intermediary depends ultimately on the portfolio preferences of wealth-holders. These in turn are affected by the relative level of interest rates an intermediary offers and any particular attributes, such as the perceived riskiness of different assets, or advantages of the liabilities of one intermediary over another. In order to encourage wealth-holders to alter the structure of their portfolios either relative interest rates or the attributes of intermediaries' deposits or loans must change.

Two specific propositions of portfolio theory concern the role of reserve requirements and interest-rate adjustments. The first states that the existence of reserve requirements causes the credit-creating process to conform to a multiplier framework. This is not, however, of importance in the Euro-market, which is not subject to reserve requirements, and is therefore by way of a slight digression and is examined in the annex to this chapter. The main conclusion of this analysis may be summarised as follows. In a general portfolio model framework, where the deposits and loans of the banking system are responsive to interest-rate movements in other markets, the balance-sheet of banks will be restricted by the supply of deposits rather than the supply of reserves. The existence of legal reserve requirements is neither a sufficient nor a necessary condition for multiplier effects. If excess reserves become available to the banking system, this need not cause it to expand automatically its balance-sheet. What matters is whether the banking system finds it profitable to make new loans, and while the existence of reserve requirements and the availability of reserves has a bearing on this so will the demand for funds from the banking system. The second proposition is that movements in

Euro-currency interest rates will tend to limit any multiplier process in the Euro-currency market. This is of some importance to estimates of the Euro-currency multiplier. The types of portfolio models which use this effect in the Euro-market are described below. Some of this analysis draws upon the result obtained in the annex.

9.2.1 *Interest-rate adjustments*

A proposition of portfolio theory is that adjustments in Euro-currency deposit rates will generally tend to limit the size of any Euro-currency multiplier. A movement of funds into the Euro-market will tend to depress interest rates there, and raise interest rates elsewhere, causing some marginal holders of Euro-currency deposits to shift their funds out of the Euro-market, partly off-setting the initial inflow. This is illustrated in Figure 9.4. An initial inflow of new deposits to the Euro-currency market of AC, at interest rate r_0, shifts the supply of deposit curve from D_s^0 to D_s' and causes the equilibrium Euro-currency interest rate to fall to r_1 and the equilibrium size of the Euro-market to expand from A to B. The initial deposit multiplier is then AB/AC, which is clearly less than unity, the fraction BC of the initial deposit inflow being lost to the Euro-currency market because of the induced fall in Euro-currency deposit rates.

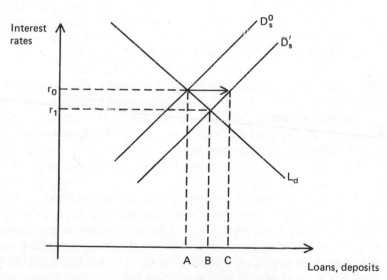

Figure 9.4   Portfolio model

Analysis of this effect on the Euro-currency multiplier, and perhaps more importantly of the interactions of Euro-markets with national banking systems and monetary policies, has been investigated by constructing small general-equilibrium models of the world's financial system.[4] Within these the Euro-banking system is highlighted and the size of the multiplier determined by examining the impact of a shift of deposits to the Euro-market on its final size. These models treat the economic system as one of short-run equilibrium in which the sum of world assets and liabilities is given and the only question is one of allocation. They abstract from the impact of financial markets on real variables and do not generally allow feedbacks from financial intermediaries to wealth, income or the price level. The type of dynamic feedback processes from bank lending to nominal incomes which multiplier theorists implicitly hypothesise are not part of the analysis. Indeed, in most models the Euro-currency banking system could be dropped out without very much loss to the final equilibrium.

The main conclusion from these models of asset distribution for the Euro-currency multiplier is that 'the leakage caused by changes in interest rates is probably larger than any other leakage'[5] or 'the interest rate leakage effect on the Euro-dollar market would be the key feature in reducing the value of the Euro-dollar multiplier'.[6] To outline the derivation of these types of conclusion, a small general-equilibrium model is described below and then iterated through the various stages which follow a shift of deposits to the Euro-currency market.

9.2.2   A general-equilibrium model

General-equilibrium models involve the specification of a consolidated balance-sheet for each sector, market-clearing conditions for each asset and certain behavioural assumptions about the substitutability between assets in the portfolios of transactors. Table 9.4 illustrates the type of balance-sheet constraints and market-clearing conditions hypothesised. To simplify, a number of restrictions are imposed on the sectoral holdings of assets.

The titles across the top of Table 9.4 identify six sectors — US and European non-banks, commercial banks and central banks; the titles along the left-hand column the assets — US and European government securities, bank deposits, loans and reserve assets, together with Euro-dollar bank deposits and loans (assumed to be issued by European banks). The right-hand column tables the interest rates on each asset and the bottom row the sectoral balance-sheet constraints. Entries in the body of Table 9.4 indicate which sectors hold or issue

Table 9.4

Balance-sheet constraints and market-clearing conditions in a simplified general-equilibrium model

Assets	SECTORS US non-banks (1)	European non-banks (2)	US banks (3)	European banks (4)	US central bank (5)	European central bank (6)	Interest rates
US government securities (S_{US})	1				-1	1	r_{US}^s
European government securities (S_E)		1				-1	r_E^s
US bank deposits (D_{US})	1		-1	1			r_{US}^d
US bank loans (L_{US})	-1		1				r_{US}^l
Euro-dollar bank deposits ($D_{E\$}$)	1	1		-1			$r_{E\$}^d$
Euro-dollar bank loans ($L_{E\$}$)	-1	-1		1			$r_{E\$}^l$
European bank deposits (D_E)		1		-1			r_E^d
European bank loans (L_E)		-1		1			r_E^l
US reserve assets (R_{US})			1		-1		r_{RUS}
European reserve assets (R_E)				1		-1	r_{RE}
Totals	US private wealth $= W_{US}$	European private wealth $= W_E$	0	0	US government deficit $= G_{US}$	European government deficit plus European balance of payments $= G_E + BOP_E$	

which assets. A '1' identifies an asset of the sector and a '−1' a liability. Market-clearing conditions are obtained by summing across the appropriate row for each asset (these determine the interest rates), and the sectoral balance-sheet by summing the appropriate column for each sector. Thus the first row of the table shows that the US central bank 'issues' government securities and these are held by US non-banks and the European central bank. The first column shows that the sum of US non-banks' holdings of US government securities, US and Euro-dollar bank deposits plus their borrowing from US and European banks adds to US private wealth, etc. The general complexity of these models can be greatly increased by introducing additional entries in the table − US non-banks might, for example, be assumed to hold US reserves, i.e. currency, or by introducing specific assumptions about the dollar/European currency exchange rate (assumed fixed), but these make the models more difficult to handle.

A further preliminary is to specify certain behavioural assumptions for each sector. These can be written in the general form:

$$F_i (B, \bar{r}) = 0 \qquad (i = 1, 2, \ldots, 6)$$

Where B is the balance-sheet constraint of sector i and $\bar{r}$ the vector of relevant interest rates. For US non-banks this would be written as:

$$F_1 (W_{US}, r^s_{US}, r^d_{US}, r^l_{US}, r^d_{E\$}, r^l_{E\$}) = 0 $$

and the demand for each asset derived under certain assumptions about the substitutability between assets. The usual assumption is that assets are gross substitutes and that a rise in the interest rate on, say, Euro-dollars will lead at least to a rise in holdings of Euro-dollars and a fall in the holdings of one or all other assets.

For example, the demand for Euro-dollars by US non-banks could then be written as:

$$D^{(1)}_{E\$} = g_{(1)} \ (\overset{+}{W}_{US}, \overset{-}{r^s_{US}}, \overset{-}{r^d_{US}}, \overset{-}{r^l_{US}}, \overset{+}{r^d_{E\$}}, \overset{-}{r^l_{E\$}})$$

where the signs over the variables are the partial derivatives of the demand for Euro-dollars by the various variables. Rises in wealth or the Euro-dollar interest rate cause US non-banks to increase − and rises in all other interest rates to reduce − their holdings of Euro-dollars. And so on for other sectors and assets.

Using this system of sectoral balance-sheet identities, market-clearing conditions and behavioural assumptions, the financial system can then be 'solved' to determine the volume of each asset held by each sector. In practice, however, algebraic analysis of the system proceeds by considering the final impact of an exogenous shock — for example, a shift of dollars from the US to the Euro-dollar market — on the structure of interest rates and size of each sector. In this way the Euro-dollar multiplier can be determined. Clearly this model is considerably more complicated than the simple filtering system described in Section 9.1, but it can be viewed as such a system, only that now explicit account is taken of the balance-sheet constraints on each sector and the impact of a deposit shift between markets on the structure of interest rates and reactions of agents in all markets. This is illustrated by considering the effect of a deposit shift from the US domestic banking system to the Euro-currency market by US non-banks using the balance-sheet identities outlined in Table 9.4.

Initially the deposit shift from the US to the Euro-dollar market will put downward pressure on Euro-dollar deposit and loan rates and upward pressure on US domestic deposit and loan rates.[7] This will entice some Euro-dollar holders to shift funds to the US market to take advantage of the higher deposit rates available there and to European deposit and security markets since Euro-dollar rates will have fallen relative to European currency interest rates. There will also be some leakage to the US market if European banks hold some precautionary reserves against their now larger stock of Euro-dollar deposits. At the same time, US and European borrowers will switch to the Euro-dollar market because Euro-dollar loan rates are now lower relative to national markets. As a first-round effect the stock of Euro-dollar deposits and loans will expand, but by something less than the initial deposit inflow, as a proportion is leaked to the US and European national markets (the model is therefore at this stage analogous to the fixed-coefficient leakage model). In the USA the transfer of dollar deposits and the demand for dollar loans to the Euro-market will cause the credit extended by the US banking system to contract somewhat and, assuming that US banks were initially 'loaned up', excess reserves will become available to the US banking system equal to the legal reserve ratio *times* the net shift of deposits by non-banks from the US to the Euro-dollar market *less* the increase in precautionary reserves held by Euro-banks with US banks. Initially any contraction in lending by US banks will partly offset the expansion of Euro-dollar lending; the offset will only be partial, however, because the increase in deposits available for lending by Euro-banks will be larger than the loss of deposits available for lending by US banks (the analogy is with the multi-stage banking model).[8] In Europe, assuming the European central bank fixes its exchange rate against the dollar, the shift of borrowing to the Euro-dollar market and of deposits out of Euro-dollars into domestic bank deposits will ease monetary conditions and add to the dollar reserves of the European central bank.

At the second round it is necessary to consider the reaction of each of the sectors to what is now a state of disequilibrium in asset markets. In the USA the rise in interest rates on bank deposits will encourage US non-banks to sell securities; some may be purchased by the European central bank, which now has larger dollar reserves, thus returning deposits to the US banking system. The US central bank may also intervene to fix the price of US securities, buying the net amount of securities offered by US non-banks. If it does, additional deposits will be made available to the US banking system, US bank deposits and loan rates will fall, the volume of US bank lending will expand towards previous levels and the impact of the deposit shift to the Euro-currency market on the overall availability of credit will be larger. Even if the US central bank does not fix security prices, the availability of free reserves may allow US banks to expand their lending, but only if this is profitable (see the annex). In Europe the fall in deposit rates will entice European non-banks to buy securities. If the European central bank intervenes to fix the price of securities, this will sterilise the impact of the dollar inflow from the Euro-market and prevent European monetary conditions from easing, and the overall expansionary impact of the shift of dollars to the Euro-market will be reduced.

There will be third-round effects from the increased availability of credit but these depend on the reaction of the central banks in their national security markets. If the US central bank does, but the European central bank does not, fix security prices, the overall expansion in credit will be greatest and this will feed back to the Euro-markets, allowing some net multiplier effects to occur. If, however, the US central bank does not intervene in its national security market, while the European central does, the effects of the deposit shift will largely be sterilised and the impact of the deposit shift will be similar to those in the first round discussed above. In this case the Euro-currency multiplier will certainly be less than unity and the overall impact on credit availability will depend on how US banks react to the availability of free reserves. If US banks find it unprofitable to expand their lending, then the increase in Euro-dollar lending will be partly compensated by a reduction in US bank lending and the overall impact on credit availability will be *smaller* than the expansion of lending in the Euro-currency market. If, however, they find it profitable to expand their lending by the full amount of free reserves available, the upper limit to the impact of the Euro-market on overall credit availability is given by the estimates derived from the fixed-coefficient multi-stage banking model.

The size of the Euro-currency multiplier will then be larger when:

(a) interest-rate adjustments in the Euro-currency market and the response of US non-banks to these are small;

(b) US banks find it profitable to expand their lending by the full amount of free reserves realeased by any deposit shift to the Euro-market;

(c) the US central bank intervencs to sterilise the effects of the shift on interest rates in the USA;

(d) the European central bank accepts any easing in monetary conditions following a decline in Euro-dollar interest rates and European non-banks are responsive to this decline.

Abstracting from condition (a) (see thc next section) the major influence on the credit-creating ability of the Euro-markets will depend crucially on the reaction of national central banks. If both target only on their domestic markets and sterilise liquidity influences on their own markets, shifts of deposits to the Euro-market will most probably have small expansionary effects. The estimates from the multi-stage banking model suggest that even in the extreme they will be fairly small.

9.3   INTEREST-RATE EFFECTS AND INSTITUTIONAL BANKING VIEWS

An assumption of portfolio model estimates of the Euro-currency multiplier is that Euro-currency interest rates adjust to non-bank deposit flows and that this leads to large leakages from the Euro-market back to national money markets. While wealth-holders will be sensitive to the relative movement in Euro-dollar and US domestic interest rates, it is very difficult to find evidence that short-term Euro-currency interest rates adjust to non-bank deposit flows. The analysis of the determination of Euro-currency interest rates (Chapter 5) has shown that, in the absence of restrictions to the free flow of capital, Euro-dollar (and Deutsche Mark) interest rates have been tied within narrow margins to the level of short-term domestic interest rates by the arbitrage activity of domestic banks. Such analysis strongly suggests that movements in Euro-currency deposit rates are largely independent of the volume of non-bank deposits in the Euro-currency market and that by implicaton the type of interest-rate effects hypothesised by portfolio models do not generally occur.

However, this conclusion is due to a more powerful arbitrage mechanism between the domestic and Euro-currency markets which, at the margin, dominates the non-bank arbitrage process: that is, interbank arbitrage. Such is the efficiency of interbank arbitrage that at the margin even small changes in the liquidity in one market are rapidly transmitted to the other without there having to be a large movement in the relative structure of domestic and Euro-currency interest rates. Inflows of non-bank deposits to the Euro-market do not lead to interest-rate movements because they are arbitraged out by banks. In such a world it might also be reasonable to believe that inflows of non-bank (or central bank) deposits would have no effect on the volume of Euro-market loans and that the concept of an independent Euro-currency multiplier is meaningless. The implication is that bank and non-bank flows to the Euro-market can be aggregated together and that Euro-banks, in their Euro-currency lending policy, do not specifically react to net increases in the volume of non-bank deposits placed with them.

Other implications for Euro-currency credit creation are drawn from the close links between domestic and Euro-currency interest rates. It has been suggested that they imply that the Euro-currency market is *demand*-determined and that the market has a near infinite capacity to expand in response to an increase in the demand for Euro-currency loans.[9] Alternatively, using the same observed linkages it is also suggested that the growth of the Euro-currency market is mainly *supply*-determined at the instigation of the banks themselves and that the expansion of Euro-dollar business by US banks is an attempt to reduce their overall holdings of reserves, determined by legal reserve ratios on domestic deposits, by expanding their reserve-free Euro-dollar business.[10] The influence of the Euro-market on credit availability then derives from reducing the effective reserve ratio on the banking system as a whole.

This analysis is very appealing as there are very close links between the Euro-market and domestic banking systems. However, it is hard to believe that the management of Euro-banks have *no scope* for independent decision-making, for example on the level of spreads, maturities or size of loans to each borrower. It seems more likely that while parent organisations determine overall lending strategies and even limits on the total volume of lending to any one country, it will be left to local managers to implement this policy as best they can, given the prevailing circumstances, which may well depend on the extent of liquidity in the Euro-market. Indeed, the analysis reported in Chapter 7 does suggest that liquidity factors are important in explaining Euro-bank lending decisions. This suggest that independent Euro-currency multiplier effects may occur, but that they would be the outcome of a more complex process involving decisions by wealth-holders to redeposit funds in the market and by intermediaries to expand their Euro-market lending. Effectively, the portfolio model and 'institutional' type banking approaches have to be combined to provide a more realistic theory of Euro-market expansion. Nevertheless, the existence of close interest-rate links certainly weakens the concept of an independent Euro-currency multiplier, as banks are not automatically dependent on the supply of deposits by non-banks and may partly expand their business simply at the instigation of parent banks. Such analysis is perhaps most relevant in explaining the impact of offshore booking countries. But more generally the linkages also suggest that it is useful to view the credit-creating influence of the Euro-market as part of the global banking system. The main influence, as Aliber (1980) has suggested, is in terms of the disintermediation of money-like balances out of national banking systems (Chapter 10).

The institutional approaches raise, however, some other problems and questions in explaining the growth of the Euro-currency system. It is difficult to believe that the Euro-market is purely demand-determined over a broad range for its size or that it has an infinite capacity to expand at given interest rates. Euro-dollar interest rates are tied to US domestic CD rates within margins determined by the level of US domestic reserve requirements and interest rates, but this does not mean that a rise in the demand for Euro-dollars has no effect on the *overall* level of deposit rates. When Euro-dollar interest rates rise above the arbitrage margins at which US domestic banks find it profitable to supply funds to the Euro-market, US domestic banks issue more domestic CDs to lend funds in the Euro-market. This action will tend to put upward pressure on US domestic and, through arbitrage, Euro-dollar interest rates. The supply of funds to the Euro-market, therefore, will not be infinitely elastic. The analysis may, however, be approximately valid if the Euro-market is small compared with the US domestic market and the amount of funds needed to arbitrage out any profitable interest-rate differential has a negligible effect on the US domestic CD market. In such circumstances the magnitude of concern about the growth of the Euro-market must also be small. Alternatively, the assumption that the Euro-market is purely demand-determined may hold if the US authorities automatically intervene to fix the domestic CD rate. If, however, the Federal Reserve targets the domestic supply of reserves, interest rates will rise as US domestic banks demand additional reserve balances to meet the reserve requirements on the new issues of domestic CDs. Even if the Federal Reserve targets interest rates, it is unlikely to accommodate passively large new issues of CDs by domestic banks.

The second 'institutional' explanation of the growth of the Euro-currency market – that it reflects attempts by banks to reduce overall reserve ratios by expanding reserve-free Euro-currency deposits – may be a factor explaining the expansion of Euro-dollar business by US banks. However, this approach is much less appropriate if applied to other nationalities of banks which are not subject to burdensome legal reserve ratios on domestic bank deposits – for example, British, Swiss or Japanese banks. These banks are also important participants in the Euro-market and a theory of Euro-market expansion should also explain their behaviour. There are other regulatory constraints on bank lending behaviour and equally these could also be used to explain the expansion of a comparatively unregulated Euro-banking system. It may, for example, reflect attempts by banks to reduce their overall capital or equity ratios. Alternatively, however, Euro-market expansion may also be a response to non-regulatory or portfolio constraints on banks' balance-sheets – for example, it may reflect attempts to reduce overall portfolio risks by enlarging the geographical location of depositors and borrowers. The influence of domestic reserve requirements can be seen as part of banks' broader portfolio considerations, of which precautionary reserve holding is only one factor.

Other underlying factors are also important in explaining the expansion of Euro-currency lending and decisions by parent banks to set up branches and subsidiaries which operate in the Euro-market – the increasing integration of national economies through trade and multinational investment, the structure of balance-of-payments surpluses and deficits, the changing portfolio preferences of wealth-holders and the needs of economic development, as well as the structure of national and international regulations. If this were not so, it would suggest that banks, and at that only certain nationalities of banks, exercise a very large degree of monopoly power in financial markets – if business were not contracted offshore it would somehow automatically be done in the same banks onshore. A principal feature of international banking is, however, its highly competitive nature. The general arguments of portfolio theory apply equally to international and national banks. The portfolio preferences of wealth-holders and competition between financial intermediaries must therefore also be taken into account in explaining Euro-market growth.

9.4   SUMMARY AND CONCLUSIONS

There is a broad range of estimates about the size of the Euro-currency multiplier, particularly where a fractional reserve multiplier theory is concerned. Most, if not all, approaches which recognise that the Euro-market is an open banking system strongly indicate, however, that its endogenous credit-creating ability is very small. These conclusions are based on plausible judgements about the size of leakages from the market into other assets. Allowing for leakages to markets outside the USA and for central bank redepositing could raise the multiplier estimate, but even under extreme assumptions it is by no means huge and many qualifications have to be made.

In an open financial system the impact of the Euro-market on credit availability will depend on the response of a number of agents. Most important is the reaction of central banks to shifts of funds to the Euro-currency market and whether the domestic liquidity effects of these are sterilised. When they are, the Euro-market will have net expansionary effects on the world stock of credit, but from the estimates reported these need not be very large. What is relevant for policy is whether any expansionary effects are controllable. The portfolio and integrated market approaches certainly suggest that they are, as national interest-rate movements will be rapidly transmitted to the Euro-market. If authorities do not target the level of interest rates, the Euro-markets may, however, complicate policy implementation (Chapter 10).

Independent movements in Euro-currency interest rates may also have a role to play in limiting the endogenous multiplier process in the Euro-currency market, but the evidence for this is not great. Alternatively, near perfect interbank arbitrage between the domestic and Euro-currency markets may mean that the concept of an independent Euro-currency multiplier is meaningless and that distinct Euro-market liquidity effects do not occur. Other banking theories of the growth of the Euro-market therefore emphasise the institutional links with national banking systems. It is difficult to believe, however, that the state of Euro-market liquidity has no influence on Eurobank lending policy or the expansion of the Euro-currency system. Independent multiplier effects may therefore still occur. The institutional approaches underline, however, the weakness of multiplier theory when applied to the Euro-markets in isolation and the need to examine more closely the process by which credit flows are disintermediated to the Euro-currency market.

9.5   ANNEX: THE ROLE OF RESERVE REQUIREMENTS IN EXPLAINING MULTIPLIER EFFECTS

It has been suggested (Crockett, 1976) that the existence of legal reserve requirements, higher than the level of reserves desired by banks on precautionary grounds, imposes a direct restraint on the banking system which prevents it equalising the marginal cost of deposits with the marginal yield on loans. As soon as the authorities remove this direct constraint by supplying more reserves, or by reducing reserve requirements, banks can thus be counted on to respond by expanding their balance-sheets.

This argument is elaborated using some diagrams. Figure 9.5 illustrates the situation for a competitive banking system subject to a legal reserve requirement, R. Bank deposit and loan rates are shown on the vertical axis and quantities on the horizontal axis. D_s is the stock of deposits supplied to the banking system, which slopes upwards, being positively related to the deposit rate r_d; L_d, the stock demand for bank loans, slopes upwards, being negatively related to the loan rate, r_l. The supply of loans by the banking system, L_s, depends on the supply of bank deposits and the legal reserve ratio, R. This can be written as

$$L_s = (1 - R)D_s$$

since a proportion R of bank deposits is sterilised by the reserve ratio and is therefore unavailable for lending by the banking system. The banking system will determine its optimal loan portfolio by attempting to equalise the marginal cost and the marginal returns on loans. The question is whether it is prevented from doing this by the imposition of legal reserve requirements.

The marginal effective cost of deposits to the banking system is not just the nominal deposit rate, r_d, but rather $r_d/(1 - R)$ since a fraction R of any marginal bank deposits is sterilised as reserves. The relevant interest rate for marginal

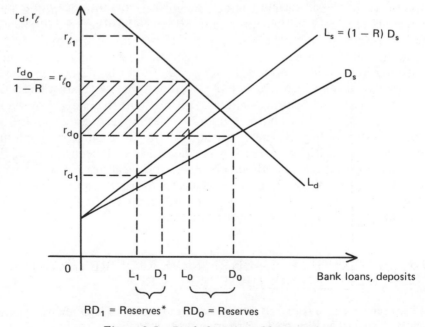

Figure 9.5   **Bank deposit and loan market**

lending behaviour of the banking system is therefore this effective deposit rate and not the nominal rate, r_d. In equilibrium banks would seek to equate this effective rate with the loan rate (assuming bank lending margins are zero) setting $r_l = r_d/(1-R)$. This is illustrated in Figure 9.5. The deposit rate is set at r_{d0}, the loan rate at r_{l0}, and the bank borrows deposits D_0, holds RD_0 as reserves and makes L_0 loans, and *the equilibrium marginal conditions for the banking system are met*. The effect of the legal reserve requirements is to place a wedge between nominal deposit and loan rates but not between the banking system's marginal effective deposit and loan rates. The result holds because it is assumed that the supply of reserves, RD_0 is determined by the demands of the banking system. But, as drawn, any expansion in the reserves made available to the banking system by the authorities beyond RD_0 would not lead to an automatic increase in bank lending. The existence of legal reserve ratios is therefore not on its own a sufficient condition for multiplier effects.

If, however, the reserves available to the banking system were constrained to RD_1 = Reserves* (see Figure 9.5), then the banking system could no longer equate the marginal effective cost of deposits with the marginal return on loans, deposit rates would fall to r_{d1}, and loan rates would rise to r_{l1}. In this case an expansion in the volume of reserves beyond RD_1 would lead to an automatic expansion in bank loans. But this analysis assumes that as the authorities restrict the volume of reserves, by (for example) open-market sales of Treasury bills, deposit rates fall relative to loan rates. This need not generally be the case as restrictive policy on the part of the authorities normally causes a rise in *all* interest rates. The reserve ratio argument is misleading because it is only a partial-equilibrium approach. General portfolio theory, however, suggests that the rise in bank loan rates will encourage borrowers to issue more securities in the primary security market, shifting the demand curve for primary loans from L_d^p to $L_d^{p'}$ (see Figure 9.6) and raising interest rates on primary securities. Together

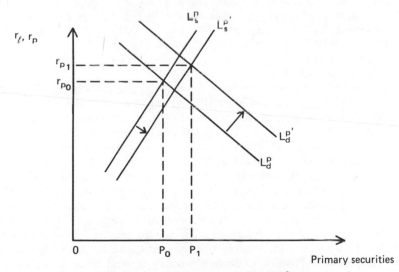

Figure 9.6   Primary security market

with the fall in bank deposit rates this will encourage a portfolio shift by wealth-holders as previous holders of bank deposits purchase more primary securities, thus shifting their supply curve to $L_s^{p\prime}$ from L_s^p (see Figure 9.6). The effect of this on the market for bank deposits and loans would be to cause upward movements in the D_s schedule, and thus bank deposit rates and downward shifts in the L_d schedule and bank loan rates in Figure 9.5 (not shown). Such shifts may well re-establish the marginal equilibrium conditions of the banking system when the banking system can once again equate the marginal effective cost of deposits with the marginal return on loans, but with the smaller totals for the stock of bank deposits and loans. The contraction of bank loans, following the action by the authorities to restrict the supply of reserves, occurs because of the portfolio shift out of bank deposits and loans to other security markets and not primarily because of the existence of reserve requirements or the discontinuity between the marginal effective cost of bank deposits and the marginal return on bank loans. Such effects occur in the absence of legal reserve ratios. The presence of reserve requirements does, however, provide a lever for the operation of monetary policy which may mean that the effects of restricting bank reserves through security sales by the authorities is more quickly transmitted to the market for bank deposits and loans.

NOTES

1. Fratianni and Savona (1972). Proxy for reserves: short-term liabilities of US banks *vis-à-vis* their foreign branches.
2. Makin (1972). Proxy for reserves: demand deposits of foreign commercial banks, exclusive of claims on home offices of branch banks.
3. For a statement of the approach see Tobin (1963) and for an application of the analysis to the Euro-currency system see Crockett (1976).
4. Freedman (1977a) and Hewson and Sakakibara (1976).
5. Freedman (1977a).
6. Hewson and Sakakibara (1976).
7. It is frequently observed that shifts of deposits from US banks to Euro-banks would not affect US domestic deposit and loan rates since Euro-banks initially hold new dollar placements as US bank deposits. The deposit shift would simply be a book-keeping operation for the US banking system, which would not alter the overall supply of domestic bank deposits. While this may be the instantaneous result of the shift of deposits to the Euro-market, it is very unlikely to be a longer-term response in a portfolio theory which allows for competition between intermediaries and variable responses of wealth-holders and other transactors. It assumes that deposits are automatically returned — indeed completely returned — to the US banking system in fixed proportions following the deposit shift to the Euro-market. However, portfolio theory is as relevant for US banks as other types of intermediaries. There is no necessary reason why all dollar deposits have to stay in the US banking system. When US banks lose deposits they will,

like everyone else, have to bid to replace them, pushing up domestic deposit and loan rates.

8. If the net deposit shift is D, and R and R_E are respectively the US legal and Euro-banks' precautionary reserve ratios, the net amount of deposits released by the deposit shift is

$$RD - R_E D + (1 - R)R_E D = R(1 - R_E)D$$

9. Heller (1979).
10. For example, Aliber (1980). Aliber does not make this point explicitly in his paper; however, it does seem to be at the heart of his analysis.

The two approaches are not necessarily inconsistent. The demand-determined approach is concerned with *interbank* flows from the domestic market to the Euro-market which consist of deposits on which domestic reserve requirements have already been imposed. The supply-determined approach, on the other hand, is concerned with taking *non-bank* deposits offshore which avoid domestic reserve requirements.

10 Euro-market Regulations and Domestic Monetary Policy

In early 1979 there began a period of intensive discussion among the central banks of the Group of Ten countries plus Switzerland on the need for direct regulation of the Euro-currency market. These discussions culminated in the issue of a press communiqué on 15 April 1980 (reproduced as an annex to this chapter) which emphasised the need to monitor the Euro-market from a national monetary and prudential point of view, the role of national regulations in stimulating Euro-market expansion and the problems which the Euro-market may pose for some national monetary authorities. This chapter and the next examine the analytical issues surrounding the discussions on Euro-market controls.

10.1 CENTRAL BANK DISCUSSIONS

The regular meetings of central banks at the BIS in Basle had long provided a forum for the discussion of macroeconomic and prudential issues raised by the growth of international banking, and in April 1971 a Euro-currency Standing Committee was formed to examine and make recommendations on policy questions arising in relation to the Euro-currency market. One result of consultations was the agreement reached among the Group of Ten central banks in June 1971 not to increase official placements of foreign exchange reserves in the Euro-currency market – the so-called 'self-denying ordinance'. The underlying reason for this agreement was that in a world of fixed exchange rates and restrictions on capital outflows from the USA central bank placements were a potentially important source of deposit growth in the Euro-currency market. However, since the agreement only covered the Group of Ten central banks, it did not affect reserve placements by other countries that were quantitatively more important. In the early 1970s there were also discussions about the need for general measures to curb the rapid expansion of the Euro-currency market. Following the 1973 oil crisis, the focus of attention shifted to the adequacy of Euro-market liquidity and the ability of the markets to withstand the recycling pressures imposed by the OPEC surplus. As it turned out, the Euro-markets adapted quickly to the demands placed upon them.

The continued rapid expansion of international bank lending in the later 1970s despite the, albeit temporary, decline in oil-induced balance-of-payments deficits led to renewed interest in the macro-economic implications of the Euro-markets. There were worries that the markets were 'over-recycling' funds to countries in balance-of-payments deficit, thus delaying balance-of-payments adjustments and adding excessively to global reserves. Others noted, however, that this recycling process had mainly allowed countries to rebuild their reserves after the first oil shock and that the reserve increases were matched by much increased external indebtedness by borrowing countries. Additionally, some monetary authorities began to express concern about the market's implications for their national monetary policy and to consider whether some system of reserve requirements on Euro-currency deposits might be appropriate. This aroused renewed interest in what were the economic implications of a large Euro-currency market. While these discussions revealed a good degree of agreement on certain monetary policy effects of the Euro-currency market (as evidenced by the April communiqué), differences appear to have remained on the balance of the argument in the 'autonomists' versus 'channelists' debate (Chapter 8) as well as on the desirability or feasibility of a system of Euro-currency reserve requirements.

10.2   MONETARY POLICY EFFECTS

Most observers, however, agree that the growth of unregulated external intermediaries may complicate the formulation and implementation of national monetary policies. Two issues can be identified. The first, which is discussed in detail below, concerns the efficiency of monetary control techniques in the short term. When domestic monetary policy is implemented through a system of controls which harms the competitive position of domestic financial intermediaries, asset holdings and credit flows will be disintermediated[1] to the Euro-currency market, which may weaken the short-term restrictive stance of domestic monetary policy. The second concerns longer-term developments in the structure of asset and money holdings.

In the USA in particular rapid structural change in the domestic financial system has raised important questions as to the appropriate definition of their national monetary aggregates.[2] Regulatory changes and historically high levels of interest rates have increased the incentive for more efficient cash management by consumers and business, resulting in the growth of a variety of highly liquid non-deposit assets.[3] By substituting for balances traditionally defined as 'narrow' money in the USA, domestic relationships between 'money' holdings and expenditure flows have become more unstable and the velocity of circulation of 'money' has tended to increase. The growth of Euro-currency markets is also seen as one element in this structural change. Purchases of Euro-currency deposits may cause wealth-holders to economise on their holdings of cash or demand deposits, or to substitute Euro-currency deposits directly for domestic bank deposits. For example, overnight Euro-dollar deposits with branches of US banks in the Caribbean offshore market can be transferred into immediately available funds without penalty and are thus a substitute for chequing accounts at US banks. In May 1981 the Federal Reserve Board had to block a move by US banks to offer smaller investors interest rates on domestic current-account deposits related to those in the Euro-dollar market. More generally, Euro-deposits are closer substitutes for domestic time deposits and may therefore cause broader 'money' or liquidity concepts to be understated.

In other countries the effects of structural changes on national monetary policy have not presented nearly the same difficulties as in the USA; and there seem to be fairly stable domestic money—expenditure relationships in West Germany and Switzerland despite the growth of Euro-markets in these countries' currencies. At present, the total size of Euro-balances excluded from national broad monetary aggregates is not very great, being of the order of some 4 per cent of total national broad money stocks. But, as noted in Chapter 3, there are some important inter-country differences. The trend by wealth-holders to 'internationalise' the structure of their asset portfolios (Chapter 4) also suggests that the volume of money-like balances held in the Euro-market may continue to expand, particularly if national regulatory frameworks provide incentives for this. There are also trends by banks to attract more investors to the market by offering smaller denominated Euro-currency depositing facilities – in which case it may be worth considering whether Euro-market deposits should be included in some monetary aggregates.

What seems clear is that on grounds of liquidity the overwhelming volume of Euro-currency deposits should be excluded from narrow definitions of money. To the extent that authorities target on narrow money, the growth of Euro-currency balances should not therefore be a major source of distortion. The efficiency of cash-management techniques in the Euro-market may, however, influence somewhat the income velocity of the narrow money stock. There is a better case for including Euro-currency deposits in broader monetary aggregates, but even here it is not overwhelming. There is, as noted in Chapter 8, a problem over the timeliness of information. Aggregates requiring policy responses need to be reported promptly but the data on Euro-currency deposits lag considerably behind the data on domestic deposits. Moreover, because of the lack of available data, only one preliminary study has attempted to examine whether the inclusion of Euro-currency deposits of non-banks would improve the stability of income velocities of broad money stocks.[4] In regressing the income velocities of various money measures on time, Brittain and Bernard (1980) found that the inclusion of Euro-currency holdings reduced somewhat the standard errors in the equation. Table 10.1 reports some of their preliminary results for the USA and the United Kingdom. In fact, the improvement is numerically rather small and in the case of the USA is mainly accounted for by US resident deposits at US branches in the Caribbean area (shown as B(ii) in the table). An implication of the analysis is that allowing for Euro-currency deposits would make more stable the relationship between 'broad' money and expenditure flows, though more detailed analysis would be needed to determine the exact importance of Euro-currency holdings and their relationship with domestic expenditure flows. The

Table 10.1
Standard errors in the regression of the log of velocity on time*

Definition of monetary aggregate		Base for the calculation		
		USA		United Kingdom
		M_2	M_3	M_3
A.	Residents' holdings of domestic currency at home banks	0.0208	0.0262	0.0880
B.	A plus residents' holdings of domestic currency (i)	0.0177	0.0249	0.0646
	abroad† (ii)	0.0175	0.0242	–
C.	B plus non-residents' holdings of the domestic currency	0.0157	0.0238	0.0870

* Estimation period 1965I–1980I.
† B(i) is based on the broadly defined Euro-currency market, while B(ii) includes only US residents' deposits at the branches of US banks in the Caribbean area.
Source: Brittain and Bernard (1980).

influence, if important, could be taken into account by redefining national monetary aggregates and by closely monitoring the expansion of the relevant Euro-currency balances. The United Kingdom does in fact closely monitor developments in the Euro-sterling market and, in the redefinition of their monetary aggregates, the USA now includes US non-bank resident overnight Euro-dollar holdings in the Caribbean area in M_2 and M_3. But even if broader money concepts are targeted, the Euro-markets may add to short-term operational problems for monetary authorities.

10.2.1   *An unregulated financial intermediary*

The basic problem is that when one group of intermediaries is regulated and another unregulated, and when the liabilities and assets of the intermediaries are close substitutes, regulation may cause sudden shifts by depositors and borrowers between one group of intermediaries and the other. The balance-sheeet of the unregulated group may expand at the expense of the regulated one, weakening the impact of the regulations. The theory of the influence of an unregulated financial intermediary on national monetary policy is well established.[5] It is still interesting, however, to examine how an unregulated external financial intermediary can affect certain techniques of national monetary policy. We do this by presenting a diagrammatic model of domestic and Euro-market intermediaries which recaps and extends the analysis in the annex to Chapter 9. Now, the diagrams examine the relationship between regulated and unregulated intermediaries rather than the relationship between regulated intermediaries and the primary security market.

This model of the influence of 'unregulated' Euro-banks is described by the following assumptions. There are only two types of financial intermediaries — domestic banks and Euro-banks. Following the principles of general portfolio theory (Chapters 4 and 9), the liabilities of these intermediaries are close (but not perfect) substitutes such that, at the margin, nominal deposit rates can differ somewhat between the two groups of intermediaries, but changes in the relative level of deposit rates will lead to deposit flows between the intermediaries. Borrowers, on the other hand, consider Euro- and domestic bank loans to be perfect substitutes and at the margin, in competitive equilibrium, lending rates on the two types of loans are the same. If not, some marginal borrowers, including the intermediaries themselves, will shift their borrowing from one market to the other until this condition is achieved. Efficient borrower arbitrage also does away with the need to consider separate currency segments of the Euro-currency market since interest-rate parity conditions can be assumed to hold between Euro-currency interest rates. Nevertheless, adjustments in domestic and Euro-currency interest rates towards interest-rate parity will cause flows across the foreign exchange markets (Chapter 8). To highlight the competing domestic currency segments of the Euro-market, floating exchange rates are therefore assumed and developments in the foreign exchange market and their effect on domestic currency segments are not considered.[6] Intermediaries' lending margins tend towards the same level because of profit arbitrage by banks (Chapter 7) and are simply assumed to be zero in the domestic and the Euro-currency market. Domestic banks are regulated by a system of non-interest-bearing (NIB) reserve requirements on domestic bank deposits. Euro-banks are free from regulation. Initially, it will also be assumed that the authorities operate monetary control by varying the level of the reserve requirements on domestic banks. This assumption is then relaxed and other techniques of monetary control are considered.

The supply of deposits and loans schedule for domestic banks subject to a reserve ratio, R, is shown in Figure 10.1. As in the annex to Chapter 9, the supply of deposits, D_s^d, is a positive function of the domestic deposit rate. This schedule is described by points of the forms (D_d, r_d). For every unit of deposits supplied, domestic banks have to hold a fraction R as NIB reserves. The volume of deposits available for lending by the domestic banking systems is thus only $\bar{D}_s^d = (1 - R)D_s^d$, since RD_s^d is sterilised as reserves. In determining their lending rates, banks will charge an interest rate which covers the full cost of their deposits, $r_d D_s^d$. Assuming lending margins are zero, this requires:

$$r_d D_s^d = r_L^d (1 - R)D_s^d$$

where r_L^d is the interest rate charged on domestic bank loans. This yields the familar formula for the effective cost of bank deposits:

$$r_L^d = \frac{r_d}{1 - R}$$

Domestic banks would therefore supply loans, L_s^d, equal to $(1 - R)$ D_s^d and charge an interest rate $r_L^d = r_d/(1 - R)$. The supply of loans schedule, which is described by points (L_d, r_L^d), will then be of the form $((1 - R)D_d, r_d/(1 - R))$ corresponding to points on the deposit supply schedule (D_d, r_d). If the supply of deposits schedule is a straight line passing through the origin, the loan supply schedule would then be described by the line $L_s^d = (1 - R)^2 D_s^d$. At the intersection of this line with the demand for loans schedule, L_D^d, the equilibrium loan rate can be read off (r_L^d) and the equilibrium volume of loans, L_d, bank deposits, D_d, and bank reserves, RD_d determined (see Figure 10.1)

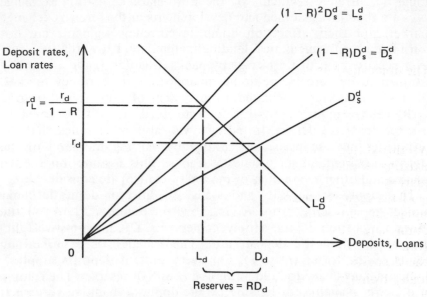

Figure 10.1   Domestic bank deposit and loan market

This analysis is now extended and unregulated Euro-banks are introduced. The segments numbered (2) in Figures 10.2 and 10.3 show the regulated domestic bank deposit and loan market. To simplify the diagrams, only the supply of domestic bank deposits *net* of reserve holdings, $\bar{D}_s^d = (1 - R)D_s^d$, and the domestic supply of loans curve, $L_s^d = (1 - R)\bar{D}_s^d$, are shown. These schedules allow the domestic deposit and loan rates to be determined in the diagram. The segments numbered (1) in the figures illustrate the supply of deposits, D_s^e, and demand for loans, L_D^e, in the domestic currency in the unregulated Euro-currency market; they are respectively upward- and downward-sloping. Since there are no Euro-currency reserve requirements, the supply of Euro-bank loans, L_s^e, is equal to the supply of Euro-currency deposits, D_s^e. Competitive equilibrium between the Euro-currency and domestic loan markets requires that the lending rate is the same in the two markets. This is determined at the intersection between the combined Euro-bank and domestic bank supply of loans, $L_s = L_s^d + L_s^e$, with the overall demand for loans, $L_D = L_D^d + L_D^e$ ($L_e + L_d$ in the segments numbered (3) in the diagrams), at r_L. Since Euro-banks, like domestic banks, are assumed not to charge a lending margin for their services, the Euro-currency deposit rate, r_e, is equal to the competitive loan rate, r_L. In turn, equilibrium in the market for domestic bank deposits and loans requires:

$$r_L = r_L^d = \frac{r_d}{1 - R}$$

The domestic/Euro-currency deposit rate differential is thus:

$$r_e - r_d = \frac{r_d}{1 - R} - r_d$$

At this differential, domestic wealth-holders are content with the existing allocation of deposits between the domestic and Euro-market.

If the domestic authorities now seek to restrict the supply of loans by raising domestic reserve requirements (say from R to R'), the immediate effect is to shift the domestic bank loan supply schedule from L_s^d to $L_s^{d'} = (1 - R')\bar{D}_s^d$ (see segment 2 of Figure 10.2), raising the domestic loan rate to $r_L^{d'}$ and reducing the domestic supply of loans from L_d to L_d' and also the combined domestic bank and Euro-bank supply of loans to $L_s' = L_s^{d'} + L_s^e$ and the loan stock to $L_e + L_d'$ (segment (3) of Figure 10.2). However, this action raises the domestic loan rate and lowers the domestic deposit rate (from r_d to r_d') relative to interest rates in the Euro-market. As the domestic/Euro-currency interest-rate differential widens from $r_e - r_d$ to $r_e - r_d'$, this will encourage some wealth-holders to move funds out of domestic and into Euro-currency bank deposits. The Euro-bank deposit and loan supply schedule will shift to the right and the domestic deposit and loan supply schedule further to the left. The rise in domestic loan rates relative to rates in the Euro-market will similarly cause an increase in Euro-market borrowing and a reduction in the demand for domestic bank loans. The loan demand schedules in the Euro- and domestic markets will therefore shift to the right and left respectively. A new competitive equilibrium will be established when domestic and Euro-currency loan rates are again at the same level. Figure 10.3 shows this position and also the shifts of the various curves. The new equilibrium loan rate is at r_L', where the new combined supply of bank loans (L_s'' rather than L_s' immediately after the rise in the domestic reserve requirement) equals the previous demand (see segment (3) of Figure 10.3). This loan rate again equals the equilibrium Euro-currency deposit rate, now r_e', and also equals

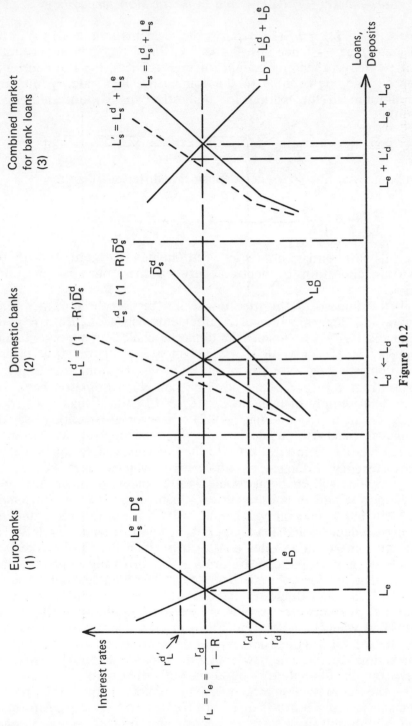

Figure 10.2

256

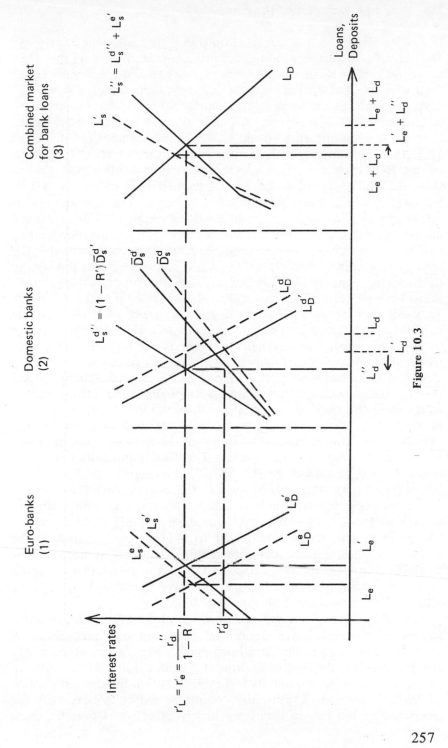

Figure 10.3

$1/(1 - R)$ times the new equilibrium domestic bank deposit rate, r_d''. The new Euro-currency/domestic interest-rate differential is thus $r_e' - r_d''$ at which wealth-holders are content to hold their now larger stock of Euro- and smaller stock of domestic bank deposits.

As a result of these portfolio shifts between the markets, the balance-sheet of Euro-banks expands relative to domestic banks. Euro-bank loans increase (from L_e to L_e' in segment (1) of Figure 10.3), while domestic bank loans contract further (to L_d'' from L_d' immediately after the increase in reserve requirements which was less than the initial position of L_d in segment (2) of Figure 10.3). Because, however, Euro-bank deposits are free from reserve requirements, the shift of deposits from the domestic to the Euro-currency market will have a larger effect on expanding Euro-currency lending than in contracting domestic lending. After the reserve change, the shift of one unit of deposits to the Euro-market reduces the supply of domestic loans by $(1 - R')$ but expands the supply of Euro-bank loans by one unit since the shift releases reserve balances of R'. This will tend to mean that the aggregate supply of loans schedule will increase beyond its position immediately following the change in domestic reserve requirements (shown as the movement from L_s' to L_s'' in segment (3) of Figure 10.3), thus weakening the restrictive stance of monetary policy. It is even theoretically possible, when the reserve change induces a very large shift of funds from the domestic to the Euro-currency market, that the effect of the restrictive increase in domestic reserve ratios can be perverse and cause an overall *expansion* in the combined volume of Euro-bank and domestic lending and a fall in lending rates. The final equilibrium stock of loans, $L_e' + L_d''$ could lie to the right of the original stock, $L_e + L_d$ (see segment (3)). It can be shown that this occurs when the elasticity of the domestic deposit supply schedule with respect to the change in the reserve ratio is close to unity.[7] But the possibility that a 1 per cent change in reserve ratios would lead to a 1 per cent change in the stock of domestic bank deposits seems somewhat remote at low levels of domestic reserve ratios, and thus the restrictive domestic monetary policy action will generally have the desired qualitative effect of reducing the overall supply of loans.

The operations of unregulated Euro-banks therefore tend to erode somewhat the restrictive action of the domestic authorities. A restrictive policy can stimulate Euro-market expansion, which partly compensates for the decline in domestic bank lending. If the authorities ignore these developments and target only on the domestic stock of bank deposits and loans, they could be led to believe that the restrictive action has in fact been highly effective. Domestic loans and deposits fall, not only because of the induced movement in domestic interest rates, but also because of portfolio shifts to the Euro-currency market. But if the authorities also examined the movement in domestic interest rates, they might suspect that all was not as it seemed, since disintermediation of flows to the Euro-market has lessened the overall rise in lending rates. This might cause the domestic authorities to raise reserve ratios further in an attempt to achieve some target for domestic lending rates. Further shifts to the Euro-market would then occur, and an increasing burden of restraint would be placed on domestic banks. Nevertheless, provided that perverse effects do not occur (and the likelihood of these will increase the higher the domestic reserve ratio), the desired stance of policy can be achieved.

Consider now two other monetary policy instruments available to domestic authorities: changing domestic interest rates and changing the supply of bank reserves with domestic reserve ratios held constant. Again, Euro-banks are free from reserve requirements. In both cases it is assumed that the authorities have some other financial instrument under their control — open-market sales or purchases of Treasury bills — which they can manipulate to achieve interest-rate or bank-reserve targets. Sales of Treasury bills reduce the overall supply of deposits to the banking system and thus the overall — domestic plus Euro — supply of bank loans. The analysis following only investigates the allocation of bank deposits and loans between the two banking systems and not this overall effect. It can be assumed that the sale of Treasury bills leads initially to an equiproportional decline in the supply of domestic and Euro-bank deposits and does not initially affect the relative positions of the supply schedules in each market.

Assume that the authorities set a target for the level of domestic deposit rates. Since they are willing to supply all reserves demanded by the banking system at these interest rates, the relationship $r_L^d = r_d/(1 - R)$ between domestic bank deposit and loan rates still holds. Under such a policy the authorities will always be able to achieve the desired degree of monetary restraint through the overall effect of Treasury bill sales on the combined Euro- and domestic supply of bank deposits and loans. However, raising the level of domestic interest rates will again lead to some shift of funds between domestic and Euro-banks. Equilibrium in all markets again requires that the relationship between domestic and Euro-currency deposit rates is given by the formula:

$$r_e = \frac{r_d}{1 - R} = r_d\,(1 + R + R^2 + \ldots)$$

and the Euro-/domestic interest-rate differential is thus:

$$r_e - r_d = r_d \, (R + R^2 + \ldots)$$

which is a function of the level of domestic interest rates, r_d. A rise in domestic interest rates widens the differential and thus encourages some depositors to shift funds to the Euro-currency market. Moreover, for certain values of r_d and R, the impact of a change in interest rates on the interest-rate differential could be as great as a change in reserve ratios. Similarly, raising domestic interest rates also raises domestic loan rates relative to those in the Euro-currency market and will encourage some borrowers to shift to the Euro-market. The effect on the balance-sheets of domestic and Euro-banks is therefore analytically the same as in the previous case. Domestic bank deposits and loans will contract relative to those of Euro-banks; shifts of funds to the Euro-market will, *ceteris paribus*, tend to be expansionary, as reserve requirements again become less onerous, and the initial contractionary effect of the sale of Treasury bills will be weakened. The authorities may therefore again have to take further restrictive action, but providing they achieve their interest-rate target the overall stance of policy will not be undermined by unregulated Euro-banks.

Finally, consider what happens if the authorities target the supply of reserves. The influence on the balance-sheets of Euro- and domestic banks will again be similar to the previous two cases. Restricting the supply of reserves is not very different from raising reserve ratios and will tend to increase domestic interest rates. However, when deposits shift to Euro-banks from domestic banks this now also reduces the demand for reserve balances by the domestic banking system. The fall in the demand for domestic bank reserves will act to equate the supply and demand for domestic bank reserves at lower levels of interest rates. The restrictive monetary policy may again be weakened and, as in the first example, perverse effects are possible when a widening Euro-currency/domestic interest-rate differential leads to very large shifts of funds to the Euro-currency market. Further restraint in the form of a reduction in the supply of bank reserves would then be necessary to achieve the desired degree of monetary tightness.

In none of these examples — raising domestic reserve requirements, raising domestic interest rates, or restricting the supply of domestic bank reserves — is monetary policy made ineffective by the operation of unregulated markets. However, perverse effects are possible, if unlikely, under the first and third examples. The existence of Euro-banks may nevertheless mean that a greater degree of restraint has to be placed on the domestic banking system, with possible effects on the allocation of credit. Borrowers who do not have access to the Euro-currency market may be more heavily constrained than those who do (Chapter 8). The analysis also suggests that domestic NIB reserve requirements may at times encourage a rapid expansion of the Euro-currency market when they place domestic banks at a competitive disadvantage.

It was also noted in the annex to Chapter 9 that restrictive action will tend to stimulate an expansion of activity in the primary securities market. As domestic bank loan rates rise, borrowers will issue more primary securities, and as domestic bank deposit rates fall relative to interest rates in the primary securities market, depositors will shift out of bank deposits into securities. Instead of disintermediation to the Euro-market, there will be disintermediation to the securities market. Larger borrowers may also be able to tap these markets and avoid somewhat the full effects of the restrictive monetary policy. An important difference is that while disintermediation to the securities market usually involves a decline in investor liquidity, disintermediation to the Euro-market may only involve a shift of liquid assets between intermediaries such that the overall liquidity in the economy is less affected. The important issue is how relevant Euro-currency deposits are for expenditures on domestic goods and services. We might generally believe that Euro-currency deposits would be closer substitutes for domestic bank deposits than primary securities (recall the highly interest-rate-sensitive nature of Euro-currency deposit holdings reported in section 4.3). Euro-currency balances also seem to bear some – although not a well-defined – relationship with expenditures on domestic goods and services. And Euro-banks do undertake some maturity transformation on non-bank deposits (Chapter 3), and although this is less than in domestic banking systems it is greater than in primary security markets. If so, disintermediation to the Euro-market may be more undesirable than disintermediation into securities as it has a larger effect in weakening the restrictive stance of policy and there may therefore be a case for extending the domestic NIB reserve requirement system to the Euro-market. Before discussing the various questions surrounding a Euro-currency reserve requirement proposal, it is instructive to examine recent experience in two countries – the USA and the United Kingdom – and to assess how important the disintermediation of money and credit flows to the Euro-market has been in practice.

10.2.2 *Recent experience*

The USA. In the USA regulated banks are subject to a system of NIB reserve requirements. At times the level of these has been varied as an instrument of monetary policy. More generally, in recent years, monetary policy has been conducted by targeting the level of domestic interest rates (the federal funds rate) and, since October 1979, by acting directly on the supply of reserves to the banking system. In 1978 and 1979 a combination of high NIB reserve requirements and high domestic interest rates led to a large disintermediation of flows to the Euro-dollar market.

As part of a larger package of measures to support the value of the dollar on the foreign exchange markets, the US authorities raised, in November 1978, the reserve requirement on large domestic time deposits (certificates of deposit) by 2 per cent to 8 per cent and simultaneously sharply increased the level of domestic interest rates. The combined effect of these measures was to widen the three-month Euro-dollar/US CD interest-rate differential by around 0.4 per cent by the end of 1978. Up to that time US non-bank resident holdings of Euro-dollars amounted to only some $6 billion, but the sharply higher interest-rate advantage encouraged a large placement of dollars in the Euro-market by US non-banks (see Figure 10.4). By end-1979 liabilities of banks in the narrowly defined (European) reporting area to US non-banks had exploded to $17.6 billion, and with a continued large interest-rate differential in favour of Euro-dollars they expanded further in 1980 and 1981.

A simultaneous development was the repatriation of dollars to the USA by US banks as they borrowed dollars in the Euro-currency market. In August 1978 the US authorities had removed the previous 4 per cent reserve requirement on US bank Euro-dollar borrowing. No longer taxed on Euro-market borrowing, and with the large movement of US non-bank funds into Euro-dollars, US banks shifted domestic funding operations to their foreign branches. Up to 1979III the volume of funds repatriated to the USA from the European Euro-currency market was, however, fairly modest and US banks only reduced their net asset position in the market by some $2 billion. In the October 1979 credit-restraint programme, marginal reserve requirements were imposed an any increase in US banks' managed liabilities, including Euro-dollar borrowing (over a given base). Because the marginal reserve requirement applied to increases in both domestic and Euro-currency liabilities, it did *not* alter the comparative costs of borrowing dollars offshore rather than domestically (see Chapter 5), and with continued strong domestic loan demand US banks borrowed a further $3.2 billion in the Euro-currency market (narrowly defined), and reduced their loans to the market by $3.4 billion in 1979III–1980I. Thus, for the first time in three years, US banks became small net users of Euro-dollars. Over all, between 1978IV and 1980I US banks reduced their net asset position with the narrowly defined Euro-currency market by some $9 billion.

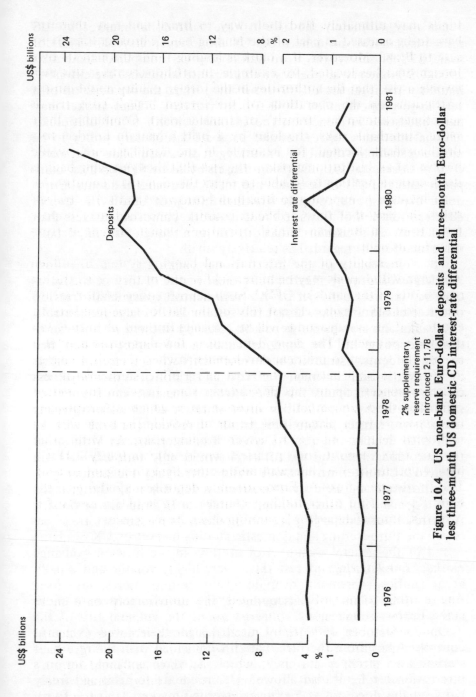

Figure 10.4 US non-bank Euro-dollar deposits and three-month Euro-dollar less three-month US domestic CD interest-rate differential

263

During this period the use of the Euro-dollar market by US residents had two influences on US monetary policy. The shift of some $11 billion to the Euro-market by US non-banks tended to cause US monetary aggregates to understate somewhat the extent of liquidity in the hands of US non-banks, while the repatriation of a very large proportion of these funds through the Euro-market may have had some influence on the income velocity of circulation of national monetary aggregates and caused US monetary policy to be more expansionary than US domestic aggregates would have suggested. Over the same period US M_2 increased by some $150 billion compared with the $11 billion increase in US non-bank residents' Euro-dollar deposits, and compared with the stock of US M_2 the overall disintermediation of flows to the Euro-market amounted to less than 1 per cent. This disintermediation effect, although still important, must therefore be regarded as relatively small.

The United Kingdom. Throughout most of the history of the Euro-currency market, Euro-sterling has represented a very small fraction of the total Euro-market. Under the system of UK exchange controls, UK banks and non-banks were not normally allowed to hold Euro-sterling deposits and the supply of funds to the market was confined to non-residents. Moreover, because of the declining role of sterling as an international currency and frequent periods of sterling weakness on the foreign exchange markets, external demands and supplies of sterling in the Euro-market remained small, so that the Euro-sterling market was largely a 'satellite' of the Euro-dollar market. Banks tended to deal in and quote Euro-sterling interest rates in terms of the Euro-dollar rate and the forward sterling discount; when a bank received a Euro-sterling deposit it would usually sell the sterling spot, cover forward and hold the funds as a dollar asset. Similarly, faced with a demand for Euro-sterling, a bank would swap out of dollars. As a result of exchange controls – which prevented arbitrage between the Euro-sterling and domestic sterling market by UK residents – and of the general weakness of sterling in the forward exchange market, Euro-sterling interest rates were highly volatile and usually at a significant premium over domestic sterling interest rates (see Figure 10.5). This also discouraged the development of a more active Euro-sterling market.

On 23 October 1979 the United Kingdom removed exchange controls. Apart from the fact that this coincided with the return of sterling as a stronger currency, which acted to enhance sterling's international role, it also allowed UK residents to arbitrage freely between the domestic and external sterling markets, and the Euro-sterling market began to expand rapidly. The premia on Euro-

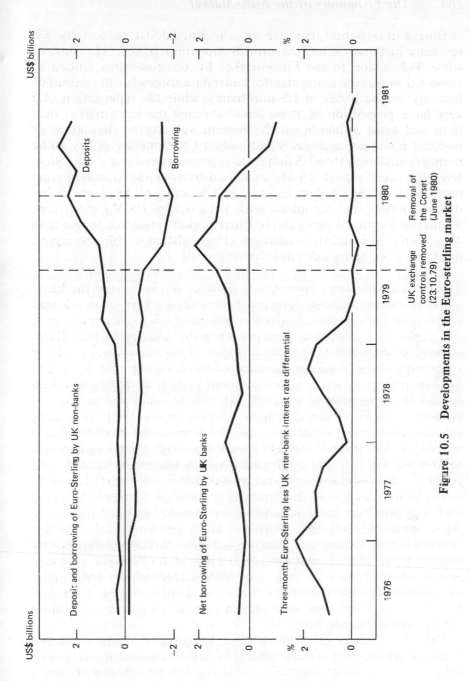

Figure 10.5 Developments in the Euro-sterling market

265

sterling deposits and loans fell (see Figure 10.5) and, as with the relationship between the US domestic and Euro-dollar markets, the UK domestic and Euro-sterling markets became much more closely integrated. UK residents could now take advantage of even small domestic/Euro-sterling interest-rate differentials when deciding whether to place or borrow funds in the Euro-currency market.

At the time of the removal of exchange control, the Bank of England was operating the Supplementary Special Deposits scheme — widely known as the 'corset' — which, *de facto*, was a system of marginal non-interest-bearing reserve requirements over a moving base.[8] This meant in practice that, for a bank exceeding the guidelines set, the effective cost of securing additional funds for on-lending was significantly above market interest rates.[9] As with other monetary control systems which tax the domestic banking system, this caused a disintermediation of funds to channels free from the regulations,[10] and with the removal of exchange controls UK banks and non-banks turned to the Euro-currency market and their borrowing and placement of Euro-sterling funds expanded rapidly. Figure 10.5 shows the increases that occurred in Euro-banks' sterling assets and liabilities *vis-à-vis* UK residents.[11] In response to the disintermediation of funds and the associated distortion of domestic money supply figures, the corset was eventually removed in June 1980. Immediately there was a fall in UK non-bank borrowing and placements of Euro-sterling and, although placement in the market expanded again in subsequent quarters, at end-March 1981 they were still below the level when the corset was removed. Indeed, it was only after the removal of the corset that UK banks became net lenders of funds to the Euro-sterling market (Figure 10.5). At present other reserve requirements on UK banks, which include a very small non-interest-bearing component, do not create a major cost incentive for banks or non-banks to do business through the Euro-sterling market; and under the approach to monetary policy adopted in the United Kingdom, which concentrates on altering the level of short-term interest rates, the Euro-sterling market need not pose a major problem for monetary policy — although, as for other countries, long delays in the reporting of Euro-currency data mean that authorities are less able to take into account recent Euro-market developments when formulating national monetary policy, and the possibilities for disintermediation limit the range of instruments which the authorities can use when implementing monetary policy.

Practical experience in the USA and the United Kingdom therefore accords with the simple theoretical model of the influence of an unregulated external financial intermediary. Taxing the domestic banking system through a system of non-interest-bearing reserve requirements causes flows to be disintermediated to the unregulated Euro-market, which expands at the expense of national banking systems. This may tend to complicate the implementation of national monetary policy and make it somewhat more expansionary than otherwise. However, for neither the USA nor the United Kingdom can it be said that the Euro-market has yet fundamentally undermined national monetary policy.

10.3 RESERVE REQUIREMENTS

The principal reason behind the proposal to place reserve requirements on Euro-currency deposits is to improve the effectiveness of national monetary policy. The presumption is, of course, that Euro-currency holdings are relevant for national monetary control. In this context the discussion of the influence of an unregulated financial intermediary suggests that a reserve requirement system might be designed to achieve two objectives:

1. *Equity*: to avoid the possible disintermediation of flows. Placing reserve requirements on Euro-banks would reduce or eliminate the competitive distortions between the Euro- and domestic banking systems. It would also make *domestic* policy variables a more accurate guide for formulating monetary policy;
2. Improved *overall* money supply control: factors other than competitive distortions may lead to the continued expansion of Euro-currency deposits. To the extent that it is the aggregate of domestic and Euro-currency bank deposits which is relevant for monetary policy formulation, a system of Euro-currency reserve requirements would allow the authorities automatically to take Euro-market developments into account *when targeting the supply of bank reserves*. If disintermediation effects occurred, they would influence the demand for bank reserves, and a policy of controlling the domestic supply of bank reserves would not be weakened.

Note that these objectives are quite different. The first concerns the general problem of the equity of treatment of different financial intermediarites. The second concerns a specific approach to monetary policy — that is, a policy of targeting the supply of domestic bank reserves. The debate about the efficiency of the techniques of monetary policy is not of direct concern here, except to note that there are other techniques of monetary policy, such as targeting directly the monetary aggregates themselves or the level of interest rates. Where there is disagreement about the techniques of monetary policy, the only generally acceptable criterion for Euro-market reserve requirements is that of equity.

In addition, Euro-currency reserve requirements might act to slow the rate of Euro-market growth and to encourage more business to be conducted 'on-shore' by increasing the costs of external inter-mediation (see Chapter 4), which itself could be seen as desirable by some national authorities. Some other advantages might also be claimed for the proposal – it could speed up the collection of Euro-market data and show the authorities' concern about global money and credit expansion. But these are not peculiar to this particular proposal.

The implementation of a scheme of Euro-currency reserve require-ments raises a general problem, however. As has been illustrated by the discussion of the influence of an unregulated financial inter-mediary, a system of, for example, NIB reserve requirements acts as a tax on the banking system and therefore provides an incentive for avoidance. The disintermediation effects which occur between the regulated banks and the unregulated Euro-banks might then occur between regulated Euro-banks and other channels, or indeed within the Euro-currency system itself. If, for example, reserves were only imposed on US banks abroad, they would be disadvantaged relative to other Euro-banks, and Euro-currency flows would move to other unregulated Euro-banks. Any system of NIB reserve requirements would then have to be applied widely across the foreign currency deposits of international banks. In practical terms any scheme would most likely be confined to the Group of Ten countries and Switzer-land. This need not pose a major problem if these countries could effect reserve requirements on *all* banks in their own countries and the branches and subsidiaries of *their own* banks in countries not party to the scheme, as at present this would cover the overwhelming majority of Euro-currency deposits. Even so, over time other centres and other countries' banks could become more important – indeed, the reserve ratios on Group of Ten banks would give them an incentive to become more active in the Euro-market – and therefore broader country agreement would have to be sought.

10.3.1   *Redenomination effects*

Similarly, any scheme would have to apply widely across currencies. If, for example, NIB reserve requirements were placed only on Euro-dollar deposits, Euro-banks would have an incentive to redenominate the deposits in another currency to avoid the reserve ratio. Instead of offering the depositor a three-month Euro-dollar deposit, they could offer, say, a three-month Euro-Deutsche Mark deposit with an accompanying three-month forward contract to buy back the Deutsche Mark for dollars. The alternative transaction, which involves a spot purchase and forward sale of Deutsche Mark, is effectively a currency swap between the bank and its customer which allows the bank to denominate its liabilities in Deutsche Mark rather than dollars, thus avoiding the reserve requirements. At no time during the transaction has the bank or its customer taken on any exchange risk. The swap is only a book-keeping operation which perhaps could even be done by the bank without the agreement of the customer. More generally, where Euro-dollars are subject to reserve requirements and Euro-Deutsche Mark deposits are not, the swap allows the bank to pay the customer a larger rate of return on dollars when they are redenominated as Deutsche Mark, and this provides the incentive for the avoidance of the reserve requirement regulations. The following technical exposition illustrates why this is so and also shows that even uniform reserve ratios on all currencies may not solve the problem.

A technical note. Consider the situation prevailing before the imposition of reserve requirements on Euro-dollar deposits and recall that arbitrage between currencies in the Euro-market implies that interest-rate parity holds. This is written:

$$r_\$ = r_{DM} + F_d$$

where $r_\$$, r_{DM} and F_d are respectively the three-month Euro-dollar and Euro-Deutsche Mark interest rates and the forward Deutsche Mark/dollar premium or discount. If the authorities now impose a NIB reserve requirement, R, on Euro-dollar deposits, this immediately raises the effective cost to the bank of Euro-dollars, which becomes $r_\$^e$:

$$r_\$^e = \frac{r_\$}{1 - R}$$

$r_\$^e$ is greater than $r_\$$ and thus greater than the prevailing three-month Euro-Deutsche Mark plus forward rate:

$$r_\$^e > r_\$ = r_{DM} + F_d$$

The bank now has an incentive to borrow (or lend) Deutsche Mark until the condition

$$r_\$^e = r_{DM} + F_d$$

is achieved, since $r_\$^e$ is now the cost of dollar deposits. However, this implies that the interest rate it would now pay on its Euro-dollar deposits has fallen to only $r_\$' = (1 - R)r_\$^e = (1 - R)(r_{DM} + F_d)$ less than $r_\$$ and the rate it would offer to its customer through the Euro-Deutsche Mark swap, $r_{DM} + F_d$. The swap involves the customer buying Deutsche Mark spot, investing them for three months, earning r_{DM}, and selling the Deutsche Mark three months forward, earning the forward premium or discount, F_d. By going through the swap transaction the customer could then increase the rate of return on his deposit by

$$r_\$^e - (1 - R)r_\$^e = Rr_\$^e = \frac{R}{1 - R}r_\$$$

The implication of the analysis is that NIB reserve requirements would have to apply to all currencies in the Euro-market. However, even imposing equal NIB reserve requirements on all deposits could still lead to incentives to redenominate the currency of the deposit. As in the unregulated intermediary example, the burden of NIB reserve requirements varies with the level of interest rates, and *thus when interest rates are different between currencies* the cost of holding reserves in one currency rather than another will also be different. Extending the above example, assume that the reserve requirement, R, on Euro-dollars is now also placed on Euro-Deutsche Mark deposits. After this change the following bank arbitrage condition would hold:

$$r_\$^e = r_{DM}^e + F_d$$

with

$$r_\$^e = \frac{r_\$'}{1 - R}, r_{DM} = \frac{r_{DM}'}{1 - R}$$

which implies the following for the relationship between Euro-dollar and Euro-Deutsche Mark deposit rates, $r_\$'$ and r_{DM}':

$$r_\$' = r_{DM}' + (1 - R)F_d$$

However, under the swap transaction, the bank would be willing to pay up to $r_{DM}' + F_d$ for dollar deposits, since F_d is the forward premium or discount it has to pay anyway on its interbank arbitrage operations. The advantage to the depositor in going through the swap transaction is therefore $RF_d = R(r_\$^e - r_{DM}^e)$.

Implications. The possibility that deposits will be redenominated in other currencies raises a major problem for the reserve requirement proposal. Suppose redenomination effects occur from dollars into Deutsche Mark because Euro-dollar rates are higher than Euro-Deutsche Mark rates and the US and West German authorities are targeting the domestic supply of bank reserves. The US authorities would observe no change – or perhaps even a fall – in the demand for their bank reserves, while the German authorities would experience an increase in the demand for their bank reserves to cover the rise in Euro-Deutsche Mark bank deposits. This may cause the US authorities to ease and the West German authorities to tighten their domestic monetary policy. However, the increased demand for Deutsche Mark reserves reflects an increased demand for *Euro-dollar* deposits, which is an American not a West German problem. The correct policy response would be for the US authorities to tighten policy and for the West German monetary policy to remain unchanged. The re-denomination of the currency of the deposits gives misleading signals to the respective monetary authorities, and this may lead to incorrect policy responses.

These effects could be avoided by adjusting the reserve ratios on different currencies to offset relative changes in interest rates, but that would be extremely complex. Alternatively, reserves could all be held in one currency so that the burden of the reserve requirement did not vary with the currency of denomination of the deposit. However, that would undermine one of the objectives of the proposal – to provide information to central banks on the volume of Euro-currency deposits held in their own currency and to take automatic account of these when targeting the domestic supply of bank reserves. Of course, if reserves were imposed uniformly at a low level, incentives for redenomination might be very small, but this might not solve the problem of inequitable treatment of domestic and Euro-currency deposits.

10.3.2 *Equity and harmonisation*

The level of reserve ratios imposed by different national authorities on domestic bank deposits varies substantially across countries and also changes over time. Some countries do not impose NIB reserve requirements at all, while in the case of one country – West Germany – reserve ratios can legally be imposed up to 100 per cent, though the more usual cross-country range might be beween zero and 16 per cent. Because of the possibility of redenomination effects, such diverse national NIB reserve requirements could not be extended to deposits in the Euro-currency market and would probably have to be introduced at some low uniform level. But the countries which would find Euro-currency reserve requirements most helpful are exactly those with high national reserve ratios. Low uniform Euro-currency reserve ratios would not remove the possibility of the disintermediation of flows to the Euro-market out of their national economies. A reduction in national reserve ratios would be required by these countries to avoid such effects.

In other countries where monetary policy is not based on a system of NIB reserve ratios, the introduction of reserve requirements on Euro-currency deposits would actually place these countries' domestic banks at a competitive advantage over Euro-banks in attracting non-resident deposits in domestic currencies. Banks could equally re-denominate Euro-currency deposits in domestic currencies to avoid the reserve requirements if national exchange controls allowed this. To make the proposal effective, the Euro-currency reserve ratios would then have to extend to non-resident, and perhaps even resident, deposits in domestic currencies in those countries not already op-erating NIB reserve ratios. Reserve ratios would have to fall in some countries and have to be introduced in others. There would have to be a move towards the harmonisation of national monetary regulations. A Euro-currency reserve requirement proposal therefore has far-reaching implications for the *harmonisation* of the conduct of national and international moletary policy, and would involve a loss of sovereignty over national monetary policy.

Against rather broader considerations, some harmonisation of domestic monetary policies and control techniques might be desirable *per se*. The problem is that in increasingly open and integrated national economies it is becoming much more difficult to distinguish what is 'money' and what balances are relevant for expenditures on domestic goods and services. In theory, at least, floating exchange rates still allow countries independent interest-rate policies; however, the stance of monetary policy is not something isolated from real economic conditions in the national economy. Monetary policy must also take account of the actual and expected levels of income and prices, which are also affected by foreign expenditures, movements in exchange rates and other countries' monetary policies. Indeed, when there is free international capital and expenditure mobility, the final outcome for the level of exchange rates, under a given national interest-rate policy, may be simply the whim of private agents as they respond to the economic conditions in different countries. The stance of national monetary policy may then be other than intended. The authorities may therefore either lose sovereignty over their national monetary policies, or domestic interest rates will have to be adjusted frequently to counter exogenous shocks. One interesting question is therefore: would the loss of national sovereignty under a system of harmonised national monetary regulations and controls be less than that which presently exists in a world of diverse national monetary policies, free capital mobility and unregulated external money markets?

In recent years many countries have moved towards adopting some form of monetary rule – such as setting a target for the rate of growth of domestic monetary aggregates. The rules are designed to provide feedbacks which lead to automatic adjustments in the instruments of monetary policy and to limit the scope for discretionary monetary policy changes. Internationally agreed and harmonised approaches to monetary policy could be seen as a very effective way of setting constraints on discretionary national monetary policies.

However, a more harmonised approach to monetary policy raises important issues for national authorities. Although authorities may have voluntarily sought to give up some sovereignty in national monetary policy by establishing monetary growth 'rules', these rules can be and are overridden, and there seems little reason why the established rules have to be mutually consistent between countries even if it is thought desirable for the international economy. Other domestic economic developments are also relevant to the setting of domestic monetary targets and to the vigour with which authorities seek to achieve them. Effectively a harmonised system would be a move to some form of global monetarism which would supersede national policy objectives. But even if authorities were to accept the loss of autonomy associated with a more harmonised system, the particular 'solution' would remain an open question – should it be based on a system of NIB reserve requirements, and at what level? The problem is that not only do regulations vary internationally but so do the traditions of monetary control depending on the institutional structure in domestic markets. Some countries act on the supply of bank reserves, others target on interest rates and still others place quantitative limits on the volume of bank lending. Institutional characteristics of different national money markets require different monetary control techniques.

10.3.3 *Interest-bearing reserve requirements*

One approach which could allow countries to extend their own reserve ratios to deposits in their own currency in the Euro-market without major disintermediation effects would be one that paid a *competitive* rate of interest on bank reserves. This would not, however, remove the problem of inequitable treatment between domestic and Euro-banks for those countries whose domestic banks continued to be subject to non-interest-bearing reserve requirements. But it would allow countries to monitor Euro-market developments in their own currency more closely and to obtain a better degree of control over these than they would otherwise have.

When a competitive interest rate is paid on reserve balances, this avoids the tax element involved in holding balances in non-interest-bearing form. Banks therefore have little cost incentive to redenominate deposits in foreign currencies when reserve requirements differ between currencies, or to seek other methods of avoiding the reserve requirements completely. Under such a system it would therefore be possible to set Euro-currency reserve ratios close to the same level and indeed to vary them in line with corresponding ratios in different domestic markets. The authorities could observe the demand for reserve assets by Euro-banks to determine whether disintermediation effects were occurring from the domestic to the Euro-currency market and adjust the stance of domestic policy accordingly. Moreover, the reserve ratio itself could act to sterilise a proportion of Euro-currency deposits and thus be used to regulate Euro-market expansion. It is unlikely, however, that national authorities could act directly on the supply of interest-bearing reserve assets, to control the size of Euro-currency liabilities denominated in different currencies, without encouraging some redenomination effects. If, for example, the quantity of Euro-dollar reserve assets were fixed, the demand for these by banks would tend to raise their price and to push the interest rate on dollar reserves below that available on other assets, including reserve balances in other currencies. The opportunity cost of holding dollar reserve balances would rise — the limiting case being the NIB variant — and banks would have an incentive to redenominate Euro-dollar deposits in other currencies.[12]

10.4   AN ASSESSMENT

The influence of the Euro-currency markets on domestic monetary policies is similar to that of an unregulated domestic financial intermediary. Deposit and credit flows may be disintermediated out of national banking systems to the Euro-market, and this may complicate the task of domestic monetary policy if authorities target only on the domestic money market. These effects will be most acute when the structure of national regulations imposes large costs on the domestic banking system. The regulations may be in the form of higher domestic non-interest-bearing reserve requirements, but the potential for disintermediation effects to occur will also rise with the level of interest rates for given NIB reserve ratios. Conventional measures of broad 'money' which cover only the domestic banking system may then understate the volume of liquid balances, and monetary policy may appear somewhat more restrictive than it actually is. Euro-markets have at times disintermediated flows out of national banking systems, weakening the effectiveness of discriminatory domestic monetary instruments. But recent experiences suggest that this has not been large enough to undermine the stance of national policies significantly.

Euro-markets, however, raise three monetary policy difficulties. The first is an information problem. Euro-currency data are presently only available with a considerable lag and cannot be readily taken into account by authorities in formulating policies. Subsequent adjustments to policy can be made when the data do become available, but it is unsatisfactory to be always 'behind the game'. Improving the timeliness of Euro-currency data is not, however, dependent on a system of direct monetary controls on Euro-currency deposits. Such controls might help shorten the delays; on the other hand, they might cause the flows to disappear from view if they encouraged them to move to other channels. Despite efforts to improve reporting dates, the data are still four to five months out of date. This fact alone gives an indication of how complex the whole problem of monitoring and regulating Euro-markets really is. The collection of timely data would be a prerequisite for any form of Euro-market control and, on its own, would greatly assist national authorities.[13]

The second difficulty has to do with the equity of treatment of different banks. The regulations imposed on domestic currency deposits do not extend to Euro-currency deposits and thus some banks are advantaged when conducting business offshore. Inequity of treatment is, however, a relative problem and varies from one banking system to another depending on the structure of national regulations. Differences in the equity of treatment between domestic and offshore bank deposits are much greater for those countries which impose high NIB reserve requirements than in other countries where reserve ratios are low or where they earn a market rate of interest. An ideal system for national monetary control might be one that could extend individual national regulations on domestic currency deposits to individual currencies in the Euro-market. Euro-deposits in different currencies are, however, nearly perfectly substitutable and can be readily transformed from one currency to another through a spot sale and forward purchase — a swap transaction. When regulations tax deposits in one currency relative to another, incentives to redenominate the currency of the deposit will exist and these will undermine the controls and give misleading signals to national authorities. Effective regulation of individual currency segments of the Euro-market is not a feasible possibility and any controls would have to be generally applied across all Euro-currency deposits.

In a world where national reserve requirement regulations are not harmonised across countries, a *uniform* system of Euro-market reserve ratios will not provide an equitable solution to all banking systems. Some will be disadvantaged and others advantaged relative to the Euro-currency market. Inequity of treatment and the potential for a disintermediation of flows to the Euro-market out of national banking systems will continue until and unless national and Euro-currency regulations are more closely harmonised. The type of regulatory framework that should be adopted by a harmonised system is an open question and could be based either on low or zero non-interest-bearing reserve ratios, or on a higher level of NIB reserve requirements. In the first case harmonisation removes inequities by moving towards the system of regulations which presently exists for Euro-currency deposits and in some domestic banking systems. In the second case harmonisation would involve the extension of NIB reserve requirements to Euro-currency deposits and some domestic banking systems. However, to the extent that regulations were extended to the Euro-market, it could encourage the growth of other 'unregulated' channels which may continue to complicate policy. Because of different national monetary traditions, a harmonisation solution is not presently feasible. Inequities in treatment will thus remain. They are a function of the diverse structure of countries' individual regulations and not solely due to the absence or otherwise of regulations in the Euro-currency market.

The third difficulty for national monetary policy, which is closely linked to the second, has to do with the techniques of domestic monetary control. Some countries conduct their policy by targeting on the supply of domestic bank reserves and these countries might find it helpful if Euro-currency deposits were also subject to reserve requirements so that they could be taken into account automatically when formulating and implementing policy. When disintermediation occurs to the Euro-market, this might weaken the indicator role of domestic bank reserves and thus their usefulness as a target variable for monetary policy. The extension of reserve ratios to Euro-currency deposits that were not uniform with domestic reserve requirements would not, however, be a complete solution. We have argued that uniform reserve ratios are not a feasible option for all banking systems and thus flows may continue to be rechannelled through the Euro-market, particularly when the burden of domestic regulations is greater than those in the Euro-currency market, e.g. during periods of monetary restraint. At such times the demand for reserves by Euro-banks will increase relative to that by domestic banks. However, when Euro-currency reserve ratios are different from national ratios, this change in the source of the demand for bank reserves will not be offsetting. If reserve ratios are less on Euro-currency than domestic deposits, the overall demand for reserve balances may actually fall and thus national monetary policy may continue to be complicated. The authorities would also need to know the source of the demand for bank reserves. The direct improvement for policy formulation, as distinct from the indirect one, due to better information, would then be smaller.

Against any benefits of the reserve requirement proposal has to be set the sheer complexity of the scheme. The general problem is that taxing certain Euro-currency deposits may cause these to move to unregulated channels which may be even more difficult to monitor than the present Euro-currency market. A system of Euro-market non-interest-bearing reserve requirements would therefore have to be very widely implemented across countries and banks at some low uniform level if such effects were not to occur on a major scale. It is possible that the Group of Ten countries, by exercising control over banks in their own countries and branches and subsidiaries of their own banks abroad, could catch the majority of Euro-currency liabilities at present. But in itself this might raise jurisdictional questions, particularly as regards overseas subsidiaries and consortium banks. Over time, other centres and banks of other countries might grow in importance and thus even wider participation would be required. The scheme would involve a much more uniform and detailed system of bank reporting on a global basis than is presently available or could be made available in the foreseeable future; and it might involve some countries changing the structure of their national as well as their international banking regulations. These technical problems are formidable. Many of the difficulties might, however, be resolved if the reserve ratios were interest-bearing and did not act as a tax on Euro-banking. Potential disintermediation effects within the Euro-currency system and thus the need for a global and uniform scheme would be less; while the benefits of being able to monitor the market more closely and take developments there into account in formulating policy would remain. Within these various issues a judgement about the desirability and practicability of direct regulation of the Euro-markets, and the form it should take, has to be made from a national monetary control viewpoint. The overall question of Euro-market regulation has to be seen, however, in the broader context of the international financial system and, especially, the role of banks in the recycling of oil surpluses.

10.5   ANNEX: PRESS COMMUNIQUÉ ISSUED BY THE BANK FOR INTERNATIONAL SETTLEMENTS, 15 APRIL 1980

1. At their meetings in Basle on 10 March and 14 April the central bank Governors of the Group of Ten countries and Switzerland exchanged views on the evolution during recent years, and the future prospects, of the international banking system in general, and the Euro-currency market in particular.
2. The Governors recognise the important part played by the banks in recycling large surpluses which have arisen during the last few years. They noted that international bank lending aggregates have been expanding at an annual rate of some 25 per cent. Moreover, the contribution of the international banking system to recycling the large OPEC surpluses that have re-emerged will lead to further substantial growth of these aggregates.
3. In view of the present volume of international bank lending and of its prospective future role, the Governors are agreed on the importance of maintaining the soundness and stability of the international banking system and of seeking to avoid any undesirable effects either worldwide or on the conduct of policy in particular countries.
4. With these considerations in mind, the Governors have decided to strengthen regular and systematic monitoring of international banking developments, with a view to assessing their significance for the world economy, for the economies of individual countries, including particularly the operation of their domestic monetary policies, and for the soundness of the international banking system as a whole. A standing Committee on Euro-markets will consider the international banking statistics compiled by the BIS and other relevant information and report to the Governors at least twice a year, and more frequently if developments call for it. These arrangements for closer surveillance could provide a framework for intensifying, if appropriate, co-operation on monetary policies between the countries concerned.
5. Recognising that individual banks, or the international banking system as a whole, could in future be exposed to greater risks than in the past, the Governors re-affirm the cardinal importance which they attach to the maintenance of sound banking standards – particularly with regard to capital adequacy, liquidity and concentration of risks. To this end they place high priority on bringing into full effect the initiatives already taken by the Committee on Banking Regulations and Supervisory Practices with regard to the supervision of banks' international business on a consolidated basis, improved assessment of country risk exposure, and the development of more comprehensive and consistent data for monitoring the extent of banks' maturity transformation.

6. The Governors note that differences in competitive conditions between domestic and international banking that arise out of offiical regulations and policies stimulate growth of international bank lending in general; and that transactions channelled through the Euro-currency market can pose problems for the effectiveness of domestic monetary policy in those countries where such differences are particularly significant. The Governors will continue efforts already being made to reduce the differences of competitive conditions, fully recognising the difficulties arising from differences in the national structure and traditions of banking systems.

NOTES

1. 'Disintermediation' in this context refers to a redistribution of asset and credit flows from regulated to unregulated intermediaries. This term is also used to refer to a shift from an intermediary to a non-intermediary.
2. For a discussion of developments in the USA see Wenninger and Sivesind (1979), and for a discussion of Euro-currency holdings see Frydl (1979–80).
3. Wenninger and Sivesind (1979).
4. Using incomplete data available at the BIS Brittain and Bernard (1980) constructed runs of non-bank Euro-currency holdings, going back in some cases to 1963, and added these to certain components of national money stocks to derive a new set of monetary aggregates which include certain Euro-currency deposits. They then regressed the measured income velocities of these aggregates on time and compared the standard errors of the regressions: the lower the standard errors, the less unstable the trend income velocity of the aggregates. While this is at best a preliminary method of examining the impact of Euro-currency deposits on national monetary policies and says little about the underlying stability of domestic demand for money functions, the first attempt explicitly to allow for the influence of Euro-currency deposits on income velocities is of some interest.
5. The analysis was developed by Gurley and Shaw (1960) and extended by Tobin and Brainard (1963).
6. A more general model might allow for the effect of exchange-rate movements on the holdings of assets denominated in any currency, (see for example, Branson, 1979 and 1980), but under the assumption that borrower arbitrage is efficient, exchange-rate movements will not affect domestic and Euro-currency interest-rate differentials or the distribution of asset holdings in any particular currency between the domestic and the Euro-currency market.
7. The combined supply of loans schedule is written as:

$$L_s = L_s^d + L_s^e$$

$$= (1 - R)^2 D_d + D_e$$

The effect of a change in the reserve ratio, R, would then be:

$$\frac{dL_s}{dR} = -2(1-R)D_d + (1-R)^2 \frac{dD_d}{dR} + \frac{dD_e}{dR}$$

$$= -2(1-R)D_d - R(2-R)\frac{dD_d}{dR}$$

since:

$$\frac{dD_d}{dR} = -\frac{dD_e}{dR}$$

when there are only two financial markets. A perverse effect of a reserve change on total loans occurs when:

$$\frac{dL_s}{dR} > 0$$

i.e.

$$-R(2-R)\frac{dD_d}{dR} > 2(1-R)D_d$$

or

$$-\frac{R}{D_d}\frac{dD_d}{dR} > \frac{2(1-R)}{(2-R)}$$

which is the elasticity of the domestic supply of deposits with respect to the reserve change. The right-hand term can be written as

$$1 - \frac{R}{2-R} \simeq 1 - \frac{1}{2}R$$

Thus, if the domestic supply elasticity is close to unity, perverse effects may well occur, and indeed the likelihood of these will be larger, the larger the size of the domestic reserve requirement.

8. The authorities set guidelines for the rate of growth of banks' 'interest-bearing eligible liabilities' expressed as a percentage rate of growth over the average level in a specified base period. To the extent that a bank exceeded these guidelines, it had to place non-interest-bearing deposits (SSDs) with the Bank of England. The rate of call for these deposits rose progressively with the amount in excess and was 50 per cent for any excess over 5 per cent.

9. In the highest penalty zone, it was nearly 2½ times market rates.

10. In this context the so-called 'Bill' leak through the domestic bankers' acceptance market was the most important.

11. The UK authorities were well aware of the potential for disintermediation through the Euro-currency markets, commenting: 'The abolition of exchange controls will clearly make it harder for the authorities in this country to rely, in the operation of monetary policy, on direct controls and constraints on financial intermediation in this country, since increased possibilities are open for offshore financial intermediation to develop' (*Bank of England Quarterly Bulletin*, vol. 19, no. 4, December 1979, Economic Commentary, p. 378). Indeed, the potential for disintermediation has been an important aspect in the discussions on approaches to monetary control in the United Kingdom (see *Monetary Control*, Cmnd 7858, March 1980, London, HMSO).

12. Strictly controlling the supply of dollar reserve assets which continued to pay market interest rates would not solve the problem. Banks would then face the costs associated with being unable to meet their reserve ratios and would again seek to redenominate deposits or to avoid the regulations altogether.

13. It is very likely, however, that the sheer mechanics of collection and compiling Euro-currency data will mean that, at best, there will still be long lags in complete reporting. A system of sampling certain important banks in certain or all Euro-currency centres may then be one way of providing current information on market developments.

11 International Banking Stability

National authorities have long been concerned with preventing or minimising the consequences of bank failures, as the collapse of a bank involves losses for depositors and may lead to wider repercussions for the financial and economic system. The stability of the international (and national) banking system involves questions about the interrelationship between agents. Depositors and other lenders of funds must remain confident that banks are soundly run and will be able to repay their debts when they fall due. Confidence may depend on the spread of banks' lending and borrowing risks and their ability to meet unexpected losses. Authorities supervise their banks to ensure that they conform to sound banking practices and in domestic money markets provide lender of last resort facilities to overcome temporary shortages of liquidity. In the Euro-market arrangements for the provision of temporary liquidity are governed by the communiqué issued on 10 September 1974 by the central banks of the Group of Ten (see Chapter 2) which stated that they were satisfied that means were available for that purpose and would be used if and when necessary, but it also concluded that it would not be practical to lay down in advance detailed rules and procedures.

Two key features in banking stability are banks' solvency and liquidity. In practice, banking supervisors find it extremely difficult to define the concept of banking solvency in any general fashion[1] and to distinguish between banking solvency and liquidity problems. For our purposes banking solvency may be taken to refer to the situation in which a bank has a positive net worth and upon liquidation is able to repay all its debts, i.e. a bank's total realisable assets exceed its total liabilities. Banking solvency is closely related to the need for the bank to maintain capital and reserves as a cushion against losses, and to engender the confidence of depositors and other trading partners. The depletion of bank reserves from financial losses, fraud or simple mismanagement are the most likely reasons for banking insolvency.

Banking liquidity may be taken to refer to the ability of the bank to meet its commitments on a day-to-day basis, for example to repay deposits or to meet contractual loan commitments and immediate operating expenses. A bank's liquidity position will depend on the maturity profile of its assets and liabilities and on its ability to liquidate assets or to attract new funds, for example from other banks (or the central bank), to meet drains on its cash reserves. A bank which is solvent may find that it is unable to meet its day-to-day commitments because of its inability to obtain immediately usable funds. Alternatively, a bank which is highly liquid may still be insolvent if its total liabilities exceed its realisable assets.

The continuing stability of the banking system requires that most banks are both solvent and liquid. Solvency and liquidity requirements might indeed be viewed as 'tolerance limits' of the banking system, and concerns about individual banking instability might be seen in terms of the types of banking practices which affect these limits and types of financial environment which could give rise to events which push the banking system beyond the limits. It is possible that even for soundly run banks chance events which lead to a loss of confidence by depositors can lead to instability, and the return of the system to stability will depend on how the banks and other agents react. To illustrate these types of processes we begin by simulating a very simple model of an international bank which is subject to various shocks. Having completed this illustrative exercise, we examine the stabilising and destabilising factors in the international banking system.

11.1 A HYPOTHETICAL MODEL

The starting-point for the model is the bank's balance-sheet identity of Chapter 7. This equates the volume of bank loans, L, to the supply of non-bank deposits placed in the bank, D, the volume of borrowing by the bank in the interbank market, B, and the bank's capital base, K:

$$L = D + B + K \qquad (1)$$

To give this balance-sheet identity some analytical content we make the following assumptions about the adjustment process by agents. The supply of non-bank deposits to the bank is assumed to depend on the past values of deposits and, to catch confidence factors, on a measure of the bank's ability to repay depositors — the ratio of non-bank deposits to the bank's capital base in the previous period.[2] If this ratio moves away from some critical level, a_1, which might be derived as some prudential norm or as an average for the banking system, non-banks adjust their volume of deposits with the bank, the speed of adjustment depending on the parameter a_0. Additionally, the supply of deposits may also be subject to exogenous shocks, u. This is written:

$$D = D_{-1} + a_0\left[a_1 - \left(\frac{D}{K}\right)_{-1}\right] + u \tag{2}$$

It is also possible that the supply of non-bank deposits will be sensitive to the relative interest rates offered by the bank on its non-bank deposits. In the simulations it is assumed, however, that this interest rate is set, as the average of market rates, at $\bar{r}$ and does not vary.

The supply of loans to the bank in the interbank market follows a similar specification, depending on the supply of interbank loans in the previous period and a measure of the bank's ability to meet its interbank borrowing commitments − the ratio of interbank borrowing to the bank's capital base in the previous period. It is also assumed that interbank loans are interest-rate sensitive and increase as the interbank interest rate the bank is willing to pay, r, rises above the average level of market interest rates, $\bar{r}$. The interest-sensitive supply is not, however, unlimited, as banks may become increasingly unwilling to lend to other banks as interbank margins widen. The interbank interest rate is an indicator of the bank's financial health which other banks may be expected to react to when lending funds in the market. To stylise this observation and to keep the model as simple as possible it is therefore assumed that if the interbank interest rate rises above some critical level, r^*, the supply of interbank lending dries up. At this point the bank will be unable to afford or attract new interbank funds and in the absence of central bank intervention and its ability to liquidate other assets the bank would be unable to meet its commitments and would become illiquid. The interbank loan supply schedule is written as:

$$B = B_{-1} + b_0(r - \bar{r}) + b_2\left[b_3 - \left(\frac{B}{K}\right)_{-1}\right] \tag{3}$$

for $r < r^*$.

The bank's supply of loans to primary borrowers, L, depends on its supply in the previous period and on its reactions to factors which affect its liquidity and solvency. We assume the bank is aware of the critical interbank interest rate at which it would be unable to borrow funds in the interbank market and will seek to adjust its balance-sheet by, for example, liquidating assets to keep its borrowing rate below this critical level. It does this sequentially, reacting to the interbank interest rate in the previous period. (If the interbank borrowing rate falls below the level of average market rates, the bank will also react by expanding its loan portfolio.) The bank also adjusts to its solvency position, which is measured as the ratio of loans outstanding to the bank's capital base in the previous period. The bank seeks to alter the volume of its total lending to bring this ratio to some optimal level, c_1. Should, however, this ratio fall below some critical value, $(L/K)^*$, it is assumed that the bank will become insolvent, as it lacks sufficient capital resources to cover future operations. The stock of bank loans outstanding also declines when there are loan losses, Z. The stock of loans equation is written:

$$L = L_{-1} + c_0 \left[c_1 - \left(\frac{L}{K} \right)_{-1} \right] - c_2 \left(\frac{r - \bar{r}}{r^* - \bar{r}} \right)_{-1} - Z \qquad (4)$$

for $L/K > (L/K)^*$. Loans losses, Z, are assumed to follow the profile

$$Z = dL_{-1} + v$$

such that a proportion, d, of loans outstanding in the previous period are expected to go bad in the next period and there may also be unexpected shocks, v.

The gross profits of the bank, π, depend on the return on non-defaulting loans, $L - Z$, the size of loan losses, and the cost of borrowing funds in the interbank market and from non-banks. The return on loans, as usual, is expressed in the form of a fixed spread, s, over average market interest rates:

$$\pi = (s + \bar{r})(L - Z) - \bar{r}D - rB - Z \qquad (5)$$

Gross profits are used to meet operating expenses, E, and, when the remaining net profits are positive (negative), as an addition to (substraction from) the capital base of the bank. The capital stock of the bank expands or contracts depending on wheter $\pi - E$ is positive or negative:

$$K = K_{-1} + \pi - E \qquad (6)$$

The bank must meet its operating expenses even if it is incurring losses and these are determined in the model simply as a proportional charge on existing capital:

$$E = eK$$

Equations (1)–(6) form a simple dynamic model of an international bank. When the bank's profits are positive (and exceed operating expenses) the bank's capital stock expands. This engenders confidence among depositors and other lenders of funds and encourages them to increase their placements with the bank. The bank will expand its lending and the overall size of its balance-sheet. The system also exhibits stabilising properties because of the bank's reaction to its liquidity and solvency positions. To illustrate this we can give the various parameters in the model some hypothetical values. As a basic case the following values are chosen:

Parameter	L	D	B	K	a_0	a_1	b_0	b_2	b_3	$\bar{r}$	r^*	c_0	c_1	c_2	$\left(\dfrac{L}{K}\right)^*$	d	s	e	u	v
Numerical value	1,000	600	300	100	50	6	2,000	25	2	0.1	0.15	50	10	20	25	0.005	0.01	0.1	0	0

Simulating the model dynamically with these parameter values shows that after ten periods the loan stock and supply of non-bank deposits to the bank have grown by around 24 per cent, interbank borrowing by 16 per cent, the bank's capital stock by 34 per cent, and the interbank interest rate has risen very marginally to 10.15 per cent (see Table 11.1). The system is dynamically stable. The bank is making profits and its total balance-sheet is expanding. Let us now shock the system and see how it responds. The immediate effects of an exogenous withdrawal of 10 per cent of non-bank deposits causes the bank to borrow funds in the interbank market to meet the withdrawal, and interbank interest rates rise to 13.75 per cent. The higher cost of funding its loans causes the bank to make losses which cut into its capital and reserves. The bank reacts by reducing its stock of lending: first, because of the higher cost of interbank borrowing, it will liquidate assets; and second, because of its losses, the loans to capital ratio rises above its optimal level and the bank will thus attempt to reduce the overall size of its balance-sheet. The losses incurred by the bank cause other agents to react: non-banks reduce further their deposits as the deposits to capital ratio rises above the 'critical' level specified in the model; and in the interbank market the rise in interest rates needed to attract residual funds to meet deposit withdrawals is larger than otherwise, because the ratio of borrowing to capital also moves above its hypothetical 'critical' level. The system, however, remains stable. The bank is able to reduce its stock of loans and thus its need to borrow funds. Subsequent earnings more than cover losses and profits replenish the bank's capital stock. Solvency and confidence ratios thus return to their starting values. After four periods the bank's balance-sheet

Table 11.1
Results for base simulations after ten periods

	Loans	Deposits	Interbank borrowing	Capital	Interbank interest rate
Starting value	1,000	600	300	100	10%
Base run	1,232	749	349	134	10.15%
Deposit loss of 10% in period 1	1,160	706	330	124	10.28%
Loan loss of 3% in period 1	962	585	275	102	10.36%

begins to expand and at the end of the ten periods it is 16 per cent larger than immediately before the deposit withdrawal (Table 11.1).

The effects of an unexpected 3 per cent loan loss on the system are analytically similar. The loan loss is borne out of the bank's gross profits, which become negative, and its capital therefore falls. All solvency and confidence ratios thus rise above their critical levels, leading to reactions by all the agents: the bank reduces its lending, non-banks reduce their supply of deposits and the cost of interbank borrowing rises as other banks become less willing to lend. Again, however, the system remains dynamically stable, as the bank success-fully cuts back its lending and thus its need to borrow funds. The loan loss, which directly depletes the bank's capital base and affects depositor confidence, has, however, a numerically larger impact on the bank's balance-sheet, and after ten periods it is still below its starting value before (Table 11.1). Interest rates in the interbank market also remain somewhat higher.

It will be evident from this discussion that certain parameters may play an important role in the dynamics and stability of the system. Three are examined here: the speed with which the bank can adjust its balance-sheet; the determinants of the bank's profitability; and the loans to capital ratio set by the bank or its regulatory authority. It is most interesting to see how varying these parameters affects the limits of tolerance at which the bank becomes unstable, i.e. the limits at which the bank becomes either insolvent or illiquid. To do this the system is therefore simulated under three alternative assumptions:

(a) halving the speed of adjustment by the bank to its optimal loans to capital ratio, i.e. reducing the parameter c_0 from 50 to 25;

(b)   halving the value of the lending spread, s, from 1.00 to 0.5; and
(c)   lowering the bank's optimal loans to capital ratio by ten per cent from 10 to 9.1.

These alternative assumptions might characterise respectively:

(a)   a situation where the bank has fewer assets that it can liquidate or where it has been lengthening the maturity of its loans;
(b)   an aggressive market environment where lending margins have been cut through competitive pressures; and
(c)   the introduction of prudential regulations which require that banks hold lower loans to capital ratios (i.e. higher capital–asset ratios).

The results of the simulations for the stability of the bank are reported in Table 11.2. The following main conclusions emerge. First, reducing the speed of adjustment of the bank has a marked effect on its tolerance to loan losses. Halving the speed of adjustment approximately halves the size of the loan shock which the bank can withstand (it also tends to alter the constraint on the bank from one of insolvency to one of illiquidity, though in the simulations where the constraint was one of illiquidity only a slightly larger loan loss would have made the bank insolvent). Second, reducing the lending spread from 1 to 0.5 per cent reduces the tolerance limits of the bank in all simulations. This result is most marked when the bank has a slower speed of adjustment and a higher loans to capital ratio (see section BI of Table 11.2). In these circumstances a loan loss of only 2.9 per cent causes the bank to become illiuqid. Third, the effect of lowering the bank's loans to capital ratio is to improve the bank's stability in all simulations: its tolerance to loan losses increases by at least 1 per cent and to deposit losses by around 4 per cent. Fourth, the tolerance of the system to deposit losses is much greater than to loan losses. Finally, the most binding constraint in the simulations is frequently one of illiquidity. This may simply reflect the arbitrary value of r^* (set 50 per cent above average market rates) chosen as the cut-off-point for the supply of funds in the interbank market and the assumption of proportional adjustments in the equations. In this model there is also no central bank willing to provide residual liquidity to the banking system, which is instead supplied through the interbank market. By introducing central bank intervention, in the form of supplying funds to the bank when the interbank interest rate reaches its critical value, it is possible to remove the liquidity constraint and to move the binding constraint on the bank to one of insolvency. Central bank intervention has, however, a very limited

Table 11.2
Percentage loan and deposit losses at which
the bank becomes unstable

A. FAST ADJUSTMENT

	I		II	
	Higher loans to capital ratio		Lower loans to capital ratio	
Value of the spread	Loans	Deposits	Loans	Deposits
1%	6.6†	13.2*	7.9†	20.6*
0.5%	6.0*	12.3*	7.4†	19.8*

B. SLOWER ADJUSTMENT

	I		II	
	Higher loans to capital ratio		Lower loans to capital ratio	
Value of the spread	Loans	Deposits	Loans	Deposits
1%	3.9*	13.2*	5.0*	17.0*
0.5%	2.9*	12.3*	4.3*	16.2*

* = 'illiquid' when $r > 0.15$.
† = 'insolvent' when $L/K > 25$.

effect on banking solvency unless there is a major element of subsidy in the interest rates at which the central bank lends to the bank.

11.2   SOURCES OF STABILITY AND INSTABILITY

The hypothetical model illustrates three potential sources of banking instability: disturbances to the supply of deposits to the bank and the costs at which they are available — bank funding risks; disturbances to the loan stock — credit risks; and trends in the parameters of the system. Each of these are now examined in turn in the context of international banking.

11.2.1   *Funding risks*

As active financial intermediaries, banks in the Euro-market mismatch the maturity and currency composition of their assets and liabilities, which exposes banks to short- and longer-term funding risks.

Short-term mismatching. In the short term a bank may not always match exactly each outgoing deposit or loan with an incoming deposit of identical amount, maturity and currency. One of the most important short-term reasons for running an unmatched book is to take a view on interest rates (see Chapter 3). A bank may also run a 'jobber's book' and refrain from matching off a lot of small 'retail' deals until a position has been built up which is big enough to trade off in the wholesale market at more favourable interest rates. Similar considerations apply to a bank's currency position where it may take a view about future exchange rates (Chapter 8). When a bank has an unmatched book it runs the risk that interest rates and exchange rates may move against it in the short-term, causing losses for the bank.

Following the large foreign exchange losses encountered by several banks in 1974 (see Chapter 2), banks carefully monitor and impose limits on their foreign exchange exposure and supervisory authorities in some countries also impose limits on banks' unmatched currency positions. The foreign exchange losses also caused banks to widen their trading margins in the foreign exchange markets to cover the risks involved, and in recent years foreign exchange trading has been a highly profitable business for some banks. The greatest proportion of foreign exchange transactions are anyway undertaken on a covered basis, and the covering operation need not expose the bank to a foreign exchange risk. In practice, short-term interest-rate risks are reasonably quantifiable as a combination of the size of the unmatched position and the period of unmatching, and the management of banks usually, and supervisors sometimes, set limits for the amount of short-term mismatching allowed. Because of the roll-over technique and the floating-rate nature of Euro-market loans, the period for short-term mismatching may be quite short, thus limiting losses. An individual bank could even eliminate all short-term interest-rate risk by borrowing funds in the interbank market at a maturity to match those of the next roll-over date. But all banks cannot avoid short-term interest-rate risks in this way. It is extremely unlikely that the initial maturity of deposits in the market will exactly match that of loans to roll-over dates and thus some banks have to mismatch the maturity of their deposits and loans.

The mismatching by individual banks need not be a problem

when each bank pays regard to its own amount of maturity transformation. There is, however, a concern that interbank trading may
accentuate this process. With a large amount of interbank trading the
link between the initial lender and ultimate borrower may expand
into a long chain as one bank passes funds on to another. If each bank
in the chain were to undertake an additional piece of maturity transformation, this could 'gear up' the maturity mismatch between *initial*
non-bank deposits and *final* non-bank loans. The system as a whole
might then become more vulnerable to a withdrawal of non-bank
deposits. We have seen (Chapter 3) that such interbank maturity
transformation does not generally happen and need not be a source
of concern. Indeed, to the extent that short-term maturity mismatching reflects a view on interest rates, it would take a rather
unusual set of expectations to expand the maturity structure in this
way, and specifically that each successive market participant expected interest rates to fall by more than the implicit market forecast. Short-term mismatch risks are thus reasonably quantifiable and
can be readily taken into account by banks. They need not be of
concern when individual banks are prudent in their policies.

Longer-term availability of funds. In the Euro-market, loans are
frequently made for much longer periods than the typical Euro-
currency deposit or the period to roll-over dates. This longer-term
maturity transformation exposes a bank to the risk that at some
time it might be unable to attract foreign currency deposits to fund
its Euro-currency lending.

Banks in the Euro-market do not have the access to central bank
discount facilities in foreign currencies that domestic banks have in
domestic currencies. If national exchange controls and other regulations allow it, banks may use their domestic currency resources to
meet a shortfall of foreign currency deposits, but that could involve
foreign exchange losses unless central banks are willing to guarantee
the rates of exchange. The view of the central banks on providing
international lender of last resort facilities, as recorded in their 1974
communiqué (see Chapter 2), is that while they would obviously
intervene to prevent a market collapse, for several reasons, they
would not provide the regular discount facilities in the Euro-market
that they do in their domestic markets. Assistance in domestic markets is given in domestic currencies; however, in international markets
it may be needed in foreign currencies, and the arrangements would
be much more complex and would involve co-operation and agreements between the authorities responsible in different countries.
Residual funding by banks to meet withdrawals of deposits is therefore achieved though borrowing in the interbank market (recall the
hypothetical model).

As long as the credit standing of individual banks is not in doubt, the interbank system functions well, and market interest rates direct funds from surplus to deficit banks on a global basis. If funds are suddenly withdrawn and placed in national banking systems (and providing there are no national capital controls), the interbank network should ensure that funds are rechannelled in some form to the Euro-currency market. The interbank mechanism does not, however, guarantee the availability of funds. For example, in a political crisis deposits might be shifted out of smaller banks into larger ones, on the simple grounds that bigger banks are on the whole more likely to stay in existence through a crisis than smaller ones, and deposits may move into national markets where they may be more protected by central banks. As in the hypothetical model deposit withdrawals may cause a bank losses, affect its solvency and liquidity and make other banks reluctant to lend. The cost of funds to the bank in the interbank market may rise sharply and in the extreme it may be unable to attract deposits from other banks. The bank would become illiquid unless it could sell off assets. Because of the potential for individual banking instability, some bankers have suggested that banks should create their own fund of liquidity to which individual banks would voluntarily pay in funds and could resort in the case of an emergency in terms of liquidity – it has been termed a private safety net (Ossola, 1980).

The linkages between banks through the interbank market raise, however, concerns for the overall stability of the system. The interbank lending means that the quality of one bank's balance-sheet is related to those of other banks it lends to. If Euro-bank B is lending funds to Euro-bank A and a borrower of A's funds (which might be another bank), call it Z (see Figure 11.1), defaults, this may affect A's liquidity and solvency and thus also the quality of B's balance-sheet and its ability to attract deposits. Similarly, if A is lending funds to B and a borrower of B's funds (say Y) defaults, this will influence A's balance-sheet. This market interdependence, which is formalised when banks form syndicates to lend to individual borrowers (X in Figure 11.1), may therefore make the structure of the international market more unstable, generalising liquidity problems throughout the market. Indeed, the failure of Herstatt – a relatively small bank – in 1974 caused a loss of confidence in other institutions and led, for a time, to general market instability. In extreme circumstances it is unlikely that a privately funded safety-net would be sufficient to maintain confidence in the market, since its resources would necessarily be limited and central bank intervention would be needed to stabilise the system. Under the 1974 communiqué it would appear that such support would be forthcoming, but perhaps

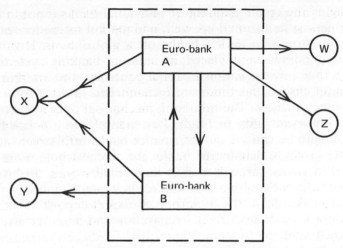

Figure 11.1   Interbank market

only when there was a generalised loss of banking confidence and possibly not when an individual bank found itself in difficulty.

In lending funds in the interbank market, banks are, however, aware of the links between their balance-sheets and of the potential risks which this may involve. There is normally some tiering in the level of interbank interest rates, reflecting the market's perception of the credit standing of different banks in the market; and in the wake of the Herstatt crisis many banks began to assess much more actively their interbank lending. A bank may, for example, make judgements about the solvency of other banks it borrows from and lends to; it may watch the percentage of funds drawn from particular banks fairly closely, to avoid too great a dependence on a small number of interbank participants, and establish informal lines of credit with a very large number of other banks in the market. Participants in the interbank market will also limit the amounts they are willing to lend to particular borrowers, and in some cases may try to discover for what purpose another bank is seeking funds. What is of concern is the soundness of individual banks, the ability of banks to discriminate between the soundness of other banks in the market when placing funds and the ultimate riskiness of final borrowers, rather than the interbank trading *per se*. Interbank risk assessment generally adds to the overall stability of the system.

The assessment of interbank risks becomes a complex matter when there is lending between different nationalities of banks in the same or different market centres. As well as institutional risks, interbank trading may involve country risks (defined below). For example, if a British bank lends funds to a Brazilian bank in London, the funds may ultimately find their way to Brazil and may therefore have to be assessed as part of the lending bank's broader loan exposure to Brazil. Moreover, if a bank is lending funds through its own foreign branches located, for example, in offshore centres, this may involve a risk that the authorities in the foreign county could impose restrictions on the operations of the foreign branch (this risk is sometimes known as 'transit' or transfer risk). Combining these various interbank risks, the loan by a British bank in London to a Brazilian bank located, for example, in the Caribbean area would involve (a) an institutional risk – the risk that the borrowing bank is itself not in a position to be able to repay the loan; (b) a country risk – an increase in exposure to Brazilian borrowers; and (c) a 'transit' risk – the risk that the Caribbean country concerned may impose restrictions on Brazilian banks' operations which prevent it from repaying its debt.

The vulnerability of the international banking system to sudden and large withdrawals may be increased because of the concentration of deposits in the hands of OPEC. Such deposit concentration means that Euro-market banks cannot rely on the 'law of large numbers' to ensure that on average funds will be returned to them when they fall due for repayment. The dependence on a few depositors may also expose the system to political developments when there is a change in the relationship between the West and a principal depositor. Because of concern about this dependence some banks in the market offer depositors uncompetitive interest rates, which either dissuade the depositor from placing new funds or provide the bank with an additional lending margin to cover funding risks. As with other funding risks, deposit concentration would only seriously affect a bank's operations if withdrawals made other banks reluctant to lend. The fixed-term nature of Euro-currency deposits may also give the bank time to find other funding sources or to liquidate assets if it fears that a major depositor is running down its placements.

11.2.2 *Lending risks*

The growing volume of indebtedness of countries to private banks (see Chapter 6) has raised concerns about the vulnerability of the banking system to defaults by countries on their debts. Concerns have been heightened by the speed with which debt charges have increased in recent years, as theoretically they can build up to a position where a sustained rate of expansion in international lending would be needed solely to cover debt payments. Domar (1950) provides the formula for the ratio of debt charges to new annual lending. It rises asymptotically to the limit

$$\frac{a + i}{a + g}$$

where a is the annual amortisation rate, i is the interest rate, and g is the rate of growth of annual lending. Thus if the rate of interest is 5 per cent and annual lending grows by 5 per cent, the debt charge will mount until it exactly equals the annual lending. The continuing transfer of new resources to developing countries requires that the rate of lending grows faster than the rate of interest.

Definition. Country risk refers to the possibility that the sovereign authorities or other borrowers in a country will be unable or unwilling to continue to service their foreign currency debt commitments. Such a risk is frequently seen as additional to normal borrower risk, though in many cases sovereign governments are themselves the principal borrower in a particular country. Instances may, however, arise where a corporation in a foreign country, while able and willing to make debt repayments, is prevented from doing so by the government. This latter risk is sometimes called 'transfer' risk and is normally a function of a country's ability to continue to generate foreign exchange through export activities, to draw on reserves or to obtain additional foreign loans. Debt repayments may also be jeopardised because of political events or motivations which may follow internal socio-political upheavals. Country risk covers all these risks in a more general way.

In recent years no major sovereign borrower has defaulted on its debts and the loan-loss experience of major banks has been much better on international than on domestic lending.[3] Average loan-loss figures obscure, however, the large number of international re-schedulings of debt, of which there have been over thirty during the past twenty years. Under a rescheduling the maturity of the loan may be lengthened, the terms made less onerous or a new loan granted simply to allow the debtor country to repay its debt obligations. At times reschedulings have been encouraged by the IMF or other friendly governments which have been unable themselves to provide official finance on a scale sufficient to make continued commitments of private capital unnecessary. Such official encouragement may have led banks to make over-optimistic assessments about the risks involved in sovereign lending on the assumption that official sources of finance will be forthcoming in a crisis. It is not unknown for sovereign borrowers to default on their debts. For example, during the 1920s about $20 billion of US dollar bonds had been issued in New York by foreign governments and by 1933 nearly one-quarter were in default.

Assessment of country risks. The most likely reason for a country finding itself unable to meet its debt obligations is a shortage of foreign exchange, perhaps because of some exogenous shock to its balance of payments or from national economic mismanagement. The reasons for a country deciding to repudiate its debts are likely, however, to be altogether more complex. It might, for example, be a political decision taken in terms of the balance of benefits and costs, or following political upheaval which brings a change of view about relationships with Western banks or simply causes the normal payments mechanism in the country to break down. To assess these types of risks many banks operate quite complex country risk-assessment systems to improve information about the risks involved, and this can be used in making lending decisions and to reduce the probability that they will have to write off or reschedule part of their loan books. Generally these systems have built up over many years and involve a blend of territorial expertise and analysis of local and international statistics. There is an extensive literature about country risk assessment and the following discussion provides only a brief summary of the techniques and issues involved.

There are basically two types of approach, though they are complementary and are often employed together. One is based on a subjective or qualitative assessment of country risks and is perhaps most widely used by banks. The second involves a quantitative or statistical assessment. Statistical approaches have the advantage that they provide more consistent frameworks within which a large volume of data on a group of countries can be analysed in a systematic fashion and they thus facilitate comparisons between the performance of different countries and over time; so far, however, they have no well-established predictive ability.

The simplest qualitative assessment system may be quite informal, based on direct contact of the management of the bank with the borrower. More usually it is formalised in the form of country reports which may be standardised and compare common statistics between countries. Qualitative approaches have the advantage that, in being more subjective, they allow for the assessment of the socio-political and managerial climate in a country in arriving at a view of its creditworthiness. But, to be effective, they require detailed knowledge of the countries under investigation, and therefore may involve a large commitment of human resources.

Quantitative assessment systems are largely concerned with the narrower question of a country's ability to pay. To measure this a large number of relevant statistics can be calculated. These might include the debt service ratio (DSR), which is the ratio of interest plus amortisation commitments to foreign exchange earnings, the ratio of debt outstanding to exports or GNP, measures of a country's vulnerability to external shocks (such as its dependence on one or two primary commodities for export earnings), and the degree of development and sophistication of the economy. The DSR is a valuable 'rule of thumb', as it measures the country's ability to meet immediate debt service commitments, but it may also be highly variable as it fluctuates with export earnings or a bunching of amortisation payments. Most individual statistics give very little indication of the dynamic aspects of a country's economy, and a check-list may therefore be drawn up within which each statistic is given a weight (perhaps subjectively) according to its assumed predictive ability of debt problems, and these weights may be added to form a summary statistic of the country's credit rating.

Some academically interesting approaches have attempted to apply econometric techniques to identify the precise set of factors, and the weights attached to them, associated with debt difficulties. To be effective these techniques require, however, a large number of observations, but sufficient data are not usually available to provide good estimates and they have hardly been used at all by banks. In a 1971 study Frank and Cline applied discriminant analysis to a sample of twenty-six countries. This analysis seeks to divide a group of countries into those which have rescheduled/defaulted on their debts and those which have not, by attaching weights to some chosen set of economic variables. Frank and Cline's study successfully identified all cases of rescheduling in their sample, while falsely predicting rescheduling in only 9 per cent of the sample. Updating the study and applying it to the post-oil crisis environment, Smith (1979) found, however, that the equation significantly over-predicted the number of reschedulings in 1977.

An improvement over discriminant analysis is logit analysis. Unlike discriminant analysis, which seeks to divide a population into two distinct groups, logit analysis attempts to estimate the probability that an observation belongs to one group rather than another. In applying logit analysis to a sample of eleven countries over the period 1965–72, Feder and Just (1977) identified several significant variables and estimated the following equation:

$$\ln[\frac{P}{1-P}] = 59.2x_1 + 0.4x_2 - 39.6x_3 - 0.1x_4 - 2.9x_5$$

$$- 52.6x_6$$

where

x_1 = debt service/exports
x_2 = imports/reserves
x_3 = amortisation/debt outstanding
x_4 = income *per capita*
x_5 = capital inflow/debt service
x_6 = average real export growth over eight years
P = probability of default or rescheduling

Again, however, Smith reports that this equation has a tendency to over-predict using recent data.

In 1978 the Federal Reserve Board introduced the requirement that, as part of the supervisory process, US bank examiners would in future require commercial banks to demonstrate that they operate an effective assessment system, though the precise structure of this would be a matter for the bank itself; and all supervisors in the Group of Ten countries are interested to see that their banks are operating risk assessment systems. Some central banks also operate their own country risk assessment systems and may transmit their views to banks involved if this is thought to be appropriate. But central banks are in no better position to assess possible lending risks than commercial banks – after all, central banks are not in the business of making commercial judgements about the creditworthiness of borrowers.

System risk. Banks may be able to limit their risk concentration in any one country by diversifying lending among a range of countries. The diversification of overall risk exposure depends, however, on the risks of default by individual borrowers being negatively correlated such that if one country defaults on its debt it is highly improbable that this will lead other countries to follow suit. If, however, country risks are positively correlated, this exposes the international banking system to the risk of cumulative defaults. Shocks such as oil price rises are global in nature and, given the relatively small demand for international bank borrowing by oil-exporting countries, it is extremely difficult for the banks to diversify effectively the risks of future oil price rises. The involvement of primarily Western banks in the financing of global deficits also raises the question of the political economy of international banking. In the short term private international financial flows may have reduced the dependency of Eastern Europe and the Third World on conditional financial flows from Western governments and institutions. In the longer term the indebtedness of sovereign governments to Western banks increases their financial dependency on the West and the vulnerability of the Western banking system to political developments in the rest of the world.

It is generally the case, however, that different countries' economic and political structures are quite diverse and that the impact of even global shocks on countries' economic positions and political developments on countries' relationships with Western banks will also be relatively diverse. Thus, although banks are unable to diversify all risks in their international portfolios, there is still considerable scope for country risk diversification. A study by Goodman (1981), which compared four country risk proxies for sixteen major borrowing non-oil developing countries, found that the bulk of the variance in the country risk proxies was non-systematic between countries and was thus diversifiable and that there was little change in cross-country relationships between the proxies after the 1974 oil price rise. Moreover, as has been discussed in Chapter 7, the growth of international bank lending is itself a diversification of bank loan portfolios away from their domestic economies. Taking domestic and international bank lending together, international bank lending may be seen as adding to the stability of the whole banking system. Still, the existence of some unquantifiable system risk and the continuing growth of country indebtedness raise the possibility that the international banking system could be subject to a large shock in the future.

11.2.3 *Recent trends*

The choice of the parameters varied in the hypothetical model was not arbitrary, for in recent years concerns have been expressed about the effect of lengthening loan maturities (which has implications for the possible speed of adjustment by the bank if a smaller proportion of the bank's total lending falls due for repayment in any period) and the decline in banks' lending margins. During the latter 1970s there was also a discernible decline in the capital asset ratios of banks in a number of countries. Because the definitions of capital vary between countries and also over time it is very difficult to make comparisons; Table 11.3 gives some indication of the trends, however. The reason for this decline appears to lie mainly in the impact of inflation on the banks' balance-sheets[4] rather than as a result of a decline in banks' profitability.[5] While the simulations in section 11.1 are only illustrative, they suggest that in a *ceteris paribus* world the effect of all three factors is to reduce the tolerance limits of the bank and its ability to cope with unexpected shocks. In the most extreme simulation a loan loss of only 2.9 per cent, which represents about 30 per cent of the bank's initial capital stock, destabilises the system. Some

Table 11.3
**Capital asset ratios of banks
in selected countries***

	1971	1976	1980
USA	5.0	4.0	3.7
United Kingdom	6.5	5.7	5.9
West Germany	3.4	3.1	2.7
Japan	4.1	3.2	3.0

* Ratios are derived as the average of the ratios of
individual banks from each country which
fall within the world's fifty largest banks.

Source: David Fairlambs, 'Capital ratios come under
scrutiny', *The Banker*, September 1981, 103–9.

banks have exposures to individual countries which exceed 30 per
cent of their capital and the number appears to be increasing.[6]

In the real world *ceteris paribus* assumptions are not, however,
likely to be even approximately valid and, as discussed in Chapter
7, the decline in Euro-market spreads and lengthening of loan maturities were accompanied by some improvement in banks' funding and
lending risks. In 1980 and 1981 there were also indications that the
trend to declining spreads and lengthening maturities was being
reversed. Average spreads for developing countries had risen from
$\frac{3}{4}$ per cent in 1979 to $1\frac{1}{8}$ per cent by mid-1981 and there was evidence
of upward movements in spreads to other borrowers and greater
price discrimination between borrowers on the basis of their credit
risks. By 1981 the average length of loan maturities had also shortened
by around three years on syndicated medium-term Euro-credits and a
much larger proportion of international bank lending was being
undertaken in short-term credits. In the second half of 1980 two-
thirds of the increase in banks' external claims were in an original
maturity of up to one year. There was, moreover, little evidence that
the maturity profile of banks' external claims had shown any tendency
to lengthen between 1978 and 1980 (see Table 11.4).

The implications of the decline in capital asset ratios for international bank lending are not precisely clear. The initial level of
banks' capital ratios may have been too high or bank lending risks
may have been declining (perhaps because of their greater international portfolio diversification). However, it is hard to believe that
the international environment is perceptibly less risky now than five

Table 11.4
Maturity distribution of banks' external assets
(in percentages of total assets)

	Less than one year	One to two years	Over two years	Unallocated
Developing countries				
Mid-1978	46.3	10.4	34.7	8.6
End-1980	49.0	7.2	35.6	8.2
All countries*				
Mid-1978	45.3	10.6	34.1	10.0
End-1980	45.5	7.7	37.2	9.6

* Excludes the reporting area defined as the Group of Ten countries, Switzerland, Austria, Denmark and Ireland and certain of their foreign affiliates.
Source: BIS Press release 'The maturity distribution of international bank lending', July 1981.

to ten years ago. The banks themselves (or their supervisory authorities) may decide that the deterioration in capital ratios has gone far enough and that they must behave more cautiously, reducing the pace at which they permit their business to grow and increasing the price they charge for their services. In either of the latter cases it may mean some reduction in the role of banks in the international intermediation process. Some commentators, however, argue that a contraction by the banks will not be so easy. Overlending in the past has meant that some banks have become hostage to their main borrowers in the sense that only by continuing to lend can the bank ensure that the borrower will service its debts and thus allow the bank to stay in business. In these circumstances the international banking system would become increasingly fragile and the erosion in banks' capital ratios could continue until the point is reached where confidence in banks can no longer be sustained.

11.3 PUBLIC CONCERNS AND RESPONSES

At first supervisory authorities were not unduly concerned with the growth of international banking, and in domestic markets prudential regulations were mainly directed at protecting depositors at the level of the individual bank. However, as banks moved increasingly towards the active management of their liabilities and as wholesale time deposit markets developed, including the borrowing and lending of funds between banks themselves in the interbank market, supervisory authorities began to pay more attention to the overall stability of the banking system. With the growth of international banking and the establishment of foreign branches and subsidiaries, the links between banks extended across national boundaries and into foreign currencies. Different nationalities of banks became more closely integrated through the Euro-currency interbank market and with the formation of international syndicates when making loans. This internationalisation and integration of banking systems led to a range of new concerns for the overall supervision of the world's banking system.

First, because different banking systems are linked through the interbank market, failures in one nation's banks or the interbank mechanism may spill over and affect the stability of another's. There is therefore concern about the functioning of the interbank market and the soundness of different nationalities of banks involved in it. Moreover, when international banking is organised through foreign banking establishments, the authorities in the country of the parent bank concerned may have less power to oversee its banks' foreign operations. Effective supervision may depend on other countries' authorities, and there is concern to ensure effective global supervision of the banking system. Second, when there is cross-border lending the legal jurisdiction of the country of the bank concerned may not extend to borrowers in other countries, and in particular there are few legal sanctions which can be taken against sovereign borrowers which default on their debts. There is therefore concern that banks should have effective credit and country risk assessment systems. Third, in the Euro-currency market the currency of denomination of bank deposits and loans is frequently other than that of the country of the authorities responsible for supervising the bank. The scope for authorities to provide lender of last resort facilities in foreign currencies is more limited than in domestic currencies. If there were to be no co-operation from other central banks, say in the form of foreign currency swaps, the most any individual central bank could do would be to commit its own foreign exchange markets. Even for important countries the amount of foreign exchange which could be made available in this way without causing a run on the domestic currency may be limited. The commitment to central bank co-operation does of course exist, but considerations relating to the immediate availability of foreign exchange still point to a greater need for effective prudential supervision.

In international banking the distribution of welfare gains and losses may also be different from those associated with domestic banking. Domestic intermediation improves the flow of savings into productive investment and the efficiency of the domestic payments transmission mechanism and generally adds to the level of domestic economic activity. There is, however, no guarantee that the distribution of final expenditures associated with international lending will be related in any systematic way to the role of the nation's banks in the international intermediation process. Indirect benefits accrue to the domestic economy because of the influence the external intermediation process has in sustaining world activity and enlarging trade flows, but these gains may be less tangible and more difficult to quantify. There are direct benefits to the country of the banks concerned when international business is profitable and generates domestic employment and invisible export earnings, but these gains might not always be seen as sufficient to compensate the country for accepting the possible welfare losses associated with international banking instability which could disrupt the country's domestic financial system. There may also, perhaps, be less concern in international markets about the protection of depositors since, in this respect, an international bank collapse would have fewer repercussions for the domestic community.

11.3.1   *Official responses*[7]

At the beginning of the 1970s the perceptions and techniques of banking supervisory authorities had not kept pace with the rapid internationalisation of the world's banking industry. The Herstatt failure and the burden of recycling the OPEC surpluses highlighted, however, the potential instability of the international banking system and led to the development of new forums and arrangements for the prudential supervision of international banking. The scope for individual national action is much more limited in the international sphere and thus in 1974 the governors of the world's major central banks created the Committee on Banking Regulations and Supervisory Practices (sometimes known as the Basle Committee) with the objective of exercising better co-ordinated surveillance over the international banking system. Earlier, in 1972, an informal group of EEC bank supervisors had been formed, which is known as the Groupe de Contact. The aim of this group is to achieve closer co-operation between EEC bank supervisors.

The work of the Basle Committee has been to develop broad principles with which different national authorities can be encouraged to conform in setting their own detailed arrangements. It does not seek to harmonise different authorities' supervisory arrangements. An aim of the group is to ensure that no foreign banking establishment escapes supervision, and to achieve this aim the supervisors reached an understanding on the division of supervisory responsibility between 'host' and 'parent' authorities. 'Host authorities' refers to the supervisory authorities in the country of location of the foreign bank, which may be a branch or subsidiary of a bank in another country. 'Parent authorities' refers to the body responsible for supervising the parent bank or head office of the foreign banking establishment. Host authorities are, for example, interested in foreign banks in their own countries as individual institutions and from the point of view of what happens in their own markets, while parent authorities are interested in foreign banks as part of larger banking institutions under their supervision. This understanding became known as the Concordat and was endorsed by the Group of Ten governors in December 1975. A guiding principle is that the supervision of foreign banking establishments is the joint responsibility of host and parent authorities.

The other guidelines are:[8]

1. No foreign banking establishment should escape supervision, and supervision should be adequate as judged by the standards of both host and parent authorities.
2. The supervision of liquidity should be the primary responsibility of host authorities. (Foreign establishments generally have to conform to local practices for their liquidity management and therefore must comply with local regulations.)
3. The supervision of solvency of foreign branches should be essentially a matter for the parent authority. (In the case of subsidiaries, primary responsibility lies with the host authority, but parent authorities should take account of the exposure of their domestic banks' foreign subsidiaries.)
4. Practical co-operation would be facilitated by transfers of information between host and parent authorities and by the granting of permission for inspections by parent authorities in the host country.

These guidelines about supervision naturally do not themselves constitute an agreement about responsibilities for the provision of lender of last resort facilities to the international banking system. As already mentioned, the governors agreed that it was not practicable for detailed rules and procedures for this to be laid down in advance.

Under the Concordat the role of parent authorities in supervising the solvency of foreign banking establishments had been recognised. A second agreement was to give effect to this principle. This was the recommendation accepted in May 1979 to monitor banks' international business on a consolidated basis. Consolidation means that the assets and liabilities of all parts of a banking group – head offices, foreign branches and foreign subsidiaries – are integrated together to form a single balance-sheet with intra-group items being netted out. This accounting technique gives a view of the overall asset, liability and exposure position of the banking group and provides better insight into its total operations. It prevents banks 'gearing up' imprudently on their capital or increasing their risk exposure bounds through the setting up of foreign banking establishments which might be subject to less rigorous prudential regulations, and allows the solvency of banks' international business to be monitored without fundamental changes in the approaches pursued at national level. In Canada, the Netherlands, West Germany, Switzerland, the USA and the United Kingdom banks' balance-sheets are already, or are in the process of being, monitored on a consolidated basis.

Another major prop of the global supervisory process has been to improve information flows between the supervisors themselves and the quality of the statistical information on international banking activities. Supervision complements but cannot take the place of commercial banks' own prudential judgements, and the information flows are also designed to ensure that banks themselves are aware of the potential risks involved in international lending.

11.4 SUMMARY AND CONCLUSIONS

The concept of banking stability or instability is a very difficult one. Invariably financial intermediation involves risks and potential losses; prudent banking involves assessing the risks and making provisions to cover losses. The issues in international banking stability are: how risky is the environment and do banks adequately take the risks into account when lending funds?

Certain factors suggest that international banking may be inherently more risky than domestic banking. The absence of detailed rules and procedures for the official provision of temporary liquidity to the Euro-market, the reliance on the interbank market for residual funding and the closely integrated nature of the market may make the international system more vulnerable to shocks which affect any of the participants. The mounting size of countries' debts, system risks and the exposure of the market to political developments raises the possibility of large loan or deposit shocks. Banks' lending margins have fallen, maturities lengthened and capital ratios declined: the tolerance limits of the system to exogenous shocks have narrowed.

Other factors point, however, to the stability of the international banking system. The international market has shown its ability to adjust and to expand in the face of numerous shocks. It is based on a network of bank branches and subsidiaries which have direct institutional links to financially strong and sound national banks. Depositors and borrowers in the market are among the most important private- and public-sector agencies, which itself evidences confidence in the market. The type of financial instruments used in the market – large denominated fixed-rate time deposits, floating-rate and syndicated loans, and the depth and sophistication of the wholesale interbank market – are designed to share lending risks and reduce funding risks and themselves suggest stability. Banks assess their funding and lending risks and diversify their risk exposures.

It remains a matter of judgement as to whether individual banks are sufficiently risk-averse. The emphasis being given by central banks to the need for extended prudential supervision suggests that they believe that commercial banks do not always assess adequately international lending risks. The official response is to move towards the global monitoring of the international banking system and to encourage banks to become more prudent themselves. The co-operation between banking supervisors is a far-sighted approach to the problems posed by international banking. Through such developments and the 'cardinal importance' which the central bank governors attached in their April 1980 communiqué to the maintenance of sound banking standards, it is possible to be reasonably optimistic about the future stability of the international banking system.

NOTES

1. Ultimately it may depend simply on how it is defined by local laws in the country of the bank concerned.
2. Some other ratios might also be considered, but since these are all interrelated through the balance-sheet identity, the simulation results reported need not be very different.
3. For example, Citibank's overseas loan losses in the 1970s averaged only 0.29 per cent of total overseas loans, compared with 0.70 per cent on domestic lending.
4. To take a simplified example – a bank with capital of 5 million, total assets of 100 million, earning a return on total assets of 1 per cent (sufficient to pay shareholders a return of 20 per cent) and with deposits of the bank expanding at a rate of inflation of, say, 10 per cent:

	Year 1	*Year 2*
Capital	5	5
Deposits	95	105
Loans	100	110
Income	1	1.1
Capital ratio	5%	4.5%

In order to maintain its capital ratio the bank would have to retain 0.5 million out of earnings. However, it can only do this by cutting its dividend, thus damaging its ability to seek capital in the market, and the bank may therefore prefer to accept a decline in its capital ratio.

5. A report prepared for the OECD provided evidence that bank profitability in many countries has been relatively stable and in some instances rising (Revell, 1980).

6. In June 1979 there were thirty-six instances where a US bank had an exposure to a single LDC in excess of 30 per cent of capital funds. By end-1980 the number of such exposures had increased to eighty (Wallich, 1981). Several authorities do, however, impose fairly tight restrictions on their banks' lending to any individual borrower as a proportion of a bank's capital.

7. For a useful discussion of the developments in co-operation among banking supervisors see Cooke (1981).

8. Cooke (1981).

Bibiliography

George C. Abbott (1979) *International Indebtedness and the Developing Countries*, London, Croom Helm.

R. Z. Aliber (1973) 'The interest rate parity theorem: a reinterpretation', *Journal of Political Economy*, vol. 81, no. 6, November–December 1973, 1451–9.

—— (1979) 'Monetary aspects of offshore markets', *Columbia Journal of World Business*, vol. 14, no. 3, Autumn 1979, 8–16.

—— (1980) 'The integration of the offshore and domestic banking system', *Journal of Monetary Economics*, vol. 6, no. 3, October 1980, 509–26.

Oscar L. Altman (1962) 'Foreign markets for dollars, sterling and other currencies', *IMF Staff Papers*, vol. 9, no. 3, November 1962, 297–316.

A. Angelini, M. Eng and F. A. Lees (1979) *International Lending Risk and the Euro-markets*, London, Macmillan.

V. Argy and Z. Hodjera (1973) 'Financial integration and interest rate linkages in industrial countries', *IMF Staff Papers*, vol. 20, no. 1, March 1973, 1–77.

V. Argy and P. J. Kouri (1974) 'Sterilization policies and the volatility of international reserves', in R. Z. Aliber (ed.), *National Monetary Policies and the International Financial System*, University of Chicago Press, Chicago, 209–30.

J. W. Bachman (1976) 'Euro-markets still tiered', *Money Manager*, 17 September 1976, 10.

Ernst Baltensperger (1980) 'Alternative approaches to the theory of the banking firm', *Journal of Monetary Economics*, vol. 6, no. 1, January 1980, 1–37.

Bank for International Settlements, *Annual Reports*, Basle, various issues.

Bank of England (1970) 'The Euro-currency business of banks in London', *Bank of England Quarterly Bulletin*, vol. 10, no. 1, March 1970, 31–40.

——, 'The foreign exchange market in London', *Bank of England Quarterly Bulletin*, vol. 20, no. 4, December 1980, 437–44.

W. J. Baumol (1952) 'The transactions demand for cash: an inventory theoretic approach', *Quarterly Journal of Economics*, vol. 66, November 1952, 545–56.

—— (1977) *Economic Theory and Operations Analysis*, Englewood Cliffs, N. J., Prentice-Hall.

Michael Beenstock (1978) *The Foreign Exchanges: Theory, Modelling and Policy*, London, Macmillan.

Geoffrey Bell (1973) *The Eurodollar Market and the International Financial System*, London, Macmillan.

R. R. Bench (1977) 'How the US comptroller of the currency analyses country risk', *Euro-money*, August 1977, 47–51.

George Blunden and Richard Farrant (1977) 'International co-operation in banking supervision', *Bank of England Quarterly Bulletin*, vol. 17, no. 3, September 1977, 325–9.

Sir George Bolton (1970) *A Banker's World: The Revival of the City, 1957–70*, London, Hutchinson.

W. H. Branson (1968) *Financial Capital Flows in the US Balance of Payments*, Amsterdam, North-Holland.

—— (1969) 'The minimum covered interest differential needed for international arbitrage activity', *Journal of Political Economy*, vol. 77, no. 6, December 1969, 1028–35.

—— (1979) 'Exchange rate dynamics and monetary policy', in A. Lindbeck (ed.), *Inflation and Employment in Open Economies*, Amsterdam, North-Holland, 189–224.

—— (1980) 'Asset markets and relative prices in exchange-rate determination', *Princeton Reprints in International Finance*, no. 20, June 1980.

W. H. Branson and R. H. Hill (1971) 'Capital movements in the OECD area', *OECD Economic Outlook, Occasional Studies* December 1971.

Andrew F. Brimmer and F. R. Dahl (1975) 'Growth of American international banking: implications for public policy', *Journal of Finance*, vol. 30, no. 2, May 1975, 341–63.

W. H. Bruce Brittain (1977) 'Developing countries' external debt and the private banks', *Banca Nazionale del Lavoro Quarterly Review*, no. 123, December 1977, 365–80.

W. H. Bruce Brittain and Henri Bernard (1980) 'The relevance of Euro-currency claims for domestic financial aggregates', unpublished BIS paper, mimeo. November 1980.

Miltiades Chacholiades (1978) *International Monetary Theory and Policy*, New York, McGraw-Hill, ch. 19.

Wayne E. Clendenning (1970) *The Euro-dollar Market*, Oxford, Clarendon Press.

Hugo Coljé (1980) 'Bank supervision on a consolidated basis', *The Banker*, vol. 130, no. 652, June 1980, 29–34.

W. P. Cooke (1981) 'Developments in co-operation among banking supervisory authorities', *Bank of England Quarterly Bulletin*, vol. 21, no. 2, June 1981, 238–44.

J. R. H. Cooper (1974) 'How foreign exchange operations can go wrong', *Euro-money*, May 1974, 4–7.

—— (1974) 'How much liquidity does a Eurobank need?' *Euro-money*, July 1974, 11–17.

Richard N. Cooper (1972) 'Euro-dollars, reserve dollars and asymmetries in the international monetary system', *Journal of International Economics*, vol. 2, no. 4, September 1972, 325–44.

Andrew D. Crockett (1976) 'The Euro-currency market: an attempt to clarify some basic issues', *IMF Staff Papers*, vol. 23, no. 2, July 1976, 375–86.

—— (1978) 'Control over international reserves', *IMF Staff Papers*, vol. 25, no. 1, March 1978, 1–24.

Andrew Crockett and Malcolm Knight (1978) 'International bank lending in perspective', *Finance and Development*, December 1978.

Richard S. Dale (1981) 'Prudential regulations of multinational banking: the problem outlined', *National Westminster Bank Quarterly Review*, February 1981, 14–24.

Robert R. Davis (1981) 'Alternative techniques for country risk evaluation', *Business Economics*, May 1981, 34–41.

Stephen I. Davis (1976) *The Euro-Bank: its origins, Management and Outlook*, London, Macmillan.

James W. Dean and Herbert G. Grubel (1979) 'Multinational banking: theory and regulation', in Franklin R. Edward (ed.), *Issues in Financial Regulation*, New York, McGraw-Hill, 405–27.

Sidney Dell and Roger Lawrence (1980) *The Balance of Payments Adjustment Process in Developing Countries*, New York, Pergamon Press.

Evsey D. Domar (1950) 'The effect of foreign investment on the balance of payments', *American Economic Review*, vol. 40, December 1950, 805–26.

G. Dufey and I. H. Giddy (1978) *The International Money Market*, Englewood Cliffs, N. J., Prentice-Hall.

J. Eaton and M. Gersovitz (1980) 'LDC participation in international financial markets: debt and reserves', *Journal of Development Economics*, vol. 7, 3–21.

—— (1981) 'Debt and potential repudiation: theoretical and empirical analysis', *Review of Economic Studies*, vol. 48, 289–309.

Paul Einzig and Brian Scott Quinn (1977) *The Euro-dollar System*, London, Macmillan.

J. G. Ellis (1980) 'Fees associated with medium-term Euro-credits', unpublished Bank of England paper, mimeo.

—— (1981) 'Euro-banks and the inter-bank market', *Bank of England Quarterly Bulletin*, vol. 21, no. 3, September 1981, 351–64.

E. J. Elton and M. J. Gruber (eds) (1975) *International Capital Markets*, Amsterdam, North-Holland.

G. Feder and R. Just (1977) 'A study of debt servicing capacity applying logit analysis', *Journal of Development Economics*, vol. 4, no. 1, March 1977, 25–38.

Federal Reserve Bank of Boston (1977) *Key Issues in International Banking*, Conference Series No. 18, October 1977.

Federal Reserve Board (1979) *A Discussion Paper Concerning Reserve Requirements on Euro-currency Deposits*, Washington, D. C., Federal Reserve Board, April 1979.

Gabriel Ferras (1967) 'Development of a European capital market' in *Banks and the Problems of Economic Expansion*, International Banking Summer School, Copenhagen, Denmark, 1969, 47–62.

Charles Fisk and Frank Rimlinger (1979) 'Non-parametric estimates of LDC repayment prospects', *Journal of Finance*, vol. 34, no. 2, March 1979, 429–36.

A. E. Fleming and S. K. Howson (1980) 'Conditions in the syndicated medium-term Euro-credit market', *Bank of England Quarterly Bulletin*, vol. 20, no. 3, September 1980, 311–18.

G. Forest and N. Mills (1979) 'Debt analysis and financing problems of developing countries', in S. Frown (ed.), *A Framework of International Banking*, Guildford, Guildford Educational Press, 152–85.

C. R. Frank Jr and W. R. Cline (1971) 'Measurement of debt servicing capacity: an application of discrimination analysis', *Journal of Development Economics*, vol. 1, no. 4, 327–44.

Michele Fratianni and Paolo Savona (1971) 'Euro-dollar creation: comments on Professor Machlup's proposition and developments', *Banca Nazionale del Lavoro Quarterly Review*, vol. 24, no. 97, June 1971, 110–28.

—— (1972) 'International liquidity: an analytical and empirical reinterpretation', in *A Debate on the Euro-Dollar Market*, Ente per gli Studi Monetari, Bancari e Finanziari, Quaderni di Ricerche, no. 11, Roma.

Charles Freedman (1979) 'Micro theory of international financial intermediation', *American Economic Association*, vol. 67, no. 1, February 1977, 172–9.

—— (1977a) 'A model of the Euro-dollar market', *Journal of Monetary Economics*, vol. 3, no. 2, April 1977, 139–61.

—— (1977b) 'The Euro-dollar market: a review of five recent studies', *Journal of Monetary Economics*, vol. 3, no. 3, October 1977, 467–78.

Edward R. Fried and Charles L. Schultze (eds) (1975) *Higher Oil Prices and the World Economy: the Adjustment Problems*, Washington, D. C., Brookings Institution.

Milton Friedman (1969) 'The Euro-dollar market: some first principles', *Morgan Guaranty Survey*, October 1969, 4–14.

Edward J. Frydl (1979–80) 'The debate over regulating the Euro-currency market', *Federal Reserve Bank of New York Quarterly Review*, vol. 4, no. 4, Winter 1979–80, 11–20.

William G. Gibson (1971) 'Euro-dollars and US monetary policy', *Journal of Money, Credit and Banking*, vol. 3, no. 3, August 1971, 649–65.

I. H. Giddy and D. L. Allen (1979) 'International competition in bank regulation', *Banca Nazionale del Lavoro Quarterly Review*, September 1979, 311–26.

Joseph Gold (1979) *Financial Assistance by the International Monetary Fund*, International Monetary Fund Pamphlet Series No. 27, Washington, D. C.

Laurance G. Goldberg and Antony Saunders (1980) 'The causes of US bank expansion overseas', *Journal of Money, Credit and Banking*, vol. 12, no. 4, November 1980, 630–43.

C. A. E. Goodhart (1975) *Money, Information and Uncertainty*, London, Macmillan, ch. 14.

L. S. Goodman (1980) 'The pricing of syndicated Euro-currency credits', *Federal Reserve Bank of New York Quarterly Review*, vol. 5, no. 2, Summer 1980, 39–49

—— (1981) 'Bank lending to non-OPEC LDCs: are risks diversifiable?', *Federal Reserve Bank of New York Quarterly Review*, vol. 6, no. 2, Summer 1981, 10–20.

S. H. Goodman (ed.) (1979) *Financing and Risk in Developing Countries*, Washington, D. C., Export–Import Bank of the United States, August 1979.

Group of Thirty (1981) *Balance-of-payments Problems for Developing Countries*, New York, Group of Thirty.

J. Gurley and E. S. Shaw (1960) *Money in a Theory of Finance*, Washington, D. C., Brookings Institute.

W. Guth (1977) 'The Working of the International Monetary System', Washington, D. C., Per Jacobsson Lecture.

Monroe Haegele (1980) 'The behaviour of spreads in the medium-term Euro-currency market', *Business Economics*, September 1980, 41–8.

H. Robert Heller (1979) 'Why the market is demand-determined', *Euro-money*, February 1979, 41–7.

H. Robert Heller and Malcolm Knight (1978) *Reserve-Currency Preferences of*

Central Banks, Essays in International Finance No. 131, Princeton, Princeton University Press, December 1978.

P. H. Hendershott (1967) 'The structure of international interest rates: the US Treasury bill rate and the Euro-dollar deposit rate', *Journal of Finance*, vol. 22, September 1967, 455–65.

Dale W. Henderson (1977) 'Modeling the interdependence of national money and capital markets', *American Economic Association*, vol. 67, no. 1, February 1977, 190–9.

Dale W. Henderson and Douglas G. Waldo (1980) 'Reserve requirements on Euro-currency deposits: implications for Euro-deposit multipliers, control of a monetary aggregate and avoidance of redenomination incentives', *International Finance Discussion Paper* no. 164, July 1980.

R. J. Herring and R. C. Marston (1977) *National Monetary Policies and International Financial Markets*, Amsterdam, North-Holland.

J. Hewson and E. Sakakibara (1976) 'A general equilibrium approach to the Euro-dollar market', *Journal of Money, Credit and Banking*, vol. 8, no. 3, August 1976, 297–323.

Zoran Hodjera (1973) 'International short-term capital movements', *IMF Staff Papers*, vol. 20, no. 3, November 1973, 683–740.

Allen R. Holmes and F. H. Klopstock (1960) 'The market for dollar deposits in Europe', *Federal Reserve Bank of New York Monthly Review*, November 1960, 197–202.

Susan Howson (1980) 'External financial markets and capital mobility', unpublished Bank of England paper, mimeo.

K. Inoue (1980) 'Determinants of market conditions in the Euro-currency market – why a borrower's market?', *BIS Working Paper*, no. 1.

International Monetary Fund (1978) *IMF Survey*, June 1978.

R. B. Johnston (1979) 'Measuring conditions in the syndicated medium-term Euro-credit market: some attempts at estimating a spread–maturity trade-off', unpublished Bank of England paper, mimeo.

—— (1980) 'Banks' international lending decisions and the determination of spreads on syndicated medium-term Euro-credits', *Bank of England Discussion Paper*, no. 12, September 1980.

—— (1982) 'Euro-market expansion: macro-economic concerns, theoretical models and preliminary empirical estimates', paper presented to the Société Universitaire Européenne de Recherches Financières Colloquium, Vienna, April 1982.

Ishan Kapur (1977) 'An analysis of the supply of Euro-currency finance to developing countries', *Oxford Bulletin of Economics and Statistics*, vol. 39, no. 3, August 1977, 171–81.

Janet Kelly (1977) *Bankers and Borders: the Case of American Banks in Britain*, Cambridge, Mass., Ballinger.

G. A. Kessler (1980) 'The need to control international bank lending', *Banca Nazionale del Lavoro Quarterly Review*, vol. 33, no. 132, March 1980, 57–81.

Tony Killick (1981) 'Euro-market recycling of OPEC surpluses: fact or myth?', *The Banker*, January 1981, 15–23.

J. A. Kirbyshire (1977) 'Should developments in the Euro-markets be a source of concern to regulatory authorities', speech to *The Financial Times* Euro-Markets Conference, London, February 1977.

Michael A. Klein (1981) 'Monetary-control implications of the Monetary Control Act', *Federal Reserve Bank of San Francisco Economic Review*, Winter 1981.

F. H. Klopstock (1968) *The Euro-dollar Market: Some Unresolved Issues*, Essays in International Finance No. 65, Princeton, Princeton University Press, March 1968.

—— (1970) 'Money creators in the Euro-dollar market – a note on Professor Friedman's views', *Federal Reserve Bank of New York Monthly Review*, January 1970, 12–15.

—— (1973) 'Foreign banks in the United States: scope and growth of operations', *Federal Reserve Bank of New York Monthly Review*, June 1973, 140–54.

Malcolm Knight (1977) 'Euro-dollars, capital mobility and the forward exchange markets', *Economica*, vol. 44, no. 173, February 1977, 1–21.

P. J. K. Kouri and M. G. Porter (1974) 'International capital flows and portfolio equilibrium', *Journal of Political Economy*, vol. 82, no. 3, May–June 1974, 433–67.

Sung Y. Kwack (1971) 'The structure of international interest rates: an extension of Hendershott's tests', *Journal of Finance*, vol. 26, no. 4, September 1971, 897–900.

Boyden E. Lee (1973) 'The Euro-dollar multiplier', *Journal of Finance*, vol. 28, no. 4, September 1973, 867–74.

Jane Sneddon Little (1979) 'Liquidity creation by Euro-banks: 1973–1978', *New England Economic Review*, January–February 1979, 62–72.

—— (1979) 'Liquidity creation by Euro-banks: a range of possibilities', *Columbia Journal of World Business*, vol. 14, no. 3, Autumn 1979, 38–45.

D. T. Llewellyn (1979a) 'International banking in the 1970s: an overview', in S. F. Frowen (ed.), *A Framework of International Banking*, Guildford, Guildford Educational Press, 25–54.

—— (1979b) 'The Eurocurrency markets and world credit', *The Banker*, January 1979, 61–9.

—— (1980) *International Financial Integration*, London, Macmillan.

David F. Lomax and P. T. G. Gutmann (1981) *The Euromarkets and International Financial Policies*, London, Macmillan.

Warren McClam (1972) 'Credit substitution and the Euro-currency market', *Banca Nazionale del Lavoro Quarterly Review*, vol. 25, no. 103, December 1972, 323–63.

—— (1973) 'The control of capital movements: comparative policy developments in the United States and Japan', *Aussenwirtschaft*, vol. 28, nos. 1–2, March–June 1973, 107–29.

Fritz Machlup (1970) 'Eurodollar creation: a mystery story', *Banca Nazionale del Lavoro Quarterly Review*, vol. 23, no. 94, September 1970, 219–60.

—— (1972) 'Eurodollars once again', *Banca Nazionale del Lavoro Quarterly Review*, vol. 25, no. 101, June 1972, 119–37.

George McKenzie (1976) *The Economics of the Eurocurrency System*, London, Macmillan.

—— (1977) 'Economic interdependence and the Eurocurrency system', unpublished paper, University of Southampton.

R. I. McKinnon (1977) *The Euro-currency market*, Essays in International Finance No. 125, Princeton, Princeton University Press, December 1977.

—— (1979) *Money in International Exchange*, New York, Oxford University Press.

C. W. McMahon (1976) 'Controlling the Euro-markets', speech given at *The Financial Times* and *Investors' Chronicle* Conference, February 1976. Reprinted in the *Bank of England Quarterly Bulletin*, vol. 16, no. 1, March 1976, 74–7.

John H. Makin (1972) 'Demand and supply functions for stocks of Euro-dollar deposits: an empirical study', *Review of Economics and Statistics*, vol. 54, no. 2, November 1972, 381–91.

—— (1973) 'Identifying a reserve base for the Euro-dollar market', *Journal of Finance*, vol. 28, no. 3, June 1973, 609–17.

H. M. Markowitz (1957) *Portfolio Selection*, New York, Wiley.

Helmut W. Mayer (1970) *Some Theoretical Problems relating to the Eurodollar Markets*, Essays in International Finance No. 79, Princeton, Princeton University Press.

—— (1971) 'Multiplier effects and credit creation in the Eurodollar market', *Banca Nazionale del Lavoro Quarterly Review*, vol. 24, no. 98, September 1971, 233–62.

—— (1976) 'The BIS concept of the Euro-currency market', *Euro-money*, May 1976, 60–6.

—— (1979a) 'The BIS statistics on international banking', paper given to the International Association for Research in Income and Wealth, Sixteenth General Conference, Austria, August 1979.

—— (1979b) 'Credit and liquidity creation in the international banking sector', *BIS Economic Paper*, no. 1, November 1979.

Geoffrey Maynard (1975) 'The recycling of oil revenues', *The Banker*, vol. 125, January 1975, 39–46.

J. E. Meade (1951) *The Theory of International Economic Policy*, Vol. 1, *The Balance of Payments*, London, Oxford University Press, ch. 19.

W. E. Moscowitz (1979) 'Global asset and liability management at commercial banks', *Federal Reserve Bank of New York Quarterly Review*, vol. 4, no. 1, Spring 1979, 42–8.

H. J. Muller (1979) 'The Concordat', *De Nederlandsche Bank N. V. Quarterly Statistics*, no. 2, September 1979, 84–91.

P. J. Nagy (1979) *Country Risk: How to Assess, Quantify and Monitor it*, London, Euro-money Publications.

Jurg Niehans and John Hewson (1976) 'The Euro-dollar market and monetary theory', *Journal of Money, Credit and Banking*, vol. 1 no. 8, February 1976, 1–27.

Bahram Nowyad and R. C. Williams (1981) *External Indebtedness of Developing Countries*, Occasional Paper No. 3, Washington, D. C., International Monetary Fund, May 1981.

OECD (1981) *Regulations Affecting International Banking Operations*, Paris, OECD.

L. H. Officer and T. D. Willett (1970) 'The covered arbitrage schedule: a critical survey of recent developments', *Journal of Money, Credit and Banking*, vol. 2, no. 2 May 1970, 247–57.

Rinaldo Ossola (1980) 'The vulnerability of the international financial system:

international lending and liquidity risk', *Banca Nazionale del Lavoro Quarterly Review*, vol. 33, no. 134, September 1980, 291–306.

M. G. Porter (1972) 'Capital flows as an offset to monetary policy: the German experience', *IMF Staff Papers*, vol. 19, no. 2, July 1972, 395–422.

J. S. Revell (1980) *Costs and Margins in Banking: an International Survey*, Paris, OECD.

Georg Rich (1972) 'A theoretical and empirical analysis of the Euro-dollar market', *Journal of Money, Credit and Banking*, vol. 4, no. 3, August 1972, 616–35.

Gordon Richardson (1979) speech given at the Annual Banquet of the Overseas Bankers' Club, February 1979. Reprinted in the *Bank of England Quarterly Bulletin*, vol. 19, no. 1, March 1979, 48–50.

Paolo Savona (1974) 'Controlling the Euro-markets', *Banca Nazionale del Lavoro Quarterly Review*, vol. 27, no. 109, June 1974, 167–74.

N. Sargen (1977) 'Use of economic indicators in country risk appraisal', *Federal Reserve Bank of San Francisco Economic Review*, Autumn 1977.

G. D. Short and B. B. While (1978) 'International bank lending: a guided tour through the data', *Federal Reserve Bank of New York Quarterly Review*, vol. 3, no. 3, Autumn 1978, 39–46.

G. Smith (1979) 'The external debt prospects of the non-oil exporting developing countries', in F Cline (ed.), *Policy Alternatives for a New International Economic Order*, New York, Praeger.

P. Stanyer and J. Whitley (1981) 'Financing world payments imbalances', *Bank of England Quarterly Bulletin*, vol. 21, no. 2, June 1981, 187–99.

Carl H. Stem (1976) 'Some Euro-currency problems: credit expansion, the regulatory framework, liquidity and petrodollars', in Carl H. Stem and John H. Makin (eds), *Euro-currencies and the International Monetary System*, Washington, D. C. American Enterprise Institute.

Alexander K. Swoboda (1968) *The Euro-dollar Market: an Interpretation*, Essays in International Finance No. 14, Princeton, Princeton University Press, February 1968.

—— (1978) 'Gold, dollars, Euro-dollars, and the world money stock under fixed exchange rates', *American Economic Review*, vol. 68, September 1978, 625–42.

—— (1980) *Credit Creation in the Euro-market: Alternative Theories and Implications for Control*, Occasional Paper No. 2, New York, Group of Thirty.

Henry S. Terrell and M. G. Martinson (1978) 'Arranging and Marketing syndicated Euro-currency loans', *Bankers' Magazine*, November–December 1978, 35–40.

Brian Tew (1977) *The Evolution of the International Monetary System, 1945–77*, New York, Wiley.

Henri Theil (1971) *Principles of Econometrics*, New York, Wiley.

James Tobin (1963) 'Commercial banks as creators of money', in Deane Carson (ed.), *Banking and Monetary Studies*, Homewood, Ill., Irwin.

—— (1965) 'The theory of portfolio selection', in F. H. Hahn and F. P. R. Brechling (eds), *The Theory of Interest Rates*, London, Macmillan.

James Tobin and W. C. Brainard (1963) 'Financial intermediaries and the effectiveness of monetary controls', *American Economic Review*, Papers and Proceedings, vol. 53, no. 2, 383–400.

US House of Representatives (1979) statements by Ralph C. Bryant. H. Robert Heller, Dennis Weatherstone and Henry C. Wallich before the Subcommittee on Domestic Monetary Policy and the Subcommittee on International Trade, Investment and Monetary Policy of the Committee on Banking, Finance and Urban Affairs.

Henry C. Wallich (1979) 'Why the Euromarket needs restraint', *Columbia Journal of World Business*, vol. 14, no. 3 Autumn 1979, 17–24.

—— (1981) speech given at the 59th Annual Meeting of the Bankers' Association for Foreign Trade, Florida, June 1981.

John Wenninger and Charles M. Sivesind (1979) 'Defining money for a changing financial system', *Federal Reserve Bank of New York Quarterly Review*, vol. 4, no. 1, Spring 1979, 1–8.

J. A. H. de Beaufort Wijnholds (1980) 'Surveillance and supervision of the international banking system', *De Nederlandsche Bank N. V. Quarterly Statistics*, no. 2, September 1980, 85–98.

Thomas D. Willett (1980) *International Liquidity Issues*, Washington, D. C., American Enterprise Institute.

R. C. Williams (1980) *International capital markets: Recent Developments and Short-term Prospects*, Occasional Paper No. 1, Washington, D. C., International Monetary Fund, September 1980.

R. C. Williams and G. G. Johnson (1981) *International Capital Markets: Recent Developments and Short-term Prospects, 1981*, Occasional Paper No. 7, Washington, D. C., International Monetary Fund, August 1981.

Manfred Willms (1976) 'Money creation in the Euro-currency market', *Weltwirtschaftliches Archiv*, band 112, heft 2, 201–30.

Rae Wiston (1980) *Domestic and Multinational Banking*, London, Croom Helm.

Index